GEORGIAN

A READING GRAMMAR

Corrected Edition

GEORGIAN
A READING GRAMMAR

Corrected Edition

Howard I. Aronson
University of Chicago

Bloomington, Indiana, 2010

SLAVICA

ISBN: 0-89357-207-1

This work was developed under a contract with the U.S. Office of Education under the provisions of Title VI, NDEA. The original book was published in July 1982; the corrected edition was published in January 1990.

Slavica Publishers
Indiana University
2611 E. 10th St.
Bloomington, IN 47408-2603
USA

[Tel.] 1-812-856-4186
[Toll-free] 1-877-SLAVICA
[Fax] 1-812-856-4187
[Email] slavica@indiana.edu
[www] http://www.slavica.com/

PREFACE TO THE CORRECTED EDITION

The present edition of *Georgian: a Reading Grammar* is basically unchanged from the original edition, except for the correction of errors and a additions to vocabularies and grammatical explanations. Since it was not possible to retype the entire book, additions have added where space was available. Such additions are indicated by the symbols ● and ■: The symbol ● indicates additions to vocabularies, which are usually to be found at the end of the vocabulary. If there is no room there for additions, the location of additions is indicated at the head of the vocabulary. The symbol ■ indicates additions to grammatical explanations. The location of the addition is given immediately after the symbol.

New illustrations have been added to the book. Whenever possible, they have been chosen to illustrate material from the exercises and the reading passages.

I want to express my gratitude to those have pointed out errors, both typographical and substantive, indicated sections lacking in clarity, and suggested improvements. First and foremost, I must thank my students at the University of Chicago. Thanks are also due to Professors Dodona Kiziria of Indiana University and Victor A. Friedman of the University of North Carolina, who sent me suggestions and corrections based on their classroom use of the textbook. I am also grateful to the reviewers of the original edition of the textbook for their corrections and suggestions. I would like to particularly thank B. G. Hewitt of Hull University for his detailed review in *Lingua*.

I hope that this corrected edition will help to make the countless riches of Georgian culture and civilization more accessible to students of the Georgian language.

PREFACE TO THE THIRD PRINTING

This reprinting differs from the corrected edition only in the addition of an *Addenda and Corrigenda* to be found following page 526. I am greatly indebted to Lia Abesaje of the Linguistic Institute of the Georgian Academy of Sciences for a number of corrections and stylistic improvements. I again express my gratitude to Professor Dodona Kiziria of Indiana University and to my students at the University of Chicago who have pointed out weaknesses in this text and who have suggested improvements.

The past few years have inaugurated a new and exciting period in the millennia-long history of Georgia. Unfortunately, these new realities of Georgian life could not be reflected in the present text. Nonetheless, it is my hope that the present edition can help to introduce readers of English to the gloriously rich past of the Georgian nation and allow them to follow what we pray will be an equally glorious future.

Chicago, Illinois—October 1991

Please see ***Addenda And Corrigenda*** following page 526.

ACKNOWLEDGMENTS

I should like to express my gratitude to the U.S. Office of Education for the grant that made the writing of this book possible and in particular to Mrs. Julia A. Petrov for her patience and help during the project. My thanks go, too, to Charles E. Gribble of Slavica Publishers for his encouragement and advice.

My task in putting together this book was greatly facilitated by the help and cooperation of Givi Kobahidze Coby, Michael LaGaly, and Dee Ann Holisky. To Prof. Holisky I am especially indebted for several grammatical analyses of the Georgian material. I have been most fortunate in having received corrections, suggestions, and criticisms from many specialists in and students of the field. In particular I should like to acknowledge the assistance of Victor Friedman, Orin Gensler, Alice Harris, and Yakov Khanukovich in the United States and of Nia Abesaje and A. A. Ǧlonṭi in Tbilisi, Georgia.

My gratitude goes, too, to Anthony Bruck, who typed the first versions of this book and to David Birnbaum and Pamela Sue Worner, who typed the English of the final version, and to Tom Gally, who typed the Georgian.

I must express my sincerest thanks to my students in Georgian classes at the University of Chicago, who worked through this material in its various forms and whose reactions and criticisms were invaluable.

Finally, I must give very special thanks to Acad. Thomas Gamkrelidze of the Georgian Academy of Sciences in Tbilisi, to Docent Šukia Apridonije of the Department of Georgian Language, Tbilisi State University, and to Prof. Dodona Kiziria of Indiana University for having painstakingly gone over the entire manuscript and for their insights into the wonders of Georgian grammar. It is impossible for me to fully express the debt I owe them.

I dedicate this book to the memory of my father, Abe Aronson.

CONTENTS

ABBREVIATIONS

abs.	absolute
arch.	archaic
adv.	adverbial case
aor.	aorist
conj.	conjugation
D.	dative case
d.o.	direct object
dat.	dative case
E.	ergative case
erg.	ergative case
f.	woman's proper name
f.pr.n.	woman's proper name
fut.	future
G.	genitive case
gen.	genitive case
Geo.	Georgian
I.	instrumental case
id.o.	indirect object
imperf.	imperfect
instr.	instrumental case
intrans.	intransitive
irr.	irregular
lit.	literally
m.	man's proper name
m.pr.n.	man's proper name
N.	nominative case
nom.	nominative case
OGeo.	Old Georgian
opt.	optative
o.s.	oneself
perf.	perfect
P/FSF	present and future stem formant
pl.	plural
plupf.	pluperfect
pp.	postposition (without further specification, takes gen.)
pr.	present
pres.	present
PSF	present stem formant
pvb.	preverb
refl.	reflexive
rel.	relative
result.	resultative
Russ.	Russian
sec.	section
sg.	singular
sing.	singular
s.o.	someone
sthg.	something

sup.	superessive
vb.	verb
V.N.	verbal noun
w.o.	without

SYMBOLS

(A)	vowel *a* syncopates (See sec. 3.2.1.1.)
(E)	vowel *e* syncopates (See sec. 3.2.1.1.)
E → I	*e* in present series of root I. conj. verbs alternates with *i* in the aorist series (See sec. 5.3.1.c, Lesson 6, vocabulary.)
H	*H*-series indirect object markers (See sec. 7.2.4, Lesson 7, vocabulary.)
∩-	indicates nontruncating vocalic stem nouns ending in *i* (See Lesson 6, vocabulary.)
(O)	vowel *o* syncopates (See sec. 3.2.1.1.)
Ø	(a) indicates the absence of a person-marker prefix or suffix (See sec. 2.2.1.) (b) indicates absence of a case ending in adjectives (See sec. 2.3.2.)
Ø=	indicates I. and II. conjugation verbs which have no preverb in the future series (See Lesson 8, vocabulary.)
+	indicates that the preverb is not dropped to form the present series forms (See sec. 2.2.2.)
=	indicates that the preverb is dropped to form the present series forms (See sec. 2.2.2.)
●	indicates addenda to vocabularies; the missing words are generally found at the end of the vocabulary--if not, the page where they can be found is indicated at the beginning of the vocabulary.
■	indicates additions to grammar sections; the page the additions can be found on is indicated after this symbol.

INTRODUCTION

Georgian, the only written member of the non-Indoeuropean Kartvelian (South Caucasian) linguistic family, is the official language of the Georgian Soviet Socialist Republic. Written Georgian goes back to the fifth century, and there is a rich and varied medieval Georgian literature. An extensive and significant scholarly literature exists in modern Georgian, covering all areas of knowledge from anatomy to zoology. Of particular importance is Georgian scholarly literature dealing with the Caucasus. No one can hope to be expert in fields such as the history, prehistory, ethnology, art, music, linguistics, folklore, etc. of the Caucasus without consulting the extensive scholarly literature on these topics written in Georgian. It is the purpose of this textbook to facilitate the acquisition of a reading knowledge of modern Georgian to enable the student to read such scholarly texts.

The textbook is designed to be used either for self-instruction or in a regular classroom. It is assumed that the student has already studied a foreign language (for instance French, Spanish, German, Russian, Greek, Latin) and is acquainted with the basic elementary terms of grammar. No other background is assumed.

The course is organized into fifteen lessons. The first lesson introduces the sound system and the Georgian alphabet. The exercises in this lesson should be repeated until the learner feels somewhat comfortable with the Georgian alphabet. (All Georgian forms in the grammar sections of Lessons 2 through 5 are given both in the Georgian alphabet and in transliteration to facilitate the learning of the alphabet.)

The remaining fourteen lessons contain grammar sections, Georgian sentences for translation into English, a vocabulary to these sentences, an English translation of the sentences, and, beginning with Lesson 5, a reading passage taken from Georgian sources and a vocabulary for that passage.

The *grammar sections* do not attempt to be exhaustive but rather are designed to cover the material of the exercises and the reading passages. Their main goal is to facilitate reading and therefore they are designed more for passive than for active mastery. In the last few lessons some grammatical material is introduced that is not drilled in the exercises or readings. This is to prepare the learner should he encounter similar forms in his later reading and also to give a better overview of Georgian grammar.

In several instances the presentation of the grammar in this textbook differs from the standard analyses of Georgian. Although I believe that the presentation in this book is linguistically justifiable, the purpose of such analyses here is purely pedagogical. So, for example, the grammatical category of *version* found in almost all analyses of Georgian will not be found here; instead the notions of indirect object and reflexive indirect object will be used.

The *Georgian sentences* for translation into English have a twofold purpose: to drill the material presented in the grammar sections and to present the student with some brief bits of information about Georgian life, culture, and history. Note that a given sentence may not contain any of the grammatical material from the lesson in which it occurs, but may rather drill material from earlier lessons. This is to prevent the student from automatically anticipating that in a given sentence a given form will occur simply because it was introduced in that particular lesson.

Every effort has been made to insure that the Georgian sentences are good, grammatical, and stylistically acceptable. At times, however, somewhat awkward sentences have been allowed if the grammatical constructions necessary for a stylistically more acceptable sentence had not been previously introduced.

The *vocabulary* to the lessons may appear to be overwhelming in size. But it must be remembered that the goal is passive rather than active mastery of the vocabulary. Further, the goal of this course is the acquisition of reading ability in Georgian, and this cannot be achieved without exposure to a large and varied vocabulary. It is recommended that the student repeat the exercises enough times (both from Georgian to English and from English to Georgian) for the vocabulary items to become familiar. A very large number of Georgian proper names are included in the exercises and the vocabulary since the absence of capital letters in Georgian makes it difficult to distinguish between common and proper nouns.

The vocabulary as a rule does not contain words occurring in the exercises that are derived from other words using affixes discussed in the wordbuilding sections of the grammar. The vocabulary to the Georgian sentences is cumulative, i.e., words introduced in the vocabulary of one lesson are not repeated in the vocabularies to following lessons. In Lessons 2 through 4, verbs are listed separately in the vocabularies from all other words, whereas in the following lessons proper nouns are listed separately in addition. Proper nouns are not given in the Georgian-English vocabulary at the end of the textbook.

The *English translation* of the Georgian sentences should be used for translating from English into Georgian. These English translations are as literal as possible and reflect the structure of the corresponding Georgian sentence. As a result, the English is often awkward or even ungrammatical! The student should pay special attention to those instances when the English of the translation differs from standard English usage; in such instances he should note how the Georgians express a comparable notion. Material in parentheses gives additional grammatical or lexical information. The material in square brackets gives, for the most part, a literal translation of the Georgian or indicates words present in English that are lacking in the Georgian.

The *reading passages* begin in Lesson 5. With the exception of the passages in Lessons 14 and 15, which are taken from a contemporary Georgian novel, they cover cultural or historical material. The vocabularies to the reading passages do not contain words that have already appeared in the vocabularies to the exercises. They also do not contain "international" words, found both in English and Georgian and common to most European languages. The vocabularies to the reading passages are not cumulative; words occurring in a given reading will be found in the vocabulary even if the words had occurred in earlier reading passages. Words from the reading passages are not included in the Georgian-English vocabulary at the end of the textbook. Entries in the vocabularies to the readings in square brackets are grammatical forms that have not yet been introduced in the grammar sections. With the exception of these, the student should be able to identify all grammatical forms occurring in the reading passages.

The reading passages should not present the student with too much difficulty if he remembers not to try to force a translation onto the grammar of the sentence. For a translation to be correct the sentence must make sense *grammatically;* one cannot simply rely on the meanings of the words and hope willy-nilly to string them together in some coherent manner.

Having completed this course, the student should be able to read most contemporary Georgian nonfiction with the aid of a good dictionary and a reference grammar. A selected listing of such works can be found in the appendixes.

The author would greatly appreciate any comments, criticisms, corrections, and suggestions for improvements. Please send these to me at the following address: Howard I. Aronson, Department of Linguistics, University of Chicago, Chicago, Illinois 60637.

LESSON 1: Phonology

1.0. In the following sections the sounds of Georgian and the corresponding letters used to denote these sounds will be given. When learning the sounds one should also learn the corresponding letters. Formation of the letters can be found in section 1.9. For practice in the pronunciation of Georgian the student is advised to read exercises 1,3,5,6,7, and 8 in the Key to the Exercises.

1.1. Stops. The major difficulty in Georgian pronunciation lies in the stops. Georgian stops, unlike English, have a three-way opposition, between voiced, voiceless aspirate, and voiceless glottalized (abruptive). The voiced stops are pronounced generally as the corresponding English voiced stops in initial position (i.e., the degree of voicing is relatively weak). The stops are labial, dental, alveolar, alveopalatal, and velar.

	Transliteration	Georgian	*Approximate* English equivalent	IPA Phonetic symbol
(1)	b	ბ	*b*ox	[b]
(2)	d	დ	*d*ot	[d]
(3)	j	ძ	*dz*	[ʣ]
(4)	ǰ	ჯ	*j*ot	[dʒ]
(5)	g	გ	*g*ot	[g]

In word-final position voiced stops are generally pronounced as the corresponding aspirates. Extremely common are the so-called *harmonic clusters* consisting here of a prevelar stop followed immediately by [g] and with only one release for the whole cluster: *bg* (ბგ), *dg* (დგ), *jg* (ძგ), *ǰg* (ჯგ) (exercise 5).

The aspirated stops are pronounced quite similarly to the corresponding English voiceless stops in absolute initial position:

(6)	p	ფ	*p*ot	[pʻ]
(7)	t	თ	*t*ot	[tʻ]
(8)	c	ც	*ts*ar	[tsʻ]
(9)	č	ჩ	*ch*op	[tʃʻ]
(10)	k	ქ	*c*ot	[kʻ]

The harmonic clusters here consist of a prevelar stop with following [kʻ] and with only one release: *pk* (ფქ), *tk* (თქ), *ck* (ცქ), *čk* (ჩქ) (exercise 5).

The glottalized voiceless stops have no equivalent in English. (In fact, the acoustic impression one often gets from these stops is that of a voiced stop!) These sounds are produced by simultaneously pronouncing a glottal stop[1] [ʔ] and the corresponding stop:

(11) ṗ პ [p']
(12) ṭ ტ [t']
(13) c̣ წ [ts']
(14) č̣ ჭ [tʃ']
(15) ḳ კ [k']

Harmonic clusters here are: *ṗḳ* (პკ), *ṭḳ* (ტკ), *c̣ḳ* (წკ), *č̣ḳ* (ჭკ).

1.2. Continuants (fricatives). Of the voiceless continuants, only *x* (ხ) might cause difficulty:

(16) s ს *s*ob [s]
(17) š შ *sh*ot [ʃ]
(18) x ხ [χ]

The Georgian *x* (ხ) is similar to the German *ach-Laut* (as in *Bach*) or the oft-cited Scottish *ch* in *loch*, or the initial sound in some American pronunciations of *chutzpah*. It differs from the latter, however, in being further back in the mouth, being a *postvelar* rather than *velar* fricative. *X* (ხ) also occurs as the second member of harmonic clusters the first member of which is a prevelar voiceless aspirated stop: *px* (ფხ), *tx* (თხ), *cx* (ცხ), *čx* (ჩხ).

The voiced fricatives correspond to the voiceless, differing from them only by the addition of voice. The *ğ* is postvelar.[2]

(19) z ზ *z*oo [z]
(20) ž ჟ mea*s*ure [ʒ]
(21) ğ ღ [ɣ]

Ğ occurs as the second member of harmonic clusters, the first member of which is a voiced prevelar stop: *bğ* (ბღ), *dğ* (დღ), *jğ* (ძღ), *ǯğ* (ჯღ).

1.3. (22) q (ყ). This sound is postvelar (pronounced in the same area as *x* and *ğ*) and glottalized.[3] It varies in pronunciation from a postvelar, glottalized stop [q'], through an affricate [qχ'], to a postvelar glottalized fricative [χ']. *Q* (ყ) serves as the second member of harmonic clusters, the first member of which is a voiceless glottalized prevelar stop: *p̣q* (პყ), *ṭq* (ტყ), *c̣q* (წყ), *č̣q* (ჭყ).

1.4. Nasals.

(23) m მ as in English [m]

(24) n ნ as in English [n]

Before velars *k* (ქ), *ḳ* (კ), *g* (გ), *n* (ნ) is pronounced as [ŋ] as in English si*ng*.

1.5 (25) v ვ. Georgian *v* (ვ) shows fluctuation in its pronunciation from [w] to [v], i.e., from the sound of English *w* in *wan* to English *v* in *van*. [v] occurs most commonly initially and intervocalically, [w] after consonants and at the end of syllables. It can also be realized as a bilabial voiced fricative [β] and, before voiceless consonants, as [f], e.g., *vc̣er* (ვწერ) 'I write' [fc̣ɛr]. Georgian *v* (ვ) in native words as a general rule does not occur before or after labial consonants [*p* (ფ), *p̣* (პ), *b* (ბ), *m* (მ)] or before rounded vowels [*u* (უ), *o* (ო); see 1.11.1]. It does occur quite commonly after simple stops, postvelars, and after harmonic clusters:

Single stop + *v*:

dv	დვ	tv	თვ	ṭv	ტვ
jv	ძვ	cv	ცვ	c̣v	წვ
ǰv	ჯვ	čv	ჩვ	č̣v	ჭვ
gv	გვ	kv	ქვ	ḳv	კვ
ǧv	ღვ	xv	ხვ	qv	ყვ

Harmonic cluster + *v*:

		dǧv	დღვ	tkv	თქვ	txv	თხვ	ṭḳv	ტკვ	ṭqv	ტყვ
jgv	ძგვ	jǧv	ძღვ	ckv	ცქვ	cxv	ცხვ	c̣ḳv	წკვ	c̣qv	წყვ
ǰgv	ჯგვ			čkv	ჩქვ	čxv	ჩხვ	č̣ḳv	ჭკვ	č̣qv	ჭყვ

1.6. Liquids and glides.

(26) r რ. Georgian *r* (რ) is generally formed by a single flap of the tip of the tongue to the alveolar ridge [ɾ]. It is very similar to the *r* in Spanish *pe/r/o* 'but' or the Russian *r* in перерыв 'break'. Between voiceless consonants it may become voiceless or drop completely.

(27) l ლ. Georgian *l* (ლ) is pronounced as the *l* of French, German, or Spanish before the front vowels *i*, *e* [l]. In other positions it is pronounced somewhat velarized (dark), similar to the American Eng-

lish *l* before back vowels [ɫ]. Between voiceless consonants it may become voiceless or drop completely.

(28) h ჰ. As in English; occurs initially only in loanwords.[4]

1.7. Vowels. Georgian has five vowels:

Neutral:

(29)	a	ა	low, open, slightly fronted [a] (cf. French *patte* [pat]).

Front unrounded:

(30)	i	ი	front, spread lips high, between close and half close [ɪ] (cf. English *bit*).
(31)	e	ე	front, spread lips, between half close and half open [ɛ] (cf. English *get*).

Back rounded:

(32)	u	უ	same height as *i* [ʊ] (cf. *book* with marked lip rounding).
(33)	o	ო	same height as *e* [ɔ] (cf. German *Glocken*).

1.8 Stress and intonation. Stress in Georgian is extremely weak and has no effect on vowel quality. The stress is so weak that linguists have not been able to agree on exactly where it falls. In words of four or fewer syllables, the stress falls on either the initial syllable or the antepenultimate syllable (third from the end). In longer words, there is a double stress: on the initial syllable and on the antepenultimate. Note that a Georgian word has as many syllables as it has vowels; m (მ), n (ნ), l (ლ), and r (რ) never form syllables. Examples:

საქართველო	Georgia	Sákartvelo or Sakártvelo
მდგომარეობა	situation	mdgómaréoba
მრგვალი	round	mrgváli
გრძელი	long	grjéli
ენათმეცნიერება	linguistics	énatmecniéreba or enatmecniéreba

There is no difference in quality between stressed and unstressed vowels. Georgian intonation is relatively even, without sharp rises or drops in tone, except in yes-no questions, where there is a sharp rise in intonation at the end of the sentence. In such yes-no questions the sentence-final vowel is often lengthened.

1.9. Assimilation. Georgian is characterized by rather long and complex consonant clusters, generally in (morpheme-) initial position. As a rule there is little or no assimilation for voicing, glottalization, or aspiration in such clusters. Harmonic clusters will have only one release, while nonharmonic clusters will have more than one release; cf. *bgera* (ბგერა) 'sound', where there is only one release for the harmonic cluster *bg*, and Tbilisi (თბილისი) 'Tbilisi' (Tiflis, capital of Georgia), which has an aspirated release for the initial *t* and a voiced release for the *b*: [tʿbɪlɪsɪ]. Examples of nonharmonic clusters:

კბილი	ḳbili	tooth
დოქტორი	dokṭori	doctor (e.g., of philosophy)
ტბა	ṭba	lake
ცდა	cda	attempt, wait
ყბა	qba	jaw

See table 1.1 on the following page, depicting the sound system of Georgian.

1.10. The Georgian alphabet. The contemporary Georgian alphabet does not distinguish upper and lower case letters; for every letter there is only one form. In distinguishing the thirty-three letters it is important to note the position of the letter with respect to the base lines. In print the following letters occur completely within the base lines:

ა თ ი ო

a t i o

ა თ ი ო

The following letters rise above the upper base line:

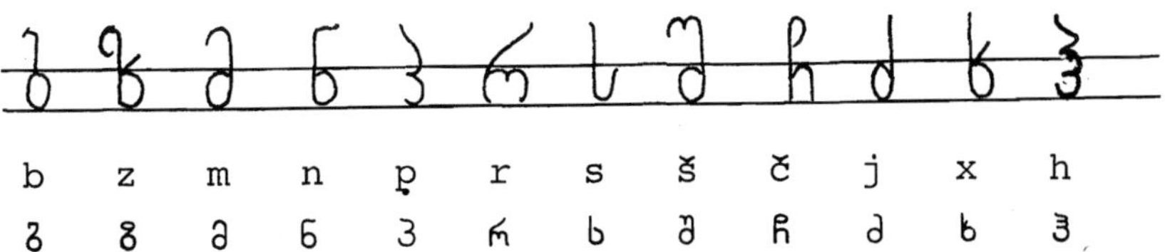

b z m n p̣ r s š č j x h

ბ ზ მ ნ პ რ ს შ ჩ ძ ხ ჰ

Table 1.1 Sound System of Georgian

		Bilabial	Dental	Alveolar	Palato-Alveolar	Velar
Stops and	vcd	ბ b [b]	დ d [d]	ძ j [dz]	ჯ ǰ [d]	გ g [g]
affricates:	asp	ფ p [pʻ]	თ t [tʻ]	ც c [tsʻ]	ჩ č [tʃʻ]	ქ k [kʻ]
	glot	პ p̣ [pʼ]	ტ ṭ [tʼ]	წ ç̣ [tsʼ]	ჭ č̣ [tʃʼ]	კ ḳ [kʼ]
Fricatives:	vcd			ზ z [z]	ჟ ž [ʒ]	
	vcls			ს s [s]	შ š [ʃ]	
Nasals:		მ m [m]	ნ n [n]			
Liquids and		ვ v [v,		ლ l [ɫ, l]		
glides:		β, w]		რ r [ɾ]		

Postvelar

	Vcd.	Vcls.	Vcls. Glott.
Stop			ყ *q* [qʼ]
Affricate			ყ *q* [qχʼ]
Fricative	ღ *ğ* [ɣ]	ხ *x* [χ]	ყ *q* [χʼ]

VOCALISM

	front		back rounded
high unr	ი *i*[ɪ]	უ *u*[ʊ]	
mid unr	ე *e*[ɛ]	ო *o*[ɔ]	mid rounded
low	ა *a*[a]		

The following letters descend below the lower base line:

g d e v ḳ l ž u p ğ q c ǯ

გ დ ე ვ კ ლ ჟ უ ფ ღ ყ ც ჯ

The following letters both rise above and descend below the base lines:

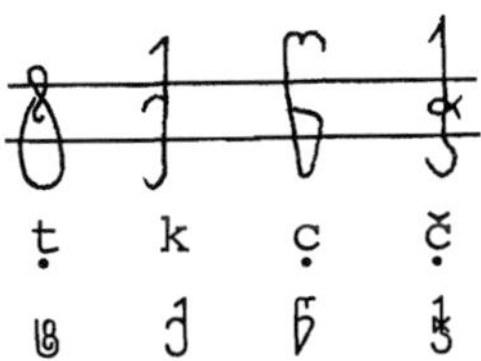

ṭ k ç č̣

ტ ქ წ ჭ

(In titles and headings it is common for all letters to be the same height; i.e., all fall between the same base lines.)

Variant shapes of letters: In some typefaces and in stylized writing, variant forms of letters are encountered:

ლ ლ l

ო ო o

რ რ r

ჯ ჯ ǯ

For the older Georgian alphabets see the Appendix to this chapter, page 30.

1.10.1. Handwriting. To form the Georgian handwritten letters, see figure 1.1.

Fig. 1.1. Georgian Handwritten Letters.

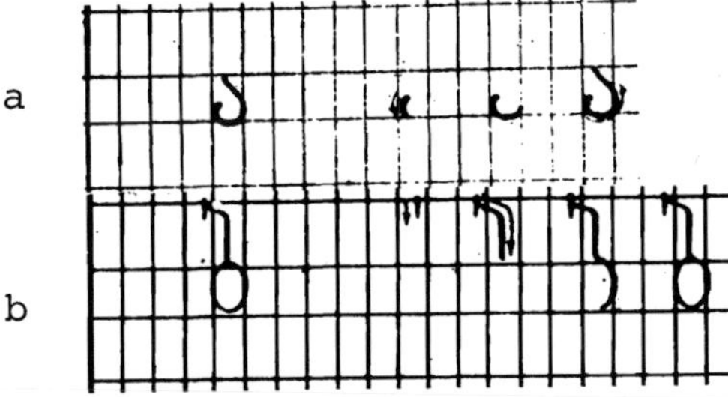

Fig. 1.1 continued:

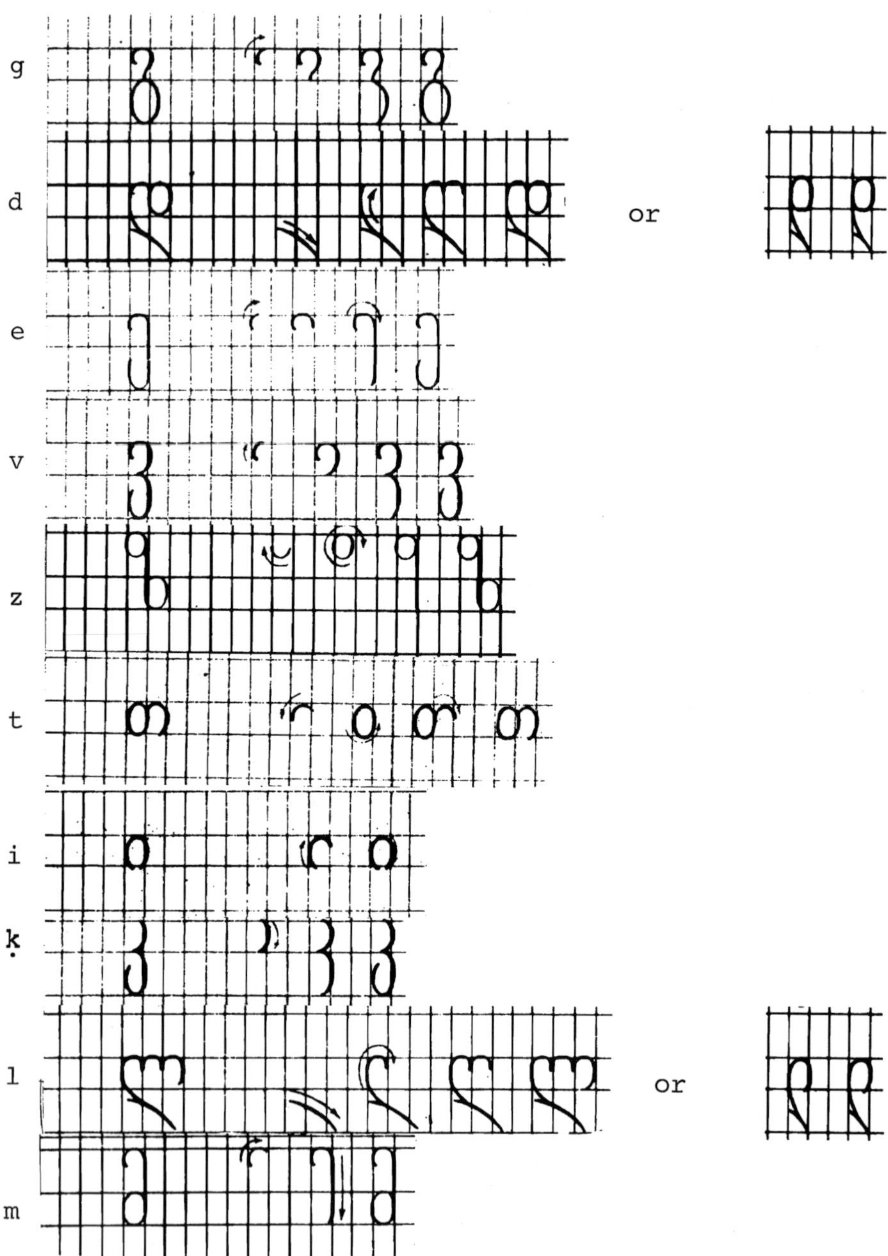

Fig. 1.1 continued:

n

o — or

p̣

ž

r — or

s

ṭ

u

p

k

Fig. 1.1 continued:

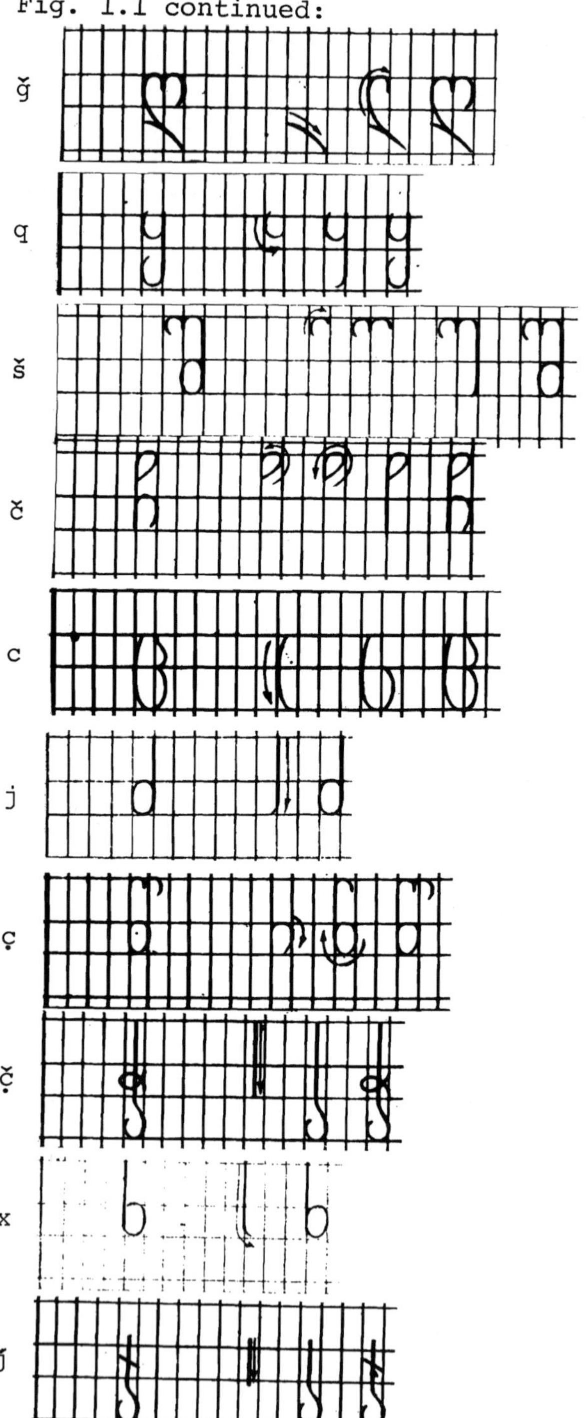

Fig. 1.1 continued:

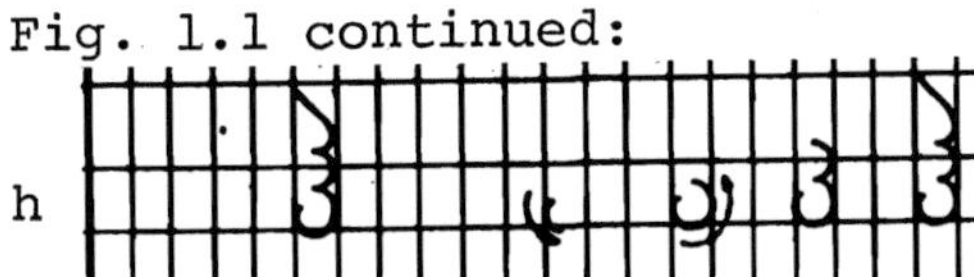

Fig. 1.2. Example of connected handwriting. See next page for transliteration.

ცოდნა სინათლეა

ცოდნა სიმდიდრეა, მერე იმისთანა მად-ლიანი სიმდიდრეა, რომ, რაც უნდა ბევრს დაუ-რიგო, ბევრს გაუნაწილო, შენ არა დაგაკლდება რა, თუ არ მოგემატება. ამ შემთხვევაში ცოდნა ანთებულ სანთელს ჰგავს: ერთი სან-თელზე რომ ათას სხვა სანთელს მოუკიდო, სანთელს იმით არც არა დააკლდება, არც სი-ნათლე, არც სიცხოველე, პირიქით, იმატებს კიდეც, რადგანაც ერთის მაგიერ ათასი სხვა სანთელი იმისთან ერთად დაიწყებს ლაპ-ლაპს.

სანთელს კიდევ იმაში ჰგავს ცოდნა, რომ თუნდაც ცოტად ბჟუტავდეს მისი სადმე ბნე-ლაში, ქურდს, მპარავს, მტერს აფრთხობს: იქ სინათლეა — ჩანს, ღვიძავთ, დაგვიანებულ მგზავრს კი იმით ახარებს, რომ იქ მღვიძარები დამხვდებიან.

Codna sinatlea

Codna simdidrea, mere imistana madliani simdidrea, rom, rac unda bevrs daurigo, bevrs gaunac̣ilo, šen ara dagaḳldeba ra, tu ar mogemaṭeba. Am šemtxvevaši codna antebul santels hgavs: ert santelze rom atas sxva santels mouḳido, santels imit arc ali daaḳldeba, arc sinatle, arc sicxovele, p̣irikit, imaṭebs ḳidec, radganac ertis magier atasi sxva santeli imastan ertad daic̣qebs lap̣lap̣s.

Santels ḳidev imaši hgavs codna, rom tundac coṭad bžuṭavdes šors sadme bnelaši, kurds, mp̣aravs, mṭers aprṭxobs: ik sinatlea -- čans, ǧvijavto, dagvianebul moqvares ḳi imit axarebs, rom ik mǧvijarebi damxvdebiano.

1.10.2. The order of the Georgian alphabet. The order of letters of the Georgian alphabet follows in general that of Greek for the first twenty-two letters:

1.	ა	a	A	17.	რ	r	P
2.	ბ	b	B	18.	ს	s	Σ
3.	გ	g	Γ	19.	ტ	ṭ	T
4.	დ	d	Δ	20.	უ	u	Y
5.	ე	e	E	21.	ფ	p	Φ
6.	ვ	v	-	22.	ქ	k	X
7.	ზ	z	Z*	23.	ღ	ǧ	
8.	თ	t	Θ	24.	ყ	q	
9.	ი	i	I	25.	შ	š	
10.	კ	ḳ	K	26.	ჩ	č	
11.	ლ	l	Λ	27.	ც	c	
12.	მ	m	M	28.	ძ	j	
13.	ნ	n	N**	29.	წ	c̣	
14.	ო	o	O	30.	ჭ	č̣	
15.	პ	p̣	Π	31.	ხ	x	
16.	ჟ	ž	-	32.	ჯ	ǰ	
				33.	ჰ	h	

*no equivalent of Greek H
**no equivalent of Greek Ξ

Notes.
Note that foreign *f* is often transcribed by Geor-

gian ფ.

Foreign *th* is often transcribed by Georgian თ.

Greek *ch* is generally transcribed by Georgian ქ.

In general, voiceless stops from European languages are transcribed in Georgian by the corresponding glottalized stops. Examples:

ḳap̣iṭani	captain	კაპიტანი
piziḳa	physics	ფიზიკა
pilosopia	philosophy	ფილოსოფია
teoria	theory	თეორია
aritmeṭiḳa	arithmetic	არითმეტიკა
arkiṭekṭori	architect	არქიტექტორი
kimia	chemistry	ქიმია
kronomeṭri	chronometer	ქრონომეტრი
p̣oliṭiḳa	policy	პოლიტიკა
ḳap̣iṭalizmi	capitalism	კაპიტალიზმი

Note that foreign *ch* (as in English *cherry*) and *ts* (as in *Tsar, tsetse*) are taken over into Georgian as ჩ and ც respectively:

čexi	Czech	ჩეხი
čeḳi	(bank) check	ჩეკი
čemp̣ioni	champion	ჩემპიონი
ciṭaṭa	citation	ციტატა
p̣rocesi	trial	პროცესი
nacia	nation	ნაცია

Foreign *ct* is generally taken over as ქტ:

subiekṭi	subject	სუბიექტი
direkṭori	director	დირექტორი

1.11. Alternations

1.11.1. *V*-loss. *V* (ვ) is generally lost when it occurs before or after a labial consonant [i.e., *b* (ბ), *p* (ფ), *p̣* (პ), *m* (მ)] as a result of vowel loss. *V* (ვ) is also generally lost when it would otherwise occur before rounded vowels, i.e., *o* (ო), *u* (უ).

1.11.2. Metathesis. Sequences involving a stop or fricative followed by a nasal or liquid [*m* (მ), *n* (ნ), *r* (რ), *l* (ლ)] followed by *v* (ვ) will generally have the *v* (ვ) shift its position to before the nasal or liquid.

Examples:

t '10' + *rva* '8' gives in the word for eighteen *tvrameṭi* (თვრამეტი) instead of the expected **trvameṭi*.

In the formation of the verbal noun of the verb *ḳl-av-s* (კლავს) 'kills', the vowel *a* is lost, which would normally result in **ḳl-v-a* [cf. *ḳer-av-s* (კერავს) 'sews', verbal noun *ḳer-v-a*]; but, as a result of this metathesis, we get the form *ḳvla* (კვლა).

This alternation can be formalized as follows:

$$\ldots \; C \left\{ \begin{matrix} r \\ l \\ m \\ n \end{matrix} \right\} v \; \ldots \; \rightarrow \; \ldots \; C \; v \left\{ \begin{matrix} r \\ l \\ m \\ n \end{matrix} \right\} \ldots$$

(*C* represents a stop or fricative consonant.) Note that application of this rule can result in *v* (ვ) occurring before *m* (მ), in which case it will be lost by the *v*-loss rule above.

Examples of the operation of these rules will be given in the following lessons.

LESSON 1: Notes

1. Most speakers of American English will have a glottal stop [?] in such words as *cotton, button, mitten,* where instead of a *t*-sound the glottal stop is heard. Some speakers will have a vague approximation of the Georgian glottalized stops in such words as *pum/p/kin, cat* (with released *t*), *pi/ck/pocket.*

2. A somewhat similar sound, although not pronounced as far back, is encountered in Spanish *la/g/o* 'lake', modern Greek αγάπη [aγápi] 'love'.

3. Since there is no contrast in modern literary Georgian between a glottalized [q'] and an aspirated [q‘], for the sake of simplicity the dot under the letter marking glottalization will not be placed on this letter in transliterations in this textbook; i.e., we shall write *q*, not *q̣*.

4. *h* (ჰ) occurs in spelling before *ṗ* (პ), *k* (ქ), *ḳ* (კ), *q* (ყ), *g* (გ) in certain grammatical forms (generally marking a third person dative object), but is generally not pronounced except in very careful speech. See below, section 7.2.4.

APPENDIX: The Georgian Alphabets

The contemporary Georgian alphabet, called *mxedruli* ('military', from *mxedari*, 'knight', 'warrior') came into use in the eleventh century. It replaced the earlier *xucuri* alphabet ('ecclesiastic', from *xucesi*, 'elder', 'priest') which, unlike the *mxedruli*, distinguished upper case ('majuscule', Georgian *asomtavruli*, 'capital') and lower case ('miniscule', Georgian *nusxuri* from *nusxa*, 'cursive hand'). *Xucuri* is first attested in the fifth century (inscriptions from the Monastery of the Cross in Jerusalem, Israel and from the Sioni cathedral in Bolnisi, Georgia). The Georgian alphabet as shown by the distinguished Georgian linguist Thomas Gamkrelidze (Tamaz Gamqrelije) is derived in its basic system from the Greek alphabet although the exact details of its creation are still unclear. Most scholars link the creation of this Georgian alphabet with the christianization of Georgia (approximately 330).

The accompanying chart, adapted from N. Marr and M. Brière, *La langue géorgienne* (Paris, 1931, p. 594), illustrates all three forms of Georgian alphabets along with the names of the letters and their numerical values. In order to show the close correspondance between the system of the Georgian alphabets and that of Greek, the corresponding Greek letters are also given. Note the identity of numerical values between the two languages.

The contemporary Georgian alphabet of thirty-three letters lacks the *he* (8), *hie* (15), *vie* (22), *qar* (35), *hoe* (38), and *fi* (39). Note that the Old Georgian ყ (*q*), then, as now, a post-velar glottalized voiceless consonant was opposed to ჴ (*q*), a post-velar aspirated voiceless stop. (This sound is still found in some Georgian dialects.) As a result, for Old Georgian, the transcription of ყ must contain an indication of glottalization, i.e., *q* with a dot underneath; the aspirated ჴ is for Old Georgian simply transcribed *q*.

Table 1.2 gives the following: 1. Order of letters; 2. *Mxedruli*; 3. *Xucuri*: a. *Asomtavruli*, b. *Nusxuri*; 4. Names of the letters; 5. Transliteration; 6. Greek alphabet; 7. Numerical value (for both Georgian and Greek alphabets).

Table 1.2. The Georgian Alphabets

1	2	3 a.	3 b.	4	5	6	7
1.	ა	Ⴀ	ⴀ	ან an	a	Α	1
2.	ბ	Ⴁ	ⴁ	ბან ban	b	Β	2
3.	გ	Ⴂ	ⴂ	გან gan	g	Γ	3
4.	დ	Ⴃ	ⴃ	დონ don	d	Δ	4
5.	ე	Ⴄ	ⴄ	ენ en	e	Ε	5
6.	ვ	Ⴅ	ⴅ	ვინ vin	v	(1)	6
7.	ზ	Ⴆ	ⴆ	ზენ zen	z	Ζ	7
8.	ჱ	Ⴡ	ⴡ	ჱე he	[ey]	Η	8
9.	თ	Ⴇ	ⴇ	თან tan	t	Θ	9
10.	ი	Ⴈ	ⴈ	ინ in	i	Ι	10
11.	კ	Ⴉ	ⴉ	კან ḳan	ḳ	Κ	20
12.	ლ	Ⴊ	ⴊ	ლას las	l	Λ	30
13.	მ	Ⴋ	ⴋ	მან man	m	Μ	40
14.	ნ	Ⴌ	ⴌ	ნარ nar	n	Ν	50
15.	ჲ	Ⴢ	ⴢ	ჲიე hie	[y]	Ξ	60
16.	ო	Ⴍ	ⴍ	ონ on	o	Ο	70
17.	პ	Ⴎ	ⴎ	პარ p̣ar	p̣	Π	80
18.	ჟ	Ⴏ	ⴏ	ჟან žan	ž	(2)	90
19.	რ	Ⴐ	ⴐ	რაე rae	r	Ρ	100
20.	ს	Ⴑ	ⴑ	სან san	s	Σ	200
21.	ტ	Ⴒ	ⴒ	ტარ ṭar	ṭ	Τ	300
22.	ჳ	Ⴣ	ⴣ	ჳე vie	[vi]	Υ	--
23.	უ	Ⴓ	ⴓ	უნ un	u	[ΟΥ]	400
24.	ფ	Ⴔ	ⴔ	ფარ par	p	Φ	500
25.	ქ	Ⴕ	ⴕ	ქან kan	k	Χ	600
26.	ღ	Ⴖ	ⴖ	ღან ğan	ğ		700
27.	ყ	Ⴗ	ⴗ	ყარ q̣ar	q̣		800
28.	შ	Ⴘ	ⴘ	შინ šin	š		900
29.	ჩ	Ⴙ	ⴙ	ჩინ čin	č		1000
30.	ც	Ⴚ	ⴚ	ცან can	c		2000
31.	ძ	Ⴛ	ⴛ	ძილ jil	j		3000
32.	წ	Ⴜ	ⴜ	წილ c̣il	c̣		4000
33.	ჭ	Ⴝ	ⴝ	ჭარ č̣ar	č̣		5000
34.	ხ	Ⴞ	ⴞ	ხან xan	x		6000
35.	ჴ	Ⴤ	ⴤ	ჴარ qar	[q]		7000
36.	ჯ	Ⴟ	ⴟ	ჯან ǰan	ǰ		8000
37.	ჰ	Ⴠ	ⴠ	ჰაე hae	h		9000
38.	ჵ	Ⴥ		ჵოე hoe	[oy]	Ω	10000
39.	ჶ			ჶი fi	[f]		

1. Older Greek Ϝ (digamma)
2. Older Greek Ϙ (koppa)

LESSON 1: Exercises

1. Cities in Georgia. Copy in Georgian, pronounce, and transliterate the following. Identify harmonic clusters.

თბილისი	ბათუმი	ცხინვალი	ჭიათურა
მცხეთა	ცხაკაია	გეგეჭკორი	ქუთაისი
ბოლნისი	სოხუმი	მახარაძე	გორი
რუსთავი	ახალციხე	ფოთი	გაგრა
ტყიბული	დუშეთი	თელავი	ყვარელი
გარდაბანი	გურჯაანი	ზესტაფონი	საჩხერე

2. World cities. Copy, pronounce, transliterate, and identify the following cities.

ჩიკაგო	სან-ფრანცისკო	დეტროიტი	გლაზგო
ლონდონი	რომი	ბუდაპეშტი	ჰამბურგი
პარიზი	ნიუ-იორკი	მოსკოვი	ჯაკარტა
ბერლინი	რიო-დე-ჟანეირო	ლენინგრადი	ფილადელფია
ტოკიო	ჰელსინკი	პეკინი	ათენი

3. Famous Georgian writers. Copy, pronounce, and transliterate. Identify any harmonic clusters.

შოთა რუსთაველი	ნიკოლოზ ბარათაშვილი
აკაკი წერეთელი	კონსტანტინე გამსახურდია
ვაჟა-ფშაველა	ნოდარ დუმბაძე
ილია ჭავჭავაძე	სულხან-საბა ორბელიანი
მიხეილ ჯავახიშვილი	ნიკო ლორთქიფანიძე
სერგო კლდიაშვილი	გალაკტიონ ტაბიძე
დავით გურამიშვილი	ალექსანდრე ყაზბეგი

4. Famous European and American writers. Copy, pronounce, transliterate, and identify.

შექსპირი	შილერი	მარკ-ტვენი	ლონგფელო
დოსტოევსკი	დანტე	ჰემინგუეი	ჰიუგო
ტოლსტოი	იბსენი	დიკენსი	არისტოფანე
გოეთე	სერვანტესი	ფლობერი	სვიფტი
ზოლა	მოლიერი	თეკერეი	პუშკინი

5. Harmonic clusters. Copy, pronounce, and transliterate.

a. voiced:		b. aspirated:	
ბგერა	sound	ფხიზელი	sober
დგას	stands	ფქვილი	flour
ჯგუფი	group	თხოვნა	request
დღე	day	თქვენ	you (pl.)
მიძღვნა	dedication	თქვა	he said
		ცხოვრება	life
		ცქერა	looking
		ცხადი	clear
		ცხვირი	nose
		ჩქარი	fast
		ჩხუბი	fight

c. glottalized:

პყრობილი	conquered
ტყე	forest
სიტყვა	word
ტკბილი	sweet
ტკივილი	pain, ache
წყალი	water
გადაწყვეტა	solution
წყება	series, row
ჭკუა	reason, intelligence
ჭკვიანი	intelligent

6. Copy, pronounce, and transliterate.

საქართველო	Georgia
ვეფხისტყაოსანი	*The Knight in the Tiger's Skin* (greatest work of Georgian literature, by Šota Rustaveli, ca. 1200)
საბერძნეთი	Greece
საფრანგეთი	France
სპარსეთი	Persia (Iran)
სომხეთი	Armenia
საბჭოთა კავშირი	Soviet Union

ჩრდილოეთი	north
სამხრეთი	south
აღმოსავლეთი	east
დასავლეთი	west
გამარჯობათ	hello (polite or plural)
გაგიმარჯოთ	hello (response to გამარჯობათ, polite or plural)
ნახვამდის	good-bye
მწვადი	shish-kabob (shashlik)
ღვინო	wine
პური	bread
წყალი	water
თავი	head
ხელი	hand, arm
ფეხი	foot, leg
გული	heart
პირი	mouth
მამა	father [sic!]
დედა	mother [sic!]
გოგონა	girl
ბიჭი	boy

7. Copy in Georgian, pronounce, and transliterate the following. (These are the first three stanzas of Šota Rustaveli's *Vepxisṭqaosani The Knight in the Tiger's Skin*).

რომელმან შექმნა სამყარო ძალითა მით ძლიერითა,
ზეგარდმო არსნი სულითა ყვნა ზეცით მონაბერითა,
ჩვენ, კაცთა, მოგვცა ქვეყანა, გვაქვს უთვალავი ფერითა,
და მისგან არს ყოვლი ხელმწიფე სახითა მის მიერითა.

2 ჰე, ღმერთო ერთო, შენ შექმენ სახე ყოვლისა ტანისა,
შენ დამიფარე, ძლევა მეც დათრგუნვად მე სატანისა,
მომეც მიჯნურთა სურვილი, სიკვდიდმდე გასატანისა,
და ცოდვათა შესუბუქება, მუნ თანა წასატანისა.

3 ვის ჰშვენის, — ლომსა, — ხმარება შუბისა, ფარ-შიმშერისა,
— მეფისა მზის თამარისა, ღაწვ-ბადახშ, თმა-გიშერისა, —
მას, არა ვიცი, შევჰკადრო შესხმა ხოტბისა, შე, რისა,
და მისთა მჭვრეტელთა უანდისა მირთმა ხამს მართ, მი, შერისა.

8. Copy, pronounce, and transliterate the following opening lines of Longfellow's *Song of Hiawatha* in Georgian translation.

შესავალი

ე თუ მკითხავენ, საიდან მოდის
ეს ლეგენდები და სიმღერები,
გაჟღენთილები ტყეთა სურნელით
და მდინარეთა სინოტივეთი,
წყნარი სოფლების ცახცახა კვამლით
და ჩანჩქერების აურზაურით...
მე ვუპასუხებ, რომ ტყეებიდან,
პრერიებიდან და მინდვრებიდან,
ოჯიბუების თბილი მიწიდან
და ჩრდილოეთის დიდი ტბებიდან,
ჭაობებიდან და ტუნდრებიდან, —
იქ სადაც ყანჩა და ყანჩის ჩრდილი
გარინდებული დგას ლერწმებს შორის.

მე ამ სიმღერებს ისევე ვმღერი,
ვით ნავადაჰა მღეროდა ადრე.
და თუ იკითხავთ, თვით ნავადაჰამ
სადღა იპოვა ეს სიმღერები:
ასე თავნება და მშვენიერი.
მე გიპასუხებთ, რომ ნავადაჰამ
ისინი ნახა ჩიტის ბუდეში,
ისინი ნახა დათვის ბუნაგში
და ბიზონების ნაფეხურებში.

9. Copy, pronounce, and transliterate the following, taken from *Romeo and Juliet*, act 2, scene 2 in the translation of Vaxṭang Čelije and beginning with "But soft! what light through yonder window breaks?" up to "O! that I were a glove upon that hand, that I might touch that cheek."

ეს რა ნათელი აელვარდა იმის სარკმელში?
აღმოსავლეთი არის იგი, მზე — ჯულიეტა.
ამოდი, მზეო, დააბნელე მოშურნე მთვარე,
ისედაც მკრთალი და სნეული მწუხარებისგან,
რადგან მის ქალწულს ელვარება მეტი გაქვს უფრო.
ნუღარ მსახურებ იმ შურიანს; ქალწულთ სამოსი
მწვანეა მეტად, უფერული — სჯობს გაიხადო
და გადააგდო, — ის მასხარებს აცვიათ მხოლოდ.

ო, ჩემო ტკბილო დედოფალო, ო, სიყვარულო!
მან რომ იცოდეს, როგორ მიყვარს!
ის ლაპარაკობს. თუმცა არა, სდუმს. სულ ერთია,
მისი თვალები მეტყველებენ, მათ ვუპასუხებ.
მაგრამ რას ვბედავ! განა ჩემთან ლაპარაკობენ!
ორ ნათელ ვარსკვლავს განუზრახავს ზეციდან წასვლა,
და ახლა სთხოვენ ჯულიეტას თვალებს ისინი—
იციმციმეთო ჩვენს ადგილზე, დაბრუნებამდე.
რა იქნებოდა, ეს თვალები ზეცას ამკობდნენ,
ხოლო ვარსკვლავნი ჩამოვიდნენ თვალების ნაცვლად!
იმისი სახის ელვარება ჩააბნელებდა
ვარსკვლავთა ციმციმს, ვით დღის შუქი ჩააქრობს ლამპარს,
თვალნი კი ზეცას დააფრქვევდნენ ისეთ სინათლეს,
რომ ფრინველები დაიწყებდნენ დილის სიმღერას.
აჰა, ეყრდნობა სახით ხელებს! ნეტავ მაქცია
ხელთათმანებად იმ ხელებზე, რომ ტურფა ღაწვებს
შევეხო მაინც!

10. Convert the transliterations in the Key to exercises 7, 8, and 9 into the Georgian alphabet. Check yourself against the Georgian in the exercises.

Key to the Exercises

1.

Tbilisi	Batumi	*Cx*invali	C̣iatura
M*cx*eta	*Cx*aḳaia	Gege*č̣ḳ*ori	Kutaisi
Bolnisi	Soxumi	Maxaraje	Gori
Rustavi	Axalcixe	Poti	Gagra
*Tq*ibuli	Dušeti	Telavi	Qvareli
Gardabani	Gurǰaani	Zesṭaponi	Sa*čx*ere

2.

Čiḳago	San-Prancisḳo	Deṭroiṭi	Glazgo (Glasgow)
Londoni	Romi	Budapešṭi	Hamburgi
Ṗarizi	Niu-Iorḳi	Mosḳovi (Moscow)	J̌aḳarṭa
Berlini	Rio-de-Žaneiro	Leningradi	Piladelpia
Ṭoḳio	Helsinḳi	Ṗeḳini (Peking)	Ateni (Athens)

3.

Šota Rustaveli	Niḳoloz Baratašvili
Aḳaḳi C̣ereteli	Ḳonsṭanṭine Gamsaxurdia
Važa-Pšavela	Ṗaolo Iašvili
Ilia Čavc̣avaje	Nodar Dumbaje
Mixeil J̌avaxišvili	Sulxan-Saba Orbeliani
Sergo Ḳldiašvili	Niḳo Lor*tḳ*ipanije
Davit Guramišvili	Galaḳṭion Ṭabije
	Aleksandre Qazbegi

4.

Šekspiri	Šileri (Schiller)	Marḳ-Ṭveni	Longpelo
Dosṭoevsḳi	Danṭe	Heminguei	Hiugo
Ṭolsṭoi	Ibseni	Diḳensi	Arisṭopane
Goete (Goethe)	Servanṭesi	Ploberi (Flaubert)	Svipṭi (Swift)
Zola	Molieri	Ṭeḳerei (Thackeray)	Ṗušḳini

5.

a.	b.	c.
bgera	pxizeli	ṗqrobili
dgas	pkvili	ṭqe
ǰgupi	txovna	siṭqva
dǧe	tkven	ṭḳbili
mijǧvna	tkva	ṭḳivili
	cxovreba	c̣qali
	ckera	gadac̣qveṭa
	cxadi	c̣qeba
	cxviri	č̣ḳua
	čkari	č̣ḳviani
	čxubi	

6. Sakartvelo, Vepxisṭqaosani, Saberjneti, Saprangeti, Ṡparseti, Somxeti, Šabč̣ota ḳavširi, črdiloeti,

samxreti, aǧmosavleti, dasavleti, gamarǰobat, gagimar-ǰot, naxvamdis, mc̣vadi, ǧvino, p̣uri, c̣qali, tavi, xeli, pexi, guli, p̣iri, mama, deda, gogona, bič̣i.

7.
Romelman šekmna samqaro jalita mit jlierita,
zegardmo arsni sulita qvna, zecit monaberita,
čven, ḳacta, mogvca kveqana, gvakvs utvalavi perita,
misgan ars qovli xelmc̣ipe saxita mis mierita.

He, Ǧmerto erto, Šen šehkmen saxe qovlisa ṭanisa,
šen damip̣are, jleva mec datrgunvad me Saṭanisa,
momec miǰnurta survili, siḳvdidmde gasaṭanisa,
codvata šesubukeba, mun tana c̣asaṭanisa.

Vis hšvenis, -- lomsa, -- xmareba šubisa, par-šimšerisa,
-- mepisa mzis Tamarisa, ǧac̣v-badaxš, tma-gišerisa, --
mas, ara vici, ševhḳadro šesxma xoṭbisa, še, risa,
mista mč̣vreṭelta qandisa mirtma xams mart, mi šerisa.

He who created the firmament, by that mighty power made beings inspired from on high with souls celestial; to us men He has given the world, infinite in variety we possess it; from Him is every monarch in His likeness.

O one God! Thou didst create the face of every form! Shield me, give me mastery to trample on Satan, give me the longing of lovers lasting even unto death, lightening the sins I must bear thither with me.

Of that lion whom the use of lance, shield, and sword adorns, of the king, the sun Tamar, the ruby-cheeked, the jet-haired, of her I know not how I shall dare to sing the manifold praise; they who look upon her cannot but taste choice sweets.

(From the translation by
Marjory Scott Wardrop)

8. Šesavali
Me tu mḳitxaven, saidan modis
es legendebi da simǧerebi,
gažǧentilebi ṭqeta surnelit
da mdinareta sinoṭiveti
c̣qnari soplebis caxcaxa ḳvamlit
da čančkerebis aurzaurit...
Me vup̣asuxeb, rom ṭqeebidan
p̣reriebidan da mindvrebidan,
oǰibuebis tbili mic̣idan
da črdiloetis didi ṭbebidan,
č̣aobebidan da ṭundrebidan, --
ik sadac qanča da qančis črdili

garindebuli dgas lerçmebs šoris.
Me am simğerebs iseve vmğeri,
vit Navadaha mğeroda adre.
Da tu iķitxavt, tvit Navadaham
sadğa iṗova es simğerebi:
ase tavṅeba da mšvenieri.
Me giṗasuxebt, rom Navadaham
isini naxa čiṭis budeši,
isini naxa datvis bunagši,
da bizonebis napexurebši.

Henri Longpelo, *Simğera Haiavataze*, Targmani inglisuridan Otar Çilajisa

9.
Es ra nateli aelvarda imis sarķmelši?
Ağmosavleti aris igi, mze J̌ulieṭa.
Amodi, mzeo, daabnele mošurne mṫvare,
isedac mķrtali da sneuli mçuxarebisgan,
radgan mis kalçuls elvareba meṭi gakvs upro.
Nuğar ṁsaxureb im šurians; kalçult samosi
mçvanea meṭad, uperuli -- sǰobs gaixado
da gadaagdo, -- is masxarebs acviat mxolod.
O, čemo ṭķbilo dedopalo, o, siqvarulo!
Man rom icodes, rogor miqvars!
Is laṗaraķobs. Tumca ara, sdums. Sul ertia,
Misi ṫvalebi meṭqveleben, mat vuṗasuxeb.
Magram ras vbedav! Gana čemtan laṗaraķoben!
Or natel varsķvlavs ganuzraxavs zecidaṅ çasvla,
da axla stxoven J̌ulieṭas tvalebs isini --
icimcimeto čvens adgilze, dabrunebamde.
Ra ikneboda, es tvalebi zecas amķobdnen,
xolo varsķvlavni čamovidnen tvalebis nacvlad!
Imisi saxis elvareba čaabnelebda
varsķvlavta cimcims, vit dğis šuki čaakrobs lamṗars,
tvalni ķi zecas daaprkvevdnen iset sinatles,
rom prinvelebi daiçqebdnen dilis simğeras.
Aha, eqrdnoba saxit xelebs! Neṭav makcia
xeltatmanebad im xelebze, rom ṭurpa ğaçvebs
ševexo mainc!

Romeo da J̌ulieṭa, II.2

LESSON 2: A General Introduction to The Georgian Verb

2.0. Conjugation. In Georgian there are four major patterns according to which the various tense and mood forms of a given verb are conjugated. These four patterns will be called *conjugations*. Unlike the conjugations of Latin, Russian, or French, verbs belonging to the same conjugation in Georgian usually also share certain grammatical or semantic features in common. Furthermore, it is often possible to derive forms of one conjugation from a verb belonging to another conjugation (e.g., see Lesson 3).

Series. Within each conjugation we find sets of tense and mood forms which are based on the same stem and share certain syntactic features in common. These will be called *series*. There are three series. The first consists of two subseries, the *future* and the *present*. The second series is called the aorist series, and the third is called the perfect series.

Parts of the verbal form. A Georgian verbal form may consist of a relatively large number of constituent parts. All verbal forms will have a *root*, which may be followed by a *present/future stem formant* (P/FSF):

c̣er-	write	(no P/FSF)
xed-av-	see	(P/FSF -*av*)
targmn-i-	translate	(P/FSF -*i*)
sv-am-	drink	(P/FSF -*am*)
ḳl-av-	kill	(P/FSF -*av*)

The root may be immediately preceded by the *preradical vowel* (PV) which may have various functions depending upon the form with which it is found. The preradical vowels are *a,e,i,u*.

a-ḳet-eb-	make	(PV *a*-, P/FSF -*eb*)
i-c̣q-eb	begin	(PV *i*-, P/FSF -*eb*)
a-ṭb-ob-	warm	(PV *a*-, P/FSF -*ob*)

The preradical vowel (if present) or the root (if there is no preradical vowel) may be immediately preceded by the person markers. In this lesson we shall learn the 1st person subject marker *v*-. The above forms, with the first person marker, would be *v-c̣er* (ვწერ) 'I write'; *v-xed-av* (ვხედავ) 'I see'; *v-targmni* (ვთარგმნი) 'I translate'; *v-sv-am* (ვსვამ) 'I drink'; *v-ḳl-av* (ვკლავ) 'I kill'; *v-a-ḳet-eb* (ვაკეთებ) 'I make'; *v-i-c̣q-eb* (ვიწყებ) 'I begin'.

The person marker (or, if there is none, the preradical vowel or the root) may be preceded by the *pre-*

verb (Pvb). These preverbs, which function somewhat similarly to the prefixes of German or Russian verbs, are listed in sec. 2.2.1. Examples of the verbs with preverbs will be found below.

Following the root and/or present/future stem formant may be (in addition to other markers) markers of the particular tense or mood forms (*screeves*, see below), the subject markers of the third person, and the markers of the plurality of subjects and objects. All of these will be discussed during the course of the lessons.

A final term must be introduced here, the *screeve* (coined by the Georgian linguist Aḳaḳi Šanije from the Georgian word *mçkrivi* 'row'). A screeve is what is traditionally called a tense, i.e., a set of six forms of a given verb differing only in person and number, as in Latin *amo, amas, amat, amamus, amatis, amant*. But since the various "tenses" do not always have temporal meaning, but may have modal or aspectual meanings instead, we prefer the more unusual but less misleading term of *screeve*.

2.1. Subject person and number. The Georgian verb generally marks subject person in the first person by means of the prefix *v-* (ვ-). Second person is generally marked by the absence of both prefix and suffix; we shall note it here by a zero-prefix, Ø-. Plurality of both the first and second person is marked by a final suffix *-t* (-თ). Third person singular and plural are both marked by suffixes which will vary from screeve to screeve and conjugation to conjugation.

Subject person prefixes occur immediately after the preverb (see sec. 2.0.) or, if there is no preverb, in absolute initial position.

Subject Markers

	Singular	Plural
1.	v-	v-......-t
2.	Ø-	Ø-......-t
3.	-suffix	-suffix

2.2. First conjugation. Verbs of the first conjugation are generally transitive, and by themselves mark both the subject and object persons. Thus a single Georgian verbal form, such as *xed-av-t*, means not simply 'you all see' but rather 'you all see him, her, it, or them'.

A third person *direct* object, independent of gender or number, i.e., corresponding to English *him, her, it, them*, is marked in Georgian by the absense of any affix.

2.2.1. Future tense of first conjugation verbs. The forms of verbs given in the vocabulary will be third person singular future tense. Most first conjugation verbs are characterized in the future tense by the presence of a *preverb*. Among the functions of the preverb is to distinguish between the *future* and *present subseries*. The preverbs can be divided into two groups, those ending in -*mo*- and those without -*mo*-. The preverbs are:

	(-*mo*- group)
a- ა- (aǧ- აღ-) 'up'	a-mo- ამო- (aǧ-mo- აღმო-)
ga- გა- (gan- გან-) 'out, away'	ga-mo- გამო-
gada- გადა- (garda- გარდა-) 'across'	gad-mo- გადმო-
da- და- (without specific direction, or sometimes 'down')	
mi- მი- 'away from speaker'	mo- მო- 'toward speaker'
še- შე- 'in, into'	še-mo- შემო-
ča- ჩა- (šta- შთა-) 'down'	ča-mo- ჩამო-
c̣a- წა- (c̣ar- წარ-) 'away'	c̣a-mo- წამო- (c̣ar-mo- წარმო-)
	mimo- მიმო- 'back and forth'

The directional meanings given for the preverbs occur almost exclusively with verbs of motion (see sec. 4.5.). The forms with -*mo*- generally indicate that the action is performed in the direction of the speaker or his addressee; forms without -*mo*- denote the direction of the action away from the speaker or his addressee. The forms in parentheses are variants of the preverbs found in "higher style" words, words somewhat equivalent to the latinate vocabulary in English.

Each screeve is marked by its characteristic set of *suffixes*, which serve to mark the screeve in the first and second persons and to mark the screeve, person, and number of the third subject person. The markers of the future tense are:

1., 2.	∅	
3.	-s (sg.)	-en (pl.)

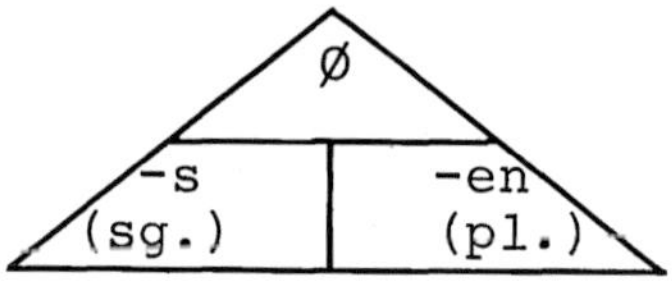

We give the characteristic suffixes of each screeve in the form of a triangle, the top of which represents the suffix of the first and second persons (both singular and plural) and the bottom of which denotes the suffixes of the third person singular and the third person plural. In the given instance, there is no suffix for the first and second persons, while the third person singular has the suffix *-s* (-ს) and the third person plural has the suffix *-en* (-ენ) [*-an* (-ან) after P/FSF *-i* (-ი)].

Verbs whose P/FSF formant ends in *-i* have *-an* in the third person plural future. These endings are added after the present/future stem formant (or, if there is none, after the root). They may be followed by the plural marker *-t* (-თ). Examples:

da= -ç̣er-s 'he (she) will write it (them)'

Singular

1. da=v-ç̣er-Ø	I will write it/them	დავწერ
2. da=Ø-ç̣er-Ø	You will write it/them	დაწერ
3. da= -ç̣er-s	He (she, it) will write it/them	დაწერს

Plural

1. da=v-ç̣er-Ø-t	We will write it/them	დავწერთ
2. da=Ø-ç̣er-Ø-t	You all will write it/them	დაწერთ [1]
3. da= -ç̣er-en	They will write it/them	დაწერენ

gada= -targmn-i-s 'he will translate it, them'

gada=v-targmn-i-Ø	გადავთარგმნი
gada=Ø-targmn-i-Ø	გადათარგმნი
gada= -targmn-i-s	გადათარგმნის
gada=v-targmn-i-Ø-t	გადავთარგმნით
gada=Ø-targmn-i-Ø-t	გადათარგმნით
gada= -targmn-i-an	გადათარგმნიან

mo= -ḳl-av-s 'he (she, it) will kill him (her, it, them)'

mo=v-ḳl-av-Ø	მოვკლავ	mo=v-ḳl-av-Ø-t	მოვკლავთ
mo=Ø-ḳl-av-Ø	მოკლავ	mo=Ø-ḳl-av-Ø-t	მოკლავთ
mo= -ḳl-av-s	მოკლავს	mo= -ḳl-av-en	მოკლავენ

As can be seen from the above examples, the first person plural differs from the first person singular only by the presence of the plural suffix *-t*. Similarly the second person plural differs from the second person singular only by the presence of the same suffix. Note also that Georgian distinguishes neither gender nor natural sex so that a third person singular subject person can correspond to English *he*, *she*, or *it*. The third person object person not only does not distinguish gender, it also does not distinguish number, so that it can be translated (depending on context) by English *him*, *her*, *it*, *them*. Henceforth in the examples we shall indicate the first person singular and plural and the second person singular and plural as follows:

Vocabulary entry form: a=a-šen-eb-s 'he will build it'

1. a=v-a-šen-eb-Ø- (t)
2. a=Ø-a-šen-eb-Ø- (t)
3. sg. a= -a-šen-eb-s 3. pl. a= -a-šen-eb-en

2.2.2. Present tense. The present tense of first conjugation verbs is normally formed by dropping the preverb. Examples:

da=v-c̣er-Ø-t	we will write it	დავწერთ
v-c̣er-Ø-t	we are writing it	ვწერთ
a=Ø-a-šen-eb	you will build it	ააშენებ
Ø-a-šen-eb	you are building it	აშენებ

The difference between the future and present tenses of I. conjugation verbs, as well as that between the remaining screeves of the future and present subseries, is basically aspectual: the future subseries is perfective and the present is imperfective. Cf. Georgian *dac̣ers* (დაწერს) and *c̣ers* (წერს) with Russian напишет and пишет.

Certain verbs which are inherently perfective in meaning, i.e., which by their very nature denote completed acts, do not have separate present tenses. Either one uses the future tense with present meaning or a paraphrase is used. In the vocabularies such verbs will be noted by a plus (+) after the preverb; verbs distinguishing future and present will have the preverb separated from the rest of the verb by an =; e.g.,

ga=a-ḳet-eb-s	he will make something
aǧ+c̣er-s	he will describe something

The above implies that to say 'he is making something' one must drop the preverb: *a-ḳet-eb-s* (აკეთებს). But to say 'he describes it' one uses the same form as the future: *aǧ+c̣er-s* (აღწერს). In a few instances the future and present differ by a feature other than the presence versus absence of a preverb. In such instances the vocabulary will give both the future and present forms, e.g.:

nax-av-s	he will see it	pres. xed-av-s
i-sc̣avl-i-s	he will study it	pres. sc̣avl-ob-s[2]

2.2.3. Conditional and imperfect. The Georgian conditional is used to express what *would happen* as a consequence of some other hypothetical action (the English conditional; see Lesson 4). The imperfect denotes ongoing (progressive) past actions, usually corresponding to English constructions of the type 'he was writing', 'he was studying', 'he was making something', etc. The imperfect is also used to express past *iterativity*, i.e., habitual actions in the past, corresponding to English 'used to' or 'would'. In this use the imperfect can be accompanied by the adverb *xolme* (ხოლმე[3]) which emphasizes the iterative use of the imperfect. Inherently perfective verbs (i.e., those which do not lose the preverb in the present tense) use the form of the conditional for the imperfect as well.

The conditional is formed from the same stem as the future and the imperfect is formed from the same stem as the present. The subject markers of the first and second persons are the same as for the future and present tenses; the suffixes are:

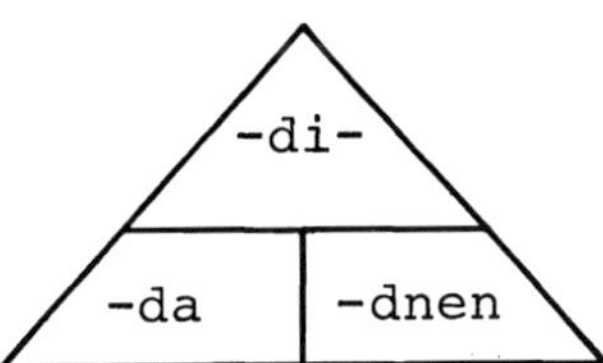

Examples:

da=v-c̣er-di(-t)	დავწერდი(თ)	I (we) {would / used to} write it
da=∅-c̣er-di(-t)	დაწერდი(თ)	you (all) {would / used to} write it
da= -c̣er-da	დაწერდა	he {would / used to} write it
da= -c̣er-dnen	დაწერდნენ	they {would / used to} write it

The imperfect is generally formed by dropping the preverb from the conditional:

v-c̣er-di(-t)	ვწერდი(თ)	I (we) was writing it
Ø-c̣er-di(-t)	წერდი(თ)	you (all) were writing it
c̣er-da	წერდა	he was writing it
c̣er-dnen	წერდნენ	they were writing it

Note that if the present tense is formed other than by just dropping a preverb, the conditional is formed from the future stem (i.e., the 3 sg. future minus the subject person ending -*s*) and the imperfect is formed from the present stem (i.e., the 3 sg. present minus the subject person -*s*):

i-ḳitx-av-s he will read it; pres.: ḳitxulob-s

This implies the following:

Conditional

v-i-ḳitx-av-di (-t) ვიკითხავდი(თ)
Ø-i-ḳitx-av-di (-t) იკითხავდი(თ)
i-ḳitx-av-da იკითხავდა i-ḳitx-av-dnen იკითხავდნენ

Imperfect

v-ḳitxulob-di (-t) ვკითხულობდი(თ)
Ø-ḳitxulob-di (-t) კითხულობდი(თ)
ḳitxulob-da კითხულობდა ḳitxulob-dnen კითხულობდნენ

(It should be noted that verbs of the type of *naxavs* (ნახავს), pres. *xedavs* (ხედავს); *isc̣avlis* (ისწავლის), pres. *sc̣avlobs* (სწავლობს); *iḳitxavs* (იკითხავს), pres. *ḳitxulobs* (კითხულობს) are quite atypical.)

2.3. Nominal system

2.3.1. Nominative and dative cases of nouns. The subject of a first conjugation verb in the screeves based on the future and present tenses is in the nominative case, i.e., the vocabulary entry form. The nominative case has the ending -*i* if the stem of the noun ends in a consonant. If the stem ends in a vowel there is no ending. The objects in these screeves, both direct and indirect, are in the dative case, which has the ending -*s*. This -*s* replaces the nominative ending -*i* of nouns whose stems end in a consonant.

N.	ena- ენა language	c̣ign-i წიგნი book	
D.	ena-s ენას	c̣ign-s წიგნს	

N. c̣eril-i წერილი letter

D. c̣eril-s წერილს

Expressions of time and measure such as 'every year', 'all day', 'three weeks', 'three miles', etc. can be in both the nominative and dative cases.[4]

2.3.2. Adjectives. Adjectives whose stems end in a vowel are always uninflected when they precede the noun they modify, no matter what case or number the noun is in. Adjectives whose stems end in a consonant have the ending *-i* for the nominative and no ending (Ø) for the dative when they precede the noun they modify:

N.	kartul-i ena-	ქართული ენა	Georgian language
D.	kartul-Ø ena-s	ქართულ ენას	
N.	axal-i mepe	ახალი მეფე	new king
D.	axal-Ø mepe-s	ახალ მეფეს	
N.	sainṭereso c̣ign-i	საინტერესო წიგნი	interesting book
D.	sainṭereso c̣ign-s	საინტერესო წიგნს	
N.	ḳarg-i p̣ropesor-i	კარგი პროფესორი	good professor
D.	ḳarg-Ø p̣ropesor-s	კარგ პროფესორს	

When an adjective is not followed by a noun it is declined as if it were a noun:

N.	axal-i	ახალი	the new one
D.	axal-s	ახალს	
N.	ḳarg-i	კარგი	the good one
D.	ḳarg-s	კარგს	
N.	sainṭereso	საინტერესო	the interesting one
D.	sainṭereso-s	საინტერესოს	

2.4. Word order. Although Georgian word order tends to be quite "free," in normal word order the verb is in sentence final position. The subject generally precedes the objects. Negatives and interrogative words and phrases *must* immediately precede the verb.

2.5. Word building. The verbal noun (masdar): The verbal noun in Georgian generally corresponds in meaning to English deverbal nouns (gerunds) in *-ing*, e.g., Georgian *dacera* (დაწერა), English '(the) writing'. It is important to note that the Georgian verbal noun is basically a nominal form and, unlike English, cannot take a direct object, so that constructions such as English 'reading the book (is difficult)' are impossible in Georgian and only the equivalent of English 'the reading of the book' (genitive case in Georgian, see Lesson 3) is possible in this construction.

The verbal noun of first conjugation verbs is usually formed from both the future and the present stems. To form the verbal noun all person and number markers are dropped as well as the preradical vowel. The P/FSFs *-av-* (-ავ-) and *-am-* (-ამ-) lose the vowel *a* (ა), a loss which we shall call syncope.[5] The P/FSF *-i* is dropped. To the resulting stems the masdar ending *-a* (ა) is added.

Future/ Present	Verbal noun stem	Verbal noun	
da=c̣er-s	da=c̣er-	da=c̣er-a (დაწერა)	writing
c̣er-s	c̣er-	c̣er-a (წერა)	writing[6]
da=xaṭ-av-s	da=xaṭ-a̸v-	da=xaṭ-v-a (დახატვა)	painting

(Similarly *xaṭ-v-a* ხატვა [from *xaṭ-av-s*] 'painting'.)

a=a-šen-eb-s	a= -šen-eb-	a=šen-eb-a (აშენება)	building
i-ḳitx-av-s	ḳitx-a̸v-	ḳitx-v-a (კითხვა)	reading

Note that no masdar is formed from the present stem *ḳitxulob-s* (კითხულობს).

gada= targmn-i-s	gada=targmn-	gada= targmn-a (გადათარგმნა)	translating
mo=ḳl-av-s	mo=ḳl-a̸v- mo-ḳvl- → (1.11.2)	mo-ḳvl-a (მოკვლა)	killing
gamo+tkv-am-s	gamo+tkv- a̸m- → gamo+ tkv̸-m- (1.11.1)	gamo+tk-m-a (გამოთქმა)	pronunciation

ağ+nišn-av-s	ağ+nišn-~~a~~v- → ağ+nišn-v- → ağ+nišvn- (1.11.2)	ağ+nišvn-a (აღნიშვნა)	meaning, definition
da=i-c̣q-eb-s	da=c̣q-eb-	da=c̣q-eb-a (დაწყება)	beginning, commencement

The verbal noun is declined just as any other regular noun ending in *a* (ა), although it often does not have plural forms. It should be noted that although the verbal noun is basically a nominal form, most Georgian dictionaries regard it as the equivalent of the infinitive of European languages and list verbs under the form of the verbal noun. This is, unfortunately, the equivalent of an English dictionary not giving the verb 'pronounce' but only the noun 'pronunciation'.

2.6. Expressions of 'and' in Georgian. The Georgian conjunction *da* (და) means 'and' in most environments. But when two contrastive clauses are joined, the conjunction *ḳi* (კი) must be used. *Ḳi* (კი) is always the *second* element in the clause. Example:

Šota c̣erils c̣ers, Ivane *ḳi* c̣igns ḳitxulobs.

შოთა წერილს წერს, ივანე კი წიგნს კითხულობს.

Šota is writing a letter and John is reading a book.

In the exercises this use of *ḳi* (კი) generally will be translated as 'however', e.g., the sentence above would read 'Šota is writing a letter; John, however, is reading a book'.

LESSON 2: Notes

1. For the sake of distinguishing between 2d person singular and plural, we shall consistently translate the 2d singular by English 'you' and the 2d plural by English 'you all'. Note that the use of 2d singular and plural in Georgian parallels their use in French or Russian, the singular form being familiar and the plural form being the polite form to one person in addition to being used to address more than one person.

2. Note that the *i-* with which *i-sc̣avl-i-s* begins is not a preverb but a preradical vowel, and thus the first person will be *v-i-sc̣avl-i* 'I shall study'.

3. *Xolme* (ხოლმე) is also used with other screeves as well to indicate habitual actions; see, e.g., sentence 31 in the exercises.

4. According to the norm, these expressions should be in the dative when the grammatical subject of the sentences is nominative and in the nominative when the grammatical subject is in a case other than nominative. But the tendency now is to use the nominative in both instances.

5. As a result of this syncope, both the *v-loss rule* (1.11.1.) and the *metathesis rule* (1.11.2.) may become operative. See the examples of *mo=ḳl-av-s* (მოკლავს) 'kill', verbal noun *mo=kvl-a* (მოკვლა) and *gamo+tkv-am-s* (გამოთქვამს) 'pronounce', verbal noun *gamo+tk-m-a* (გამოთქმა) below.

6. The difference in meaning between *c̣era* (წერა) and *dac̣era* (დაწერა) is one of aspect, the former being imperfective and the latter perfective.

LESSON 2: Exercises

1. რას აკეთებ?
   ინგლისურ წიგნს ვკითხულობ.
2. დავითი რას აკეთებს?
   ქართულ წიგნს კითხულობს.
3. წერილს წერ?
   არა, არ ვწერ.
4. მასწავლებელს ხედავ?
   დიახ, ვხედავ. სტატიას წერს.
5. რას აკეთებენ დავითი და ელისაბედი?
   წიგნს კითხულობენ.
6. რას აკეთებდა შენი მამა გუშინ?
   გუშინ საინტერესო წიგნს კითხულობდა. დღეს კი წერილს წერს. ხვალ ჩემი ძმა წერილს დაწერს.
7. ხვალ რას გააკეთებთ? ხვალ გაზეთს წავიკითხავთ. დედა წერილს დაწერს, მარიამი კი რუსულ ლექსს ისწავლის.
8. რას სწავლობ? ქართულ გრამატიკას ვსწავლობ.
9. რას ხედავ? მასწავლებელს ვხედავ. მოწაფეს ხედავ? დიახ, ქართულ გაკვეთილს თარგმნის. ელისაბედი გაკვეთილს ხვალ გადათარგმნის.
10. გუშინ რა ენას სწავლობდი? გუშინ რუსულ ენას ვსწავლობდი. ინგლისურ გაკვეთილს გადავწერ ხვალ. ახლა ქართულ გაზეთს ვკითხულობ.
11. მარიამი ქართულ ანბანს სწავლობს. სიტყვას გადაწერს და შემდეგ წარმოთქვამს. ქართულ სიტყვას კარგად წარმოთქვამს.
12. რას აღნიშნავს სიტყვა „მამა"? „მამა" აღნიშნავს „father"-ს. ქართული სიტყვა „დედა" აღნიშნავს „mother"-ს.
13. ხვალ მარიამს ვნახავ. მარიამი და ელისაბედი საქართველოს აღწერენ. შემდეგ ქართულ გაკვეთილს წაიკითხავენ.
14. კონცერტს ისმენთ? არა, ქართულ სავარჯიშოს ვწერთ.

საღამოს კინოფილმს ვნახავთ, შემდეგ კი გაკვეთილს ვისწავლით.

15. მასწავლებელს ხედავთ? ახლა წერილს წერს. გუშინ საინტერესო სტატიას კითხულობდა.
16. რას აკეთებდით გუშინ? ქართულ ლექსს ვიხილავდით.
17. გუშინ წითელ წიგნს ვკითხულობდი. ვანო კი თეთრს კითხულობდა.
18. რას ისმენთ? ახლა ქართულ ოპერას ვისმენთ. ხვალ რუსულს მოვისმენთ.
19. ზურაბი რადიოგადაცემას ისმენს? არა, ყურნალს კითხულობს. შოთა და შალვა ისმენენ რადიოგადაცემას.
20. მასწავლებელი სავარჯიშოს იხილავს? დიახ, სავარჯიშოს იხილავს. ხვალ ახალ სავარჯიშოს განიხილავს.
21. დღეს ქართულ ზმნას სწავლობენ, ხვალ კი დიდ ქართულ ლექსს წაიკითხავენ.
22. გუშინ ქართულ გრამატიკას სწავლობდით? არა, ქართულ გრამატიკას არ ვსწავლობდით. რუსულ პიესას ვთარგმნიდით.
23. ხვალ რას გავაკეთებთ? ქართულ სტატიას წავიკითხავთ, შემდეგ კი განვიხილავთ. თბილისს აღვწერთ.
24. რას აკეთებდნენ შოთა და შალვა? შოთა ინგლისურ წიგნს კითხულობდა, შალვა კი ქართულს.
25. რას იხილავდი გუშინ? „ანა კარენინას" ვიხილავდი.
26. მასწავლებელი დაიწყებს თარგმნას, მოწაფე კი გააგრძელებს.
27. ხვალ ელისაბედი და შალვა მნიშვნელოვან სტატიას გადათარგმნიან. შემდეგ ქართულ ენას განიხილავენ.
28. ქართულ სტატიას კითხულობდი? არა, ინგლისურს ვკითხულობდი.
29. ხვალ რუსულ სავარჯიშოს გადაწერთ? არა, ქართულს გადავწერთ.
30. რას აკეთებდნენ შოთა და შალვა გუშინ? შოთა და

შალვა ქართულ გაზეთს კითხულობდნენ. ზურაბი და მარიამი კი ლინგვისტიკას სწავლობდნენ. ხვალ სულიკო ქართულ ანბანს გადაწერს.

31. როცა ქართულ ენას ვსწავლობთ, მასწავლებელი სიტყვას დაწერს ხოლმე, ვანო და მარიკო კი გადაწერენ. მასწავლებელი სიტყვას წარმოთქვამს, და შემდეგ ვანო გაიმეორებს. ხვალ ვანო და მარიკო განიხილავენ ქართულ რომანს.

32. ვიქტორი ლექსს ისმენს. შემდეგ სავარჯიშოს გადაწერს.

33. როცა მამა წერას დაიწყებს, დედა კითხვას დაიწყებს, მარიკო კი გაზეთს წაიკითხავს.

34. ვიქტორი კლასიკურ მუსიკას ისმენდა ხოლმე. ახლა კი, როცა ქართულ გრამატიკას სწავლობს, ქართულ ხალხურ მუსიკას ისმენს.

35. როცა ქართულ გრამატიკას ვსწავლობდით, მასწავლებელი ხშირად აღწერდა ხოლმე ქართულ წარმოთქმას. ყოველ ახალ ქართულ სიტყვას წარმოთქვამდა ხოლმე. შემდეგ სიტყვას გადავწერდი ხოლმე. ვიმეორებდი ხოლმე, როცა ვკითხულობდი ქართულ გრამატიკას.

36. დღეს ვიქტორი სიმფონიას ისმენს. გუშინ კვარტეტს ისმენდა.

37. როცა ვანო და თამარი რუსულ ენას სწავლობდნენ, რუსულ ლექსს ხშირად თარგმნიდნენ ხოლმე.

38. ფიზიკას როდის ისწავლით? ფიზიკას ხვალ საღამოს ვისწავლით.

39. შენს ქართულ ლექსს როდის დაწერ? ჩემს ქართულ ლექსს საღამოს დავწერ.

40. რას აკეთებდით გუშინ საღამოს? გუშინ საღამოს ქართულ გაკვეთილს ვწერდით და ლინგვისტიკას ვსწავლობდით. დღეს საღამოს ჩვენს ახალ ოპერას მოვისმენთ.

41. ახალ სავარჯიშოს როდის გადათარგმნი? ახალს დღეს საღამოს გადავთარგმნი, შემდეგ კი ვისწავლი ქიმიას.

42. როცა მასწავლებელი სიტყვას დაწერს, გადავწერთ. შემდეგ წარმოვთქვამთ.
43. წითელ წიგნს ხედავ? არა, მხოლოდ თეთრს ვხედავ.
44. ახალ გაკვეთილს ხვალ გადათარგმნიან? არა, ხვალ ძველს გადათარგმნიან.
45. ვიქტორი კითხვას სწავლობს, მარიამი კი წერას.
46. ელისაბედი გუშინ სწავლობდა ქართულ წარმოთქმას, დღეს კი ქართულ ლექსს კარგად წარმოთქვამს.
47. ვიქტორი და ზურაბი ქართულ ზმნას ისწავლიან.
48. ძველ ქართულს სწავლობთ? არა, ახალს.
49. როცა შოთა წერილს წერდა, ვანო და სულიკო თარგმნას იწყებდნენ.
50. ახლა „ვფრცქვნი"-ს წარმოვთქვამ. „ვფრცქვნი" „I'm peeling it"-ს აღნიშნავს. კარგად წარმოვთქვამ!

Vocabulary

ანბანი	alphabet
არ	not [has the form არა when not immediately before the verb]
არა	no
ახალი	new
ახლა	now
გაზეთი	newspaper
გაკვეთილი	lesson
გრამატიკა	grammar
გუშინ	yesterday
და	and
დავითი	David [m.pr.n.]
დედა	mother
დიახ	yes
დიდი	great, big, large
დღეს	today [D. of დღე 'day']
ელისაბედი	Elizabeth
ენა	language
ვანო	Vano [m.pr.n. from ივანე 'John']
ვიქტორი	Victor
ზმნა	verb
ზურაბი	Zurab [m.pr.n.]
თამარი	Tamar [f.pr.n.]
თარგმანი	translation [i.e., book, article, etc.]
თბილისი	Tbilisi
თეთრი	white
თქვენი	your, yours**
ინგლისური	English [adj.]*
კარგად	well [adverb]
კინოფილმი	movie, cinema film
კვარტეტი	quartet
კი	however, and [see sec. 2.6]
კლასიკური	classical
კონცერტი	concert
ლექსი	poem
ლინგვისტიკა	linguistics
მამა	father
მარიამი	Mary [f.pr.n.]
მარიკო	Mary [dimin. of მარიამი]
მასწავლებელი	teacher
მნიშვნელოვანი	important
მოწაფე	pupil
მუსიკა	music
მხოლოდ	only
ოპერა	opera
პიესა	[theater] play
ჟურნალი	magazine

რა	what? [interr.]
რადიოგადაცემა	radio broadcast
როდის	when? [interr.]
რომანი	novel
როცა or როდესაც	when [relative]
რუსული	Russian* [adj.]
სავარჯიშო	exercise
საინტერესო	interesting
საქართველო	Georgia
საღამოს	in the evening [D. of საღამო 'evening']
სიმფონია	symphony
სიტყვა	word
სტატია	article
სულიკო	Suliḳo [f. or m.pr.n.]
ფიზიკა	physics
ფილმი	film
ქართული	Georgian* [adj.]
ქიმია	chemistry
ყოველი	every
შალვა	Šalva [m.pr.n.]
შემდეგ	then [=afterwards]
შენი	your, yours [sg.]**
შოთა	Šota [m.pr.n.]
ჩემი	my, mine**
ჩვენი	our, ours**
ძველი	old [of things]
ძმა	brother
წერილი	letter; article
წიგნი	book
წითელი	red
ხალხური	folk [adj.]
ხოლმე	[indicates iterativity; see sec. 2.2.3]
ხვალ	tomorrow
ხშირად	often

Verbs.

Verbs will be listed alphabetically by root. (Roots will be italicized.) If several verbs have the same root, they will be alphabetized by prefix.

გააგრძელებს	ga=a-*grjel*-eb-s	continue
გადათარგმნის	gada=*targmn*-i-s	translate
წარმოთქვამს	c̣armo+*tkv*-am-s:pr=fut. [VN წარმოთქმა (1.11.1)]	pronounce
გააკეთებს	ga=a-*ḳet*-eb-s	do, make
(წა)იკითხავს: კითხულობს	(c̣a+)i-*ḳitx*-av-s: pr. ḳitxulob-s [both forms of future used]	read
გაიმეორებს	ga=i-*meor*-eb-s	repeat

ნახავს: ხედავს	*nax*-av-s: pr. *xed*-av-s	see
აღნიშნავს	ağ=/ağ+*nišn*-av-s [VN აღნიშვნა (1.11.2)]	mean
მოისმენს	mo=i-*smen*-s	listen to
ისწავლის: სწავლობს	i-*sc̣avl*-i-s: pr. sc̣avlob-s	study, learn
აღწერს	ağ+*c̣er*-s	describe
გადაწერს	gada+*c̣er*-s	copy
დაწერს	da=*c̣er*-s	write
დაიწყებს	da=i-*c̣q*-eb-s	begin
ხედავს	[see ნახავს]	
განიხილავს	gan=i-*xil*-av-s	discuss, examine

*Not used of persons; see sec. 4.6.3.
**The possessive adjectives *čemi* (ჩემი) 'my', *čveni* (ჩვენი) 'our', *šeni* (შენი) 'your', and *tkveni* (თქვენი) 'you all's' generally take the dative ending *-s* when modifying a noun in the dative. *Mati* (მათი) 'their' (sec. 7.4.) also takes this dative ending.

Key to the Exercises

1. What are you doing?
   I am reading an English book.
2. What is David doing?
   He is reading a Georgian book.
3. Are you writing a letter?
   No, I am not writing.
4. Do you see the teacher?
   Yes, I see him. He is writing an article.
5. What are David and Elizabeth doing?
   They are reading a book.
6. What was your father doing yesterday?
   Yesterday he was reading an interesting book. Today, however, he is writing a letter. Tomorrow my brother will write a letter.
7. What will you all do tomorrow? Tomorrow we will read the newspaper. Mother will write a letter, Mary however will learn a Russian poem.
8. What are you studying?
   I am studying Georgian grammar.
9. What do you see?
   I see the teacher.
   Do you see the pupil?
   Yes, he is translating the Georgian lesson.
   Elizabeth will translate the lesson tommorow.
10. What language were you studying yesterday?
    Yesterday I was studying the Russian language. I will copy the English lesson tomorrow. Now I am reading a Georgian newspaper.
11. Mary is studying the Georgian alphabet. She will copy a word and then will pronounce it. She will pronounce the Georgian word well.
12. What does the word *mama* mean?
    Mama means 'father'. The Georgian word *deda* means 'mother'.
13. I shall see Mary tomorrow. Mary and Elizabeth will describe Georgia. Then they will read the Georgian lesson.
14. Are you all listening to the concert?
    No, we are writing the Georgian exercises. In the evening we will see a film, then however we will learn the lesson.
15. Do you all see the teacher?
    Now he is writing a letter. Yesterday he was reading an interesting article.
16. What were you all doing yesterday?
    We were discussing a Georgian poem.
17. Yesterday I was reading a red book. Vano, however, was reading a white one.
18. What are you all listening to?

Now we are listening to a Georgian opera. Tomorrow we will listen to a Russian one.

19. Is Zurab listening to the radio broadcast?
No, he is reading a magazine. Šota and Šalva are listening to the radio broadcast.

20. Is the teacher discussing the exercise?
Yes, he is discussing the exercise. Tomorrow he will discuss the new exercise.

21. Today they are studying the Georgian verb; tomorrow, however, they will read a great Georgian poem.

22. Were you all studying Georgian grammar yesterday?
No, we were not studying Georgian grammar. We were translating a Russian play.

23. What will we do tomorrow?
We will read a Georgian article; then, however, we will discuss it. We will describe Tbilisi.

24. What were Šota and Šalva doing?
Šota was reading an English book; Šalva, however, a Georgian one.

25. What were you discussing yesterday?
I was discussing *Anna Karenina*.

26. The teacher will start the translating [verbal noun]; the student, however, will continue it.

27. Tomorrow Elizabeth and Šalva will translate an important article. Then they will discuss the Georgian language.

28. Were you reading a Georgian article?
No, I was reading an English one.

29. Will you all copy the Russian exercise tomorrow?
No, we will copy the Georgian one.

30. What were Šota and Šalva doing yesterday?
Šota and Šalva were reading a Georgian newspaper. Zurab and Mary, however, were studying linguistics. Tomorrow Suliḳo will copy the Georgian alphabet.

31. When we study Georgian the teacher writes [use ხოლმე] a word; Vano and Mariḳo, however, will copy it. The teacher will pronounce the word, and then Vano will repeat it. Tomorrow Vano and Mariḳo will discuss a Georgian novel.

32. Victor is listening to the poem. Then he will copy the exercise.

33. When father will begin the writing, mother will begin the reading; Mariḳo, however, will read the newspaper.

34. Victor used to listen to classical music. Now, however, when he studies Georgian grammar he listens to Georgian folk music.

35. When we were studying Georgian grammar, the teacher often would describe the Georgian pronuncia-

tion. He would pronounce every new Georgian word. Then I would copy the word. I would repeat it when I was reading a Georgian grammar.

36. Today Victor is listening to a symphony. Yesterday he was listening to a quartet.
37. When Vano and Tamar were studying the Russian language, they would often translate a Russian poem.
38. When will you all study physics?
    We will study physics tomorrow evening.
39. When will you write your Georgian poem?
    I will write my Georgian poem in the evening.
40. What were you all doing yesterday in the evening? Yesterday in the evening we were writing the Georgian lesson and studying linguistics. Today in the evening we will listen to our new opera.
41. When will you translate the new exercise?
    Today I will translate the new one in the evening; then, however, I will study chemistry.
42. When the teacher will write the word, we will copy it.
    Then we will pronounce it.
43. Do you see the red book? No, I see only the white one.
44. Will they translate the new lesson tomorrow?
    No, tomorrow they will translate the old one.
45. Victor is studying reading, Mary, however, writing.
46. Elizabeth was studying Georgian pronunciation yesterday; today, however, she will pronounce the Georgian poem well.
47. Victor and Zurab will study the Georgian verb.
48. Are you all studying old Georgian? No, new!
49. When Šota was writing a letter, Vano and Suliḳo were beginning the translating [use verbal noun].
50. Now I will pronounce ვფრცქვნი. ვფრცქვნი means 'I am peeling it'. I will pronounce it well!

LESSON 3

3.1. Second conjugation. The second conjugation, generally derived from verbs of the first conjugation, is usually (though not always) intransitive in meaning with respect to the meaning of the first conjugation forms. This intransitivity can be manifested as a simple intransitive, e.g., *v-mal-av* (ვმალავ) 'I hide something', II. conjugation form *v-i-mal-eb-i* (ვიმალები) 'I am hiding' (i.e., myself), cf. French *je me cache*. Most commonly II. conjugation forms correspond to English passives, e.g., *daçers* (დაწერს) 'he will write it', II. conjugation form *daiçereba* (დაიწერება) 'it will be written', or to *inceptives* or *inchoatives*, forms indicating 'becoming', e.g., *gaalamazebs* (გაალამაზებს)he will beautify it,' II. conjugation form *galamazdeba* (გალამაზდება) 'it will become beautiful'.

3.1.1. The endings of the future and present screeves of II. conjugation verbs are:

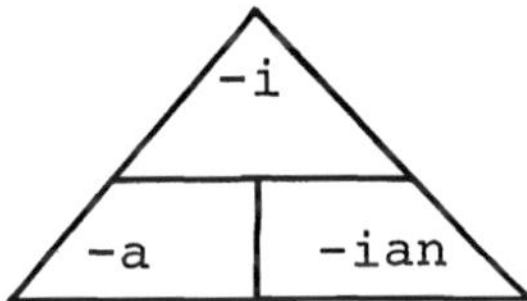

There are two productive ways of deriving II. conjugation forms from I. conjugation forms, depending on the present stem formant of the I. conjugation forms.

3.1.2. II. conj. in *d* (დ) (დონიანი ვნებითი).

I. conjugation verbs that have the following three features:

(1) Preradical vowel *-a-* (-ა-), sometimes *-i-* (-ი-),
(2) Syllabic root (i.e., root contains a vowel),
(3) Present/future stem formant *-eb-* (-ებ-)

form their II. conjugation forms in *-d-* (-დ-). This is a highly productive class consisting largely of verbs derived from nouns or adjectives (see wordbuilding, this lesson). II. conjugation forms in *d* most commonly have the *inceptive* or *inchoative* meanings mentioned above, i.e., they denote a change of state, a "becoming."

The II. conjugation stem of these verbs is formed by dropping the preradical vowel [*-a-* (-ა-) or *-i-* (-ი-)] and the suffixes of the present or future screeve and adding the II. conjugation marker *-d-* (-დ-) immediately before the present/future stem marker *-eb-* (-ებ-). The personal endings of the second conjugation (see above) are then added to this stem. Examples:

Vocabulary entry form: ga=a-c̣itl-eb-s 'he will make s.o. blush' (I. conjugation)

(a) drop preradical vowel: ga= -c̣itl-eb-
(b) insert *-d-*: ga= -c̣itl-d-eb-
(c) add suffixes:

გავწითლდები (-თ)	ga=v-c̣itl-d-eb-i (-t)	I/we shall blush
გაწითლდები (-თ)	ga= -c̣itl-d-eb-i (-t)	you (all) will blush
გაწითლდება	ga= -c̣itl-d-eb-a	
გაწითლდებიან	ga= -c̣itl-d-eb-ian	

The present tense is formed by dropping the preverb.

Vocabulary entry form: a=a-šen-eb-s (ააშენებს) 'he will build it' (I. conjugation)

(a) drop preradical vowel: a= -šen-eb-
(b) insert *-d-*: a= -šen-d-eb-
(c) add suffixes:

აშენდება	a=šen-d-eb-a	it will be built
აშენდებიან	a=šen-d-eb-ian	they will be built
შენდება	šen-d-eb-a	it is being built
შენდებიან	šen-d-eb-ian	they are being built

3.1.3. II. conj. in *-i* (-ი) (ინიანი ვნებითი). Most remaining I. conjugation forms form their II. conjugation with *-i-* (-ი-) as preradical vowel, replacing any other preradical vowel that there may be in the I. conjugation form. The present/future stem formant is dropped and replaced by *-eb-* (-ებ-). The personal suffixes are then added. Examples: da=xaṭ-av-s (I) 'he will paint it'.

დავიხატები (-თ)	da=v-i-xaṭ-eb-i (-t)	I/we shall be painted
დაიხატები (-თ)	da= -i-xaṭ-eb-i (-t)	you (all) will be painted
დაიხატება	da= -i-xaṭ-eb-a	he will be painted
დაიხატებიან	da= -i-xaṭ-eb-i-an	they will be painted

I. conjugation verbs with F/PSF *-ob* with a root *not* containing a vowel, and with a preradical vowel (generally *-a-* or *-i-*) form the II. conjugation irregularly; see sec. 9.1.2.1.

Other types of irregularities are discussed below or will be given in the vocabularies to the exercises or the reading passages.

3.1.4. Irregularities.

3.1.4.1. Root verbs with vowel *e*. A *root verb* is a verb which has no present/future stem formant. In some of the root verbs which have the root vowel *e*, this *e* changes to *i* in the II. conjugation. These will be indicated in the vocabularies. Examples:

I. conj.

da=i-č̣er-s	დაიჭერს	catch
še=ḳreb-s	შეკრებს	collect, gather
mo=i-smen-s	მოისმენს	listen to

II. conj.

da=i-č̣ir-eb-a	დაიჭირება
še=i-ḳrib-eb-a	შეიკრიბება
mo=i-smin-eb-a	მოისმინება

Note that some root verbs with *e* do not have this alternation: da=c̣er-s დაწერს (I.), II. conjugation *da=i-c̣er-eb-a* (დაიწერება).

3.1.4.2. Root verbs ending in *-ev*. Such verbs tend to be irregular in the formation of the II. conjugation forms. See sec. 15.1.4.

3.1.4.3. Verbs in *-am*. The small number of verbs in *-am* (all of which are members of an irregular class) can form their II. conjugation forms with the preradical vowel *-i-*, and with the loss of the *a* from the P/FSF *-am*. The endings in the present/future then are:

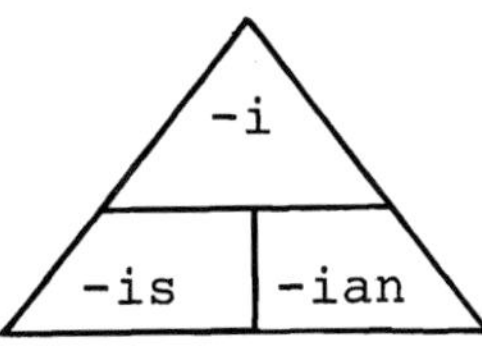

Example: c̣armo+tkv-am-s (წარმოთქვამს) 'pronounce'

3 sg. c̣armo+i-tk-m-is წარმოითქმის

3 pl. c̣armo+i-tk-m-ian წარმოითქმიან[1]

Normally, though, they take the regular endings added to the stem ending in *m*: *c̣armo+i-tk-m-eb-a* (3 sg.) (წარმოითქმება).

3.1.4.4. Verbs in *-av* with no root vowel and ending in *l, r, n*. These verbs keep the present/future stem formant *-av* in II. conjugation forms, but with loss of the vowel *a*. The syncopated *-v-* (from *-av*) precedes the II. conjugational *-eb-*. These forms generally undergo metathesis (1.11.2): *mo=ḳl-av-s* (მოკლავს) 'kill'.

II. conj.:
mo=i-ḳl-a̸v-eb-a →
mo=i-ḳl-v-eb-a →
mo=i-ḳvl-eb-a მოიკვლება

3.1.4.4.1. One may occasionally encounter an older form of the II. conjugation of verbs in *-av* which is formed analogously to sec. 3.1.4.3. The preradical vowel is *-i-*, and the P/FSF loses the vowel *-a*. Example: da=mal-av-s (დამალავს) 'hide'

II. conj. forms:

Regular

დავიმალები (-თ)	da=v-i-mal-eb-i (-t)
დაიმალები (-თ)	da= -i-mal-eb-i (-t)
დაიმალება	da= -i-mal-eb-a
დაიმალებიან	da= -i-mal-eb-ian

Old

დავიმალვი (-თ)	da=v-i-mal-v-i (-t)
დაიმალვი (-თ)	da= -i-mal-v-i (-t)
დაიმალვის	da= -i-mal-v-is
დაიმალვიან	da= -i-mal-v-ian

3.1.4.5. Verbs in *-eb* with nonsyllabic roots. The small number of verbs in *-eb* with roots that do not contain any vowel form the II. conjugation forms as in 3.1.3., i.e., with the II. conjugation in *-i-*. Examples:

გააღებს ga=a-ğ-eb-s open გაიღება ga=i-ğ-eb-a

დაიწყებს da=i-c̣q-eb-s begin დაიწყება da=i-c̣q-eb-a

3.1.4.6. Verbs in *-ob*. Most verbs in *-ob* without preradical vowel form the II. conjugation by adding the preradical vowel *i-* and the II. conjugation endings to the stem; e.g., *mo=sṗ-ob-s* (მოსპობს) 'destroy', II.

conjugation *mo=i-sp̣-ob-a* (მოისპობა) 'be destroyed'. I. conjugation verbs in *-ob* which have a preradical vowel form the II. conjugation irregularly; see sec. 9.1.2.

3.1.5. Conditional and imperfect of II. conj. verbs. The conditional and the imperfect of II. conjugation verbs are formed basically the same way as the corresponding screeves of the I. conjugation. The endings of these screeves are the same as for the I. conjugation except that the II. conjugation forms begin with *-od* instead of just *-d*:

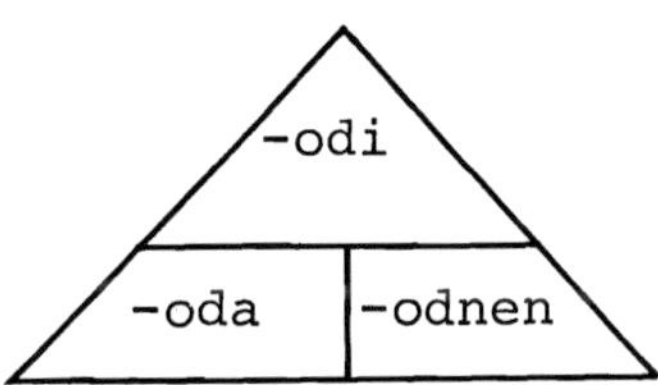

Examples:

Imperfect II. conj. of da=mal-av-s დამალავს 'hide':

II. conj. future (3 sg) da=i-mal-eb-a დაიმალება

1. v-i-mal-eb-odi (-t) ვიმალებოდი (-თ)
2. -i-mal-eb-odi (-t) იმალებოდი (-თ)
3. -i-mal-eb-oda იმალებოდა
   -i-mal-eb-odnen იმალებოდნენ

(The corresponding conditional would have the preverb *da=* in all forms.)

Imperfect II. conj. of a=a-šen-eb-s ააშენებს 'build':

II. conj. future (3sg) a=šen-d-eb-a აშენდება

1. v-šen-d-eb-odi (-t) ვშენდებოდი (-თ)
2. -šen-d-eb-odi (-t) შენდებოდი (-თ)
3. -šen-d-eb-oda შენდებოდა
   -šen-d-eb-odnen შენდებოდნენ

(The corresponding conditional would have the preverb *a=* in all forms.)

3.1.6. The verbal noun of II. conj. verbs. The verbal noun of II. conjugation verbs is the same as the verbal noun of the corresponding I. conjugation verb.

3.1.7. The verb 'to be' [verbal noun *qopn-a* (ყოფნა) 'being']. As in many other languages, the Georgian verb 'to be' is quite irregular. In this lesson we shall learn the present tense, the future, and the conditional. This verb does not have any imperfect forms.

Present:	sg.		pl.			
1. v-ar	I am	v-ar-t	we are		ვარ	ვართ
2. x-ar	you are	x-ar-t	you all are		ხარ	ხართ
3. ar-i-s	is	ar-i-an	they are		არის	არიან

Note that in this verb the marker of the second person is *x*-.

The marker of the third person singular of 'to be' can also be the enclitic -*a* which can be added to another word in the sentence. If such a word ends in a consonant the enclitic is -*aa*. Examples:

Bavšvebi ik arian. ბავშვები იქ არიან.

The children are there.

Çigni ik aris (ikaa). წიგნი იქ არის (იქაა).

The book is there.

Daviti kartveli aris. დავითი ქართველი არის.

Daviti kartvelia. დავითი ქართველია.

David is a Georgian.

Elisabedi ak aris. ელისაბედი აქ არის.

Elisabedi akaa. ელისაბედი აქაა.

Elizabeth is here.

Future: The future tense of 'to be' is a second conjugation verb *i-kn-eb-a*:

v-i-kn-eb-i (-t) ვიქნები (-თ)
i-kn-eb-i (-t) იქნები (-თ)
i-kn-eb-a იქნება
i-kn-eb-i-an იქნებიან

Conditional: This is formed regularly from the future:

v-i-kn-eb-odi (-t) ვიქნებოდი (-თ)
i-kn-eb-odi (-t) იქნებოდი (-თ)
i-kn-eb-oda იქნებოდა
i-kn-eb-odnen იქნებოდნენ

3.2.0. Noun.

3.2.1. Genitive, instrumental, and adverbial cases.

Note the following examples:

	man		writer		street	
N.	ḳac-i	კაცი	mc̣eral-i	მწერალი	kuča-	ქუჩა
G.	ḳac-is	კაცის	mc̣erl-is	მწერლის	kuč-is	ქუჩის
I.	ḳac-it	კაცით	mc̣erl-it	მწერლით	kuč-it	ქუჩით
A.	ḳac-ad	კაცად	mc̣erl-ad	მწერლად	kuč-ad	ქუჩად

	window		month		Peru	
N.	panǰara-	ფანჯარა	tve-	თვე	P̣eru-	პერუ
G.	panǰr-is	ფანჯრის	tv-is	თვის	P̣eru-s	პერუს
I.	panǰr-it	ფანჯრით	tv-it	თვით	P̣eru-ti	პერუთი
A.	panǰr-ad	ფანჯრად	tve-d	თვედ	P̣eru-d	პერუდ

	Georgia	
N.	Sakartvelo-	საქართველო
G.	Sakartvelo-s	საქართველოს
I.	Sakartvelo-ti	საქართველოთი
A.	Sakartvelo-d	საქართველოდ

The endings of the genitive *-is* and the instrumental *-it* are added to (a) the stem of nouns ending in a consonant, (b) the *truncated stem* of nouns endings in *-a* and *-e*. The truncated stem is the stem minus the vowel in absolute final position; see *kuča* (ქუჩა), *panǰara* (ფანჯარა), *tve* (თვე) above.

The endings genitive *-s* and instrumental *-ti* are added to the stems of nouns ending in *o* and *u*. These are nontruncating stems; see *Sakartvelo* საქართველო and *P̣eru* პერუ above. (Note that with nontruncating stems, the dative and genitive forms are identical: N. *Sakartvelo*, D. *Sakartvelo-s*, G. *Sakartvelo-s*; N. *P̣eru*, D. *P̣eru-s*, G. *P̣eru-s*.[2]

The ending of the adverbial case is *-ad* after consonantal stems and stems in *-a* (with truncation of stem-final *a*). Stems in *e* and nontruncating stems (in *o*, *u*) take the ending *-d*.

3.2.1.1. Syncope. In many words the last vowel in the stem of a noun is lost before the endings of the genitive, instrumental, and adverbial. This is particularly common before stem-final consonants *r*, *l*, *n*, and *m*. This *syncope* is most common in consonantal stems and the larger the resulting consonant cluster would be, the more likely is syncopation to occur. The vowels affected by syncopation are *a*, *e*, and, less commonly, *o*.[3] Note, in addition to *mc̣erali* მწერალი and *panǯara* (ფანჯარა) above, the following examples:

N.	generAl-i	გენერალი	mǧvdEl-i	მღვდელი
D.	generAl-s	გენერალს	mǧvdEl-s	მღვდელს
G.	generl- is	გენერლის	mǧvdl- is	მღვდლის
I.	generl- it	გენერლით	mǧvdl- it	მღვდლით
A.	generl- ad	გენერლად	mǧvdl- ad	მღვდლად
	general		priest	

N.	obOl-i	ობოლი
D.	obOl-s	ობოლს
G.	obl- is	ობლის
I.	obl- it	ობლით
A.	obl- ad	ობლად
	orphan	

Note also the irregular noun *ǦmErti* (ღმერთი) 'God', which, in the singular has the syncopated stem *Ǧvt-*, e.g., G. *Ǧvt-is* ღვთის I. *Ǧvt-it* ღვთით: the plural is regular. In the vocabularies, alternating vowels will be indicated by capital letters *A*, *E*, *O*.

3.3. Functions of the cases.

3.3.1. Genitive. The Georgian genitive case functions similarly to the genitive of Greek, Latin, or Russian. It is used to indicate possession as well as in general corresponding to the English preposition *of*. English constructions of two nouns like *stone house*, *university professor*, etc., correspond to Georgian constructions, the first member of which is a genitive, e.g. *kvis saxli* 'stone (gen.) house', *universiṭeṭis p̣ropesori* 'university professor'.

Left branching: Georgian is a so-called "left branching" language. This means that modifying words precede the word modified. More specifically, both adjectives and genitives precede the nouns that they modify. Note the following:

Ameriḳis šeertebuli šṭaṭebi
ამერიკის შეერთებული შტატები
America's United States (USA)

Sabčota *ḳavširis* ḳomunisṭuri *parṭiis* cenṭraluri
საბჭოთა კავშირის კომუნისტური პარტიის ცენტრალური
Soviet Union's Communist Party's Central

ḳomiṭeṭi

კომიტეტი

Committee

(= Central Committee of the Communist Party of the Soviet Union; *ḳavširis* and *parṭiis* are genitives.)

Čiḳagos universiṭeṭis isṭoriis ḳatedris gamocema

ჩიკაგოს უნივერსიტეტის ისტორიის კათედრის გამოცემა

Chicago's University's History Department's publication

(= A publication of the Department of History of the University of Chicago; all genitives are italicized.)

3.3.1.2. Genitive with verbal nouns. The genitive case with a verbal noun marks the *direct object* of the corresponding I. conj. verb and the *subject* of the corresponding II. conj. verb. Examples:

Vikṭori ċerils daċers.

ვიქტორი წერილს დაწერს.

Victor will write the letter.

moulodnel-i 'unexpected':

Ċeril-is daċera moulodnelia.

წერილის დაწერა მოულოდნელია.

The writing of the letter is unexpected.

3.2.2. Instrumental. The most common function of the instrumental is to indicate the instrument *with which* an action is performed, e.g., *kalmit vċerdi* (კალმით ვწერდი) 'I was writing with a pen', *danit ṗurs č̣rian* (დანით პურს ჭრიან) 'with a knife they are cutting the bread', etc. The instrumental is not normally used to express accompaniment as in 'I went there with my friend'; it often corresponds to the Russian instrumental case without preposition.

3.3.3. Adverbial. The adverbial case is the least common of the Georgian cases. Its main function is to form adverbs from adjectives. Adverbs in Georgian are derived from adjectives by putting the adjective into the adverbial case, declining the adjective as a noun:

ღრმა	ğrma	deep →			
			ღრმად	ğrmad	deeply
აშკარა	ašḳara	clear →			
			აშკარად	ašḳarad	clearly
ხშირი	xširi	frequent →			
			ხშირად	xširad	frequently
იშვიათი	išviati	rare →			
			იშვიათად	išviatad[4]	rarely

The adverbial case is also used with certain verbs. These uses will be indicated in the vocabulary. An example is the verb *ča=tvl-i-s* (ჩათვლის) 'consider s.o., sthg. (D.) as sthg. (adv.)' : *Davits ḳarg megobrad tvlidit* (დავითს კარგ მეგობრად თვლიდით) 'You all used to consider David (d.) a good friend (adv.)'.

3.4. Adjectives. As was mentioned above (2.3.2), adjectives ending in a vowel are uninflected in all cases when they precede the noun they modify. Consonantal stem adjectives have the ending *-i* in the genitive and instrumental (i.e., in those cases which have an *i* in the ending) and have no ending in the adverbial. Examples:

N.	sainṭereso teoria	ḳarg-i amindi
	საინტერესო თეორია	კარგი ამინდი
D.	sainṭereso teorias	ḳarg- aminds
	საინტერესო თეორიას	კარგ ამინდს
G.	sainṭereso teoriis	ḳarg-i amindis
	საინტერესო თეორიის	კარგი ამინდის
I.	sainṭereso teoriit	ḳarg-i amindit
	საინტერესო თეორიით	კარგი ამინდით
A.	sainṭereso teoriad	ḳarg- amindad
	საინტერესო თეორიად	კარგ ამინდად
	interesting theory	good weather

N.	axAl-i	Sakartvelo
	ახალი	საქართველო
D.	axAl-	Sakartvelos
	ახალ	საქართველოს

G.	axAl-i	Sakartvelos
	ახალი	საქართველოს
I.	axAl-i	Sakartveloti
	ახალი	საქართველოთი
A.	axAl-	Sakartvelod
	ახალ	საქართველოდ
	new Georgia	

When the adjective is not followed by a noun, it is declined as if it were a noun. Adjectives so declined can have syncope. Examples:

N.	maǧAl-i	c̣itEl-i	mc̣vane-	parto-
	მაღალი	წითელი	მწვანე	ფართო
D.	maǧAl-s	c̣itEl-s	mc̣vane-s	parto-s
	მაღალს	წითელს	მწვანეს	ფართოს
G.	maǧl- is	c̣itl- is	mc̣van- is	parto-s
	მაღლის	წითლის	მწვანის	ფართოს
I.	maǧl- it	c̣itl- it	mc̣van- it	parto-ti
	მაღლით	წითლით	მწვანით	ფართოთი
A.	maǧl- ad	c̣itl- ad	mc̣vane-d	parto-d
	მაღლად	წითლად	მწვანედ	ფართოდ
	the high one	the red one	the green one	the wide one

3.5. Wordbuilding.

3.5.1. Denominatives: I. conjugation verb forms can be formed from most nouns, adjectives, and adverbs with the preradical vowel *a-* and the P/F stem formant *-eb*.[5] Such verbs generally have the meaning 'to make something X', where X stands for the noun or adjective from which the verb is derived. The preverb with denominatives is usually *ga=*, less frequently, *da=*. These verbs all form their second conjugation forms with *d-*; these forms have the meaning 'to become X'. Examples:

Nominal form	I. conj.	II. conj.
grjeli	ga=a-grjel-eb-s	ga=grjel-d-eb-a
გრძელი	გააგრძელებს	გაგრძელდება
long	lengthen, contin-	become longer,

	ue	be continued
mzad	da=a-mzad-eb-s	da=mzad-d-eb-a
მზად	დაამზადებს	დამზადდება
ready(adverb)	prepare	be(come) prepared
lamazi	ga=a-lamaz-eb-s	ga=lamaz-d-eb-a
ლამაზი	გაალამაზებს	გალამაზდება
beautiful	beautify	become beautiful
rigi	ga=a-rig-eb-s	ga=rig-d-eb-a
რიგი	გაარიგებს	გარიგდება
order	put into order, arrange	become arranged
Ğmerti	ga=a-ğmert-eb-s	ga=ğmert-d-eb-a
ღმერთი	გააღმერთებს	გაღმერთდება
God	deify s.o.	become deified
inṭeresi	da=a-inṭeres-eb-s	da=inṭeres-d-eb-a
ინტერესი	დააინტერესებს	დაინტერესდება
interest	to interest s.o.	to become interested

In the following lessons, denominative verbs which are formed regularly from nouns or adjectives and the meanings of which are predictable in terms of the nouns or adjectives from which they are derived will not be listed in the vocabularies. Rather, only the relevant noun or adjective will be given.

3.5.2. Syncope and truncation in wordbuilding. As a general rule, those nouns and adjectives which have truncation or syncope in their declension (see secs. 3.2.1. and 3.2.1.1.) also have truncation or syncope before derivational suffixes beginning with a vowel. So, for example, the following denominatives:[6]

წითელი	(E)	red	გააწითლებს	make red
ახალი	(A)	new	გააახლებს	make new
მაგარი	(A)	strong	გაამაგრებს	make strong
მწვანე		green	გაამწვანებს	make green
ფორმა		form	გააფორმებს	form, give form to

Examples of syncope and truncation before other suffixes will be seen in the wordbuilding sections of the remaining lessons.

Georgian SSR Government House

LESSON 3: Notes

1. For the loss of the *v*, see *v*-loss rule, sec. 1.11.1.

2. First names and last names (except for last names ending in *švil-i*, *-je*, or an adjectival ending, which are declined regularly) ending in a vowel are declined according to the nontruncating pattern; e.g., შალვა *Šalva*, D. შალვას *Šalva-s*, G. შალვას *Šalva-s*, etc.; პავლე *P̣avle* (Paul), D., G. პავლეს *P̣avle-s*. In certain names the final *i* is not the N. ending but part of the stem. Such names are also declined without truncation: გიორგი *Giorgi-* (George), D., G. გიორგის *Giorgi-s*, I. გიორგით *Giorgi-t*, A. გიორგიდ *Giorgi-d*. (Note that with such names the I. ending is *-t* and not *-ti*.)

When a first name and last name are used together, the first name is not declined; e.g.,

N. ტიციან ტაბიძე Ṭician- Ṭabije-

D. ტიციან ტაბიძეს Ṭician- Ṭabije-s

G. ტიციან ტაბიძის Ṭician- Ṭabij-is etc.

N. კონსტანტინე გამსახურდია
Ḳonsṭanṭine Gamsaxurdia

D. კონსტანტინე გამსახურდიას
Ḳonsṭanṭine Gamsaxurdia-s

G. კონსტანტინე გამსახურდიას
Ḳonsṭanṭine Gamsaxurdia-s etc.

Combinations of names with titles are treated similarly; only the last member of the name is declined. So, in the following combinations of names only the last word is declined:

თამარ მეფე	Tamar mepe	Queen Tamara
მეფე ალექსანდრე მესამე	Mepe Aleksandre mesame	Tsar Alexander III
დავით მეოთხე აღმაშენებელი	Davit meotxe aǧmašenebeli	David IV, the Rebuilder

The words მამა (*mama*) 'father' and დედა (*deda*) 'mother' are generally declined without truncation when used to refer to one's own parents.

Monosyllabic nontruncating stems can take in the genitive and instrumental cases either the endings *-is* and -*it* or the endings -*s* and -*ti*; e.g., *dro*- (დრო) 'time', Gen. *dro-is* დროის or *dro-s* დროს; Instr. *dro-it* დროით or *dro-ti* დროთი.

3. Syncopation of *o* often results in an environment allowing a *v* lost due to the labialized vowel to reappear; e.g., N. *mindOri* (მინდორი) 'field', G. *mindvris* (მინდვრის); *ṗamidOri* (პამიდორი) 'tomato', G. *ṗamidvris* (პამიდვრის); N. *nigOzi* (ნიგოზი) 'walnut', G. *nigvzis* (ნიგვზის). Forms in which this *v* reappears will be indicated in the vocabularies.

4. Some adverbs are formed from adjectives by the addition of only -*a* (instead of -*ad*) to the stem. Such forms will be indicated in the vocabulary, e.g. *čkari* (ჩქარი) 'fast, rapid', adverb: *čkara* (ჩქარა) 'quickly, rapidly'. Note that *čkara* (ჩქარა) is the adverb derived from *čkari* (ჩქარი); it is not the adverbial case, which is still *čkarad* (ჩქარად).

5. In a few instances the denominative is formed with a preradical vowel other than -*a*-; e.g., from *meore* (მეორე) 'second' (2nd) the denominative has the preradical vowel -*i*-: *ga=i-meor-eb-s* (გაიმეორებს) 'repeat'. The II conjugation forms are regular: *ga=meor-d-eb-a* (გამეორდება) 'be repeated'.

6. Although truncation of final *a* is usual before most derivational suffixes, such truncation often does not occur in the formation of denominatives; e.g., სუფთა 'clean' but გასუფთავებს 'make clean', ღრმა 'deep' but გაღრმავებს 'make deep'.

LESSON 3: Exercises

1. ლურჯი რვეული აქაა, წითელი კი იქაა. მხოლოდ წითელია ჩემი.
2. ხვალ კლასი ქართული სახელის სწავლას გააგრძელებს. ზეგ ქართული ზმნის სწავლას დავიწყებთ.
3. ქართული სიტყვა ადვილად იწერება. ქართული გრამატიკის სწავლა კი ხშირად ძნელია.
4. ვანოს კალამი მწვანეა, ჩემი კი თეთრია. მწვანეს ხედავ? —არა, თეთრს ვხედავ.
5. ხვალ დავიწყებთ ჩვენი მოთხრობის წერას. სულიკო ალბათ გაწითლდება, როცა სოსოს ახალი მოთხრობა გადაითარგმნება.
6. კალმით ვწერ. ვანო ფანქრით წერს. ვანო შავი მელნით წერს, სულიკო კი ლურჯით.
7. როდის დამთავრდება პროფესორის ლექცია? —ხვალ დამთავრდება ლექცია. ახლა მეორე ნაწილს წერს, ხვალ კი მესამე ნაწილი დაიწერება. ზეგ ლექციას წაიკითხავს.
8. პროფესორი დღეს დიდ სიას ამზადებს. სია ხვალ იქნება მზად. ზეგ სია გადიდდება.
9. რას წერს ბავშვი? —ბავშვი საქართველოს აღწერის პირველ ნაწილს წერს.
10. პროფესორი ნიკოლოზ ორჯონიკიძე წიგნს დაწერს. ქართულ სინტაქსს გამოიკვლევს. წიგნი გამოქვეყნდება და მაშინ პროფესორი ორჯონიკიძე ცნობილი იქნება.
11. რუსული გრამატიკის მეორე თავის წერა ძნელი იქნება, მესამე თავის წერა კი — ადვილი.
12. ხვალ აქ ვიქნები. —ხვალ აქ იქნებით? —არა, ხვალ მხოლოდ ვანო იქნება აქ. შინ ვიქნები. ზეგ აქ ვიქნები.
13. ივანე ქართული ენის წრის წევრია, პავლე კი მათემატიკის წრის წევრია.
14. ხვალ მოწაფე ხელით გადაწერს გაკვეთილს. გაკვეთილი

ნელა და ფრთხილად გადაიწერება.

15. ზინაიდა გიორგაძე ახალ გამოკვლევას წერს. ძველი ქართული ზმნის მორფოლოგიას იკვლევს. მალე ხელნაწერი გასწორდება, შემდეგ კი დაიბეჭდება.

16. ივანე ამერიკის საენათმეცნიერო საზოგადოების წევრია? —დიახ, ივანე საზოგადოების მთავარი საბჭოს წევრია.

17. როცა დაიწყება კლასის კრება, მასწავლებელი ახალი გაკვეთილის განხილვას დაიწყებს. როცა დაბნელდება, კლასის კრება დამთავრდება.

18. როცა რუსული კლასის კრება დამთავრდება, საშინაო დავალების შედგენას დავიწყებ. საშინაო დავალებას დავამთავრებ, შემდეგ კი მასწავლებელი გუშინდელი სავარჯიშოს გასწორებას დაიწყებს. როცა სავარჯიშოს გასწორება დამთავრდება, ხვალინდელ სავარჯიშოს დავამზადებთ.

19. როცა ავტორი ახალი სტატიის წერას იწყებდა, რედაქტორი უკვე ამთავრებდა ძველის გასწორებას.

20. მასწავლებელი თეკლეს ცუდ სტუდენტად თვლის, თუმცა თეკლე მუდამ ბეჯითად სწავლობს ეკონომიკის გაკვეთილს. აკაკი კი ძალიან კარგ სტუდენტად ითვლება.

21. მასწავლებელი კმაყოფილია ვანოთი? —დიახ, მასწავლებელი კმაყოფილია ვანოთი. ვანო ქართულ გაკვეთილს მუდამ ბეჯითად სწავლობს და ქართულ სიტყვას მუდამ კარგად წარმოთქვამს.

22. ქართული სიტყვა „გვფრცქვნის" ძნელად წარმოითქმება/წარმოითქმის.

23. მათემატიკის კლასის კრება როდის დამთავრდება? —კლასის კრება მალე დამთავრდება. შემდეგ ფიზიკის კლასის კრება დაიწყება.

24. რატომ ჭრის დედა პურს დანით? პურის ჭრა კოვზით ძალიან ძნელია.

25. საბჭოს სხდომა გვიან მთავრდებოდა.

26. მალე ვიქტორის სტატია გამოქვეყნდება. თბილისის უნივერსიტეტის ახალი ისტორიის ჟურნალის რედაქტორი სტატიას გამოაქვეყნებს.
27. როცა გარეთ დაბნელდება, შინ ვიქნებით. ქართულ გრამატიკას ვისწავლით. ხვალ გამოცდა იქნება. იქ იქნებით? —დიახ, როცა გამოცდა დაიწყება, იქ ვიქნებით.
28. წუხელ რას აკეთებდი? —წუხელ შინ ფიზიკას ვსწავლობდი. დღეს გამოცდა იქნება.
29. ხვალ მეორე გაკვეთილის კითხვა გაგრძელდება. შემდეგ სავარჯიშო გასწორდება და ვიქტორი და შოთა ახალი გაკვეთილის წერას დაიწყებენ.
30. ივანე სად იმალება? —ივანე აქ იმალება. ვხედავ. —ივანე წიგნს სად დამალავს? —აქ დამალავს.
31. როცა პავლე ყიფშიძე ახალ წიგნს გაათავებს, ზინაიდა ხელნაწერს გაასწორებს. შემდეგ საქართველოს აკადემიის სტამბა წიგნს დაბეჭდავს და აკადემია წიგნს გამოაქვეყნებს.
32. ჩვენი უნივერსიტეტის გამომცემლობა მხოლოდ მეცნიერულ მასალას ბეჭდავდა ხოლმე, მაგრამ გამოაქვეყნებს ლიდა ზარათაშვილის ახალ რომანს, როცა რომანი გადაითარგმნება.
33. ივანე „მზიან ღამეს" დიდ რომანად თვლის. მალე ავტორის ბიოგრაფიის წერას დაამთავრებს. როცა ხელნაწერის გასწორებას გაათავებს, წიგნი გამოქვეყნდება.
34. როდის გამოქვეყნდება მწერლის ბიოგრაფია? როცა ავტორი პირველი თავის გასწორებას დაამთავრებს, წიგნი დაიბეჭდება.
35. გუშინ, როცა ბნელდებოდა, ქიმიის გაკვეთილს ვსწავლობდით.
36. სოსო დღეს მოთხრობას წერს. —რა აღიწერება? —იქ საქართველო აღიწერება.
37. როცა რუსული ლიტერატურის კლასის კრება დაიწყება,

„ბორის გოდუნოვის" კითხვა გაგრძელდება. შემდეგ ილია ჭავჭავაძის ლექსის გადაწერას გავათავებთ.

38. ხვალინდელი გაკვეთილი როდის დამზადდება?
—ხვალინდელი გაკვეთილი დღეს დამზადდება.

39. სადა ხარ ახლა? —ახლა გარეთ ვარ, გარეთ ბნელდება.

40. ქართული ანბანის კითხვა გაადვილდება, თუ ბეჯითად ისწავლი. ბეჯითი სწავლა გააადვილებს ქართული ანბანის კითხვას.

41. როცა დაბნელდება, ქალაქი გალამაზდება.

42. ქართული სიტყვის წარმოთქმა გაძნელდება, თუ ხშირად არ გაიმეორებ.

43. გუშინდელი ქართული ფილმი ხვალ გამეორდება.

44. წერილს როდის წერდნენ? წერილი გუშინ იწერებოდა.

45. მალე დაბნელდება.

46. ზინაიდას ლამაზად თვლი? ივანე ზინაიდას ლამაზად თვლის.

Tbilisi
Right Bank of Mtkvari River, Second Half of XIX Century

Vocabulary

ადვილი [Vb. გაადვილებს]	easy
ავტორი	author
აკადემია	academy
აკაკი	Aḳaḳi [m.pr. n.] (dat. აკაკის)
ალბათ	probably
ამერიკა	America
აქ	here
ახალი	(A) new
ბავშვი	child, baby
ბეჯითი	diligent
ბიოგრაფია	biography
ბნელი [Vb. დააბნელებს]	dark
ბორის გოდუნოვი	Boris Godunov
გამომცემლობა	publishing house
გამოცდა	examination
გარეთ	outside
გვიან	late(adverb)
გიორგაძე	Giorgaje [surname]
გუშინდელი	(E) yesterday's (adj.) [cf. გუშინ]
დანა	knife
დიდი [Vb. გაადიდებს]	large, great
ეკონომიკა	economics
ზეგ	day after tomorrow
ზინაიდა	Zinaida [f.pr.n.]
თავი	head, chapter
თეკლე	Teḳle [f.pr.n.]
თუ	if
თუმცა	although
ისტორია	history
იქ	there
კალამი	(A) pen
კარგი	good
კითხვა[cf. იკითხავს]	reading(VN); question
კლასი	class
კმაყოფილი	satisfied [+instr.]
კოვზი	spoon
კრება	meeting, gathering
ლამაზი[Vb. გაალამაზებს]	beautiful
ლექცია	lecture
ლიდა	Lida [f.pr.n.]
ლიტერატურა	literature
ლურჯი	blue
მაგრამ	but
მათემატიკა	mathematics
მალე	soon
მასალა	material
მასწავლებელი	(E) teacher

მაშინ	then, at that time
მელანი	(A) ink
მეორე	second
მესამე	third
მეცნიერული	scientific [მეცნიერი = 'scientist']
მზად	ready
მზიანი	sunny [cf. მზე 'sun']
მთავარი	(A) main
მოთხრობა	story
მორფოლოგია	morphology
მუდამ	always
მწერალი	(A) writer
მწვანე	green
ნაწილი	part, section
ნელი	slow (adverb= ნელა)
ნიკოლოზი	Nicholas [m.pr.n.]
ორჯონიკიძე	Orǰoniḳije [surname]
პავლე	Paul [m.pr.n.]
პირველი	first
პროფესორი	professor
პური	bread
რატომ	why?
რედაქტორი	editor
რვეული	notebook
საბჭო	council
სად [სადა before monosyllables]	where?
საენათმეცნიერო	linguistic (cf. ენათმეცნიერი 'linguist')
საზოგადოება	society
საშინაო დავალება	homework
სახელი	name, noun
სახელოვანი [cf. სახელი]	(A) famous
სია	list
სინტაქსი	syntax
სოსო	[m.pr.n. from იოსები 'Joseph']
სტამბა	printing house
სტუდენტი	[university] student
სწავლა	[VN] learning
სხდომა	session, meeting
უკვე	already
უნივერსიტეტი	university
ფანქარი	(A) pencil
ფრთხილი	careful
ქალაქი	city
ყიფშიძე	Qipšije [surname]
ღამე	night
შავი	black
შედგენა	[VN] composing, composition
შინ	[adverb] in,

	(at) home
ცნობილი	well-known, famous
ცუდი	bad
ძალიან	very
ძნელი [Vb. გააძნელებს]	difficult
წევრი	member
წითელი	(E) red [Vb. გააწითლებს 'make red, make blush']
წრე	circle, club
წუხელ	yesterday evening
ჭავჭავაძე ილია	Ilia Čavčavaje (Geo. writer, 1837-1907)
ხელი	hand
ხელნაწერი	manuscript
ხვალინდელი	(E) tomorrow's [adj.]

Verbs. Verbs will be listed alphabetically by root. (Roots will be italicized.) If several verbs have the same root, they will be alphabetized by prefix, etc. N.B. For denominative verbs (sec. 3.5) not listed below, see the relevant nominal form in the vocabulary above.

დაბეჭდავს	da=*beč̣d*-av-s	print
გაათავებს	ga=a-*tav*-eb-s	finish
ჩათვლის	ča=*tvl*-i-s	consider (as = adv.)
გამოიკვლევს	gamo=i-*ḳvlev*-s	investigate
დამალავს	da=*mal*-av-s	hide
დაამზადებს	da=a-*mzad*-eb-s	prepare
დაამთავრებს	da=a-*mtavr*-eb-s	finish, end
გაასწორებს	ga=a-*sc̣or*-eb-s	correct
გამოაქვეყნებს	gamo=a-*kveqn*-eb-s	publish
მოჭრის	mo=*č̣r*-i-s	cut, cut off

Key to the Exercises

1. The blue notebook is here, the red one however is there. Only the red one is mine.
2. Tomorrow the class will continue the studying of the Georgian noun. The day after tomorrow we will begin the studying of the Georgian verb.
3. A Georgian word is easily written. The studying of Georgian grammar, however, is often difficult.
4. Vano's pen is green, mine however is white. Do you see the green one? No, I see the white one.
5. Tomorrow we will begin the writing of our story. Suliḳo probably will blush when Soso's new story will be translated.
6. I am writing with a pen. Vano is writing with a pencil. Vano is writing with black ink; Suliḳo, however, [is writing] with blue.
7. When will the professor's lecture be finished? The lecture will be finished tomorrow. Now he is writing the second part; tomorrow, however, the third part will be written. The day after tomorrow he will read the lecture.
8. The professor is preparing a big list today. The list will be ready tomorrow. The day after tomorrow the list will be enlarged.
9. What is the child writing? The child is writing the first part of a description of Georgia.
10. Professor Niḳoloz Orǯoniḳije will write a book. He will investigate Georgian syntax. The book will be published and then Professor Orǯoniḳije will be famous.
11. The writing of the second chapter of the Russian grammar will be difficult; the writing of the third chapter, however, [will be] easy.
12. I will be here tomorrow. Will you all be here tomorrow? No, only Vano will be here tomorrow. I will be at home. I will be here the day after tomorrow.
13. John is a member of the Georgian Language Circle; Paul, however, is a member of the Mathematics Circle.
14. Tomorrow the pupil will copy the lesson by hand. The lesson will be copied slowly and carefully.
15. Zinaida Giorgadze is writing a new investigation. She is investigating the morphology of the Old Georgian verb. Soon the manuscript will be corrected; then, however, it will be printed.
16. Is John a member of the Linguistic Society of America? Yes, John is a member of the Society's main council.
17. When the class meeting [gathering] will begin,

the teacher will begin the discussion of the new lesson. When it will get dark, the class meeting will end.

18. When the Russian class meeting will end, I will begin the composition of the homework. I will finish the homework, and then the teacher will begin the correction of yesterday's exercise. When the correcting of the exercise will be finished, we will prepare tomorrow's exercise.
19. When the author was beginning the writing of the new article, the editor was already finishing the correcting of the old one.
20. The teacher considers Teḳle a poor student although Teḳle always studies the economics lesson diligently. Aḳaḳi, however, is considered a very good student.
21. Is the teacher satisfied with Vano? Yes, the teacher is satisfied with Vano. Vano studies the Georgian lesson always diligently, and he always pronounces the Georgian word well.
22. The Georgian word *gvprckvnis* ['He is peeling us'] is difficult to pronounce [= is pronounced difficultly].
23. When will the mathematics class meeting be finished? The class meeting will be finished soon. Then the physics class meeting will begin.
24. Why does mother cut bread with a knife? The cutting of bread with a spoon is very difficult.
25. The council session was ending late.
26. Soon Victor's article will be published. The Tbilisi University's Journal of Modern [= new] History's editor will publish the article.
27. When it will get dark outside we will be at home. We will study Georgian grammar. There will be an examination tomorrow. Will you all be there? Yes, when the examination will begin, we will be there.
28. What were you doing yesterday evening? Yesterday evening I was studying physics at home. Today there will be a test.
29. Tomorrow the reading of the second lesson will be continued. Then the exercise will be corrected, and Victor and Šota will begin the writing of the new lesson.
30. Where is John hiding? John is hiding here. I see him. Where will John hide the book? He will hide it here.
31. When Paul Qipšije will finish the new book, Zinaida will correct the manuscript. Then the Georgian Academy [= Georgia's Academy] printing house will print the book and the Academy will publish

the book.
32. Our university publishing house used to print only scientific material, but it will publish Lida Baratashvili's new novel when the novel will be translated.
33. John considers *Sunny Night* a great novel. Soon he will finish the writing of the author's biography. When he will finish the correcting of the manuscript, the book will be published.
34. When will the author's biography be published? When the author will finish the correcting of the first chapter, the book will be printed.
35. Yesterday when it was getting dark, we were studying the chemistry lesson.
36. Soso is writing a story today. What will be described? Georgia will be described there.
37. When the Russian literature class meeting will begin, the reading of *Boris Godunov* will [be] continue[d]. Then we will finish the copying of Ilia Čavčavaje's poem.
38. When will tomorrow's lesson be prepared? Tomorrow's lesson will be prepared today.
39. Where are you now? I am outside now. It is getting dark outside.
40. The reading of the Georgian alphabet will become easy if you will study it diligently. Diligent study will make the reading of the Georgian alphabet easy.
41. When it becomes dark, the city will become beautiful.
42. The pronunciation of a Georgian word will become difficult if you don't repeat it often.
43. Yesterday's Georgian film will be repeated tomorrow.
44. When were they writing the letter? The letter was being written yesterday.
45. It will soon become dark.
46. Do you consider Zinaida beautiful? John considers Zinaida beautiful.

LESSON 4

4.0. Series. The screeves of the Georgian verb are divided into a number of *series*, groups of screeves built upon the same stem. For I. conjugation verbs the first series consists of two subseries, the *future (perfective) subseries* and the *present (imperfective) subseries*. Of the screeves covered thus far, the future and the conditional belong to the future subseries and the present and imperfect belong to the present subseries.

4.1. The conjunctive. The conjunctive is the final screeve of the future and present series. Conjunctives formed from the future stem are *perfective* in meaning, i.e., they denote completed actions while conjunctives formed from the present stem do not focus on the completion of the action.[1]

4.1.1. The conjunctive is formed from the future or present stems of I. and II. conjugation verbs. The endings are:[2]

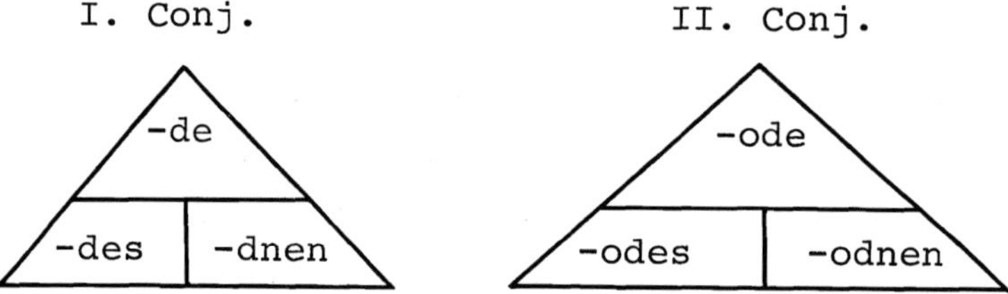

Note that the 3 pl. of the conjunctive is formally identical to the 3 pl. of the corresponding imperfect or conditional. Examples of the conjunctive:

Vocabulary entry form:

დამალავს	da=mal-av-s 'hide' (I. conj.)

Conjunctive (perfective):

დავმალავდე (-თ)	da=v-mal-av-d-e (-t)
დამალავდე (-თ)	da= -mal-av-d-e (-t)
დამალავდეს	da= -mal-av-d-es
დამალავდნენ	da= -mal-av-d-nen

II. Conjugation future:

დაიმალება	da=i-mal-eb-a

Conjunctive (perfective):

დავიმალებოდე (-თ)	da=v-i-mal-eb-od-e (-t)

დაიმალებოდე (-თ) da= -i-mal-eb-od-e (-t)
დაიმალებოდეს da= -i-mal-eb-od-es
დაიმალებოდნენ da= -i-mal-eb-od-nen

To form the corresponding conjunctive imperfective simply drop the preverb *da=*.

Vocabulary entry form:

გაიმეორებს ga=i-meor-eb-s 'repeat' (I.)

Conjunctive (perfective):

გავიმეორებდე (-თ) ga=v-i-meor-eb-d-e (-t)
გაიმეორებდე (-თ) ga= -i-meor-eb-d-e (-t)
გაიმეორებდეს ga= i-meor-eb-d-es
გაიმეორებდნენ ga= i-meor-eb-d-nen

II. Conjugation future

გამეორდება ga=meor-d-eb-a

Conjunctive (perfective):

გავმეორდებოდე (-თ) ga=v-meor-d-eb-od-e (-t)
გამეორდებოდე (-თ) ga= -meor-d-eb-od-e (-t)
გამეორდებოდეს ga= meor-d-eb-od-es
გამეორდებოდნენ ga= meor-d-eb-od-nen

Again, the conjunctive imperfective is formed by dropping the preverb.

4.1.2. Function of the conjunctive. The Georgian conjunctive is a modal screeve very similar in its function to the French subjunctive present. It is most commonly used with the conditional in sentences containing a condition counter to fact and what the result would be if the counterfactual were or were to be realized, e.g.,

> *If Victor pronounced the Georgian word well* [counterfactual condition; he doesn't; Georgian conjunctive], *Elizabeth would understand.* [result; Georgian conditional].
>
> In Georgian: ვიქტორი რომ ქართულ სიტყვას კარგად წარმოთქვამდეს [conj.] ელისაბედი გაიგებდა [conditional]
>
> Viktori rom kartul siṭqvas ḳargad c̣armo+tkv-am-d-es, Elisabedi ga=i-g-eb-d-a.

გზას რომ ააშენებდნენ [conj.], კარგი იქნებოდა [conditional]

Gzas rom a=a-šen-eb-d-nen, ḳargi iknebodа. 'If they were to build a road [they won't], it would be good.'

სტატია რომ დაიწერებოდეს [conj.], ნესტორი წაიკითხავდა [conditional]

Sṭaṭia rom daic̣erebodes, Nesṭori c̣aiḳitxavda. 'If the article were to be written, Nestor would read it.'

The conjunctive denotes counterfactual conditions which are valid either at the present moment or for the future. For conditions valid in the past, see sec. 10.1.3.2. Note that 'if' in such constructions is რომ *rom*, which occurs immediately before the verb, generally as the second element in the clause.

Potential conditions. If a condition is *potential*, but not counterfactual, both the condition and the result are often expressed by the future tense; English 'if' is expressed by Georgian თუ *tu*, which may occupy first or second position in its clause. Example:

ტარიელს თუ ვნახავ [fut.], მოვკლავ [fut.].

Ṭariels tu v-nax-av, mo-v-ḳl-av. 'If I [will] see Tariel, I'll kill him.'

4.2. Plural of nouns. The marker of the plural is *-eb-*, which comes immediately after the stem and immediately before the case endings. The case endings are the same in the plural as in the singular. In vocalic stems, *a* truncates before the *-eb-*; *e*, *o*, and *u* do not. If there is syncope in the G., I., and A. of the singular there will be syncope throughout the plural. Examples:

	c̣ign-i	mc̣erAl-i	muša	moc̣ape
	წიგნი	მწერალი	მუშა	მოწაფე
	book	writer	worker	pupil
N.	c̣ign-eb-i	mc̣erl-eb-i	muš-eb-i	moc̣ape-eb-i
	წიგნები	მწერლები	მუშები	მოწაფეები
D.	c̣ign-eb-s	mc̣erl-eb-s	muš-eb-s	moc̣ape-eb-s
	წიგნებს	მწერლებს	მუშებს	მოწაფეებს

G. c̣ign-eb-is mc̣erl-eb-is muš-eb-is moc̣ape-eb-is
წიგნების მწერლების მუშების მოწაფეების

I. c̣ign-eb-it mc̣erl-eb-it muš-eb-it moc̣ape-eb-it
წიგნებით მწერლებით მუშებით მოწაფეებით

A. c̣ign-eb-ad mc̣erl-eb-ad muš-eb-ad moc̣ape-eb-ad
წიგნებად მწერლებად მუშებად მოწაფეებად

savarǰišo სავარჯიშო exercise

N. savarǰišo-eb-i სავარჯიშოები

D. savarǰišo-eb-s სავარჯიშოებს

G. savarǰišo-eb-is სავარჯიშოების

I. savarǰišo-eb-it სავარჯიშოებით

A. savarǰišo-eb-ad სავარჯიშოებად

Adjectives which precede the noun they modify do not change for number. Adjectives used independently are declined in the plural exactly as nouns: კარგი მუშები (*ḳargi mušebi*) 'good workers', gen. კარგი მუშების (*ḳargi mušebis*), dat. კარგ მუშებს (*ḳarg mušebs*), etc.; საინტერესო წიგნები (*sainṭereso c̣ignebi*) 'interesting books', gen. საინტერესო წიგნების (*sainṭereso c̣ignebis*), etc.

Number agreement with verbs. When the subject of a third person verb is a *plural* noun denoting inanimate things (or two or more singular inanimate nouns) the verb is generally 3d person *singular*; when the subject is a plural noun (or more than one singular noun) denoting persons or animals, the verb is generally 3d person plural. Examples: სტუდენტები (დავითი და მარიამი) წიგნის წერას ხვალ დაიწყებენ.

Sṭudenṭebi (Davidi da Mariami) c̣ignis c̣eras xval da=i-c̣q-eb-en. 'The students (David and Mary) will begin the writing of the book tomorrow.'

გაკვეთილები მალე მომზადდება.

Gaḳvetilebi male mo=mzad-d-eb-a.
'The lessons will soon be ready.'

4.3. "Extended" case forms. The vowel *a* can be added to the endings of the dative, genitive, instrumental, and adverbial cases. These extended case forms are used before certain postpositions (see below, sec. 4.4.), before the short form of არის, -ა *aris*, *-a* (sec. 3.1.7.) and immediately before და *da* 'and' (and other conjunctions) when two or more nouns are conjoined by the conjunction, e.g., სოფიოს, ანტონსა და ელენეს ვხედავ (*Sopio-s, Anṭon-s-a da Elene-s v-xed-av*) 'I see Sophie, Anthony, and Helen.' When a genitive is not followed by the noun to which it refers, it takes the extended ending, e.g.: საქართველოს დედაქალაქი თბილისია და ამერიკისა — ვაშინგტონი (*Sakartvelo-s dedakalak-i Tbilis-i-a da Amerik-is-a — Vašingṭon-i.*) 'Georgia's capital is Tbilisi and America's — Washington.' For other conditions for this use of the extended form of the genitive, see sec. 8.6.

4.4. Postpositions. Instead of the prepositions of English and many other European languages, Georgian has postpositions, i.e., forms which follow (rather than precede) the noun phrase. As in other languages the Georgian postpositions can govern various cases. A few postpositions are written together with the noun that they follow:

4.4.1. Postpositions with the dative case. *-ši* 'into', 'to', 'in'. This postposition is attached to the bare stem of the noun. This is, however, a variant form of the dative case, and adjectival agreement, etc., is as with the dative. Examples: ქალაქი (*kalaki*) 'city'; ქალაქში (*kalakši*) 'to, in the city'; საქართველო (*Sakartvelo*) 'Georgia'; საქართველოში (*Sakartvelos̆i*) 'in, to Georgia'; ახალი სახლი (*axali saxli*) 'new house'; ახალ სახლში (*axal saxlši*) 'in, to the new house'. When two nouns conjoined by და (*da*) 'and' are both governed by the same postposition *-ši*, the first noun takes the extended dative ending: მოსკოვსა და ლენინგრადში (*Mosḳov-s-a da Leningrad-ši*) 'in, to Moscow and Leningrad'.

-ze 'on, onto'. As with *-ši*, this postposition is added on to the bare stem variant of the dative case: მაგიდა (*magida*) 'table'; მაგიდაზე (*magidaze*) 'on, onto the table'; კედელი (*ḳedEli*) 'wall'; კედელზე (*ḳedElze*) 'on the wall'. Note also იატაკსა და კედელზე (*iaṭaḳ-s-a da ḳedEl-ze*) 'on, onto the floor and wall'; ქართულ ენაზე (*ḳartul ena-ze*) 'into Georgian [language]'. As in English, *-ze* can mean 'on' in the sense of 'about': ცხოვრებაზე (*cxovreba-ze*) 'on [= about] life'.

-tan 'near, at'. This is the equivalent of French *chez*, German *bei*, Russian *у* or *к*. It is added to the bare stem of consonantal stem nouns and to the dative of vocalic stem nouns. As with *-ši* and *-ze*, the noun is syntactically dative. Examples: ფანჯარა (*panǰAra*) 'window'; ფანჯარასთან (*panǰara-s-tan*) 'near the window'; დავითი (*Davit-i*) 'David'; დავითთან (*Davit-tan*) 'at David's'; ვანო (*Vano*) 'Jack'; ვანოსთან (*Vano-s-tan*) 'at Jack's'.

Note the forms ჩემთან (*čem-tan*) 'at my place';

ჩვენთან (*čven-tan*) 'at our place'. Similarly: შენთან (*šen-tan*) 'at your place'; თქვენთან (*tkven-tan*) 'at your (pl.) place'.

-vit 'like'. This postposition is attached to the extended ending of the dative case: კაცსავით (*ḳac-s-a-vit*) 'like a man'; მუშასავით (*muša-s-a-vit*) 'like a worker'; სავარჯიშოსავით (*savarǰišo-s-a-vit*) 'like an exercise'.[3]

4.4.2. Postpositions with the genitive. *-tvis* 'for'. This is added either directly to the genitive or to the extended genitive form. Examples: პროფესორისთვის (*p̣ropesor-is-tvis*) or პროფესორისათვის (*p̣ropesor-is-a-tvis*) 'for the professor'; მწერლებისთვის (*mc̣erl-eb-is-tvis*) or მწერლებისათვის (*mc̣erl-eb-is-a-tvis*) 'for the writers'; მუშის(ა)თვის (*muš-is(-a)-tvis*) 'for the worker' (from მუშა *muša* 'worker'), საქართველოს(ა)თვის (*Sakartvelo-s(-a)-tvis*) 'for Georgia'.

-gan 'from'. This postposition has the meaning of 'made from', 'made out of', or 'for' (a given reason). It is also used to mark 'from' or 'by' whom, i.e., with personal nouns, but does not denote 'from where'. This postposition is added to the genitive or to the extended genitive form. Examples: რკინა (*rḳina*) 'iron'; რკინის(ა)გან (*rḳin-is(-a)-gan*) 'made out of iron'; სტუდენტი (*sṭudenṭi*) 'student'; სტუდენტების(ა)გან (*sṭudenṭ-eb-is(-a)-gan*) 'from the students'.

-ḳen 'toward'. Added to the genitive or extended genitive. Examples: სკოლა (*sḳola*) 'school'; სკოლის(ა)კენ (*sḳol-is(-a)-ḳen*) 'toward the school'; კედელი (*ḳedEl-i*) 'wall'; კედლის(ა)კენ (*ḳedl-is-(-a)-ḳen*) 'toward the wall'.

-dan 'from'. This is in answer to the question 'from where'. It is added to the unextended genitive with loss of the final *s* of the genitive ending.* Examples: თბილისიდან (*Tbilis-is̸-dan* → *Tbilis-i-dan*) 'from Tbilisi'; საქართველოდან (*Sakartvelo-s̸-dan* → *Sakartvelo- -dan*) 'from Georgia'.

4.4.2.1. When two nouns joined by a conjunction, such as და (*da*) 'and', are both governed by the same postposition, either the postposition is repeated on both nouns or else the first noun is placed in the proper case with the extended case form and the second noun takes the postposition regularly; e.g., 'in Europe and America' can be expressed either ევროპაში და ამერიკაში

*Historically this postposition is derived from *-gan* added to the ending of the instrumental: *Tbilis-it-gan* → *Tbilis-idan*.

Evropaši da Amerikaši or ევროპასა და ამერიკაში *Evropasa da Amerikaši*.

4.4.3. Postposition with the adverbial. *-mdis* or *-mde* 'up to', 'until'. This is added to the adverbial with loss of the final *d* of the case ending, e.g., სახლამდე (*saxl-ad-mde* → *saxl-a-mde*) 'up to the house'; წყარომდის (*çqaro-d-mdis* → *çqaro- -mdis*) 'up to the spring'; შუადღემდის (*šuadğe-d-mdis* → *šuadğe- -mdis*) 'until noon'.

4.4.4. The remaining postpositions are written separately after the noun that forms the head of the postpositional phrase. With the exception of შუა (*šua*) 'between' and შორის (*šoris*) 'between', 'among', which take the dative, *all remaining postpositions take the genitive*. These 'independent' postpositions will be listed in the vocabularies of the various lessons.

4.4.5. Circumfix *u-.....-o*. This circumfix corresponds to the English suffix *-less* but also to the English preposition *without*.[4] Examples:

კბილი ḳbili	tooth	უკბილო uḳbilo	toothless, without teeth
სიტყვა siṭqva	word	უსიტყვო usiṭqvo	wordless, without a word
ნიშანი nišAni	sign	უნიშნო unišno	signless, without a sign

4.4.6. Suffix *-ian-*. This suffix corresponds to the English preposition *with* in the meaning of having as a possession, attribute, or characteristic.[5] Examples:

სურათები suratebi	pictures	სურათებიანი suratebiani	with pictures, illustrated
შვილი švili	child	შვილიანი šviliani	having a child
ცოლი coli	wife	ცოლიანი coliani	having a wife, married (of a man)
ცხენი cxeni	horse	ცხენიანი cxeniani	having a horse, with a horse
სუფიქსი supiksi	suffix	სუფიქსიანი supiksiani	having a suffix, suffixed

4.5. Verb of motion *svla* სვლა.

4.5.1. მოდის *modis* (verbal noun მოსვლა *mosvla*) 'come'.

Present
mo+v-di-var(-t) მოვდივარ(თ)
mo+ -di-xar(-t) მოდიხარ(თ)
mo+ -di-s მოდის
mo+ -di-an მოდიან

Imperfect
mo+v-di-od-i(-t) მოვდიოდი(თ)
mo+ -di-od-i(-t) მოდიოდი(თ)
mo+ -di-od-a მოდიოდა
mo+ -di-od-nen მოდიოდნენ

Future
mo+v-val(-t) → mo+ -val(-t) მოვალ(თ)
mo+x-val(-t) მოხვალ(თ)
mo+va მოვა
mo+vl-en მოვლენ

Conditional
mo+v-vid-od-i(-t) → mo+ -vid-od-i(-t) მოვიდოდი(თ)
mo+x-vid-od-i(-t) მოხვიდოდი(თ)
mo+ -vid-od-a მოვიდოდა
mo+ -vid-od-nen მოვიდოდნენ

The conjunctives are formed similarly from the imperfect and conditional.

Note that the present screeve has as endings in the 1st and 2d persons forms of the verb 'to be'. In the future screeve and the screeves formed from it the *v* of the first person is dropped before the *v* beginning the root of the verb. Note also that *all* forms based on the future screeve have as marker of 2d person the prefix *x*-; *svla* სვლა and *xar* ხარ (2d person present of *qopna* ყოფნა 'be') are the only verbs with this person prefix.

4.5.2. go. The verb 'go' is conjugated exactly as the verb 'come' above, except that the preverb in the screeves based on the present is მი- *mi*- and the preverb in the future series of screeves is წა- *ça*-. Pres. 3sg. *mi+di-s* მიდის, Fut. 3sg. *ça+va* წავა.[6]

4.5.3. The remaining verbs of motion are also conjugated as the verb 'come', differing only in preverb. These are (forms given are 3 sg. present and future):

a+di-s / a+va	a-mo+di-s / a-mo+va
ადის ავა	ამოდის ამოვა
go up	come up
ga+di-s / ga+va	ga-mo+di-s / ga-mo+va
გადის გავა	გამოდის გამოვა
go away	come out
gada+di-s / gada+va	gad-mo+di-s / gad-mo+va
გადადის გადავა	გადმოდის გადმოვა
go across	come across
še+di-s / še+va	še-mo+di-s / še-mo+va
შედის შევა	შემოდის შემოვა
go in	come in
ča+di-s / ča+va	ča-mo+di-s / ča-mo+va
ჩადის ჩავა	ჩამოდის ჩამოვა
go down	come down, arrive

4.5.4. The verbal nouns of these verbs are formed by adding the relevant preverb to *-svl-a*, e.g., *mi+svl-a* მისვლა, *mo+svl-a* მოსვლა, *a+svl-a* ასვლა, *a-mo+svl-a* ამოსვლა, etc.

4.6. Wordbuilding: formation of adjectives from nouns.

4.6.1. Circumfix *sa-.....-o*. Examples:

inṭeresi	sainṭereso
ინტერესი	საინტერესო
interest	interesting
quradɣeba	saquradɣebo
ყურადღება	საყურადღებო
attention	important (worthy of attention)
liṭeraṭura	saliṭeraṭuro
ლიტერატურა	სალიტერატურო
literature	literary

enatmecnieri	saenatmecniero
ენათმეცნიერი	საენათმეცნიერო
linguist	linguistic
sḳola	sasḳolo
სკოლა	სასკოლო
school	school-
p̣aṭivi	sap̣aṭio (see sec. 1.11.1)
პატივი	საპატიო
respect, honor	respected, honorable

4.6.2. Suffix *-ur-/-ul-*. The variant form *-ul-* occurs when the stem of the noun contains an *r*.

kimia	kimiuri
ქიმია	ქიმიური
chemistry	chemical
xalxi	xalxuri
ხალხი	ხალხური
people, folk	popular, folk-
ḳomunisṭi	ḳomunisṭuri
კომუნისტი	კომუნისტური
communist	communist (adj.)
jaǧli	jaǧluri
ძაღლი	ძაღლური
dog	canine
gmiri	gmiruli
გმირი	გმირული
hero	heroic
liṭeraṭura	liṭeraṭuruli
ლიტერატურა	ლიტერატურული
literature	literary
gramaṭiḳa	gramaṭiḳuli
გრამატიკა	გრამატიკული
grammar	grammatical

mxaṭvAri	mxaṭvruli
მხატვარი	მხატვრული
artist	artistic

4.6.3. Formation of adjectives from place names. The names of many countries end in *-et-*; this suffix is dropped in the formation of adjectives. Two distinct types of adjectives can be formed from the names of countries, cities, and other place names. The first takes the suffix *-ur-/-ul-* (distribution as above, sec. 4.6.2.) and refers to nonpersonal nouns. The second takes the suffix *-el-* and refers to persons. The adjective in *-el-* also forms the noun of nationality.

P̣oloneti	Poland	p̣oloneli	p̣olonuri
პოლონეთი		პოლონელი	პოლონური
Bulgareti	Bulgaria	bulgareli	bulgaruli
ბულგარეთი		ბულგარელი	ბულგარული
Esp̣aneti	Spain	esp̣aneli	esp̣anuri
ესპანეთი		ესპანელი	ესპანური
Ungreti	Hungary	ungreli	ungruli
უნგრეთი		უნგრელი	უნგრული
Indoeti	India	indoeli	induri
ინდოეთი		ინდოელი	ინდური
Čineti	China	čineli	činuri
ჩინეთი		ჩინელი	ჩინური
Ameriḳa	America	ameriḳeli	ameriḳuli
ამერიკა		ამერიკელი	ამერიკული
Germania	Germany	germaneli	germanuli
გერმანია		გერმანელი	გერმანული
Iṭalia	Italy	iṭalieli	iṭaliuri
იტალია		იტალიელი	იტალიური
Evrop̣a	Europe	evrop̣eli	evrop̣uli
ევროპა		ევროპელი	ევროპული
Inglisi	England	ingliseli	inglisuri
ინგლისი		ინგლისელი	ინგლისური
Tbilisi	Tbilisi	tbiliseli	tbilisuri
თბილისი		თბილისელი	თბილისური

Mosḳovi	Moscow	mosḳoveli	mosḳovuri
მოსკოვი		მოსკოველი	მოსკოვური

Note also:

ucxoeti		ucxoeli	ucxo
უცხოეთი		უცხოელი	უცხო
abroad, foreign countries		an alien, foreigner	or
			ucxouri
			უცხოური
			foreign

In many instances the (personal) noun/adjective of nationality serves as the starting point from which the name of the country (or region) and the impersonal adjective are derived. Such formations are common for locations in the Caucasus. Examples:

rusi	Russian	Ruseti	Russia	rusuli
რუსი		რუსეთი		რუსული
somExi	Armenian	Somxeti	Armenia	somxuri
სომეხი		სომხეთი		სომხური
osi	Ossetian	Oseti	Ossetia	osuri
ოსი		ოსეთი		ოსური
svani	Svan	Svaneti	Svanetia	svanuri
სვანი		სვანეთი		სვანური

Irregular formations include:

kartveli	Georgian	Sakartvelo	Georgia	kartuli
ქართველი		საქართველო		ქართული
prangi	French(man)	Saprangeti	France	pranguli
ფრანგი		საფრანგეთი		ფრანგული
berjEni	Greek	Saberjneti	Greece	berjnuli
ბერძენი		საბერძნეთი		ბერძნული
megreli	Mingrelian	Samegrelo	Mingrelia	megruli
მეგრელი		სამეგრელო		მეგრული

Examples:

kartveli poeṭi	a Georgian poet
ქართველი პოეტი	

kartuli p̣oezia	Georgian poetry
ქართული პოეზია	
ingliseli romanisṭi	English novelist
ინგლისელი რომანისტი	
inglisuri romani	English novel
ინგლისური რომანი	

Note also: ამერიკელი ვარ (Amerikeli var) 'I am (an) American'.

Sioni Cathedral in Tbilisi

LESSON 4: Notes

1. In general the distinction between the future and present stem forms in Georgian is analogous to the distinction between the perfective and imperfective forms of the Russian verb; წერს *c̣er-s* is to Russian пишет as დაწერს *da-c̣er-s* is to Russian напишет.

2. It should be clear that the suffix *-d-* (I. conj.) or *-od-* (II. conj.) serves to distinguish the conjunctive, imperfect, and conditional from the present and future. Thus, the actual screeve suffixes for the imperfect or conditional would be:

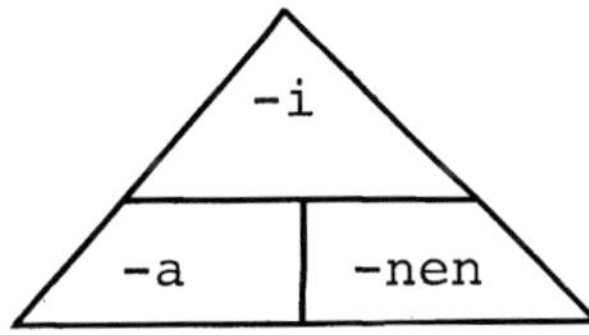

and those for the conjunctive would be:

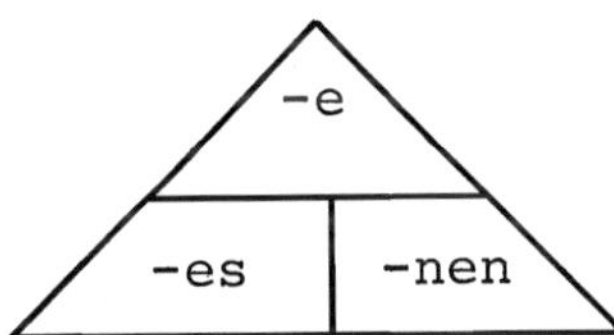

We shall henceforth mark them this way.

3. *-vit* can also occur with the nominative case, but *only* with consonantal stems; e.g., *ḳac-i-vit* კაცივით alongside *ḳac-s-a-vit* კაცსავით, *vard-i-vit* (ვარდივით) 'like a rose' alongside *vard-s-a-vit* ვარდსავით.

4. Note that this circumfix can be used with phrases as well as with individual words; e.g. უამაფიქსო (*u-am-apiks-o*) 'without this (*am*) affix (აფიქსი *apiks-i*),' უთავკიდურბგეროდ (*u-tavḳidur=bger-o-d*) 'without the initial (თავკიდური *tavḳiduri*) sound' (ბგერა *bgera*) (adverbial case). Truncation and syncope generally occur with this circumfix.

5. "With" in the sense of accompaniment is expressed by the postposition -თან *-tan* followed immediately by ერთად (*ertad*) 'together'; e.g.,

> თბილისში ვიქნებით მარიამთან ერთად.
>
> Tbilisši viknebit Mariamtan ertad.
>
> We shall be in Tbilisi [together] with Mary.

6. Forms with the preverb *mi+* (i.e., *mi+va*) also occur, though less frequently. The preverb *ca+* usually conveys here the meaning of setting out for a given destination, while the preverb *mi+* usually underlines the actual reaching of the destination.

Courtyard in Old Tbilisi
(Artist: A. Cimakurije)

LESSON 4: Exercises

1. კარგი იქნებოდა, რომ ვკითხულობდეთ წიგნებს ქართული ცხოვრების შესახებ.
2. ბიბლიის პირველი თარგმანი ძველ ქართულზე ბერძნულიდანაა.
3. დავითი მოსკოველია? —არა, უკრაინიდანაა.
4. ჩემს ქართულ წიგნებს შორის ფრანგული ტექსტის ფონეტიკური ანალიზია. უნივერსიტეტში რომ ვკითხულობდე, ფრანგულ ბგერებს უფრო სწორედ წარმოვთქვამდი.
5. ზურაბი თუ მხოლოდ ქართულ, ესპანურ და იტალიურ რომანებს კითხულობს, გერმანულ და ჰოლანდიურ რომანებს მაგიდაზე რატომ ვხედავ? —იმიტომ, რომ ხვალ აქ ზურაბის და სოფიკო მოვა. ბათუმის საშუალო სკოლაში ჰოლანდიურ და გერმანულ ლიტერატურას ასწავლის.
6. სად მიდიხართ? —ელისაბედთან მივდივართ. —კითხვას რომ ვამთავრებდე, წავიდოდი, მაგრამ ხვალ ვანოსთან წავალ.
7. მასწავლებელი თუ ოთახიდან გავა, ჩინურ ენაში გაკვეთილს არ ვისწავლით.
8. შენი სომხურ-რუსული ლექსიკონი სად არის? —მაგიდაზეა ფანჯარასთან. —იქ არ არის. —იქ თუ არ არის, უჯრაში ჩემი კალმებისა და ფანქრების უკან იქნება.
9. თამარისაგან პასუხს რომ მივიღებდე, თამარის ძმასთან ერთად თეატრში წავიდოდი.
10. მზე აღმოსავლეთიდან ამოდის და დასავლეთით ჩადის.
11. ქართული ენის სწავლის შემდეგ ნიკო და ოლღა ქუჩაზე გადავლენ და ანტონთან წავლენ. ანტონი ერევნიდან მეგობრებისაგან კლასიკური მუსიკის ახალ ფირფიტებს მიიღებს.
12. თუ პარიზიდან წერილს მიიღებ, შენთან მოვალ.
13. წიგნს კატოსაგან თუ მიიღებ, ჩვენთან მოხვალ.

14. ვინაა (ვინ არის) შოთა რუსთაველის „ვეფხისტყაოსნის" პირველი ინგლისური თარგმანის ავტორი? —მარჯორი უორდროპია. საქართველოში „ვეფხისტყაოსანი" ახლა სხვა ენებზეც ითარგმნება.
15. საენათმეცნიერო წრის წევრები ქართულ ენაზე რომ კითხულობდნენ, ქართული ზმნის სტრუქტურას აღვწერდი.
16. მოსკოვში კრემლის წინ წითელ მოედანზე ლენინის მავზოლეუმია.
17. ომის გამო ჯარისკაცები ფრონტზე არიან და სამწუხაროდ დედაქალაქში საჭმელი ცოტაა. ომის დროს ცხოვრება დიდ ქალაქებში ძალიან ძნელია, მაგრამ ომის შემდეგ ყველაფერი გაუმჯობესდება.
18. არდადეგების დროს ყოველთვის მთაში ავდივარ. ივლისშიც იქ ავალ, როცა ჩემი ცოლი ჩემს დასთან ერთად ევროპაში წავა.
19. ზურაბი რომ ახალ ფრანგულ-ქართულ ლექსიკონს დაამთავრებდეს სოფიკოს მოსვლამდის, მთელ მოთხრობას გადათარგმნიდით.
20. ნოდარ დუმბაძე ცნობილი ქართველი მწერალია. მაიაკოვსკი საქართველოდანაა. მაიაკოვსკი ქართველი კი არ არის, არამედ რუსი პოეტია.
21. უცხო ენების ინსტიტუტის მასწავლებლები ქართველი სტუდენტებისათვის წერენ ძველი ბერძნული ენის გრამატიკას.
22. ანტონი ახალი რომანისათვის ჯილდოს მიიღებს. ჯილდოს წყალობით გამდიდრდება.
23. სახლში შევდიოდით, როცა ექიმი გამოდიოდა.
24. ცუდი ამინდის გამო გივისთან სტუმრად დღეს არ წავალთ.
25. ჩვენი პროფესორის წიგნები რომ უფრო გარკვეულად იწერებოდეს, სტუდენტები უფრო ადვილად გაიგებდნენ.
26. გამოცდის გამო ვკითხულობთ წიგნებს საქართველოს ისტორიის შესახებ.
27. რომელი ქალაქია უფრო ძველი, თბილისი თუ მოსკოვი?

—თბილისი უფრო ძველი ქალაქია.

28. კაცისათვის კარგი ღვინო და კარგი ყველი ძალიან მნიშვნელოვანია.

29. კლასის კრება რომ უფრო ადრე იწყებოდეს, დროზე მოვიდოდი.

30. საქართველოს აკადემია გამოაქვეყნებს ახალ წიგნს ქართული ლიტერატურული ენის ისტორიის შესახებ.

31. გივი ინგლისურ სიტყვებს უაქცენტოდ წარმოთქვამს.

32. ქართული ტექსტის კითხვა ულექსიკონოდ ძალიან ძნელია.

33. დიდ ქართულ ქალაქებს შორის არის თბილისი, ქუთაისი და ბათუმი.

34. წიგნს თუ ბოლომდე წავიკითხავ, ყველაფერს გავიგებ.

35. სოფიო რადიოგადაცემას უსიტყვოდ ისმენს. ვენერა და მედეა მოისმენდნენ, პროგრამა რომ უფრო საინტერესო იქნებოდეს?!

36. გზაზე თბილისსა და მცხეთას შორის ძველი საინტერესო ეკლესიებია.

37. ქართველურ ენებს შორის წერილობითი ენა მხოლოდ ერთია — ქართული

38. ადრე რომ არ დაბნელდებოდეს, დღეს საღამოს რესტორანში წავიდოდით.

Vocabulary

ადრე	early
ამინდი	weather
ანალიზი	analysis
ანტონი	Anthony [m.pr.n.]
არამედ	but rather (cf. Ger. *sondern*, Russ. *a*)
არდადეგები	vacation [pl.]
აქცენტი	accent
აღმოსავლეთი	east(ern)
ბათუმი	(city in Georgia)
ბგერა	sound
ბერძენი	(E) Greek (person)
ბიბლია	Bible
ბოლო	end, conclusion
გამო	because of, on account of [pp.]
გარკვეული	clear, explicit, (a) certain
გზა	road, way
გივი	Givi [m.pr.n.]*
და	sister
დასავლეთი	west(ern)
დედაქალაქი	capital city (lit. 'mother city')
დრო	time; დროზე on time
დროს	during [pp.] (cf. დრო time)
დუმბაძე ნოდარი	(contemporary Soviet Georgian writer)
ევროპა	Europe
ეკლესია	church
ელენე	Helen [f.pr.n.]*
ერევანი	(A) Yerevan (capital of Armenia)
ერთად	together (see note 5)
ერთი	one
ექიმი	doctor (M.D.)
ვენერა	Venera, Venus [f.pr.n.]*
ვეფხისტყაოსანი	(A) *The Hero in the Tiger Skin*, poem of Šota Rustaveli; lit. tiger (ვეფხ(ვ)ი) skin (ტყავი) wearing-one (-ოსანი)
ვინ	who? [Dat. and Gen. ვის?]

ვინაიდან	because
თეატრი	theater
თუ	(a) if [with fut.; see sec. 4.1.2.] (b) or [in questions]
ივლისი	July
იმიტომ	for that reason
იმიტომ, რომ	because
ინსტიტუტი	institute
კატო	Kate [f.pr.n.; from ეკატერინე]
კრემლი	Kremlin
ლენინი	Lenin
ლექსიკონი	dictionary
მაგიდა	table
მავზოლეუმი	mausoleum
მაიაკოვსკი*	Mayakovsky (20th century Russian writer)
მდიდარი	(A) rich
მეგობარი	(A) friend
მედეა	Medea [f.pr.n.]*
მზე	sun
მთა	mountain(s)
მთელი	whole, entire
მიერ	by [pp.]
მოედანი	(A) (public) square
მოსკოვი	Moscow
მცხეთა	Mtskheta (first capital of Georgia)
ნიკო	Nick [m.pr.n.; from ნიკოლოზი]
ოთახი	room
ოლღა	Olga [f.pr.n.]*
ომი	war
პარიზი	Paris
პასუხი	answer
პირველი	first
პოეტი	poet
რესტორანი	(A) restaurant (also without syncope)
რომ	if [in conditionals; see sec. 4.1.2.]
რომელი	(E) which? what?
რუსთაველი შოთა	(Georgia's greatest poet, ca. 1172-1216)
რუსი	Russian (person)
სამწუხარო	unfortunate
საშუალო	middle, average; საშუალო სკოლა middle school (equivalent of U.S. high school)
საჭმელი	(E) food (cf. ჭამს 'eat')
სახლი	house
სომეხი	(E) Armenian (person)
სოფიო	Sophia [f.pr.n.]
სოფიკო	diminutive of

სოფიო	[f.pr.n.]
სტრუქტურა	structure
სტუმარი	(A) guest
სწორი, სწორე	precise, correct
სხვა	(an)other
ტექსტი	text
უკან	behind [pp.]
უკრაინა	the Ukraine
უორდროპი მარჯორი	Marjorie Wardrop (1869-1909)
უფრო	more
უცხო, უცხოური	foreign
უჯრა	drawer
ფანჯარა	(A) window
ფირფიტა	(phonograph) record
ფონეტიკა	phonetics
ფრანგი	French (person)
ფრონტი	front (here: military)
ქართველური	Kartvelian (the linguistic family to which Georgian belongs)
ქუთაისი	(city in Georgia)
ქუჩა	street
ღვინო	wine [Gen. and Instr. irreg.: Gen. ღვინის Instr. ღვინით]
ყველაფერი	(E) everything
ყველი	cheese
ყოველთვის	always
შემდეგ	after [pp.]; then (adverb)
შესახებ	about [pp.]
შორის	among [pp. with Dat.; sec. 4.4.3.]
შუა	between [pp. with Dat.; sec. 4.4.3.]
-ც (-აც after consonants)	(written together with the preceding word) also; ც . . . და -ც both ... and
ცოლი	wife
ცოტა	little [quantifier]*
ცხოვრება	life
წერილობითი	written (of a language)
წინ	in front of, before [pp.]; before (adverb)
წყალობით	thanks to [pp.]
ჯარისკაცი	soldier (cf. ჯარი army, კაცი man)
ჯილდო	prize
ჰოლანდიური	Dutch

*Nontruncating

Verbs.

გაიგებს	ga=i-*g*-eb-s	understand, learn, find out; hear
გაამდიდრებს see მდიდარი		
ასწავლის	a-*sc̣avl*-i-s (present = future)	teach
გააუმჯობესებს	ga=a-*umǰobes*-eb-s	improve
მიიღებს	mi=i-*ğ*-eb-s	receive, get

Jvari Cathedral
(Mcxeta; end of VI-beginning of VII centuries)
ჯვარი

Key to the Exercises

1. It would be good if we read books about Georgian life.
2. The first translation of the Bible into Old Georgian is from Greek.
3. Is David a Moscovite? No, he is from the Ukraine.
4. Among my Georgian books is a phonetic analysis of a French text. Were I to read it in the university, I would pronounce French sounds more accurately.
5. If Zurab reads only Georgian, Spanish, and Italian novels, why do I see German and Dutch novels on the table? Because Zurab's sister Sopiḳo will come here tomorrow. She teaches Dutch and German literature in a Batumi high school (literally 'middle school').
6. Where are you all going? We are going to Elizabeth's. If I were finishing the reading, I would go. But tomorrow I shall go to Vano's.
7. If the teacher will go out from the room, we will not study the lesson in the Chinese language.
8. Where is your Armenian-Russian [*Armenian* has no case ending; only *Russian* is declined] dictionary? It is on the table near the window. It isn't there. If it isn't there, it will be in the drawer behind my pens and pencils.
9. Were I to receive an answer from Tamar, I would go to the theatre with Tamar's brother.
10. The sun rises from the east and sets in the west (instr.).
11. After studying Georgian Nick and Olga will go across on the street and go to Anthony's. Anthony will receive new records of classical music from friends from Erevan.
12. If I receive a letter from Paris, I will come to your place.
13. If you receive a book from Kate, you will come to our place.
14. Who is the author of the first English translation of Šota Rustaveli's *The Knight in the Tiger's Skin* (ვეფხისტყაოსანი)? It is Marjorie Wardop. In Georgia now *The Knight in the Tiger's Skin* is being translated into other languages also.
15. If the members of the linguistic circle read [on] Georgian, I would describe the structure of the Georgian verb.
16. In front of the Kremlin on Red Square in Moscow is Lenin's mausoleum.
17. Because of the war the soldiers are on the front and unfortunately there is little food in the capital city. During the war life in the big cities

is very difficult but after the war everything will improve.

18. I always go up to the mountains [= in mountain] during vacation. I will go up there in July also when my wife will go to Europe with my sister.
19. If Zurab would finish the new French-Georgian dictionary before Sopiḳo's coming, you all would translate the whole story.
20. Nodar Dumbaje is a well-known Georgian writer. Mayakovsky is from Georgia. Mayakovsky, however, is not a Georgian but is a Russian poet.
21. The teachers of the Institute of Foreign Languages are writing a grammar of ancient Greek for Georgian students.
22. Anthony will receive a prize for [his] new novel. Thanks to the prize he will become rich.
23. We were entering into the house when the doctor was coming out.
24. Because of the bad weather we will not visit Givi today (= go to Givi's as guest).
25. If our professor's books were being written more clearly, the students would understand them more easily.
26. Because of the examination we are reading books about Georgia's history.
27. Which city is older (= more old), Tbilisi or Moscow? Tbilisi is the older city.
28. For a man, good wine and good cheese are very important.
29. If the class meeting began [use conjunctive imperfective] earlier (= more early) I would come on time.
30. The Georgian Academy will publish a new book about the history of the Georgian literary language.
31. Givi pronounces English words without an accent.
32. Reading a Georgian text is very difficult without a dictionary.
33. Among the large Georgian cities are Tbilisi, Kutaisi, and Batumi.
34. If I read the book up to the end, I will understand everything.
35. Sophie is listening to the radio broadcast without a word. Would Venera and Medea listen if the program were more interesting?
36. On the road between Tbilisi and Mtskheta there are interesting old churches.
37. Among the Kartvelian languages there is only one written language -- Georgian.
38. If it didn't become dark [so] early, we would go to the restaurant this evening (= today in the evening).

LESSON 5

5.0. Regular verbs. In this course verbs are considered regular if the root *in the present or future tenses* contains a vowel. Verbs such as დაწერს (*da=-c̣er-s*) [root *cer*] 'write'; გადათარგმნის (*gada=-targmn-i-s*) [root *targmn*] 'translate'; ააშენებს (*a=a-šen-eb-s*) [root *šen*] 'build'; აღნიშნავს (*aǧ+ -nišn-av-s*) [root *nišn*] 'mean'; etc. are regular. Verbs such as მოკლავს (*mo= -ḳl-av-s*) 'kill'; წარმოთქვამს (*c̣armo+tkv-am-s*) 'pronounce'; ჩათვლის (*ča=tvl-i-s*) 'consider'; მოსპობს (*mo=sp̣-ob-s*) 'destroy'; etc. are considered irregular since their roots (*-ḳl-*, *-tkv-*, *-tvl-*, *-sp̣-*) contain no vowels in the future or present series.

5.1. The aorist series. The second series of Georgian verbs is the aorist series. Whereas the future and present subseries consist of three screeves each (future subseries: future, conditional, conjunctive perfective; present subseries: present, imperfect, conjunctive imperfective), the aorist series consists of only two screeves, the aorist and the optative. In general, the aorist screeves are formed most frequently from future (i.e., perfective) series stems.

I. conjugation forms have a special case for the subject of aorist series screeves. This case could well be called the I.-conjugation-aorist-series-subject case, but it is traditionally called the *ergative* case (მოთხრობითი [*motxrobiti*] 'narrative case'). The direct object is in the nominative case (the same case which marks the subject in the present and future series). Indirect objects continue to be marked by the dative case. II. conjugation verbs have the same subject marker in the aorist series as in the present and future series, i.e., the nominative case. This can be summarized by the following table:

	I. Conj.			II. Conj.
	Subject	D.O.	Id.O.	Subject
Future and Present Series	Nominative	Dative		Nominative
Aorist Series	Ergative	Nominative	Dative	Nominative

Please note that the choice of subject case for I. conjugation verbs is purely mechanical. If the screeve is present, future, imperfect, conditional or conjunctive, the subject will be in the nominative case (and the direct and indirect objects in the dative); if the screeve is aorist or optative, the subject will be in the ergative, the direct object in the nominative, and the indirect object in the dative.[1]

5.2. The ergative case. The ergative case has the ending *-ma* which is added to consonantal stem nouns and the ending *-m* which is added to vocalic stem nouns (i.e., nouns ending in *a, e, o, i, u*).[2] Examples:

N.	ḳac-i	generAl-i	mindOr-i
	კაცი	გენერალი	მინდორი
E.	ḳac-ma	generAl-ma	mindOr-ma
	კაცმა	გენერალმა	მინდორმა
	man	general	field
N.	gramaṭiḳa	moçape	gogo
	გრამატიკა	მოწაფე	გოგო
E.	gramaṭiḳa-m	moçape-m	gogo-m
	გრამატიკამ	მოწაფემ	გოგომ
	grammar	pupil	girl

Plural forms are regular: კაცებმა *ḳac-eb-ma*, გენერლებმა *generl-eb-ma*, მინდვრებმა *mindvr-eb-ma*, გრამატიკებმა *gramaṭiḳ-eb-ma*, მოწაფეებმა *moçape-eb-ma*, გოგოებმა *gogo-eb-ma*. Note that there is no syncope in the singular ergative forms.

The ergative case of ვინ (*vin*) 'who'? is exceptional in that it is identical to the nominative, i.e., nom. and erg. = ვინ.

5.2.1. As noted in sec. 2.3.2 and sec. 3.4, adjectives ending in a vowel have no endings when preceding the noun they modify. Adjectives whose stems end in a consonant have the same endings as nouns in the ergative case when they precede the noun they modify:

N.	kartuli ena	meore gaḳvetili
	ქართული ენა	მეორე გაკვეთილი
E.	kartul-ma ena-m	meore gaḳvetil-ma
	ქართულმა ენამ	მეორე გაკვეთილმა
	Georgian language	second lesson
N.	maǧAl-i mta	
	მაღალი მთა	

E. maǧal-ma mta-m მაღალმა მთამ

high mountain

5.3. The aorist. The Georgian aorist of I. and II. conjugation verbs is almost always formed from the future (perfective) stem.[3] It is a past tense which lacks the durative, ongoing meaning of the imperfect. Nor is it generally iterative in meaning, unlike the imperfect or the conditional with *xolme* ხოლმე. A vague notion of its meaning can be gotten from approximate counterparts in other languages:

Georgian

Aorist		Imperfect	
დაწერა	da-c̣er-a	წერდა	c̣er-da
დაიწერა	da-i-c̣er-a	იწერებოდა	i-c̣er-eb-od-a
დამალა	da-mal-a	მალავდა	mal-av-d-a
დაიმალა	da-i-mal-a	იმალებოდა	i-mal-eb-od-a

English

Simple past	Past progressive
wrote	was writing
was written	was being written
hid something	was hiding (something)
hid (oneself)	was hiding (oneself)

French

passé composé or *passé defini*	*imparfait*
il a écrit, il écrivit	il écrivait
il a été écrit, il fut écrit	il s'écrivait
il l'a caché, il le cacha	il le cachait
il s'est caché, il se cacha	il se cachait

Russian

past perfective	past imperfective
он написал	он писал
он был написан	он писался
он скрыл	он скрывал
он скрылся	он скрывался

5.3.1. Aorist of regular verbs: I. conjugation.

Regular verbs of the I. conjugation form the aorist from the future stem by:

a. dropping the future stem formant, if any, and
b. adding the aorist endings:

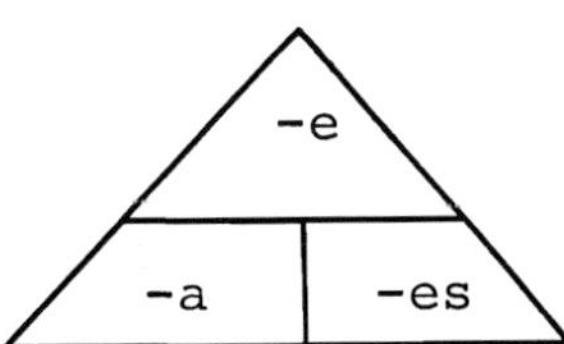

c. Some, though not all, root verbs (i.e., verbs without a present/future stem formant) having root vowel *e* alternate that vowel with *i* in the aorist series. Root verbs ending in *-ev* have the alternation but also lose the root-final *v* throughout the aorist. (Note the similar alternation in forming II. conjugation forms of these root verbs [sec. 3.1.4.1]). For examples, see sec. 5.3.2.2 below.

5.3.2. Aorist of regular verbs: II. conjugation. Remember that the subject of II. conjugation verbs in the aorist series is in the *nominative*.

5.3.2.1. II. conjugation in *-i-*. The aorist of II. conjugation verbs with *-i-* derived from regular I. conjugation verbs is formed in exactly the same manner as for I. conjugation verbs, except that the 3pl. ending differs:

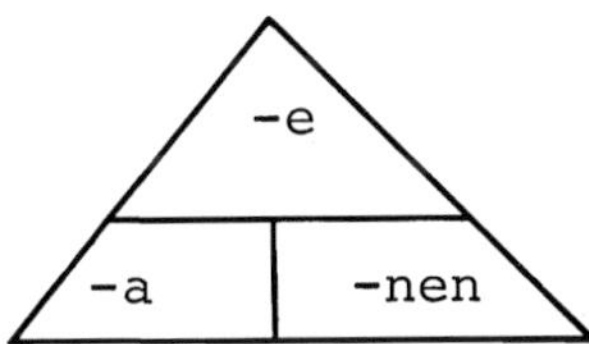

The only differences between I. conjugation aorists and the corresponding II. conjugation in *-i-* aorist will be in the ending of the 3pl. (I. conjugation *-es*, II. conjugation *-nen*) and the presence of the preradical vowel *-i-* in the II. conjugation form. The I. conjugation aorists usually do not have the preradical vowel *-i-*.[4] Root verbs in *-ev* form the II. conjugation aorist irregularly (see sec. 15.1.4). For examples see sec. 5.3.2.2 below.

5.3.2.2. Examples:

I. conj.	II. conj. in *i-*
Root verbs:	
da= -grex-s 'twist'	da= -i-grix-eb-a 'become twisted'
da=v-grix-e(-t)	da=v-i-grix-e(-t)
da= -grix-e(-t)	da= -i-grix-e(-t)
da= -grix-a da=grix-es	da= -i-grix-a da= -i-grix-nen
დავგრიხე(თ)	დავიგრიხე(თ)
დაგრიხე(თ)	დაიგრიხე(თ)
დაგრიხა დაგრიხეს	დაიგრიხა დაიგრიხნენ
a=a-rčev-s 'choose'	
a=v-a-rči-e(-t)	(see sec. 15.1.4)
a= -a-rči-e(-t)	
a= -a-rči-a a= -a-rči-es	
ავარჩიე(თ)	
აარჩიე(თ)	
აარჩია აარჩიეს	
da= -ç̣er-s 'write'	da= -i-ç̣er-eb-a 'be written'
da=v-ç̣er-e(-t)	
da= -ç̣er-e(-t)	
da= -ç̣er-a da= -ç̣er-es	da= -i-ç̣er-a da= -i-ç̣er-nen
დავწერე(თ)	
დაწერე(თ)	
დაწერა დაწერეს	დაიწერა დაიწერნენ
a= -ç̣on-i-s 'weigh'	a= -i-ç̣on-eb-a 'be weighed'
a=v-ç̣on-e(-t)	a=v-i-ç̣on-e(-t)
a= -ç̣on-e(-t)	a= -i-ç̣on-e(-t)
a= -ç̣on-a a= -ç̣on-es	a= -i-ç̣on-a a= -i-ç̣on-nen
ავწონე(თ)	ავიწონე(თ)
აწონე(თ)	აიწონე(თ)
აწონა აწონეს	აიწონა აიწონნენ

da= -mal-av-s 'hide (something)'	da= -i-mal-eb-a 'hide oneself'
da=v-mal-e(-t)	da=v-i-mal-e(-t)
da= -mal-e(-t)	da= -i-mal-e(-t)
da= -mal-a da= -mal-es	da= -i-mal-a da= -i-mal-nen
დავმალე(თ)	დავიმალე(თ)
დამალე(თ)	დაიმალე(თ)
დამალა დამალეს	დაიმალა დაიმალნენ

5.3.2.3. II. conjugation in *-d-*. The aorist of II. conjugation verbs in *-d-* is formed from the future stem by:

a. dropping the future stem formant
b. adding the aorist endings:

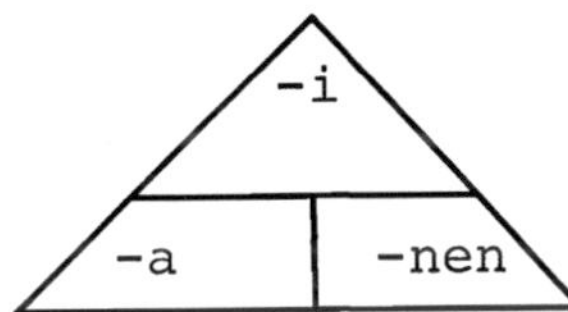

(Note that these are the same endings as for the imperfect and conditional; these two screeves differ from the aorist in having both the P/FSF (*-eb*) and the suffix *-od-*.) Example:

I. conj.	II. conj. in *-d-*
ga= -a-çitl-eb-s 'make red'	ga= -çitl-d-eb-a 'blush'
ga=v-a-çitl-e(-t)	ga=v-çitl-d-i(-t)
ga= -a-çitl-e(-t)	ga= -çitl-d-i(-t)
ga= -a-çitl-a	ga= -çitl-d-a
ga= -a-çitl-es	ga= -çitl-d-nen
გავაწითლე(თ)	გავწითლდი(თ)
გააწითლე(თ)	გაწითლდი(თ)
გააწითლა	გაწითლდა
გააწითლეს	გაწითლდნენ

Other examples (all forms are third person singular):

Noun	I. conj. fut.	II. conj. fut.	Aor. II. conj.
meore	ga=i-meor-eb-s	ga=meor-d-eb-a	ga=meor-d-a
მეორე	გაიმეორებს	გამეორდება	გამეორდა
second	repeat	be repeated	

tavi	ga=a-tav-eb-s	ga=tav-d-eb-a	ga=tav-d-a
თავი	გაათავებს	გათავდება	გათავდა
head	end	end (intr.)	
---	a=a-šen-eb-s	a=šen-d-eb-a	a=šen-d-a
	ააშენებს	აშენდება	აშენდა
	build	be built	

5.3.3. Examples:

I.

დაწერს	write	აღმოაჩენს	discover
დავწერე(თ)		აღმოვაჩინე(თ)	
დაწერე(თ)		აღმოაჩინე(თ)	
დაწერა	დაწერეს	აღმოაჩინა	აღმოაჩინეს
ნახავს	see	ააშენებს	build
ვნახე(თ)		ავაშენე(თ)	
ნახე(თ)		ააშენე(თ)	
ნახა	ნახეს	ააშენა	ააშენეს
შერევს	mix	გადათარგმნის	translate
შევრიე(თ)		გადავთარგმნე(თ)	
შერიე(თ)		გადათარგმნე(თ)	
შერია	შერიეს	გადათარგმნა	გადათარგმნეს

II. -*i*-.		II. -*d*-.	
დამალავს		გააწითლებს	
დაიმალება	hide	გაწითლდება	blush
დავიმალე(თ)		გავწითლდი(თ)	
დაიმალე(თ)		გაწითლდი(თ)	
დაიმალა	დაიმალნენ	გაწითლდა	გაწითლდნენ

5.4. Aorist of irregular verbs.

5.4.1. Verbs in -*eb* and -*ob* with nonsyllabic roots form the aorist of both the I. and II. conjugation forms from the future stem in the normal manner, i.e., by dropping any future stem formant and by adding the aorist endings. These aorist endings, however, are irregular in the 3sg. in that they take -*o* instead of -*a*; i.e.,

I. conj.

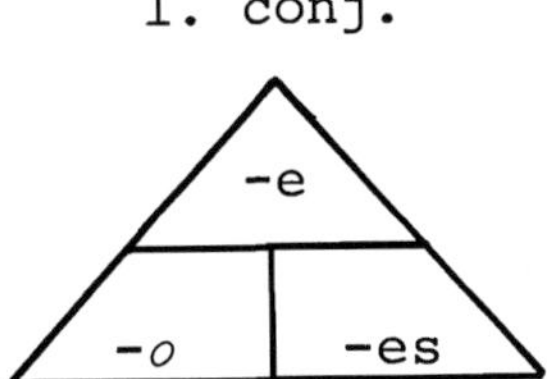

II. conj.

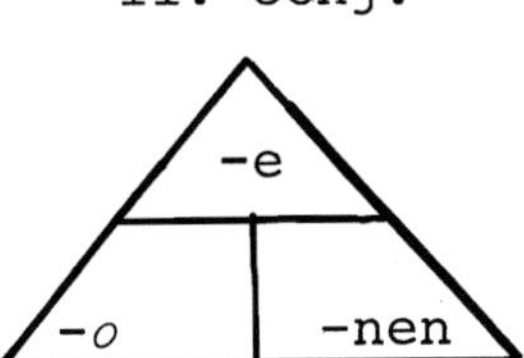

Examples:

Fut. I.	Aorist I.	Fut. II.	Aorist II.
ga=a-ğ-eb-s	ga=a-ğ-o	ga=i-ğ-eb-a	ga=i-ğ-o
გააღებს	გააღო	გაიღება	გაიღო
open			
da=i-çq-eb-s	da=i-çq-o	da=i-çq-eb-a	da-i-çq-o[5]
დაიწყებს	დაიწყო	დაიწყება	დაიწყო
begin			
mi=i-ğ-eb-s	mi=i-ğ-o	mi=i-ğ-eb-a	mi=i-ğ-o[5]
მიიღებს	მიიღო	მიიღება	მიიღო
receive			

5.4.2. Aorist/Imperfect of ყოფნა. Subj. is nom.

ვიყავი(-თ)	v-i-qav-i(-t)	
იყავი(-თ)	i-qav-i(-t)	
იყო	იყვნენ i-q-o	i-qv-nen

5.4.3. Aorist of სვლა svla. (*Subject in nominative*)
[*Pvb*+v-ved-i(-t) →] 1. *Pvb*+ved-i(-t)
2. *Pvb*+x-ved-i(-t)

3sg. *Pvb*+vid-a 3pl. *Pvb*+vid-nen

Pvb stands for the preverb found in the future series of screeves. So, from pres. მიდის *mi+di-s*, fut. წავა *ça+va* we get aorist 3sg. წავიდა *ça+vid-a*. Note that as in the future screeves, the 2d person has the marker *x*-. Note also the vowel alternation between the 1st and 2d person and the 3d person forms. Example:

მოდის comes		მოვედი(-თ)
		მოხვედი(-თ)
	მოვიდა	მოვიდნენ

5.5. Demonstrative pronouns and adjectives.

5.5.1. The demonstrative *adjectives* N. ეს (*es*) 'this', 'these' and ის (*is*) 'that', 'those' have one form for all the remaining cases. Note that these forms modify both singular and plural nouns.

N.	es ეს	is ის
E.D.G.I.A.	am ამ	im იმ

5.5.2. The demonstrative *pronouns* N. sg. ეს (*es*) 'this (one)' and ის (*is*) or იგი (*igi*) 'that (one)' form all remaining singular case forms from the stems *ama-* and *ima-* respectively. These are declined like a regular noun stem in *a*, except for the E., which takes the ending *-n*:[6]

	this:		that:			
Nom.	es	ეს	is ის	or	igi იგი	
Erg.	ama-n	ამან	ima-n	იმან		
Dat.	ama-s	ამას	ima-s	იმას		
Gen.	am- is	ამის	im- is	იმის		
Inst.	am- it	ამით	im- it	იმით		
Adv.	am- ad	ამად	im- ad	იმად		

In the plural only two forms are found, a nominative and an ergative-dative-genitive:

	these:		those:		
Nom.	ese-ni	ესენი	isi-ni ისინი	or	იგინი igini
E.D.G.	ama-t	ამათ	ima-t	იმათ	

5.6. Nouns: the stylistically marked plural. In addition to the plural formation described in sec. 4.2 there is a less frequent plural formation of nouns (which was typical of the older Georgian literary language). This system opposes a nominative to an ergative-dative-genitive plural, much as in the plural of the demonstrative pronoun. In the stylistically marked plural there is neither syncope nor truncation; the endings are added directly to the stem of the noun. These endings are:

Nom.	-ni
E.D.G.	-t(a)

Examples:

	სახელი	saxel-i	ძმა	jma
N.pl.	სახელნი	saxel-ni	ძმანი	jma-ni
E.D.G.pl.	სახელთ(ა)	saxel-t(a)	ძმათ(ა)	jma-t(a)
		name		brother

	კალამი	ḳalAm-i	კაცი	ḳac-i
N.pl.	კალამნი	ḳalAm-ni	კაცნი	ḳac-ni
E.D.G.pl.	კალამთ(ა)	ḳalAm-t(a)	კაცთ(ა)	ḳac-t(a)
		pen		man

It should be noted that the ending *-ta* is commonly used to form adjectives from nouns; cf. საბჭო (*sabč̣o*) 'council, Soviet' (noun), საბჭოთა (*sabč̣ota*) councils', Soviets' (g.pl.), and 'Soviet' (adj.) as in საბჭოთა კავშირი (*Sabč̣ota ḳavširi*) Soviets' Union, i.e., Soviet Union.[7]

5.7. Wordbuilding: formation of *nomina agentis*. Nouns generally denoting persons in terms of profession or actions they perform can be derived from nouns and from verbs.

5.7.1. Denominals with circumfix *me-.....-e*.

ბაღი	baği	garden	მებაღე	me-bağ-e	gardener
პური	p̣uri	bread	მეპურე	me-p̣ur-e	baker
დუქანი	dukAni	shop	მედუქნე	me-dukn-e	shopowner
საათი	saati	watch, clock	მესაათე	me-saat-e	watchmaker
ცხვარი	cxvAri	sheep	მეცხვარე	me-cxvar-e	shepherd

5.7.2. Deverbals with prefix *m-*. Nomina agentis are generally formed from the *present* stem of verbs, minus any preradical vowel. Often there is a suffix *-el-* (*-El-*), or, less commonly, *-Ar-* (*-Al-* when the verbal root contains an *r*). The present stem formants *-av-* and *-am-* undergo syncope before these suffixes, and PSF *-i* is dropped. Examples:

(a) with *-el-*

gada=targmn-i-s	m-targmn-el-i
გადათარგმნის	მთარგმნელი
translate	translator
mo=ḳl-av-s	m-ḳvl-el-i
მოკლავს	მკვლელი
kill	killer (see sec. 1.11.2)
∅=mart-av-s[8]	m-mart-v-el-i
მართავს	მმართველი
manage	manager

mo=i-smen-s	m-smen-el-i
მოისმენს	მსმენელი
listen	listener
a=a-šen-eb-s	m-šen-eb-El-i
ააშენებს	მშენებელი
build	builder

Note the following formed from the future stem:

i-ḳitx-av-s	m-ḳitx-v-el-i
იკითხავს	მკითხველი
read	reader
še=a-pas-eb-s	še-m-pas-eb-El-i
შეაფასებს	შემფასებელი
estimate	estimator

(Note that the prefix *m- follows* any preverb.)

(b) with no suffix. (This group is less common than the group with *-el-*.)

še=ḳer-av-s	m-ḳer-av-i
შეკერავს	მკერავი
sew	tailor, sewer
ağ-mo+a-čen-s	ağ-mo+m-čen-i
აღმოაჩენს	აღმომჩენი
discover	discoverer

These forms are also known as the *present active participle* (see sec. 11.5).

LESSON 5: Notes

1. If one noun is the subject of two or more verbs governing different subject cases, the noun takes the case demanded by the *nearest* verb to it. Example:

> ნიკო კართან მივიდა და გააღო.
>
> Nick went up to the door and opened it.
>
> ნიკომ კარი გააღო და გავიდა.
>
> Nick opened the door and went out.

In the first sentence the subject, ნიკო, is in the nominative because the nearest verb, მივიდა, always takes a nominative subject, this despite the fact that გააღო demands a subject in the ergative, being a I. conjugation verb in the aorist. In the second sentence, the situation is reversed.

2. The ending *-m* also occurs with proper names with stems ending in *i* (see Lesson 3, note 3); e.g. გიორგიმ, გივიმ. The ending *-m* also occurs with the small number of loanwords with stems ending in *i* such as ჩაი tea, ტრამვაი streetcar, ტაქსი taxicab. Such nouns are declined the same as names like გიორგი. Note also that the erg. of ვინ who? is irregular, being identical to the nom. The full declension of this interrogative pronoun is nom., erg. ვინ; dat., gen. ვის.

3. Much less common is the *imperfective* aorist, formed from the present stem (i.e., generally without preverb). It can indicate that the action ended without achieving the desired result: კარი ვაღე I tried to open the door (unsuccessfully) as opposed to კარი გავაღე I opened the door (perfective aorist). Note that the use of the imperfect, კარს ვაღებდი I was opening the door generally implies that the door will be opened. The imperfective aorist (often repeated) can also indicate a series of such unsuccessful attempts: კარი ვაღე ვაღე და ძლივს გავაღე I tried and tried to open the door and just barely (ძლივს) opened (perfective aorist) it.

4. For an example of a I. conjugation verb with preradical vowel *-i-*, see the examples of დაიწყებს (*da=i-c̣q-eb-s*) 'begin', below.

5. Note that for these particular verbs the aorist forms of the I. and II. conjugation are formally identical, particularly in the 3sg., where both are *da=i-c̣q-o* დაიწყო. The semantic distinction between the two

conjugations can be determined by either context or by the case of the subject in the third person; cf. მეორემ დაიწყო (*meorem (E.) daiçqo*) 'the second (one) began it'; and მეორე დაიწყო (*meore (N.) daiçqo*) 'the second (one) began'. In the first example (with the E.) the verb is transitive, cf. French *le deuxième l'a commencé*, Russian второй начал. The second example (with the N.) has an intransitive verb; cf. French *le deuxième s'est commencé*, Russian второй начался. (There is a difference in endings in the 3pl.: I. conjugation *-es*, II. conjugation *-nen*, but since the subjects of II. conjugation verbs are generally inanimate, this latter ending is rather rare in occurrence (see sec. 4.2).

6. Georgian has a third, less common demonstrative: adjective N. *eg* ეგ, E.D.G.I.Adv. *mag* მაგ and pronoun N. *eg* ეგ, stem of other cases *maga-*, pl. N. *egeni* ეგენი E.D.G. *magat* მაგათ. *Eg* ეგ indicates a distance intermediate between that of *es* ეს and *is* ის, somewhat similar to Latin *iste, ista, istud*.

It should be noted that before the particle *-c* 'also' the nominative forms *es* ეს and *is* ის add *e* and *i* respectively: *esec* (ესეც) 'this too', *isic* (ისიც) 'that too'.

7. Consonantal stem adjectives modifying nouns in the stylistically marked plural generally take *-i* in the nominative and no ending in the E.D.G. Adjectives ending in a vowel take no ending in either form. Compare the adjective endings in the stylistically marked plural of *sxva saxelovan-i ḳac-i* 'another famous man':

N.	sxva-	saxelovan-i	ḳac-ni	სხვა სახელოვანი კაცნი
E.D.G.	sxva-	saxelovan-	ḳac-t(a)	სხვა სახელოვან კაცთა

8. This verb has no preverb in the future series; as a result there is no formal difference between it and the present series.

LESSON 5: Exercises

1. ვინ აღმოაჩინა ამერიკა? —ქრისტეფორე კოლუმბმა.
2. შოთა რუსთაველის დიდი პოემა ინგლისურად პირველად ვინ გადათარგმნა? —მარჯორი უორდროპმა.
3. გუშინ რადიოთი ხალხური მუსიკის პროგრამა მოვისმინეთ. იმ დროს, როდესაც ვისმენდით, შალვა გაზეთს კითხულობდა.
4. გუშინ მედეა სად წავიდა? —გუშინ მედეა უნივერსიტეტში წავიდა და შემდეგ მნიშვნელოვანი სტატიის კითხვა დაიწყო.
5. შალვამ კი სავარჯიშოები დაამზადა და შემდეგ მარიამთან წავიდა.
6. ჯორჯ ვაშინგტონი სად დაიბადა? —ვაშინგტონი ვირჯინიაში დაიბადა. —სად დაიბადე? —ჩიკაგოში დავიბადე.
7. მცხეთა საქართველოს პირველი დედაქალაქი იყო. მეექვსე საუკუნეში დედაქალაქი მცხეთიდან თბილისში გადავიდა.
8. ივანემ პროფესორის სიტყვები მოისმინა და წავიდა.
9. როცა ომი დაიწყო, მეცხვარეები მთაში დაიმალნენ. ომის შემდეგ ბარში ჩამოვიდნენ.
10. საინტერესო წერილი მივიღე პეტრესაგან, ჩემმა ძმამ კი ბათუმიდან მიიღო პაკეტი.
11. შექსპირის პირველი მთარგმნელი ქართულ ენაზე იყო დიმიტრი ყიფიანი.
12. ყველაფერს რომ ისწავლი, ყველაფერს კარგად გაიგებ. —ხომ ვისწავლე ყველაფერი!
13. იმ კაცმა ყველაფერი გაიგო, რაც წაიკითხა. ამან კი მხოლოდ ცოტა წაიკითხა და ახლა ძალიან ცოტას გაიგებს ამ საქმეების შესახებ.
14. მედუქნის მამა ომის წინ გამდიდრდა.
15. „ვეფხისტყაოსანი" პირველად 1712 (ათას შვიდას თორმეტ) წელს გამოქვეყნდა. გაიგე? მეფე ვახტანგ VI (მეექვსემ) „ვეფხისტყაოსანი" 1712 (ათას შვიდას

თორმეტ) წელს გამოაქვეყნა. იგი ამ პოემის პირველი გამომქვეყნებელი იყო.

16. როცა ლადომ პარიზული გაზეთის კითხვა დაამთავრა, ივანე ჯავახიშვილის ბიოგრაფიის კითხვა დაიწყო. —ივანე ჯავახიშვილი ვინ იყო? —დიდი ქართველი ისტორიკოსი და თბილისის უნივერსიტეტის მამა იყო. დაწერა ცნობილი „ქართველი ერის ისტორია."

17. როცა ამ კითხვაზე პასუხი აღმოაჩინე, გავმდიდრდი.

18. საქართველო, სომხეთი და აზერბაიჯანი ამიერკავკასიის საბჭოთა რესპუბლიკებია. საქართველოს დედაქალაქი თბილისია, სომხეთის დედაქალაქი ერევანია, აზერბაიჯანისა კი ბაქოა.

19. გუშინ ის სტუდენტი ნახე? —არა, ეს ვნახე. იმას ხვალ ვნახავ.

20. პროფესორმა ლექცია დღეს ადრე დაიწყო. ლექცია გუშინაც ადრე დაიწყო.

21. როცა გავდიოდი, თამარმა კარი გააღო და შემოვიდა.

22. წერილი მივიღეთ შენი ძმისაგანაც და ანტონის დისაგანაც. ანტონმა კი წერილი ჩემი დისაგან მიიღო.

23. ომის შემდეგ ცხოვრება ამ ქვეყანაში დიდად გაუმჯობესდა. საუკუნის ბოლომდე უმჯობესდებოდა. ახალი ომი თუ დაიწყება, მდგომარეობა ცუდი იქნება.

24. ამას წინათ იერუსალიმის ქართულ ეკლესიაში შოთა რუსთაველის სურათი აღმოაჩინეს. ის ქართულ მონასტერში ბერად იყო.

25. რევაზმა ლექცია მოისმინა, შემდეგ კი ეს ძველი სავარჯიშოები გაიმეორა. ლექციებს თუ მოისმენთ და შემდეგ ამ სავარჯიშოებს გაიმეორებთ, რევაზივით (= რევაზსავით) ყველაფერს გაიგებთ.

26. გასული საუკუნის დიდმა ქართველმა პოეტმა, აკაკი წერეთელმა, დაწერა ცნობილი ლექსი „სულიკო."

27. ქართული ენის პირველი გრამატიკა ვინ დაწერა? —პირველი გრამატიკა რომში გამოქვეყნდა (1643).

ავტორი იყო იტალიელი ბერი მაჯო. ანტონ პირველმა ამ ენის პირველი ქართული გრამატიკა დაწერა (1753). —ანტონ პირველი ვინ იყო? —საქართველოს კათალიკოსი იყო. —კათალიკოსი რას ნიშნავს? ეკლესიის მეთაურს ნიშნავს.

28. „ვეფხისტყაოსანი" რუსულ ენაზე პირველად გასულ საუკუნეში გადაითარგმნა. მთარგმნელი იყო სახელოვანი რუსი პოეტი ბალმონტი.

29. ის წიგნები ბერძნულიდან ითარგმნა,* ესენი კი, ძველი სომხურიდან. ის გუშინ წავიკითხე, ამას კი, ახლა ვკითხულობ.

30. პასუხი თემოსაგან გუშინ მივიღეთ. იმ წერილში თემომ აღწერა ცხოვრება კავკასიაში. ომის შემდეგ თემო და ლადო სტუდენტები იყვნენ თბილისში. იმ დროს ჩემი დებიც თბილისში იყვნენ.

31. იმ დროს, როდესაც ჩემი მეგობრები პოემას კითხულობდნენ, რევაზმა და ლადომ კარი გააღეს და შემოვიდნენ.

32. გუშინ როდის გახვედით? —გუშინ გვიან გავედით, ვინაიდან ჩვენთან ძალიან გვიან მოხვედით. —დაიგვიანეთ, ვინაიდან ლექციები გვიან დამთავრდა.

33. ეს პური ვინ გამოაცხო? —მეპურემ. მეპურე გუშინ პურს აცხობდა.

34. გუშინ პური გამოაცხვეთ? —დიახ, პური გამოვაცხვეთ.

35. პირველი დამოწმებული ქართული ტექსტები მეხუთე საუკუნეში დაიწერა. ეს ტექსტები პირველი ქართული ანბანით დაიწერა. ამ ანბანის სახელი „ხუცური" იყო. ახალი ქართული ანბანის სახელი „მხედრულია."

36. როცა მოსკოვში ვიყავი, წითელი მოედანი და კრემლი ვნახე. მოსკოვში თუ წახვალთ, წითელ მოედანსა და კრემლს ნახავთ.

37. მასალით ძალიან კმაყოფილი ვიყავით. იმ მასალით

ივანეც კმაყოფილი იყო.

38. ეს წიგნიც წავიკითხე და ისიც. იმას ვკითხულობდი, როცა თემო შემოვიდა სახლში.
39. მწერალთა კავშირის წევრი ხარ? —არა, მასწავლე-ბელთა კავშირის წევრი ვარ.
40. ლადო ამ ლურჯი კალმით დაწერს, რევაზი კი — იმით. —ის ლურჯი არ არის, წითელია. ჩემიც წითელია.
41. საქართველოს რუსეთთან შეერთების შემდეგ (1801) საქართველოს ისტორიაში ახალი პერიოდი დაიწყო.
42. ეს წიგნები პროფესორისათვისაა, ისინი კი — სტუდენტებისათვის.
43. პირველი ქართული წიგნები მეფე ვახტანგ მეექვსის სტამბაში დაიბეჭდა.
44. ავტორმა ხელნაწერი ფრთხილად გაასწორა. როცა ხელნაწერი გასწორდა, რედაქტორები კმაყოფილნი იყვნენ.
45. როცა ყველაფერი დამზადდა, მამამ კარი გააღო და სახლში შემოვიდა.
46. რუსი პოეტი მაიაკოვსკი საქართველოში დაიბადა.
47. გასულ საუკუნეში თბილისი იყო კულტურის ცენტრი არა მხოლოდ ქართველებისათვის, არამედ სომხებისათვისაც. საქართველოს ქალაქებში სომხებს დღესაც ვხედავთ.
48. როცა დავიბადე, აღმოსავლეთში ომი ჯერ კიდევ გრძელდებოდა. ომი გათავდა იმ დროს, როცა სკოლაში ვსწავლობდი.
49. წუხელ ზურაბმა არაყი და ღვინო დალია და დღეს ძალიან ავადაა. ღვინოსა და არაყს თუ დალევს, ვახტანგიც ავად იქნება.
50. სკოლაში რომ არ ვსწავლობდე, ამ სულელურ გაკვეთილს არ ვისწავლიდი!

*Note the use of the imperfective (nonprefixed) form of the aorist here to mark a series of independent past completed actions.

Vocabulary ●131

ავად	sick
ამას წინათ	recently
ამიერკავკასია	Transcaucasia
არ	not
არაყი	vodka (A)
ბარი	valley (no pl.)
ბერი	monk
გამომქვეყნებელი	publisher (E)
გასული	last (previous)
დამოწმებული	attested
ერი ●	people, nation
იმ დროს, როდესაც (როცა)	while
ისტორიკოსი	historian
კავშირი	union
კათალიკოსი	catholicos (Georgian patriarch)
კარი	door, gate
კაცი	man
კითხვა	question
კულტურა	culture
მდგომარეობა	situation
მედუქნე	shopowner (cf. დუქანი [A] shop)
მეექვსე ●	sixth (cf. ექვსი six)
მეპურე	baker (cf. პური bread)
მეხუთე	fifth (cf. ხუთი five)
მეფე	king
მეცხვარე	shepherd (cf. ცხვარი [A] sheep)
მთარგმნელი	translator
მონასტერი	monastery (E)
პაკეტი	package
პერიოდი	period
პოემა	[longer] poem
პროგრამა	program
რადიო	radio
რაც	what, which, that (rel.)
რესპუბლიკა	republic
საუკუნე	century
საქმე	matter, affair, job
სახელოვანი	famous (A) (only of persons)
სკოლა	school
სულელური	silly (non-person)
სურათი	picture
ქვეყანა	country, world (A)
შეერთება	unification, union
შეკითხვა	question
ცენტრი	center
წელი	year (E)
ხომ	but, however (German

	doch, Russian ведь)	
ჯერ კიდევ	still, yet	

Verbs.

დაბადებს	da=*bad*-eb-s	bear, bring into the world ([II] დაიბადება be born)
დაიგვიანებს	da=*i-gvian*-eb-s	be late (intransitive)
დალევს	da+*lev*-s: pr. სვამს sv-am-s	drink (aor. დალია)
სვამს	see დალევს	
მოისმენს	mo=i-*smen*-s	listen to (aor. მოისმინა)
გააღებს	ga=a-*ğ*-eb-s	open
აღმოაჩენს	ağmo+a-*čen*-s	discover (aor. აღმოაჩინა)
გამოაცხობს	gamo=a-*cxv*-ob-s*	bake

*Although the root of this verb is *cxv*, the *v* disappears before a following *o* (see sec. 1.11.1). As a consequence the future, გამოაცხობს, lacks the *v*, which reappears in the aorist: გამოვაცხვე, გამოაცხვე, 3pl. გამოაცხვეს (but 3sg. გამოაცხო).

Proper nouns.

აზერბაიჯანი	Azerbaijan	იტალია	Italy
ბაქო	Baku	კავკასია	The Caucasus
გერმანია	Germany	რომი	Rome
ვირჯინია	Virginia (state)	ჩიკაგო	Chicago
იერუსალიმი	Jerusalem		

ბალმონტი კონსტანტინე	Konstantin Bal'mont (1867-1942)
ვაშინგტონი ჯორჯი	George Washington
კოლუმბი ქრისტეფორე	Christopher Columbus
მაჯო	Maggio (Francesco Mario)
შექსპირი	Shakespeare
ყიფიანი დიმიტრი	(1814-1887)
წერეთელი აკაკი	(1840-1915)

ვახტანგი [m.] პეტრე [m.] Peter რევაზი [m.]
თემო [m. from თეიმურაზი] ლადო [m. from ვლადიმერი]

Key to the Exercises

1. Who discovered America? Christopher Columbus.
2. Who first translated Shota Rustaveli's great poem into English (adv.)? Marjory Wardrop.
3. Yesterday we listened to the program of folk music on the radio (instr.). While we were listening, Šalva was reading the newspaper.
4. Where did Medea go yesterday? Yesterday Medea went to the university and then began the reading of an important article.
5. Šalva however prepared the exercises and then went to Mary's (place).
6. Where was George Washington born? Washington was born in Virginia. Where were you born? I was born in Chicago.
7. Mcxeta was the first capital of Georgia. In the sixth century the capital moved [went across] from Mcxeta to Tbilisi.
8. John listened to the professor's words and went away.
9. When the war began shepherds hid in the mountains. After the war they came down into the valley(s).
10. I received an interesting letter from Peter; my brother however received a package from Batumi.
11. The first translator of Shakespeare into Georgian was Dimitri Qipiani.
12. If you will study everything you will understand everything well. But [however] I studied everything!
13. That man understood everything that he read. This (one), however, read only a little and now will understand very little about these matters.
14. The shopowner's father became rich before the war.
15. "The Knight in the Tiger Skin" was first published in 1712 (ათას შვიდას თორმეტ წელს). Did you understand? King **Vaxṭang** VI published "The Knight in the Tiger Skin" in 1712. He [that one] was the first publisher of this poem.
16. When Lado finished the reading of the Paris newspaper he began the reading of Ivane J̌avaxišvili's biography. Who was Ivane J̌avaxišvili? He was a great Georgian historian and the father of Tbilisi University. He wrote the famous *History of the Georgian People* (ერი).
17. When I discovered the answer to [on] this question I became rich.
18. Georgia, Armenia, and Azerbaidjan are the Transcaucasus's Soviet republics. Georgia's capital is Tbilisi, Armenia's capital is Yerevan, and Azerbaid-

jan's is Baku.
19. Did you see that student yesterday? No, I saw this (one). That one I shall see tomorrow.
20. The professor began the lecture early today. Yesterday the lecture began early too.
21. When I was going out, Tamar opened the door and came in.
22. We received a letter from both your brother and from Anthony's sister. Anthony, however, received a letter from my sister.
23. After the war life in this country greatly improved. It was improving until the end of the century. If a new war will begin, the situation will be bad.
24. Recently they discovered Shota Rustaveli's picture in Jerusalem's Georgian church. He [that one] was a monk (adv.) in the Georgian monastery.
25. Revaz listened to the lecture, then, however, repeated these old exercises. If you all listen to the lectures and then repeat these exercises, like Revaz you all will understand everything.
26. The great Georgian poet of the last century, Aḳaḳi C̣ereteli, wrote the famous poem "Suliḳo".
27. Who wrote the first grammar of the Georgian language? The first grammar was published in Rome (1643). The author was the Italian monk Maggio. Anthony I wrote the first Georgian grammar of this language (1753). Who was Anthony I? He was the Catholicos (Patriarch) of Georgia. What does "catholicos" mean? It means head of the church.
28. "The Hero in the Tiger Skin" was first translated into Russian in the last century. The translator was a famous Russian poet, Balmont.
29. Those books were translated from Greek, these, however, from Old Armenian. I read that one yesterday and I am now reading this one.
30. We received an answer from Temo yesterday. In that letter Temo described life in the Caucasus. Temo and Lado were students in Tbilisi after the war. At that time (dat. without preposition) my sisters too were in Tbilisi.
31. While my friends were reading the (longer) poem, Revaz and Lado opened the door and came in.
32. When did you all go out yesterday? Yesterday we went out late because you all came to our place very late. We were late because the lectures ended late.
33. Who baked this bread? The baker. The baker was baking bread yesterday.
34. Did you all bake bread yesterday? Yes, we baked bread.

35. The first attested Georgian texts were written in the fifth century. These texts were written with the first Georgian alphabet. The name of this alphabet was *xucuri*. The name of the new Georgian alphabet is *mxedruli*.
36. When I was in Moscow I saw Red Square and the Kremlin. If you all go to Moscow, you all will see Red Square and the Kremlin.
37. We were very satsified with the material. John, too, was satisfied with that material.
38. I read both this book and that one . I was reading that one when Temo came into the house.
39. Are you a member of the writers' union? No, I am a member of the teachers' union.
40. Lado will write with this blue pen, Revaz, however, will write with that one. That one is not blue; it is red. Mine, too, is red.
41. After the union of Georgia with (-თან) Russia (1801) a new period in Georgia's history began.
42. These books are for the professor, those, however, for the students.
43. The first Georgian books were printed in King Vaxṭang VI's printing house.
44. The author carefully corrected the manuscript. When the manuscript was corrected, the editors were satisfied (use stylistically marked plural).
45. When everything was prepared, father opened the door and came into the house.
46. The Russian poet Mayakovsky was born in Georgia.
47. In the past century Tbilisi was the center of culture not only for the Georgians but for the Armenians also. Today, too, we see Armenians in Georgia's cities.
48. When I was born, the war was still continuing in the east. The war ended at that time, when I was studying in school.
49. Last night Zurab drank vodka and wine and today he is very sick. If he drinks wine and vodka, Vakhtang, too, will be sick.
50. If I weren't studying in school, I wouldn't study this silly lesson.

●ADDENDA TO VOCABULARY

იმ დროს	at that time
მეთაური	head (of an organization)

5.8.0. General Note to the Reading Passages. Beginning with this lesson, each lesson will contain an unedited reading passage taken from Georgian sources. The vocabularies to these reading passages, as a general rule, will contain all words *except* (a) those which have previously occurred in the vocabularies to the exercises, (b) derivatives of words which have already occurred in the exercises and whose formation and meaning should be easily predictable, (c) easily recognizable proper names (both of persons and places), and (d) internationalisms and other words which are identical or similar in both English and Georgian.

Constructions which have not yet been introduced in the grammar sections of the lessons will be enclosed in square brackets. Except for such forms, all other grammatical constructions occurring in the reading passages should be identifiable.

5.8.1. Hints on reading Georgian. Reading Georgian texts presents the learner with some problems not usually encountered in most other European languages. Many of these problems are due to left branching (see sec. 3.3.1 and below) and to the variation in the case marking of the subject and direct object, both of which characterize Georgian. A phenomenon found in other European languages, embedding of participial phrases (see below) can also cause difficulty, especially when combined with left-branching. The following hints should facilitate the reading of Georgian texts.

5.8.1.1. Breaking the sentence down into phrases. In reading Georgian it is very important to be able to break a sentence down into its constituent phrases. The ends of noun phrases are usually marked by nouns in the *nominative*, *dative*, or *ergative* cases. The end of a phrase can also be marked by nouns in the instrumental or adverbial cases or nouns followed by postpositions, although these can form a part of a larger phrase (see embedding, below). As a rule, nouns in the genitive case or nouns with "extended" case forms (sec. 4.3), which usually occur before და or another conjunction do not mark the end of a phrase. Adjectives, of course, except when declined as nouns, usually do not mark the end of a phrase. Note the following example of an analysis of a sentence into constituent phrases:

1	2	3	4
თბილისის	გიმნაზიის	დამთავრების	შემდეგ
Tbilisi G.	*gymnasium* G.	finishing G.	after (pp.)

5 6

ივანე ჯავახიშვილი

Ivane J̌avaxišvili (nom.)

7

პეტერბურგს

St. Petersburg (dat.)

8 9

გაემგზავრა და

verb: II. conj. aor. 'he travelled to' (+dat.) and

10 11

უმაღლესი განათლება

higher (adj.) education (nom.)

12 13

პეტერბურგის უნივერსიტეტში

St. Petersburg (G.) university + pp. in

14

მიიღო

verb: I. conj. aor. 'he received'

After finishing the Tbilisi *gymnasium* Ivane J̌avaxišvili travelled to St. Petersburg and received (his) higher education in St. Petersburg University.

5.8.1.2. Left-branching. In Georgian, word order within a phrase will often be the reverse of that found in English. We have already seen how strings of genitives in Georgian precede the noun they refer to, while in English strings of prepositional phrases with 'of' *follow* the noun (sec. 3.3.1). Other examples of this reverse order include:

1	2		2	1
ჩვენთვის	საჭირო (არის)	(it is)	necessary	for us
1	2		2	1
უკან	დაბრუნება		(re)turning	back
1	2		2	1
თბილისში	აღზრდილი		raised	in-Tbilisi

5.8.1.3. Embedding. In English we can often replace a relative clause by a participial construction, which will *follow* the noun phrase it refers to; e.g.:

Relative clause: Have you seen Tbilisi University, *which was founded by Ivane J̌avaxišvili in 1918?*

Participial construction: Have you seen Tbilisi University, *founded by Ivane J̌avaxišvili in 1918?*

In Georgian, such participial constructions often *precede* the noun phrase they modify; they are said to be *embedded* within the sentence. Embedded participial constructions are also found in German and Russian. Examples:

> German: Die *noch heute im Gottesdienst verwandte* altgeorgische Bibelübersetzung ist schwer verständlich. 'The Old Georgian Bible translation *still used today in church services* is difficult to understand' (lit.: The still-today-used-in-church-services Old Georgian Bible translation).

> Russian: Наряду с известиями *о прикованном к горным вершинам* Прометее ... ходили легенды и о необычайном многоязычии кавказских гор. 'Alongside reports about Prometheus (who was) chained to the mountain peaks there circulated also legends about the unusual polyglossy of the Caucasus mountains' (lit.: Alongside reports *about-the-fettered-to-the-mountain-peaks* Prometheus).

Georgian has similar participial constructions. The formation of Georgian participles will be discussed in greater detail in Lesson 11 (particularly sec. 11.1). For purposes of reading at this stage, however, it is sufficient to mention that the Georgian perfect participle, corresponding in general to the English past participle, consists of the preverb, the verbal root, usually (though not always) the P/FSF followed by a suffix, most commonly *-il-* (root verbs and verbs with P/FSF *-i*) or *-ul-* (with most other verbs). (For examples, see sec. 11.1.) The present active participle, usually corresponding to English participles in *-ing* also occurs in embedded constructions. Its formation was described in sec. 5.7.2. Note that if the verb from which the participle is formed has a preverb, that preverb will occur in the participle before the formant *m-*.

In the vocabularies to the reading passages in Lessons 5 through 10 participles will be listed. Georgian words translated by English participles (i.e., in *-ed, -en, -ing*, etc., e.g., 'broken, built, prepared, living, writing,' etc.) give warning of potential embedded participial constructions. Examples of embedded constructions are:

1 2 3 4
მტრის მიერ მიტაცებული ტერიტორია
enemy by captured territory

4 3 2 1
territory captured by the enemy

(Note the left-branching within the embedded participial construction.)

1 2
(ამ სისტემით) (დათარიღებული)
By this system is dated

3 4
((ძველ საისტორიო ძეგლებში) აღწერილი))
in old historical monuments described

5
(ბევრი საინტერესო მოვლენა)
many interesting phenomenon

5 4
Many interesting phenomena described

3 2
in old historical monuments are dated

1
by (means of) this system.

Note that the participle აღწერილი modifies the noun მოვლენა and agrees with it in case and that the preceding phrase ძველ საისტორიო ძეგლებში forms part of the embedded construction and is left-branching in comparison with the English order.

5.8.1.4. Verbal nouns. The reader should be reminded that although the Georgian verbal noun is very often translatable by an English infinitive, it differs from the latter in that it cannot take a direct object, taking rather a noun in the genitive case. Compare English with Georgian:

John began *to read the book.*

ივანემ დაიწყო წიგნის კითხვა (lit.: John began the reading of the book.)

5.8.1.5. Word order and case. As in many other languages with relatively free word order, in reading Georgian one cannot rely on word order to determine the subject and objects of the verb. But unlike many other languages with case systems (e.g., Latin, Russian), in Georgian one cannot rely solely on case to determine what is subject, what is direct object, and what is indirect object. This is because in Georgian the subject can be marked by the nominative or ergative case, as well as the dative (see Lessons 10 and 12), and the direct object can be marked by the dative or nominative. To find the subject and objects of a Georgian sentence, it is necessary first to determine the structure of the verb (i.e., what conjugation it belongs to, and, if it is I. conjugation, then what series it is). The structure of the verb should allow determination of the proper cases for subject and objects. Example:

ბავშვი დამალა	Verb is I. conjugation aorist. Therefore the nominative case marks the *direct object.* He hid the child.
ბავშვი დაიმალა	Verb is II. conjugation (aorist). Therefore the nominative marks the *subject.* The child hid.

Reading Passage

თბილისი

თბილისი უძველესი ქალაქია. ის ძალიან დაწინაურდა მეოთხე-მეხუთე საუკუნეებში. მეექვსე საუკუნეში თბილისი ქართლის დედაქალაქად გადაიქცა, მანამდის კი დედაქალაქად მცხეთა ითვლებოდა.

თბილისის ზრდას მისმა მდებარეობამაც შეუწყო ხელი. აქ გადიოდა სამხედრო და სავაჭრო გზები.

ბევრი მტერი ჰყავდა თბილისს, ყველა ცდილობდა მის ხელში ჩაგდებას.

მეშვიდე საუკუნეში არაბებმა[1] დაიპყრეს ქართლი და თბილისიც აიღეს.

მერვე საუკუნეში ქართველები აუჯანყდნენ არაბებს, მაგრამ ვერაფერს გახდნენ. არაბთა სარდალმა მურვან ყრუმ[2] ააოხრა საქართველო და მთელი კავკასია დაიპყრო. 853 წელს ბუღა თურქმა[3] დაწვა თბილისი და 50 ათასი კაცი გაჟლიტა.

თბილისი უცხოელი დამპყრობლების ხელში დიდხანს იტანჯებოდა და მხოლოდ მეთორმეტე საუკუნეში გათავისუფლდა მტრებისაგან.

მეცამეტე საუკუნეში ხვარაზმელებმა[4] აიღეს თბილისი. ერთი წლის შემდეგ ქართველებმა განდევნეს ხვარაზმელები, მაგრამ ისინი 1227 წელს კვლავ წამოვიდნენ თბილისზე. ქართველებმა დაცალეს თავიანთი დედაქალაქი და დაწვეს.

ხვარაზმელების შემდეგ მონღოლებმა[5] აიკლეს თბილისი, მერე სპარსელებმა[6] ააოხრეს — ჯერ შაჰ-აბასისა[7] და შემდეგ აღა-მაჰმად-ხანის[8] მეთაურობით. ქართველი ხალხი მედგრად ებრძოდა სპარსელებს.

---

[1] არაბები — არაბეთის ნახევარკუნძულზე მოსახლე ხალხი.

[2] მურვან ყრუ — არაბების სარდალი, რომელმაც 736 — 8 წლებში გამოილაშქრა საქართველოს წინააღმდეგ და სასტიკად ააოხრა იგი.

[3] ბუღა თურქი — მონღოლების სარდალი, რომელიც 853 წელს თავს დაესხა საქართველოს.

[4] ხვარაზმელები — ხვარაზმი უძველესი სახელმწიფო შუა აზიაში.

[5] მონღოლები — ეხლანდელი მონღოლეთის ტერიტორიაზე მცხოვრები ძველი მომთაბარე ტომები.

[6] სპარსელები — (ირანელები) აზიის ცენტრალურ ნაწილში მცხოვრებნი.

[7] შაჰ-აბასი — ირანის მეფე, საქართველოს დაუძინებელი მტერი, რომელმაც 1616 წელს კახეთი ააოხრა.

[8] აღა-მაჰმად-ხანი — ირანის მეფე, რომელიც 1795 წელს თავს დაესხა საქართველოს.

Vocabulary

უძველესი	very old, oldest (cf. ძველი old)
ის	here: it
ძალიან	here: very much
და=წინაურდება	progress (II. conj. -*d*-)
მეოთხე	fourth (cf. ოთხი four)
ქართლი	Kartli (province in central Georgia)
[გადა=იქცა]	became (3sg. aorist + adv.)
მანამდის	until then
ზრდა	growth
მისი	his; her; its (not referring to the subject)
მდებარეობა	location
[შეუწყობს ხელს]	lend (s.o. [dat.]) a hand, help (s.o. [dat.]) (še=u-ç̣q-ob-s)
სამხედრო	military
სავაჭრო	commercial (cf. ვაჭარი (A) merchant)
ბევრი	much; many (followed by singular)
ყველა	all; everybody (non-truncating)
მტერი	enemy (E)
[ჰყავდა]	he (dat.) had s.o. (nom.) (imperf. 3sg.)
[ცდილობდა]	attempt; try to
[ხელში ჩაგდება]	capture (VN)
მეშვიდე	seventh (cf. შვიდი seven)
არაბი	Arab (person)
და=იპყრობს	conquer (aor. irreg.)
აიღებს	take, capture (a=i-ğ-eb-s)
მერვე	eighth (cf. რვა eight)
[აუჯანყდება]	revolt against s.o. [dat.] (II. conj.)
[ვერაფერს გახდნენ]	they couldn't accomplish anything (aor. 3sg.)
სარდალი	general (A)
ყრუ	deaf

ააოხრებს lay waste; destroy (a=a-oxr-eb-s)
853 წელს = რვაას ორმოცდაცამეტ წელს
მთელი whole, entire
თურქი Turk (person)
და=წვავს burn (aor. irr.)
50 = ორმოცდაათი
ათასი thousand (followed by singular)
კაცი man
გა=ჟლეტს annihilate; slaughter (aorist root: -žliṭ-)
დამპყრობელი conqueror (E) (cf. დაიპყრობს conquer)
ხელი hand; arm
დიდხანს for a long time
და=ტანჯავს cause to suffer
მეთორმეტე twelfth (cf. თორმეტი twelve)
თავისუფალი free (A)
მეცამეტე thirteenth (cf. ცამეტი thirteen)
ხვარაზმი Khorezm (khanate in what is present-day Uzbekistan)
გან=დევნის drive out; exile
1227 = ათას ორას ოცდაშვიდ
კვლავ again
წამოვა come (fut. of მოდის, sec. 4.5.3)
-ზე here: against
და=ცლის evacuate
თავიანთი their own
ა=იკლებს destroy (aor. irr.)
მერე then; later; afterwards
სპარსელი Persian (person)
ჯერ at first
მეთაურობა leadership, command

მედგარი	steadfast, resolute (A)
[ებრძოდა]	he was fighting s.o. (dat.) (imperfect 3sg.)

Vocabulary to footnotes

ნახევარკუნძული	peninsula (cf. ნახევარი half, კუნძული island)
მოსახლე	inhabitant; living; inhabiting
ხალხი	people; folk
რომელიც (erg. რომელმაც)	which, that, who (rel. pronoun) (E)
736-8 = შვიდას ოცდათექვსმეტ-ოცდათვრამეტ	
გამო=ილაშქრებ	fight
წინააღმდეგ	against (pp.)
სასტიკი	cruel; merciless
მონღოლი	Mongol (person)
[დაესხა თავს]	he overran s.o. (dat.) (aor. 3sg.)
სახელმწიფო	[national] state
შუა	here: middle; central (adj.)
აზია	Asia
ეხლანდელი	present-day (cf. ეხლა, ახლა now) (E)
ტერიტორია	territory
მცხოვრები	inhabitant; living; inhabiting
მომთაბარე	nomad; nomadic
ტომი	tribe
ირანი	Iran
ცენტრალური	central
მეფე	king
დაუძინებელი	unsleeping; sleepless (E)
1616 = ათას ექვსას თექვსმეტ	
კახეთი	Kakhetia (province in Eastern Georgia)

1795 = ათას
შვიდას
ოთხმოცდათხუთმეტ

"Mother of Kartli"
Statue overlooking Tbilisi

ქართლის დედა

LESSON 6

6.1. Optative of regular verbs. The optative of regular verbs is formed from the same stem as the aorist. It takes the same cases as the corresponding aorist. The screeve endings are:

Regular I. conjugation verbs and regular II. conjugation verbs in *i-*:

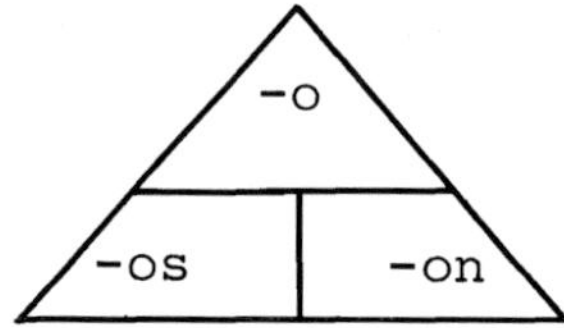

Regular II. conjugation verbs in *-d-*:[1]

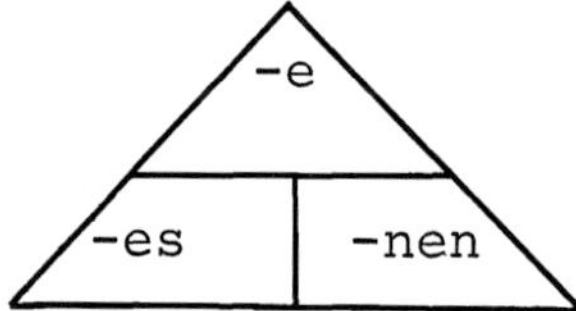

Examples:[2]

I. conjugation

და(ვ)წერო(თ), დაწეროს, დაწერონ	write
გა(ვ)აკეთო(თ), გააკეთოს, გააკეთონ	make
გა(ვ)აღო(თ), გააღოს, გააღონ	open

II. conjugation in *i-*:

და(ვ)იბადო(თ), დაიბადოს, დაიბადონ	be born
და(ვ)იხატო(თ), დაიხატოს, დაიხატონ	be painted

II. conjugation in *-d-*:

გა(ვ)წითლდე(თ), გაწითლდეს, გაწითლდნენ	blush
გა(ვ)ლამაზდე(თ), გალამაზდეს, გალამაზდნენ	become beautiful

The optative forms of the verbs 'be' and 'go' are:

ყოფნა be (ვ)იყო(თ), იყოს, იყონ

სვლა go 1. Pvb+ვიდე(თ), 2. Pvb+სვიდე(თ)
3sg. Pvb.+ვიდეს 3pl. Pvb.+ვიდნენ

(e.g. 1. წავიდე(თ), 2. წასვიდე(თ), 3sg. წავიდეს, 3pl.

წავიდნენ 'go'[3]

Verbs in the optative have the subject and objects in the same cases as in the aorist (see sec. 5.0).

6.2. Function of the optative. The optative, like the conjunctive, is modal. It is used after present- or future-tense-form verbs indicating desire, intention, necessity, possibility, and in such uses often corresponds to the English infinitive (and to the French subjunctive or the Russian conditional).[4] Examples of the Georgian optative corresponding to such English infinitives are:

ვაპირებ ეს წიგნი ხვალ ვიკითხო.

I intend *to read* this book tomorrow.

მზექალა უბრძანებს შალვას, კარი გააღოს.

Mzekala will order Šalva *to open* the door (lit.: Mzekala will order to Šalva that he open the door).

ეგნატე ბრძანებს წერილები დაიწეროს.

Egnaṭe will order the letters *to be written*.

The Georgian optative also corresponds to English subordinate clauses introduced by *that* and indicating the same modal notions as mentioned above; in both English and Georgian the subordinating conjunction (რომ in Georgian) can be omitted:

შესაძლებელია (რომ) ნიკო გვიან მოვიდეს.

It is probable (that) Nick might come late.

საჭიროა (რომ) ეს წიგნი წავიკითხოთ.

It is necessary that we read this book.[5]

დროა (რომ) შინ წავიდეთ.

It is time (that) we went home.

შეუძლებელია (რომ) პიესის კითხვა დროზე დაამთავრონ.

It is impossible (that) they'll finish the reading of the play in time.

The optative is regularly used after the following forms:

უნდა have to, must, should (not conjugated; cf.

Russian должен, надо)

შეიძლება[6] be possible, can, may (has only 3sg. forms in the present, imperfect, შეიძლებოდა and conjunctive, შეიძლებოდეს; cf. Russian можно.)

იქნებ(ა)[7] perhaps

Examples:

ჩემი ახალი კოსტიუმი უნდა ნახოთ.

You all have to see my new suit.

შეიძლება შემოვიდე?

May I come in?

ეს ორ დღეში შეიძლება გაკეთდეს.

This can be done in two days.

იქნებ(ა) ვიქტორი ხვალ მოვიდეს.

Perhaps Victor will come tomorrow.

The optative with the conjunction რომ can be used to form a purpose clause, translatable by English 'in order to':

თბილისში მივდივარ, რომ ქართული ენა ვისწავლო.

I am going to Tbilisi in order to study Georgian.

(რომ can introduce most other subordinate clauses containing an optative, but it is generally omitted.)

The optative is used in questions where it corresponds to English 'to be to', 'to be supposed to'; e.g., ხვალ აქ მოვიდე? Am I to come here tomorrow?

The optative can often be replaced by the verbal noun. In such uses the Georgian verbal noun corresponds to the use of infinitive in English. Examples:

ვაპირებ ამ წიგნის კითხვას.

I intend to read this book (lit., the reading of this book).

საჭიროა ამ წიგნის წაკითხვა.

It is necessary to read this book (lit.: the reading of this book is necessary).

6.3. Imperative. The Georgian positive imperative (2d person) is identical in form to the second person aorist; e.g. დაწერე(თ) write!; დაბრუნდი(თ) return!; იყავი(თ) be!; ააშენე(თ) build!, etc. The imperative of სვლა is irregular: მოდი(თ), წადი(თ), გადი(თ) etc. Any direct objects will be in the nominative (i.e., the syntax is as for the aorist). The "imperative" of other persons is formed with the optative. Most common is the use of the 1pl. optative with the meaning of 'let's'; e.g., წავიდეთ! let's go!; ეს წიგნები წავიკითხოთ! let's read these books!; განვიხილოთ! let's discuss it. Examples of the third person "imperative" use of the optative are: ივანემ დაამთავროს! let John finish it!; გაკვეთილი გაიმეორონ! let them repeat the lesson!, etc.

Negative imperatives are generally formed with the negative particle ნუ 'don't' plus the present or future tense. ნუ can occur with all persons (most commonly, of course, with the second person). Examples are ნუ წარმოთქვამ(თ) don't pronounce it!; ნუ კითხულობ(თ) don't read it!; ნუ (და)წერ(თ) don't write it!; ნუ განვიხილავთ let's not discuss it!; ნუ ნახავს he is not to see it!; ნუ ხარ(თ) don't be!; ნუ მიდიხარ(თ) don't go!; etc. A less polite form of the negative imperative is formed with არ and the optative: არ იკითხო don't read it.

The use of cases with the imperative is the same as for the corresponding screeve, i.e., aorist, present or future, optative.

6.4. Negation. Georgian has three negating particles, ნუ, ვერ, and არ. The use of ნუ 'don't' has been explained above, sec. 6.3. ვერ is the equivalent of English *can't* and is followed by a personal form of the verb: ვერ ვწერ I can't write; ვერ დავწერ I won't be able to write; ვერ გადათარგმნე you couldn't translate; ვერ დაბრუნდებიან they won't be able to return, etc. In all other instances არ is used.[8]

Corresponding to არა 'no' is the form ვერა 'no', (I, you, etc. can't): სანდრო ხვალ თეატრში წავა? ვერა, ვერ წავა. თბილისში არ იქნება. Will Sandro go to the theater tomorrow? No, he won't be able to go. He won't be in Tbilisi.

6.4.1. With the addition of the affix *-ğa(r)-* we get აღარ 'no longer', 'no more'; ვეღარ 'can't any longer', 'can't any more'; and ნუღარ 'don't ... any longer', 'don't ... any more'. Examples:

პავლე გერმანულ ენას აღარ სწავლობს.

Paul no longer studies German.

დავითი ქართულ სიტყვებს უაქცენტოდ ვეღარ წარმოთქვამს.

David no longer can pronounce the Georgian words without an accent.

ნუღარ იმეორებ ამ სიტყვებს!

Don't repeat these words any more!

6.4.2. With the same three negators the following negative pronouns and adverbs are formed:

არავინ	ვერავინ	ნურავინ	no one (declined as ვინ, Lesson 2, note 5)
არაფერი (E)	ვერაფერი (E)	ნურაფერი (E)	nothing
არსად	ვერსად	ნურსად	nowhere
არასოდეს	ვერასოდეს	ნურასოდეს	never

"Double negatives" can occur but this is not obligatory unless a form containing a negator is not immediately before the verb. Examples:

არავინ არაფერს (არ) აკეთებდა.	Nobody was doing anything.
ნურაფერს (ნუ) ჭამ!	Don't eat anything.
ნუ გაგზავნით ნურსად!	Don't send it anywhere.
შენი წიგნი ვერსად (ვერ) ვნახე.	I couldn't see your book anywhere.

The infix *-ǧa(r)-* (sec. 6.4.1 above) can be added to these forms; e.g., აღარაფერი nothing ... any more; ნუღარსად don't ... anywhere any more; etc.

6.5. Vocative form. The vocative form of *proper names* is identical to the bare stem without any endings; e.g., დავით! from დავითი; მოთა! from მოთა; ილიკო! from ილიკო; გიორგი! from გიორგი (the *i* is not the nominative ending but part of the stem; cf. dat. გიორგის, erg. გიორგიმ).

Consonantal stem common nouns and adjectives form the vocative with the ending *-o*, e.g., ქართველი 'Georgian' voc. ქართველო; ბატონი 'Mr.' voc. ბატონო; მკი-

რფასი ამხანაგი 'dear comrade' voc. ძვირფასო ამხა-
ნაგო.

Polysyllabic vocalic stems form the vocative in common nouns with either the ending *-v* or with no ending whatsoever, e.g., the bare stem. Examples: საქართველო 'Georgia' voc. საქართველოვ or საქართველო; კოლმეურნე 'kolkhoznik' (collective farmer) voc. კოლმეურნევ or კოლმეურნე; მამა 'father' voc. მამა or მამავ.

Monosyllabic vocalic stems form the vocative in common nouns with either the ending *-o* or with the ending *-v*. Examples: და 'sister' voc. დაო or დავ; ძე 'son' voc. ძეო or ძევ. (It should be noted that in the plural all common nouns take the vocative ending *-o*, since the plural declension is always a consonantal stem declension.)

Vocalic stem adjectives do not take any endings when modifying a noun. When used independently they follow the same rules as for nouns.

In the stylistically marked plural (sec. 5.6) the vocative form has the ending *-no*: ქართველნო, ბატონნო, ამხანაგნო, კოლმეურნენო, მამანო, დანო, ძენო.

6.6 Numerals and other quantifiers. In Georgian numerals and other quantifiers are always followed by the *singular* form of the noun and, in verb agreement, by singular forms of the verb. Such forms include:

ყველა all; ბევრი, მრავალი much, many; ზოგი, ზოგიერთი, რამდენიმე some, several; ცოტა few, a few; რამდენი how much?, how many?; and all cardinal numbers.

In this lesson we shall learn the numerals from one to twenty-nine. Numerals are declined just like any other adjectives.

1. ერთი	11. თერთმეტი	21. ოცდაერთი
2. ორი	12. თორმეტი	22. ოცდაორი
3. სამი	13. ცამეტი	23. ოცდასამი
4. ოთხი	14. თოთხმეტი	24. ოცდაოთხი
5. ხუთი	15. თხუთმეტი	25. ოცდახუთი
6. ექვსი	16. თექვსმეტი	26. ოცდაექვსი
7. შვიდი	17. ჩვიდმეტი	27. ოცდაშვიდი
8. რვა	18. თვრამეტი	28. ოცდარვა
9. ცხრა	19. ცხრამეტი	29. ოცდაცხრა
10. ათი	20. ოცი	

The initial *t-* in the teens is from ათი 10; მეტი means 'more'.

t-cam-meṭ-i is simplified in spelling to *cameṭi* '13'.

t-švid-meṭ-i is simplified in spelling to *čvid-meṭi* '17'.

For თვრამეტი '18' from *t-rva-meṭ-i*, see sec. 1.11.2.

t-cxra-meṭ-i is simplified in spelling to *cxra-meṭi* '19'.

Examples:

ჩემი სამი ძმა ქართულ ენას სწავლობს.

My three brothers are studying Georgian.

ზაფხულში ბევრი რუსი სტუმრად ჩამოდის საქართველოში.

Many Russians visit [come as guest] Georgia in the summer.

რამდენი ინგლისური რომანი უნდა წაიკითხო?

How many English novels do you have to read?

6.6.1. Ordinals are formed with the circumfix *me*-.. ...-*e* which is added to the truncated stem of the cardinal for 2 to 20 and to the unit in numerals from 21 to 29. First is პირველი. Examples:

2d მეორე; 8th მერვე; 10th მეათე; 15th მეთხუთმეტე; 20th მეოცე; 21st ოცდაპირველი or ოცდამეერთე; 25th ოცდამეხუთე; 29th ოცდამეცხრე.

6.7 Wordbuilding: abstract suffixes.

6.7.1 Derivation of (abstract) nouns from adjectives.

Circumfix *si*-.....-*e*. Examples:

ხშირი	frequent	სიხშირე	frequency
მაღალი	high, tall (A)	სიმაღლე	height
ლამაზი	beautiful	სილამაზე	beauty
ახალი	new (A)	სიახლე	newness
ბრძენი	wise (E)	სიბრძნე	wisdom
ნათელი	light, clear (E)	სინათლე	light
დიდი	big, large	სიდიდე	bigness, size

Suffix *-ob-a* / *-eb-a*. Examples:

საშუალო	mediocre	საშუალოობა	mediocrity
რეალური	real	რეალობა	reality
თავაზიანი	courteous	თავაზიანობა	courtesy
ინერტული	inert	ინერტულობა	inertia
სერიოზული	serious	სერიოზულობა	seriousness
თავისუფალი	free (A)	თავისუფლება	freedom
ბედნიერი	happy	ბედნიერება	happiness
დამოუკიდებელი	independent (E)	დამოუკიდებლობა	independence

6.7.2. Derivation of abstract nouns from nouns (denoting human agents). Suffix *-ob-a* / *-eb-a*. Examples:

ოსტატი	artisan, craftsman	ოსტატობა	skill, craftsmanship
ძმა	brother	ძმობა	fraternity
მეგობარი	friend (A)	მეგობრობა	friendship
ბავშვი	child	ბავშვობა	childhood
მეურნე	farmer	მეურნეობა	farm, farming
ქურდი	thief	ქურდობა	theft
მეცნიერი	scientist	მეცნიერება	science
მწერალი	writer (A)	მწერლობა	literature

6.7.3. Derivation of abstract nouns from verbs. The verbal noun (or masdar) with the suffix *-a* is the deverbal abstract noun; for rules of formation see sec. 2.5. Examples:

შეადარებს	compare	შედარება	comparison
წარმოადგენს	perform	წარმოდგენა	performance
ბრძანებს	command	ბრძანება	command
დააბრუნებს	return	დაბრუნება	return

LESSON 6: Notes

1. Note that these are the same endings as those of the conjunctive screeves of the present and future series.

2. Henceforth examples will be abbreviated so that the 1st and 2d persons, singular and plural, will be indicated by one form, e.g., და(ვ)წერო(თ), which is to be interpreted as:

1sg. დავწერო	1pl. დავწეროთ
2sg. დაწერო	2pl. დაწეროთ

The forms of the 3sg. and 3pl. are given separately.

3. As is true in general of irregular verbs (see Lesson 9), the optative is based on the 3sg. of the aorist, იყო, and *Pvb* + ვიდა respectively. The optative of 'be' follows the pattern of a II. conjugation verb in *i*- and that of 'go', 'come' resembles a II. conjugation verb in -*d*-. Note that the latter shares two features of other screeves of this verb: (1) in the 1st person Pvb+*v-vid-e(-t)* is simplified to Pvb+*vid-e(-t)* and (2) the 2d person has the subject person marker *x*-.

4. If the verb in the principal clause is a past tense, the optative is generally not used but rather is replaced by the pluperfect (see Lesson 10).

5. Note that many of these constructions can be paraphrased with 'for' plus infinitive: It is necessary for us to read this book. It is time for us to go home.

6. შეიძლება does not denote physical ability (for which the verb შემიძლია is used; see sec. 11.1.2.3). It corresponds to Russian можно, возможно and expresses possibility or permission. In the spoken language it is usually pronounced შეილება.

7. Note that the form იქნება is homophonous with the 3sg. future of ყოფნა be: იქნება he will be.

8. A less common synonym of არ is როდი which is somewhat less categorical in meaning. Note, too, that არ and ვერ can be replaced by არა and ვერა in some circumstances, particularly before monosyllabic verbal forms.

9. The nouns ბატონი 'Mr.' and ქალბატონი 'Ms.', 'Miss',

'Mrs.' followed by the first (given) name is the usual *formal* way of addressing people in Georgian, corresponding to the English *Mr.*, *Ms.* plus last name or to the Russian use of first name and patronymic. So, a Georgian named ვიტა დოლიძე would be addressed formally as ბატონო ვიტა, corresponding to the formal English *Mr. Dolidze*. Remember, too, that the second person *plural* is used to address one person formally.

ბატონი and ქალბატონი used with proper names behave somewhat differently from other titles (Lesson 3, note 2). They behave like regular adjectives in the nominative, ergative, and vocative: ბატონი დავითი, ბატონმა დავითმა, ბატონო დავით! In the remaining cases they generally have no ending: ბატონ დავითს, დავითის, etc.

LESSON 6: Exercises

1. განვიხილოთ საქართველოს ისტორია! —ასეთი განხილვისათვის საჭიროა წავიკითხოთ ივანე ჯავახიშვილის ისტორია.
2. მეექვსე საუკუნეში ჩვენს ერამდე, პირველი ორი ქართული სახელმწიფო ჩამოყალიბდა: კოლხეთი — დასავლეთ საქართველოში და იბერია აღმოსავლეთში. ესენი ბერძნული სახელებია და ქართულ ენაზე შეიძლება ასე გადაითარგმნოს: ეგრისი და ქართლი.
3. გაიმეორე ეს სახელები! —ეგრისი და ქართლი. კოლხეთის შესახებ გუშინ ვკითხულობდი. ეს ის ადგილი უნდა იყოს, სადაც ბერძენი გმირი იასონი წავიდა.
4. მცხეთაში უნდა დავბრუნდე, რომ მეთერთმეტე საუკუნის ცნობილი ეკლესია, სვეტიცხოველი, კვლავ ვნახო.
5. ნუ დაივიწყებთ, რომ ყველა ქართული ტერიტორია გაერთიანდა მეთორმეტე საუკუნის ოცდამეორე წელს, როდესაც მეფე იყო დავით აღმაშენებელი. საქართველოს გაერთიანება ძალიან მნიშვნელოვანი თარიღია ამიერკავკასიის ისტორიაში.
6. თბილისში შეიძლება ნახო მეათე, მეთერთმეტე და მეთორმეტე საუკუნეების ლამაზი ქართული ხატები.
7. შეიძლება ნახო საქართველოს უდიდესი მმართველის, თამარ მეფის პორტრეტებიც. თამარი გიორგი მესამის ქალიშვილი იყო.
8. საქართველოს ისტორიის გაგებისათვის ძველი ქართული წყაროები და ხელნაწერები უნდა წაიკითხოთ. —სამწუხაროდ, ძველ ქართულ ანბანს, ხუცურს, ვერ ვკითხულობ; მხოლოდ ახალს, მხედრულს, ვკითხულობ.
9. სტუდენტებო, ქართველურ ენათა სახელები გადაწერეთ! —აქ კალამი არ არის. ლადომ სახელები გადაწეროს! კალამი ლადოსთან არის ახლოს. —არ დავივიწყოთ ეს ენები: სვანური, მეგრული, ლაზური ანუ ჭანური და, რასაკვირველია, ქართული.

10. ქალბატონო მარიამ, რამდენი საბჭოთა რესპუბლიკაა? —ბატონო გივი, თხუთმეტი. საქართველოს საბჭოთა სოციალისტურ რესპუბლიკაში ორი ავტონომიური საბჭოთა სოციალისტური რესპუბლიკაა (ასსრ): აფხაზეთის ასსრ და აჭარის ასსრ. ერთი ავტონომიური ოლქია: სამხრეთ ოსეთის ავტონომიური ოლქი.
11. დავით, ბიბლიის ძველ ქართულ თარგმანებს კითხულობ? —ვერა, ბატონო გივი, ვერ ვკითხულობ. სამწუხაროდ, ჩვენს კლასში ვერავინ (ვერ) კითხულობს. —იქნებ ელისაბედმა წაიკითხოს ძველი ქართული ტექსტები. —არა, ბატონო გივი, ვერ ვკითხულობ.
12. სტუდენტებო, მეშვიდე გაკვეთილს ნუ მოამზადებთ; მეექვსე მოამზადეთ! —მეექვსე გაკვეთილიც მოვამზადოთ და მეშვიდეც!
13. საჭიროა ყველა კავკასიური ენა შეისწავლო, რომ შეადარო. ბევრი ლინგვისტი ამტკიცებს, რომ შეუძლებელია გენეტიკური ურთიერთობა ქართველურ ენებსა და ჩრდილო კავკასიის ენებს შორის. სხვა ლინგვისტები კი ამტკიცებენ, რომ უნდა იყოს ასეთი ურთიერთობა ამ ენებს შორის. მაგრამ თითქმის ყველა ლინგვისტის მიხედვით, ბასკურ ენასა და ქართულს შორის გენეტიკური ურთიერთობის დამამტკიცებელ საბუთს ვერავინ (ვერ) წარმოადგენს.
14. ქალბატონო ლილი, ნურაფერს ნუ წერთ ახლა. წერილი დაწერეთ ქალბატონ ელისაბედის მოსვლის შემდეგ.
15. ბატონო თამაზ, აღწერეთ საქართველო თამარის მეფობის დროს. —სამწუხაროდ, ვერ აღვწერ, ვინაიდან თამარი მეფედ იყო მეთორმეტე საუკუნეში, გუშინ კი ვკითხულობდი საქართველოს შესახებ გიორგი მეორის მეფობის დროს. არ უნდა დაივიწყოთ, რომ ეს „დიდი თურქობის" პერიოდი იყო, როცა თურქებმა საქართველო ააოხრეს.
16. გიორგი მეორის ვაჟიშვილი იყო დავით მეორე, ე.ი. (ესე იგი) დავით აღმაშენებელი, თამარ მეფის პაპის

მამა.

17. ქალბატონო დიანა, რამდენი ქართველური ენაა? —ზოგის მიხედვით, ოთხია: ქართული, სვანური, ლაზური (ანუ ჭანური) და მეგრული. ზოგი ლინგვისტი კი ამტკიცებს, რომ მხოლოდ სამი ენაა: ქართული, სვანური და ზანური. ამ ლინგვისტების მიხედვით, ზანური ერთი ენაა; ზანურის ორი მთავარი კილო მეგრული და ლაზურია.
18. საქართველო მეფის რუსეთთან რომელ საუკუნეში გაერთიანდა? ქალბატონო ლილი, ეს იყო მეცხრამეტე საუკუნის პირველ წელს.
19. აფხაზები ქართველური ერი არაა. ქართველებსავით მრავალი აფხაზი ქრისტიანი არის, მაგრამ უმეტესი მუსლიმანები არიან. აჭარლები ქართულ ენაზე მოლაპარაკენი არიან, მაგრამ მუსლიმანები არიან.
20. დედა, მოდი ნახე ქართული ხალხური ხელოვნების ეს საინტერესო გამოფენა!
21. საბჭოთა კავშირიდან ნიუ-იორკში აგვისტოში დავბრუნდები. ჩემი დაბრუნების შემდეგ ვაპირებ რამდენიმე სტატია დავწერო საბჭოთა საქართველოს ცხოვრებაზე.
22. სპარსული ენა უნდა შევისწავლო, ვინაიდან ბევრი ქართული სიტყვა სპარსულიდან მოდის. ქართველები სიტყვებს ბევრი უცხო ენიდან სესხულობენ. სიტყვები „ვარდი", „ამხანაგი", „თამაში", „ბაღი" ქართველებმა საშუალო სპარსულიდან ისესხეს.
23. ამ ცნობების წყარო უნდა აღმოვაჩინოთ.
24. ძვირფასო მეგობრებო, ეს წიგნები დავაბრუნოთ ბიბლიოთეკაში! ისინი რამდენიმე კვირის წინათ მივიღეთ ბიბლიოთეკიდან. ახლა მეცხრამეტე საუკუნის ქართველი მწერლების რამდენიმე წიგნი უნდა წავიკითხოთ.
25. ამხანაგებო, სტუდენტები ლექციაზე მოვიდნენ, რომ

მეოცე საუკუნის ქართული ხელოვნების განხილვა მოისმინონ.

26. საენათმეცნიერო საზოგადოების სხდომაზე მოხსენება უნდა წარმოვადგინო. ამ მოხსენებაში წარმოვადგენ ბევრ ფაქტს ქართული კილოების შესახებ. აღმოსავლური და დასავლური კილოები უნდა შევადარო.

27. შინ ნუ დაბრუნდები ექვს საათამდე! შინ დაბრუნდი რვა საათის შემდეგ!

28. რამდენი წლის წინათ დაიბადე? —ოცდარვა წლის წინათ დავიბადე. მალე ოცდაცხრა წლისა ვიქნები.

29. რამდენია ქართულ ენაზე მოლაპარაკე? —თითქმის ოთხი მილიონი.

30. შესაძლებელია, რომ ხვალ თამაზი ბიბლიოთეკაში დაბრუნდეს, რომ დაამთავროს სტატია ქართული ფოლკლორის შესახებ.

31. ფრანგულ ენას აღარ ვსწავლობ. ფრანგულს ვეღარ ვსწავლობ, ვინაიდან ჩემი ფრანგული ენის მასწავლებელი ჩიკაგოში აღარ არის.

32. ბატონო გივი, პროფესორმა ბრძანა, რომ სტუდენტები უნივერსიტეტში ხვალ დილით ადრე მოვიდნენ? ვინაიდან ადრე უნდა ვიყოთ უნივერსიტეტში, საშინაო დავალება ამ საღამოს უნდა გავაკეთო.

33. მცხეთა საქართველოს დედაქალაქი აღარაა. როცა იქნები მცხეთაში, შედი სვეტიცხოვლის ეკლესიაში. ქართული საეკლესიო არქიტექტურის მნიშვნელოვანი ნიმუშია.

34. ჩვენს უნივერსიტეტში სწავლა ჩვეულებრივ დილის ცხრა საათზე იწყება და საღამოს ხუთ საათზე მთავრდება.

35. ჩვენი უნივერსიტეტის თეატრი წარმოადგენს აკაკი წერეთლის ერთ პიესათაგანს.* მეგობრებო, მოდით წარმოდგენაზე ამ საღამოს ექვს საათზე.

36. შემოდით, ბატონო იოსებ! მოვისმინოთ ათი საათის რადიოპროგრამა, ოპერა „დაისი". —ეს ოპერა ვინ დაწერა? ქართველმა კომპოზიტორმა ზაქარია ფალიაშვილმა.

*See sec. 8.6.1.

Vocabulary

აგვისტო	August
ადგილი	place
ავტონომიური	autonomous
ამხანაგი	comrade
ანუ	or (in other words)
არქიტექტურა	architecture
ასე	so
ასეთი	such (a)
აფხაზი	an Abkhaz
აღმაშენებელი	builder; restorer (E) (cf. ააშენებს build)
აჭარელი	an Adjar (E)
ახლოს	near (adverb), (cf. ახლო near)
ბასკი	a Basque
ბატონი	Mr.
ბაღი	garden
ბევრი	much; many
ბიბლიოთეკა	library
გაერთიანება	unification
გამოფენა	exhibit(ion)
გენეტიკა	genetics
გმირი	hero
დაახლოებით	approximately (adverb)
დილა	morning
ერა	era (ჩვენს ერამდე B.C.)
ესე იგი (ე.ი.)	i.e.
ვაჟიშვილი	son
ვარდი	rose
ზანური	Zan
ზოგი	some
თამაში	game
თარიღი	date
თითქმის	almost
თურქი	a Turk
იქნებ(ა)	perhaps(+opt.)
კვირა	week; Sunday
კვლავ	again
კილო	dialect
კომპოზიტორი	composer
ლაზი	a Laz
ლინგვისტი	linguist
მაგალითი	example
მეგრელი	Mingrelian
მეფე: მეფის	tsarist (gen. used as adjective)
მეფობა	reign
მილიონი	million
მიხედვით	according to (pp.)
მმართველი	ruler; administrator
მოლაპარაკე	speaker
მოხსენება	report
მუსლიმანი	a Muslim
ნიმუში	model; specimen
ოლქი	region
პაპა	grandfather

პორტრეტი	portrait
რამდენი	how many? how much?
რამდენიმე	several
რასაკვირველია	of course
რომ	that (conjunct.)
საათი	hour; watch; clock; o'clock
საბუთი	document; proof
დამამტკიცებელი საბუთი	evidence
სადაც	where (rel.) pron.)
საჭიროა	it is necessary (+opt.)
სახელმწიფო	state (national)
სვანი	a Svan
სოციალისტი	a socialist
სპარს(ელ)ი	a Persian
ტერიტორია	territory
უდიდესი	greatest (cf. დიდი)
უმეტესი	most (greatest number)
უნდა	must (+opt.) (sec. 6.2)
ურთიერთობა	relationship
ფაქტი	fact
ფოლკლორი	folklore
ქალბატონი	Ms.; Mrs.; Miss
ქალიშვილი	daughter
ქრისტიანი	a Christian
ყველა	all; everybody (nontruncating)
შეერთება	union
შეიძლება	be permitted, be possible, may (+opt.)
შესაძლებელია	it is probable (+opt.)
შეუძლებელია	it is impossible (+opt.)
ჩვეულებრივი	usual, ordinary (adverb: ჩვეულებრივ)
ჩრდილო	north(ern)
ცნობები	information (pl.)
ძვირფასი	dear
წარმოდგენა	performance; representation (see -dgen-)
წინათ	ago (pp.)
წყარო	source; spring (water)
ჭანი	a Chan (Laz)
ხატი	icon
ხელოვნება	art

Verbs.

დააბრუნებს	da=a-*brun*-eb-s	return sthg. (II. conj. დაბრუნდება return, go back)
ბრძანებს	*brjan*-eb-s	order, command (pres. = fut.)
შეადარებს	še=a-*dar*-eb-s	compare sthg. (d.o.) to sthg. (id.o.)
წარმოადგენს	ç̣armo+a-*dgen*-s	perform; present (aor. E → I)[1]
გააერთიანებს	ga=a-*ertian*-eb-s	unite; join
დაივიწყებს	da=i-*viç̣q*-eb-s	forget
მოამზადებს	mo=a-*mzad*-eb-s	prepare (= დაამზადებს)
დაამტკიცებს	da=a-*mṭḳic*-eb-s	maintain; prove
აოხრებს	a=a-*oxr*-eb-s	overrun; ravage; devastate
დააპირებს	da=a-*p̣ir*-eb-s	intend (to)
ისესხებს:	i-*sesx*-eb-s;	borrow
სესხულობს	pres. sesxulob-s	
შეისწავლის	še+i-*sç̣avl*-i-s	learn
ჩამოაყალიბებს	čamo=a-*qalib*-eb-s	form

Proper nouns.

აჭარა	Adjaria
ეგრისი	Colchis (West Georgia)
იბერია	Iberia (East Georgia)
კავკასია	the Caucasus (region of USSR; the Caucasus mountain chain itself is called კავკასიონი in Georgian)
კოლხეთი	Colchis
ნიუ-იორკი	New York
სამხრეთ ოსეთი	South Ossetia
სვეტიცხოველი	XI. cent. church in Mcxeta (lit.: 'Living column' from სვეტი column, ცხოველი living) (E)

ქართლი	Kartli		
იასონი	Jason	ზაქარია ფალიაშვილი	composer, 1871-1933
დიანა	Diana (f.)	იოსები	Joseph (m.)
თამაზი	(m.)	ლილი-[2]	Lily (f.)

Notes to the vocabulary.

1. The notation (aor. E → I) will indicate root verbs which alternate the vowel *e* in the present series and the vowel *i* in the aorist series (see sec. 5.3.1). Such I. conjugation verbs will also have *i* in the II. conjugation forms (see sec. 3.1.4.1).

2. A hyphen after a proper name ending in *i* indicates that the *i* is a part of the stem and not the nominative case ending. So, the dative of ლილი will be ლილის and the ergative ლილიმ.

Sveṭicxoveli
(Mcxeta)

სვეტიცხოველი

Key to the Exercises

1. Let's discuss Georgia's history! For such a discussion it is necessary that we read Ivane J̌avaxišvili's history.
2. In the sixth century B.C. [up to our era] the first two Georgian states were formed: Colchis in Western Georgia and Iberia in Eastern. These are Greek names and they can be so translated into Georgian: Egrisi and Kartli.
3. Repeat these names! Egrisi and Kartli. I was reading about Colchis yesterday. This must be that place where the Greek hero Jason went.
4. I must return to Mcxeta in order to again see the famous church of the eleventh century, Sveṭicxoveli [living pillar].
5. Don't forget (pl.) that all the Georgian territories were united in the twenty-second year of the twelfth century, when the king was David the Builder. The unification of Georgia is a very important date in Transcaucasia's history.
6. In Tbilisi you can see beautiful Georgian icons of the tenth, eleventh, and twelfth centuries.
7. You can also see portraits of Georgia's greatest ruler, Queen Tamara [Tamara King]. Tamara was the daughter of George III.
8. For an understanding of Georgia's history you all must read the old Georgian sources and manuscripts. Unfortunately I cannot read the old Georgian alphabet, the *xucuri*; I only read the new one, the *mxedruli*.
9. Students, copy the names of the Kartvelian languages! There is no pen here. Let Lado copy the names. There is a pen near to Lado (+ -*tan*). Let's not forget these languages: Svan, Mingrelian, Laz or Ç̣an, and, of course, Georgian.
10. Ms. Mary, how many Soviet Republics are there? Mr. Givi, fifteen. In the Georgian Soviet Socialist Republic there are two Autonomous Soviet Socialist Republics (ASSR): the Abkhaz ASSR and the Adjar ASSR. There is also one autonomous region, the South Ossetian Autonomous Region.
11. David, do you read the old Georgian Bible translations? No, Mr. Givi, I cannot read them. Unfortunately no one can read them in our class. Perhaps Elizabeth reads old Georgian texts. No, Mr. Givi, I cannot read them.
12. Students, don't prepare the seventh lesson; prepare the sixth! Let's prepare both the sixth lesson and the seventh also!
13. It is necessary that you learn all the Caucasian

languages in order to compare them [that you (may) compare them]. Many linguists maintain that a genetic relationship between the Kartvelian languages and the languages of the North Caucasus is impossible. Other linguists however maintain that there must be such a relationship between these languages. But according to almost all linguists no one can present evidence of a genetic relationship between the Basque language and Georgian.

14. Ms. Lily, don't write anything now. Write the letter after Ms. Elizabeth comes (use VN).
15. Mr. Tamaz, describe Georgia during Tamara's reign! Unfortunately, I cannot describe it because Tamar was queen (adv.) in the twelfth century, and yesterday I was reading about Georgia during the reign of George II (1072-1089). You must not forget that this was the period of the *Didi Turkoba* [Great Turkish Conquests], when the Turks overran Georgia.
16. George II's son was David II, i.e., David the Builder, Tamara King's great-grandfather [grandfather's father].
17. Ms. Diana, how many Kartvelian languages are there? According to some, there are four: Georgian, Svan, Laz (or Ç̌an), and Mingrelian. Some linguists, however, maintain that there are only three languages: Georgian, Svan, and Zan. Zan, according to these linguists, is one language; Zan's two main dialects are Mingrelian and Laz (or Ç̌an).
18. In which century was Georgia united with (*-tan*) Tsarist [King's] Russia? Ms. Lily, this union was in the first year (dat.) of the nineteenth century (1801).
19. The Abkhaz are not a Kartvelian people. Like the Georgians, many Abkhazians are Christians, but most are Muslims. The Adjarians are speakers of [on] the Georgian language, but they are Muslims.
20. Mother, come [and] see this interesting exhibit of Georgian folk art!
21. I shall return to New York from the Soviet Union in August. After my return I intend to write several articles on life in Soviet Georgia [Soviet Georgia's life].
22. I must learn Persian, because many Georgian words come from Persian. Georgians borrow words from many foreign languages. The Georgians borrowed the words *vardi* 'rose', *amxanagi* 'comrade', *tamaši* 'game', *baği* 'garden' from Middle Persian.
23. We must discover the source of this information.

24. Dear friends, let us return these books to the library! Several weeks ago we got those from the library. Now we must read several books of nineteenth century Georgian writers.
25. Comrades, let the students come to the lecture in order that they may listen to the discussion of twentieth century Georgian art!
26. I have to present a report at the session of the linguistic society. In this report I shall present many facts about Georgian dialects. I must compare the eastern and western dialects.
27. Don't return home until six o'clock! Return home after eight o'clock!
28. How many years ago were you born? I was born twenty-eight years ago. Soon I shall be twenty-nine years old [of 29 year (gen.)].
29. How many speakers of [on] the Georgian language are there? Almost four million.
30. It is probable that Tamaz may return to the library tomorrow in order to finish the article about Georgian folklore.
31. I am not studying French any more. I can no longer study French because my French teacher is no longer in Chicago.
32. Mr. Givi, did the professor order the students to come to the university early tomorrow morning [instr.]? Because we must be at the university early, I must do the homework this evening.
33. The capital of Georgia is no longer Mcxeta. When you will be in Mcxeta go into the Sveṭicxoveli church. It is an important model of Ġeorgian ecclesiastic architecture.
34. In our university, learning usually begins at [on] 9 o'clock in the morning (gen.) and ends at five o'clock in the evening (gen.).
35. Our university theatre will perform one of the plays* of Aḳaḳi Çereteli. Friends, come to the performance, this evening at six o'clock.
36. Come in, Mr. Joseph! Let's listen to the ten o'clock radio program, the opera "Daisi." Who wrote this opera? The Georgian composer, Zachary Paliašvili.

*See sec. 8.6.1.

1 **კავკასიური ენები.** ცალკე უნდა შევჩერდეთ ე. წ. „კავკასიურ ენებზე“. ასე იწოდება ენათა წყება, რომელთაც ამჟამად კავკასიაში ვხვდებით და რომელთა მონათესავე ენები სხვაგან თითქმის არ დარჩენილა. კავკასიაში გვხვდება აზერბეიჯანული, ყუმიკური, ოსური, ქურთული, სომხური, ბერძნულიც, მაგრამ მათგან პირველი ორი ურალურ-ალტაური ოჯახის თურქულ ჯგუფს ეკუთვნის, უკანასკნელი ოთხი ინდო-ევროპულ ენებს უკავშირდება გენეალოგიურად.

2 ამიტომ: ყველა ენა, რომელიც კი გვხვდება კავკასიაში, როდი იწოდება „კავკასიურად“; „კავკასიური“ ეწოდება კავკასიის ენათა გარკვეულ წყებას.

3 კავკასიურ ენებში ოთხი ჯგუფი გაირჩევა: **I. ქართველურ** ენათა ჯგუფი, **II. აფხაზურ-ადიღეური ჯგუფი, III. ჩაჩნური ჯგუფი** და **IV. დაღისტნურ** ენათა ჯგუფი.

4 **I. ქართველურ** ენათა ჯგუფი სამი წევრისაგან შედგება; ესენია: 1. **ქართული** თავისი კილოებით (როგორიცაა: ქართლური, კახური, ქიზიყური, ინგილოური, თუშური, ფშაური, ხევსურული, მთიულური; მესხურ-ჯავახური, იმერული, რაჭულ-ლეჩხუმური, გურული, აჭარული); 2. **ზანური** ანუ **ჭანურ-მეგრული** — კილოკავებითურთ; ჭანურის კილოკავებია: ათინური, ვიწურ-არქაბული და ხოფური; მეგრულის კილოკავებია: ზუგდიდურ-სამურზაყანული და სენაკური; 3. **სვანური**. პროფ. ა. შანიძის კლასიფიკაციით სვანური ოთხი კილოსაგან შედგება; ესენია: ბალს-ზემოური, ბალს-ქვემოური, ლაშხური და ლენტეხური; პირველი ორი ინგურის ხეობაშია, დანარჩენი ორი — ცხენისწყლისაში.

5 ხშირად ჭანური და მეგრული ცალკე ენებად მიაჩნიათ, შეცთომაა. ჭანური და მეგრული ისე ახლოს დგას ერთმანეთთან, როგორც, მაგალითად, ხევსურული და გურული; როგორც ეს ორი უკანასკნელი ვერ ჩაითვლება ცალკე ენებად, ისე ჭანური და მეგრული. ჭანური და მეგრული ისეთივე ორი კილოა ერთი ენისა, როგორც ხევსურული და გურულია ქართული ენის კილო. საერთო სახელად ჭანურისა და მეგრულისათვის პირობით ნახმარი გვაქვს *ზანური* („კოლხური“ არარეალური იქნებოდა, „ლაზური“ უხერხულია, რადგანაც „ჭანურის“ სინონიმს წარმოადგენს).

6 ტერმინი „ქართველური ენები“ შემოღებულია ცნობილი ავსტრიელი ენათმეცნიერის ჰუგო შუხარდტის მიერ.

7 **II. აფხაზურ-ადიღეურ** ჯგუფში შედის: *აფხაზური ენა*, *უბიხური ენა* და *ადიღეური* (*ჩერქეზული*) ქვეჯგუფი — *ყაბარდულის*, *კიახურისა* (ანუ ქვემო-ადიღეურის) და *ბასლინეურის* შემადგენლობით. ყაბარდულ-ბალყარული ავტონომიური რესპუბლიკის ცენტრია ნალჩიკი, ადიღეური ავტონ. ოლქისა — ქ. მაიკოპი (1936 წ.). უბიხური ამჟამად კავკასიაში არა გვხვდება: გასული საუკუნის მესამოცე წლებში მეფის რუსეთმა რომ დაიპყრო კავკასიის მთიანეთი, უბიხები გადასახლდენ თურქეთში; იქ მათი მოსახლეობის მთავარი მასა ქალ. იზმიდის მიდამოებშია.

Vocabulary

(See note at end of vocabulary.)

1.

ცალკე	individual(ly); separate(ly)
შე=აჩერებს	stop (for a moment) + -ze = on
ე.წ. =	so-called
ეგრეთ წოდებული	
იწოდება	be called sthg. (II. conj., + adv.) (only present series)
წყება	group, series
რომელთაც	which (erg., dat., gen. pl.) (relative)
ამჟამად	at present; now (cf. ეს, ამ this, ჟამი time)
[ვხვდებით]	we encounter s.o., sthg. (dat.)(II. conj.)
რომელთა •	which (relative) (here = gen. pl.)
მონათესავე	related; cognate
სხვაგან	elsewhere
თითქმის არ	here: barely
[დარჩენილა]	it (nom.) has remained; survived
[გვხვდება]	we (dat.) find; come across s.o., sthg. (nom.)
აზერბეიჯანი	now: აზერბაიჯანი
ყუმიკური	Kumyk
ოსი	an Ossetian (person)
ქურთი	a Kurd (person)
[მათგან]	of them
ურალურ-ალტაური	Ural-Altaic
ოჯახი	family
ჯგუფი	group
[ეკუთვნის]	s.o., sthg. (nom.) belongs to s.o., sthg. (dat.)
უკანასკნელი	last
ინდო-ევროპული	Indo-European
[უკავშირდება]	it (nom.) is linked, connected to s.o.,

	sthg. (dat.) (II. conj.)
გენეალოგიური	genealogical (here: genetically)
2.	
ამიტომ	for this reason; therefore (cf. რატომ)
რომელიც	which (relative); რომელიც კი: here: even though
როდი	in no way; not at all
[ეწოდება]	it (dat.) is called sthg. (nom.)
გარკვეული	(a) certain
3.	
ადიღე	an Adyghe (person)
გა=არჩევს	distinguish (II. conj. = გაირჩევა, aor. irr., 3sg. გაირჩა)
ჩაჩანი	a Chechen (person) (A)
დაღისტანი	Daghestan (A) (now: დაღესტანი)
4.	
[შე+დგება]	consist (II. conj.) (only present series)
თავისი	its (own) (See sec. 7.4.)
კილოებით	(Note use of instr. with meaning of 'with'.)
როგორიც	such as
ქართლური	adj. from ქართლი province of East Georgia; (distinguish ქართლური Kartlian from ქართული Georgian)
კილოკავი	sub-dialect
-ურთ	with (pp. + instr.)
პროფ.	პროფესორი
შანიძე აკაკი	leading Georgian linguist (1887-)
კლასიფიკაციის	classification (კლასიფიკაციით according to the classification)
ინგური	Ingur (river) (now: ენგური)
ხეობა	mountain valley
დანარჩენი	remaining
ცხენისწყალი	Cxenisçqali (A) (lit.: Horsewater) (river in W. Gerogia; ცხენისწყლისაში=ცხენისწყლის

	ხეობაში; see sec. 8.6.)
5.	
[მიაჩნიათ]	they (dat.) consider sthg. (nom.) as sthg. (adv.)
შეცთომა = შეცდომა	mistake; error
ისე... როგორც...	as..., as...
[დგას]	stand(s) (irr.)
ერთმანეთი	each other
მაგალითი	example; მაგალითად for example, e.g.
როგორც... ისე...	as..., so...
ისეთივე... როგორც...	just as much... as...
ერთი ენისა	(Note the long form of the gen. when it is postposed.)
საერთო	common; general
პირობითი	arbitrary; პირობით conditionally
[ნახმარი გვაქვს]	we(dat.) have used sthg. (nom.)
კოლხური	Colchidian (from Colchis)
არარეალური	unreal; unrealistic
უხერხული	awkward
რადგანაც	for; since; because
სინონიმი	synonym
წარმო+ადგენს	represent (aor. E → I)
6.	
ტერმინი	term
შემოღებული	introduced
ავსტრია	Austria
ენათმეცნიერი	linguist
შუხარდტი ჰუგო	Hugo Schuchardt (1842-1928)
7.	
ჩერქეზი	a Circassian (person)
ქვეჯგუფი	subgroup (ქვე = under, sub)
ქვემო	lower
შემადგენლობა	composition (შემადგენლობით with a

	composition, i.e., composed of)
ნალჩიკი	Nalchik (city)
ავტონ.	ავტონომიური
ოლქისა	ოლქის ცენტრი; see sec. 8.6.
ქ.	ქალაქი
მაიკოპი	Maikop (city)
1936 წ.	ათას ცხრაას ოცდათექვსმეტ წელს
არა	არ
მესამოცე	sixtieth; here: the 60s
რომ	here: when; დაიპყრობს conquer
მთიანეთი	mountain region (cf. მთიანი mountainous)
გადა=ასახლებს	move; exile; გადასახლდენ = გადასახლდნენ
მათი	their
მოსახლეობა	population
მასა	mass
ქალ.	ქალაქი
მიდამო	environs, neighborhood; suburb

Note: Place names and derivatives of place names generally are not given in the vocabulary if there are no special equivalents in English. Locations of some of the regions of Georgia mentioned in the reading can be found on the attached map (fig. 6.1).

• რომელთა მონათესავე ენები languages related to which

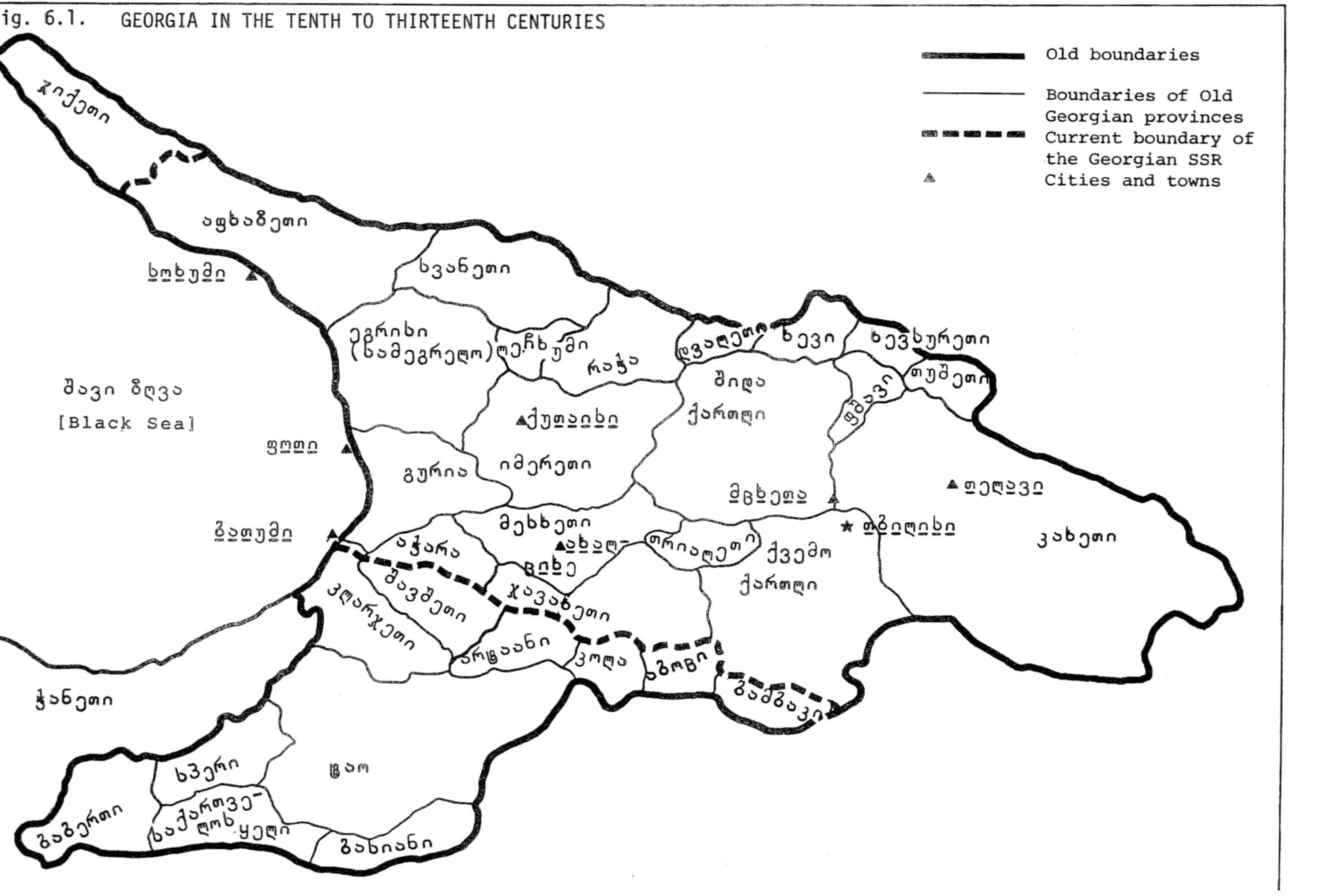

Fig. 6.1. GEORGIA IN THE TENTH TO THIRTEENTH CENTURIES

LESSON 7

7.1. Object markers. The Georgian verb, in addition to marking the subject of the sentence also marks the direct and indirect objects. These are marked by prefixes which occur immediately before the preradical vowel, or, if there is none, immediately before the root of the verb. Number is distinguished for objects of the first and second persons; number is not distinguished for third person objects (but see p. 345■).

It must be noted that, in general, indirect objects denote human beings (and therefore can be first, second, and third persons) while direct objects tend to denote things (and therefore are most commonly third person only). Although the concept of the indirect object in Georgian is broader than in English, nonetheless not all verbs can take indirect objects. As a rule, indirect objects are found more commonly with I. conjugation verbs than with II. conjugation verbs. In fact, there are many I. conjugation verbs that occur with indirect objects while their corresponding II. conjugation forms do not. In normal word order the indirect object precedes the direct object, e.g.: ივანემ ექიმს წერილი გაუგზავნა John sent the doctor (id.o.) a letter (d.o.).

7.1.1. Direct object markers. The direct object markers are:

	Singular	Plural
1st	m-	gv-
2d	g-	g-.....-t
3d	Ø	

Note that the plural marker of the second person is the same as the plural marker of the first and second person subject markers and it occupies the same position.

7.1.2. Rules for the object marker.

Rule 1 A first person object cannot occur with a first person subject, nor can a second person object occur with a second person subject (see sec. 7.4.3).

Rule 2 The *v-* marking first person subject is always dropped before the *g-* marking second person object. (The *presence* of a second person *object* marker *g-* and the *absence* of a third person *subject* marker *suffix* is generally sufficient to indicate a first person subject; e.g., გხედავ I see you; გნახე I saw you. In both forms the presence of the prefix *g-* indicates that the subject cannot be second person; the absence of a suffix *-s* or *-en* in the first form, *-a* or *-es* in the second, indicates that the subject cannot be third person. Therefore, the subject must be first person, and this despite the absence of the subject prefix *v-*.)

Rule 3 When the subject of a verb is first person plural and the object is second person plural, only one plural marker *-t* can occur; e.g., გაგიგებთ *ga=g-i-g-eb-t* can mean:

a. I (*v-*; rule 2) will understand you all (*g-.....-t*).

b. We (*v-.....-t*; rule 2) will understand you (*g-*).

c. We (*v-.....-t*; rule 2) will understand you all (*g-.....-t*).

The determination of the meaning of such a form is either through context or by the use of personal pronouns (see section 9.2).

Rule 4 When a 3sg. subject marker ending in *s* occurs with a second person plural object (*g-.....-t*) the *-s* is lost. Thus the form გაგიგებთ above can also have the meaning:

d. He (*-s*) will understand you all (*g-.....-t*).

Again, context or pronouns will eliminate ambiguity.

Rule 5 When a third pl. subject ending occurs with a second pl. object (*g-.....-t*), the object plural marker *-t* is dropped. Thus, a form such as გაგიგებენ can mean:

a. They (*-en*) will understand you (*g-*).

b. They (*-en*) will understand you all (*g-.....-t*).

A similar loss of the plural marker *-t* of the second person object marker occurs in the third person plural of the remaining screeves: imperfect, conditional, conjunctive (ending *-nen*), aorist (ending *-es*), and optative (ending *-on*); e.g., (გა)გიგებდნენ *(ga=)g-i-g-eb-d-nen* can refer to a plural object as well as a singular. გაგიგეს *ga=g-i-g-es*, the aorist, can also refer to both singular and plural second person objects. Similarly, in the optative, გაგიგონ *ga=g-i-g-on*.

7.1.3. Examples: მოკლავს (mo=ḳl-av-s) 'kill'.

Future/Present:

Subject	1sg. obj.	2sg. obj.
1sg.	—	(მო)გკლავ
2sg.	(მო)მკლავ	—
3sg.	(მო)მკლავს	(მო)გკლავს
1pl.	—	(მო)გკლავთ[a]
2pl.	(მო)მკლავთ	—
3pl.	(მო)მკლავენ	(მო)გკლავენ[c]
	1pl. obj.	**2pl. obj.**
1sg.	—	(მო)გკლავთ[a]
2sg.	(მო)გვკლავ	—
3sg.	(მო)გვკლავს	(მო)გკლავთ[b]
1pl.	—	(მო)გკლავთ[a]
2pl.	(მო)გვკლავთ	—
3pl.	(მო)გვკლავენ	(მო)გკლავენ[c]

Imperfect/Conditional:

	1 sg. obj.	2sg. obj.
1sg.	—	(მო)გკლავდი
2sg.	(მო)მკლავდი	—
3sg.	(მო)მკლავდა	(მო)გკლავდა
1pl.	—	(მო)გკლავდით[a]
2pl.	(მო)მკლავდით	—
3pl.	(მო)მკლავდნენ	(მო)გკლავდნენ[c]
	1pl. obj.	**2pl. obj.**
1sg.	—	(მო)გკლავდით[a]
2sg.	(მო)გვკლავდი	—
3sg.	(მო)გვკლავდა	(მო)გკლავდათ
1pl.	—	(მო)გკლავდით[a]
2pl.	(მო)გვკლავდით	—
3pl.	(მო)გვკლავდნენ	(მო)გკლავდნენ[c]

The *conjunctive* patterns analogously to the imperfect/iterative-conditional and presents special patterns only with a 3sg. subject and 2pl. object, e.g. (მო-)გკლავდეთ (rule 4).

ნახავს (nax-av-s) 'see'.

Aorist:

	1sg. obj.	2sg. obj.	1pl. obj.	2pl. obj.
1sg.	—	გნახე	—	გნახეთ[a]
2sg.	მნახე	—	გვნახე	—
3sg.	მნახა	გნახა	გვნახა	გნახათ
1pl.	—	გნახეთ[a]	—	გნახეთ[a]
2pl.	მნახეთ	—	გვნახეთ	—
3pl.	მნახეს	გნახეს[c]	გვნახეს	გნახეს[c]

Optative:

	1sg. obj.	2sg. obj.	1pl. obj.	2pl. obj.
1sg.	—	გნახო	—	გნახოთ[a]
2sg.	მნახო	—	გვნახო	—
3sg.	მნახოს	გნახოს	გვნახოს	გნახოთ[b]
1pl.	—	გნახოთ[a]	—	გნახოთ[a]
2pl.	მნახოთ	—	გვნახოთ	—
3pl.	მნახონ	გნახონ[c]	გვნახონ	გნახონ[c]

a. See sec. 7.1.2, rule 3.
b. See sec. 7.1.2, rule 4.
c. See sec. 7.1.2, rule 5.

(Forms with direct object in the third person were already presented in section 2.2.)

As a general rule, only I. conjugation verbs may take both direct and indirect object markers; II. conjugation verbs as a rule can take only indirect object markers.

7.2. Indirect object markers. Both I. and II. conjugation verbs may take an indirect object. The notion of "indirect object" in Georgian is significantly broader than the same notion in English (see 7.2.3, below), particularly for II. conjugation verbs. It should be noted that certain verbs (both I. and II. conjugation) occur only with indirect object markers; absolute (i.e., objectless) forms of such verbs do not occur. For all verbs, nominal and pronominal indirect objects are always in the dative case.

7.2.1. Indirect object markers with I. conjugation verbs. I. conjugation verbs can mark an indirect object in two ways, either with the special preradical vowels *i-/u-* or without the addition of special preradical vowels. Although one must learn which verb takes which type of indirect object marking, by far the more common type of marking is that with the preradical vowels *i-/u-*.

7.2.2. The *u*-series of indirect object markers. We shall call the series of indirect object markers with preradical vowels *i-/u-* the *u-series*.[1] Before adding these markers to a given screeve form, any preradical vowel (*a-* or *i-*) must be dropped. Then the *u-series* markers are inserted immediately before the root. These markers are:

	Singular	Plural
1st.	mi-	gvi-
2d.	gi-	gi-.....-t
3d.	u-	

[See also ■, p. 345.]

Note that the *u-series markers* in the first and second persons consist simply of the (direct) object markers plus the preradical vowel *i-*. In the third person (both sg. and pl.) we find the vowel *u-*.[2] *Note also that the rules for object markers (sec. 7.1.2) apply also to u-series markers.* The first person marker *v-* is kept before the third person object marker *-u-*.

7.2.3. Meanings of indirect objects. As mentioned above, the notion of indirect object in Georgian is broader than in English. The indirect object of a I. conjugation verb can correspond to the English indirect object (with or without the preposition *to*), to the English preposition *for*, and to English possessives. Examples are:

ძმას წერილს გაუგზავნის	He will send (his) brother a letter.
ძმას საჩუქარი უყიდა	He bought a gift for (his) brother.
შვილს თმა დაუვარცხნა	She combed (her) child's hair.[3]

The meanings of the indirect object can cover an even greater range with II. conjugation verbs. These meanings will be pointed out in the vocabularies.

7.2.4. Less common is the *h-series of indirect object markers*. This series is identical in the first and second persons to the direct object markers (sec. 7.1.1); in the third person the marker can be *h-*, or *s-*, or nothing, depending on the following sound:

h- before g, k, ḳ, q, p

s- before d, t, ṭ, j, ċ, ç, ǯ, č, č̣

(Ø-) before all remaining consonants and all vowels.[4]

s- and *h*- are added immediately before the verbal root. The markers *s*- and *h*- do not cause the loss of the first person marker *v*-: მივსწერ I shall write him; ვჰკითხავ I (shall) ask him (sthg.).

Just as all other object markers, the h-series markers are subject to the rules in 7.1.2.

The *h-series* indirect object markers occur most commonly with verbs with the preverbs *mi*- (with third person id.o.) and *mo*- (with first and second person id. o.'s), i.e., when the focus is on the direction of the action, toward the speaker and adressee or toward the person spoken about. Also, *h-series* markers occur with causatives of transitive verbs (see section 11.4). An example will be *mi=s-c̣ers* and *mo=m-c̣ers* both meaning 'write someone'. Note the following (aorist) forms:

მომწერა He wrote me

მოგწერა He wrote you

მისწერა He wrote him/them

Verbs taking the *h*-series markers will be indicated in the vocabularies.

7.2.5. A number of verbs with preverbs *not* of the *mo*-group (see sec. 2.2.1) add *mo*- when the id.o. is first or second person. Note the following:

გამომიგზავნა He sent it to me

გამოგიგზავნა He sent it to you

გაუგზავნა He sent it to him/them

Verbs which add *mo*- to the preverb when there is a first or second person object will be indicated in the vocabularies.[5]

7.3. Absolute and relative verbs. Verbs having an indirect object marker will be called *relative* verbs while verbs without such an indirect object marking will be called *absolute*. In the relative form of II. conjugation verbs the id.o. markers differ depending on how the II. conjugation forms are derived from base I. conjugation forms.

7.3.1. Relative forms of the II. conjugation in *i*-. II. conjugation forms in *i*- become relative by (a) changing the preradical vowel from *i*- to *e*-; (b) adding the *h-series* markers before the new preradical vowel *e*-. (Note that since the markers always precede the vowel *e*- the marker of a third person id.o. is always Ø, and therefore the *h*-series markers become identical to the direct object markers.) *These object person markers are subject to the rules in 7.1.2.* Examples:

გაიგზავნება	be sent	გაეგზავნება	be sent to s.o.
დაიმალება	hide (o.s.)	დაემალება	hide (o.s.) from s.o.

7.3.2. Relative forms of the II. conjugation in -*d*-. II. conjugation forms in -*d*- become relative by the addition of the *u*-series of indirect object markers. These *u*-series markers are subject to the rules in 7.1.2. Examples are:

მომზადდება be prepared	მოუმზადდება be prepared for s.o.
აშენდება be built	აუშენდება be built for s.o.
შეერთდება be united	შეუერთდება be united to sthg.

(In some instances one encounters relative II. conjugation in -*d*- forms with *h*-series markers or with *a*-series markers [the superessive; see sec. 13.3]. Most commonly such forms have no absolute [i.e., non-relative] forms.)

It must be noted that in general II. conjugation in -*d*- forms with indirect objects are quite infrequent. In place of such forms, Georgians tend to prefer the corresponding I. conjugation form in the third person plural (without personal pronoun; see sec. 9.2) or the II. conjugation absolute form with a postpositional phrase with -*tvis* 'for'. So in the following examples instead of *a* one would prefer *b* or *c*.

(a) ეს სახლი ივანეს აუშენდა.
This house was built for John (indirect object).

(b) ეს სახლი ივანეს აუშენეს.
They (French *on*, German *man*) built this house for John (indirect object).

(c) ეს სახლი ივანესათვის აშენდა.
This house was built for John (postpositional phrase).

7.3.3. Meaning of relative II. conjugation forms. Relative II. conjugation forms have an indirect object which can correspond to a number of constructions in

English, most commonly to constructions with 'to' or 'for'. When the II. form is derived from a relative I. conjugation form with id.o., it generally preserves the meaning of the I. conjugation id.o. (although it should be noted that a very large number of verbs cannot form relative II. conjugation forms). Examples:

დაუმალავს	da=u-mal-av-s	hide something *from* someone
დაემალება	da=e-mal-eb-a	hide (oneself) *from* someone
შეადარებს	še=a-dar-eb-s	compare s.o./sthg. to s.o./sthg. (*h*-series)
შეედარება	še=e-dar-eb-a	be compared to s.o./sthg.

There are a number of relative II. conjugation verbs which are not derived from corresponding I. conjugation verbs and which do not have absolute (i.e., objectless) II. conjugation forms. Such verbs and their meanings will be given in the vocabulary.[6] Examples are:

დაეხმარება	da=e-xmar-eb-a	help someone
შეეხება	še=e-x-eb-a	concern s.o./sthg.
ელოდება	Ø=e-lod-eb-a	wait for s.o./sthg.

7.3.4. The irregular verb მიცემა 'give sthg. to s.o.'. The stem of this verb changes depending upon the series. In the present series, forms are based on 3sg. present აძლევს *a-jlev-s* (with *h*-series indirect object markers). In the future series the forms are based on 3sg. future მისცემს *mi+s-cem-s*. With first or second person indirect objects the preverb is *mo+*, e.g., მომცემ 'you will give it to me'.

In the aorist the screeve endings are:

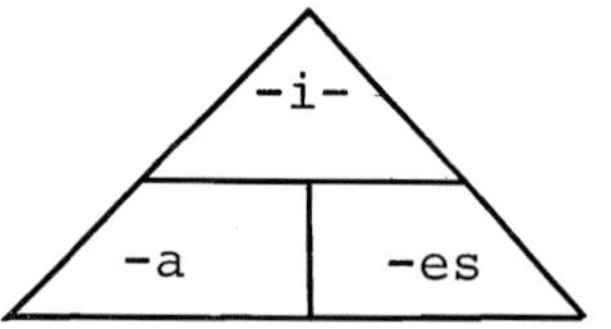

The root varies according to the person of the *subject*. If the subject is third person, the root is *-c-*; if the subject is first or second person, the root is *-ec-*. The preverb is *mi+* with a third person indirect object and *mo+* with a first or second person:

Subject:		3 singular	3 plural
Object:	1sg.	მომცა	მომცეს
	1pl.	მოგვცა	მოგვცეს
	2sg.	მოგცა	მოგცეს
	2pl.	მოგცათ	მოგცეს
	3d.	მისცა	მისცეს

Subject:		1sg.	1pl.	2sg.	2pl.
Object:	1sg.	-	-	მომეცი	მომეცით
	1pl.	-	-	მოგვეცი	მოგვეცით
	2sg.	მოგეცი	მოგეცით	-	-
	2pl.	მოგეცით	მოგეცით	-	-
	3d.	მივეცი	მივეცით	მიეცი	მიეცით

The optative has the endings in the following figure, which are added to the stem of the 3sg. aorist (-*c*-).

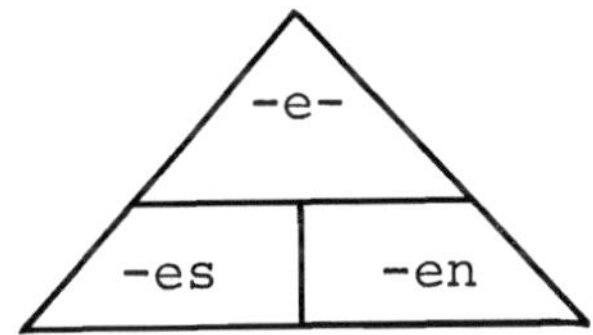

As in other screeves, the optative takes the *h*-series id. o. markers and has the preverb *mi+* with a 3d person id.o. and *mo+* with 1st and 2d. Example: მისცეს let him give it to her.

Summary

Present	აძლევს
Imperfect	აძლევდა
Conjunctive	აძლევდეს

	Object	
	3d.	1sg.
Future	მისცემს	მომცემს
Conditional	მისცემდა	მომცემდა
Conjunctive	მისცემდეს	მომცემდეს
Aorist	მისცა	მომცა
Optative	მისცეს	მომცეს

7.4. Reflexive possessives. The third person possessives may be distinguished according to whether the possessive's antecedent is the subject of the sentence (reflexive possessive) or whether it is not:

	3d. singular	3d. plural
reflexive	თავისი his own, her own its own	თავიანთი their own
nonreflexive	მისი his, her(s), it(s)	მათი their(s)

თავისი and თავიანთი are similar to Russian свой (3d person) or Latin *suus*; მისი and მათი are the equivalents of Russian его, её, их or Latin *eius, eorum*. Examples:

> სოსომ თავის დას საჩუქარი გაუგზავნა.
>
> Soso sent *his* sister a gift.
>
> საჩუქარი მის ქმარსაც გაუგზავნა.
>
> He also sent *her* husband a gift.

7.4.1. The emphatic pronoun, corresponding to Russian сам or Latin *ipse* is თვითონ; e.g., ელენემ თვითონ დაწერა წერილი Helen herself wrote the letter. თვითონ is not declined.

7.4.2. Possessives. These are declined like adjectives when used attributively (adjectivally) and like nouns when used pronominally. Note however that when used adjectivally, the datives of the first and second person possessives take the full dative ending *-s* as does the third person plural: ჩემს, ჩვენს, შენს, თქვენს, მათს.

	Singular	Plural
1st.	ჩემი	ჩვენი
2d.	შენი	თქვენი
3d.	მისი	მათი
Reflexive	თავისი	თავიანთი

7.4.3. Reflexive pronouns. When the subject and object of a sentence are one and the same person, the object is marked by a reflexive pronoun.[7] These are:

	Singular	Plural
1st.	ჩემი თავი myself	ჩვენი თავი ourselves
2d.	შენი თავი yourself	თქვენი თავი yourselves

3d. თავისი თავი — himself (herself, itself)
თავიანთი თავი — themselves

These are all declined regularly; note that grammatically these are all third person forms consisting of the possessive pronoun + თავი 'head' and therefore take third person object markers. Examples:

ელგუჯამ თავისი თავი სარკეში ნახა.
Elguǯa saw himself in the mirror.

ჩემს თავს ბეჯით სტუდენტად ვთვლი.
I consider myself a diligent student.

Reflexive indirect objects can be paraphrased by the pronoun plus postposition *-tvis*; e.g., ჩემთვის ვიყიდე I bought it for myself. See also sec. 13.1.

7.4.4. Reciprocal pronoun. The reciprocal pronoun, meaning 'each other' (Russian *друг друга*, French *l'un l'autre*, German *einander*) is ერთმანეთი, which is regularly declined.

7.5. Relative and interrogative pronouns. Relative pronouns are derived from interrogatives by adding the particle *-c* to the interrogative. The *-c* is added to the extended case forms (sec. 4.3), if the relative is declined. In nondeclinable forms ending in a consonant, the vowel *-a-* is usually inserted before the *-c* (but note ვინც and როგორც). Examples:

Interrogative			Relative	
რომელი? (E)		which	რომელიც[8]	
ვინ?		who	ვინც[9]	
რა?		what	რაც	
სად?		where	სადაც	
როგორ?	how?		როგორც	as
რამდენი?	how many?		რამდენიც	as many, so many

Note როდის? when?; but relative როდესაც or როცა when.

Of the first three relatives, რომელიც is by far the most common, corresponding to English *who, which, what, that*. Examples of რომელიც:

კაცი, რომელიც ვნახე
The man whom (that) I saw

წიგნი, რომელსაც ვკითხულობდი
The book that (which) I was reading

ექიმი, რომელმაც გნახა
The doctor who saw you

When the relative pronoun is used with a postposition, the *-c* is added to the postposition. If the postposition ends in a consonant, *-a-* is added before the *-c*. Examples:

რომელშიც (also რომელშიდაც)	in which
რომელზეც (also რომელზედაც)	on which
რომლის შესახებაც	about which

7.6. Wordbuilding: derivatives in *sa-*.

7.6.1. Denominal derivatives in *sa-.....-o*. In sec. 4.6.1 the use of the circumfix *sa-.....-o* in forming adjectives was presented. The same circumfix is also used to form nouns derived from other nouns. The meaning of such derivatives can be "place where":

ბაჟი	customs duty	საბაჟო	custom house
აგენტი	agent	სააგენტო	agency
ელჩი	ambassador	საელჩო	embassy
მზარეული	cook	სამზარეულო	kitchen
საფლავი	grave	სასაფლაო	cemetery (sec. 1.11.1)
ავადმყოფი	patient, sick person	საავადმყოფო	hospital
სტუმარი	guest (A)	სასტუმრო	hotel, inn

7.6.2. Other denominatives in *sa-.....-o* and *sa-.....-e* can mean 'to be used for', 'designated for':

ზეთი	oil	საზეთე	oiler, lubricator
თვალი	eye	სათვალე	eyeglasses
თამაში	game, playing	სათამაშო	toy
ზრდა	growth	საზრდო	food

7.6.3. Deverbal derivatives in *sa-*. These forms, traditionally called the future passive participle, generally have a meaning paraphrasable as 'for ...ing', 'to be + past participle'. Examples:

ბეჭდავს	print	საბეჭდი მანქანა	typewriter (lit., machine

			for printing)
წერს	write	საწერი მაგიდა	writing table (lit., table for writing)
კერავს	sew	საკერავი მანქანა	sewing machine (lit., machine for sewing)
გააღებს	open	გასაღები	key (lit., something for opening)
დალევს	drink (fut.)	დასალევი	beverage
აღნიშნავს	denote, mark	აღსანიშნავი	notable
იცვამს	dress s.o.	ფეხსაცმელი	shoes (sec. 1.11.1; ფეხი =foot)
		ტანსაცმელი	clothes (ტანი= body)
ჭამს	eat	საჭმელი	food

Note that the prefix *sa-* follows the preverb (if any) and any preradical vowel is dropped. Some of these derivatives take the suffix *-el-* before which the P/FSFs *-am*, *-av* undergo syncope (cf. საჭმელი). The P/FSF *-i* is dropped. The suffix *-el-* is particularly common with verbs in P/FSF *-eb-*. Note too that verbs in *-av* in certain instances lose the P/FSF (e.g., ბეჭდავს → საბეჭდი print).

Since these derivatives are nominal they cannot take objects in the dative or nominative but instead take the genitive. Compare:

წიგნების საბეჭდი დაზგა

a press for printing books

ავადმყოფების მისაღები ოთახი

a room for receiving patients

The deverbal derivatives in *sa-* in the adverbial case correspond to the English use of the infinitive with 'in order to'. Examples:

in order to write a letter წერილის დასაწერად

in order to open the door კარის გასაღებად

LESSON 7: Notes

1. More traditionally these markers are called the *objective version markers* (Tschenkéli: *OVZ* -- *Personalzeichen der Objektiven Version;* Vogt: *préfixe de VO (version objective);* Rudenko: *pokazatel' tret'ej porody*). The term *objective version* comes from Šanije, who regards these markers as denoting the person (other than the subject) for whose benefit the action is performed, სასხვისო ქცევა 'the designated-for-someone-else version'.

2. Note that the sequences *mi-, gvi-, gi-* do not necessarily indicate the *u*-series of indirect object markers. In rare instances they may represent direct object markers followed by the preradical vowel *i-*. Compare the following (examples are with third person singular subject):

Direct Object	Obj. Person	*u*-series indirect object
'he will receive s.o.'		'he will build it for s.o.'
მიმიღებს	1st.	ამიშენებს
mi=m-i-ǧ-eb-s		a=mi-šen-eb-s
მიგიღებს	2d.	აგიშენებს
mi=g-i-ǧ-eb-s		a=gi-šen-eb-s
მიიღებს	3d.	აუშენებს
mi= -*i*-ǧ-eb-s		a= *u* -šen-eb-s

Note the differences between third person direct and indirect objects.

3. Note that these correspond to datives in other languages: cf. Russian *Он купил брату подарок* 'He bought a gift for his brother'; French *Il lui a lavé le visage (à son fils)*, German *Sie hat ihrem Sohne das Haar gekämmt* 'She combed her son's hair'.

4. These are the normative rules. In actual practice, however, many modern Georgian writers have no marker for the third person indirect object marker; for them the *h*-series has merged completely with the direct object markers and the student should be aware that a form without *h-* or *s-* where the grammar calls for them can still refer to a third person indirect object, even when there is no indirect object noun or pronoun in the sentence. For most writers *s-* or *h-* are

dropped after the *v*- of the first person, e.g. ვკითხავ for ვჰკითხავ 'I shall ask him'.

5. The addition of the prefix -*mo*- is possible also with a third person id.o. in circumstances such as the following, where the speaker and the recipient are both together in Tbilisi: ამერიკიდან თბილისში გამოუგზავნეს. 'They sent it to him [here] from America to Tbilisi'.

6. The verb შეადარებს is irregular in that its relative II. conjugation form has -*e*- rather than -*d*- as an id.o. marker: შეედარება. Some relative II. conjugation verbs are not derived either from corresponding I. conjugation verbs or II. conjugation absolute verbs, but are themselves base forms. Examples include: დაეხმარება 'help s.o.', დაეთანხმება 'agree with s.o.' Such verbs form the verbal noun in -*eb-a:* დახმარება, დათანხმება.

7. In some cases when one might expect an indirect object reflexive in the dative, e.g., ჩემს თავს, a special construction of the verb, the (dative) reflexive, is used. See section 13.1.

8. With the genitive, the -*c* is not added to რომლისა but rather to the noun which forms the head of the phrase or to the end of a following postposition taking the genitive, for example:

> საქართველო, რომლის დედაქალაქიც თბილისია, საბჭოთა კავშირშია.
>
> Georgia, the capital of which is Tbilisi, is in the Soviet Union.
>
> ვანომ გადათარგმნა წიგნი, რომლის შესახებაც მოგწერეთ.
>
> Vano translated the book about which I wrote you all.

In both instances, the noun phrase can also occur without -*c:* რომლის დედაქალაქი..., რომლის შესახებ....

9. The declension is as for ვინ: nom., erg. ვინც, gen., dat. ვისაც.

LESSON 7: Exercises

1. ხვალ უნივერსიტეტში გნახავ.
2. ქეთევანი გიცნობს? —დიახ, ძალიან კარგად მიცნობს. დიტომ გასულ წელს სოჭში გაგვაცნო ერთმანეთი.
3. მიხო! სადა ხარ? ამ ხალხში ვერ გხედავ.
4. ჩვენმა პროფესორმა შეგვაქო, ვინაიდან ძალიან ვრცელი წერილი მივსწერეთ.
5. მოგვწერეთ უფრო ხშირად და არ დაგვივიწყებთ!
6. ქალბატონო რუსუდან, შემოდით! ექიმი ახლა მიგიღებთ.
7. ბავშვებო, ნუ დაივიწყებთ ჩვენი ქვეყნის ომის გმირებს!
8. ამ ახალი რომანის მოკლე რეცენზია ჩვენს ინგლისური ლიტერატურის პროფესორს უნდა გავუგზავნოთ.
9. მეგობრებო, დამეხმარეთ, გთხოვთ! —დიდი სიამოვნებით დაგეხმარებით.
10. ფულს გამოგიგზავნი. წადი მაღაზიაში და, გთხოვ, რამდენიმე ახალი პერანგი მიყიდე.
11. როცა ქართულ ენას ვსწავლობთ, ჩვენი კარგი ქართველი მეგობრები ძალიან გვეხმარებიან.
12. მამას ქართულ-ინგლისური ლექსიკონი უნდა ვუყიდო, ვინაიდან მალე ინგლისში სტუმრად წავა.
13. როცა ლონდონში იქნება, ჩვენს კარგ მეგობრებს მიხეილსა და ვერას უნდა დაურეკოს.
14. შეიძლება დაგეხმაროთ? —დიახ, გთხოვთ. ჩემს ცოლს კაბა უნდა ვუყიდო.
15. ჩემმა ცოლმა ჰალსტუკი მიყიდა.
16. სარკეში ვის ხედავ? —ჩემს თავს ვხედავ!
17. ივანე თავის კარგ მეგობარს ერევანში საჩუქარს უგზავნის.
18. ქურდებს ფული დაუმალე! ქურდებს დაემალე!
19. კაცი, რომელსაც წერილი გავუგზავნე, სადგურში მელოდებოდა.

20. კაცმა, რომელმაც სადგურში გნახა, გუშინ დამირეკა.
21. კაცი, რომელიც სადგურზე ნახე, ხვალ დაგირეკავს.
22. პაპაჩემმა* თავისი სახლი თვითონ ააშენა. სახლი, სადაც დავიბადე, თავის ვაჟიშვილს აუშენა.
23. ჩვენმა მშობლებმა რამდენიმე საინტერესო წიგნი და ჟურნალი გამოგვიგზავნეს. —მაშინ თქვენს მშობლებს ვრცელი წერილი უნდა მისწეროთ.
24. ვის ელოდებით? —ელგუჯასა და რუსუდანს ველოდებით.
25. სად იყავით? სადგურში გელოდებოდით!
26. როდესაც დამირეკავ, ჩემს თავს ისე აგიწერ, რომ, როცა სადგურზე მნახავ, მიცნობ, ვინცა ვარ. [When it occurs before a monosyllabic word, the pronoun ვინც usually adds *-a:* ვინცა.]
27. ჩემმა დამ გამომიგზავნა ეს ლურჯი კალამი, რომლითაც გწერ. საჩუქარი უნდა გავუგზავნო, ვინაიდან მალე იქნება მისი დაბადების დღე.
28. ჩემს თავს ვერ ვეხმარები. სხვები უნდა დაეხმარონ იმას, ვინც თავის თავს ვერ ეხმარება.
29. ივანემ დაურეკა თავის ძმებს? —არა, მათს მეზობელს დაურეკა, ვინაიდან სახლში არ იყვნენ.
30. გენერალმა თავის ჯარს საზღვარზე გადასვლა უბრძანა.
31. უსათვალოდ ვერ გხედავთ, ჩემო ძვირფასო მეგობრებო.
32. როცა საბჭოთა კავშირის საელჩოში ვიყავი, ელჩს საქმე განვუმარტე. თავის მთავრობას მისწერა მეტი ცნობების მისაღებად.
33. ერთმანეთს იცნობთ? —რასაკვირველია, ვანოს ვიცნობ და ვანო მიცნობს. ძალიან კარგი მეგობრები ვართ და ერთმანეთთან ხშირად ვართ სტუმრად.
34. ძველი ქართული ტექსტების წასაკითხავად საჭიროა ხუცურის ცოდნა.
35. აეროპორტში შესაძლებელია შენს შვილიშვილებს უბაჟოდ უყიდო საჩუქრები.
36. თბილისის მთავარ სადგურზე პაპიროსები ძალიან იაფად შეიძლება იყიდო.

37. ნუღარ გველოდები. ქალაქში უნდა წავიდე ახალი ჰალსტუკის საყიდლად.
38. შენმა კატამ შემაშინა, როცა უცებ ოთახში შემოვიდა. მაგრამ ახლა აღარაფერი მაშინებს.
39. როდესაც მესაზღვრემ თურქეთის საზღვარზე გაგვაჩერა, ეს ჩვენთვის საოცარი იყო.
40. გავაჩერებ ამ ახალგაზრდა კაცს ქუჩაზე. იქნებ ეს ქართული სიტყვა განმიმარტოს. მაგრამ უცხოელია და სიტყვას ვერ განმარტავს.
41. პაპა და ბებია ლამაზ ქართულ ნოხს გამოგიგზავნიან.
42. სიტყვა „პაპა" განმიმარტე! —„პაპა" მამის მამას ან დედის მამას ნიშნავს.
43. შენი სახლი ამიწერე! პატარა სახლია, რომელშიც ოთხი ოთახია: სამზარეულო, სასტუმრო, სასადილო და საწოლი ოთახი.
44. ბატონმა აკაკიმ სახლი ვის აუშენა? თავის შვილებს აუშენა.
45. გენერალმა გვიბრძანა, რომ საზღვარზე ღამით გადავიდეთ, რომ მტრის ჯარს მოულოდნელად შევუტიოთ.
46. ეს წერილი წამიკითხე, გთხოვ. —დიდი სიამოვნებით წაგიკითხავ.
47. რამდენი წიგნი გამოგიგზავნა შენმა ბიძამ? ექვსი წიგნი გამომიგზავნა. ახლა უნდა მივწერო წერილი.
48. ომის დროს მეცხვარეები მტერს მთაში დაემალნენ.
49. პროფესორი: მესამე გაკვეთილის სავარჯიშოები უნდა მომიმზადოთ. სტუდენტები: დიახ, ბატონო, ამ სავარჯიშოებს მოგიმზადებთ.
50. ამ საკითხის გასაგებად ჩემი ახალი წიგნი უნდა წაიკითხოთ.
51. ეს წერილი ვის გაეგზავნება? ეს ქალაქის საბჭოს გაეგზავნება.
52. ეს სასახლე მეფეს აუშენდა.
53. მამა შვილს პირს ხვალ დაბანს, დღეს კი პირი დედამ დაბანა.

54. მღვდელმა ვინ შეაქო? თავისი ეპისკოპოსი აქო. ეპისკოპოსმა კი მღვდელს ვაჟიშვილები უქო.
55. ეს ბოთლი არაყი ვის უყიდე? ჩემთვის ვიყიდე. გამყიდველმა მომყიდა. ივანესაც ერთი ბოთლი არაყი მიჰყიდა.
56. ფულს თუ მომცემთ, ქართული საესტრადო მუსიკის ამ ახალ ფირფიტას გიყიდით.
57. საესტრადო მუსიკის ფირფიტას ნუ მიყიდით. —ფულს მოგცემთ; ქართული ხალხური მუსიკის ფირფიტა მიყიდეთ! —გამყიდველი დიდი სიამოვნებით მომყიდის. მის მაღაზიაში საესტრადო და ხალხური მუსიკის ფირფიტებს ყიდიან.
58. ფულს ახლა ნუ მაძლევთ. როცა ფირფიტას მოგცემთ, ფული მაშინ მომეცით. ასე უფრო ადვილი იქნება.
59. გივის მიეცით ფული! —თხუთმეტი მანეთი უკვე მივეცი! —რამდენი?! —თხუთმეტი მანეთი და ოცი კაპიკი!
60. ამ საწყალ ხალხს ფული მივსცეთ! —რამდენი? —უნდა მისცეთ იმდენი, რამდენიც შეიძლება.
61. ვანომ იმ სტუდენტს ცხრა მანეთი და ათი კაპიკი მისცა. ამ სტუდენტსაც ფული უნდა მისცე!
62. მამაჩემს* უნდა დავეხმარო; მისწერს თავის ბიძას, რომელმაც ლენინგრადიდან დიდი პაკეტი გამოგვიგზავნა.
63. საქართველო მეფის რუსეთს 1801 (ათას რვაას ერთ) წელს შეუერთდა.
64. ერთმანეთს ხვალ კრებაზე ვნახავთ. რომელ კრებაზე? იმ კრებაზე, რომლის შესახებ (შესახებაც) მოგწერე.
65. შენი შარვალი მეტისმეტად მოკლეა; ფეხები დაგიგრძელდა!
66. გასაღებები, რომლებიც დედაშენმა მოგცა, მოგვეცი, გთხოვ!
67. ეს სუფრა ვისთვის მომზადდა? სტუდენტებმა თავიანთ პროფესორს მოუმზადეს.

68. ეს სკამი ჩემს ბებიას ლონდონში გაუკეთეს.

---

*For certain kinship terms the most common form in Georgian is with the possessive adjective following the kinship term and the possessive adjective alone being declined. Such forms are written as one word. Examples: დედაჩემი, Erg. დედაჩემმა, Gen. დედაჩემის etc. 'my mother'; დედაშენი 'your mother'; დედამისი 'his/her mother,' etc.

Georgian National Costumes

Vocabulary

აეროპორტი	airport
ან	or (noninterrogative; cf. თუ)
აღარაფერი	nothing any more (see sec. 6.4.2) (E)
ახალგაზრდა	young; youth (person)
ბაჟი	[customs] duty
ბებია	grandmother
ბიძა	uncle
ბოთლი	bottle
გამყიდველი	salesperson (cf. ყიდის)
გასაღები	key (cf. გააღებს)
გენერალი	general (military) (A)
გთხოვ(თ)	please (with -*t* = polite or plural)
ელჩი	ambassador
ეპისკოპოსი	bishop
ერთმანეთი	each other
ვრცელი	long (extensive)
ზოგიერთი	several
იაფი	cheap; inexpensive
იმდენი	that much
კაბა	dress
კაპიკი	copeck
კატა	cat
მანეთი	ruble
მაღაზია	store
მეზობელი	neighbor, neighboring (E)
მესაზღვრე	border guard (cf. საზღვარი)
მეტი	more
მეტისმეტად	too (overly)
მთავრობა	government
მოკლე	short
მოულოდნელი	unexpected
მტერი	enemy (E)
მღვდელი	priest (E)
მშობლები	parents (pl.)
ნოხი	carpet; rug
ოსტატი	master; craftsman
პაპიროსი	cigarette
პატარა	small; little (nontruncating)
პერანგი	shirt
პირი	face; mouth
რამდენიც	as much (rel.)
რეცენზია	review; critique
სადგური	station
საელჩო	embassy (cf. ელჩი)
საესტრადო	pertaining to the stage (ესტრადა); "popular"
საზღვარი	border; frontier; limit (A)
სათვალე	[eye]glasses

საკითხი	question
სამზარეულო	kitchen
საოცარი	surprising (A)
სარკე	mirror
სასადილო	dining room
საყიდელი, საყიდი	(E), (cf. *qid-* 'buy' and sec. 7.6.3)
სასახლე	palace
საჩუქარი	gift (A)
საწოლი	bed; bedroom
საწყალი	poor (pitiable) (A)
სიამოვნება	pleasure
სკამი	chair
სუფრა	table; tablecloth; banquet
უცებ	suddenly
ფეხი	foot; leg
ფული	money
ქურდი	thief
შარვალი	trousers (A)
შვილიშვილი	grandchild
ჩვენთვის	for us
ცოდნა	knowledge
ხალხი	people; folk
ჯარი	army
ჰალსტუკი	necktie
ინგლისი	England
ლენინგრადი	Leningrad
ლონდონი	London
სოჭი	Sochi (popular Black Sea resort in the RSFSR)
დიტო	from დიმიტრი Dmitri [m.]
ელგუჯა	[m.]
ვერა	Vera [f.]
მიხეილი	Michael [m.]
მიხო	from მიხეილი Mike [m.]
რუსუდანი	[f.]
ქეთევანი	[f.]

Verbs

დაბანს	da=*ban*-s	wash sthg.
დაბანს	da=(H-)*ban*-s*	wash s.o.'s sthg.
ბრძანებს	*brjan*-eb-s: pr.=fut.	order
უ-ბრძან-ებ-ს		order s.o. (to do something)
გაგზავნის	ga=*gzavn*-i-s	send
გა(მო)უ-გზავნის		send s.o. sthg. (see sec. 7.2.5)
დააგრძელებს	da=a-*grjel*-eb-s	lengthen
შეაერთებს	še=a-*ert*-eb-s	unite
-(e)c-	see *-cem-*	
უკითხავს	u-*ḳitx*-avs: pr.=fut.	(rel. form of იკითხ-

ავს, pr. კითხულობს) read s.o. sthg.

ელოდება e-*lod*-eb-a: pr.=fut. wait (for s.o./sthg.), expect (s.o./sthg.)

დაუმალავს da=u-*mal*-av-s hide from s.o.

განმარტავს gan-*marṭ*-av-s explain

სიტყვას განმარტავს define (a word)

დარეკავს da=*reḳ*-av-s ring

დაურეკავს telephone s.o. (id.o.) (NB: this verb occurs without a direct object.)

განსაზღვრავს gan+*sazğvr*-av-s define

შეუტევს še=u-*ṭev*-s attack (only id.o.; no d.o.)

აქებს a-*k*-eb-s: pr.=fut. (fut. შე=აქებს also used) praise. უქებს pr.=fut. (fut. შე=უქებს also used) praise s.o.'s (dat.).

იყიდის: ყიდულობს i-*qid*-i-s: qidulob-s buy (conditional იყიდდა or იყიდიდა; conjunctive იყიდდეს or იყიდიდეს)

უყიდის (rel. form of იყიდის, pr. ყიდულობს) u-*qid*-i-s (pr.=fut.) buy sthg. for s.o.

მიჰყიდის mi=h-*qid*-i-s (mo-: see sec. 7.2.4) sell to s.o. (impf./cond. (მი)ჰყიდდა or (მი)ჰყიდიდა; conj. (მი)ყიდდეს or (მი)ჰყიდიდეს)

გაყიდის ga=*qid*-i-s sell (impf./cond. (გა)ყიდდა or (გა)ყიდიდა; conj. (გა)ყიდდეს or (გა)ყიდიდეს)

გააჩერებს ga=a-*čer*-eb-s stop

ააშენებს a=a-*šen*-eb-s build

შეაშინებს še=a-*šin*-eb-s frighten

-c-, *-cem-* see sec. 7.3.4. give

იცნობს Ø=i-*cn*-ob-s 1: know, be acquainted with, Fr. *connaître* Ger. *kennen*. (Pr. series only) 2: recognize (aor. (ვ)იცანი(თ), იცნო, იც(ვ)ნეს)

გააცნობს ga=a-*cn*-ob-s introduce s.o. to s.o. (make acquainted) (aor. irr. გა(ვ)აცანი(თ), გააცნო, გააც(ვ)ნეს).

a-*jlev*-s	see -*cem*-	
მისწერს:მოსწერს	mi=s-*c̣er*-s (mo-: see sec. 7.2.4)	write to s.o.
აუწერს	a+u-*c̣er*-s**	describe to s.o.
დაეხმარება	da=e-*xmar*-eb-a	help s.o. (dat.); relative II. conj. only.

*Henceforth (H-) will indicate that indirect objects are marked by the *h*-series of markers.

**Note that with *u*-series markers the preverb is *a+*, not *ağ+*.

Key to the Exercises

1. I shall see you tomorrow at the university.
2. Does Ketevan know you? Yes, she knows me very well. Diṭo introduced us (to) each other (d.o.) last year in Sochi.
3. Mike, where are you? I can't see you among [in] these people.
4. Our professor praised us because we wrote him a very long letter.
5. [You all] write us more often and we won't forget you!
6. Ms. Rusudan, come in. The doctor will receive you now.
7. Children, don't forget our country's war heroes!
8. We have to send a short review of this new novel to our professor of English literature.
9. Friends, help me, please! We shall help you with great pleasure.
10. I will send you money. Go to the store and please buy me several new shirts.
11. When we study Georgian language our good Georgian friends help us very [much].
12. I have to buy father a Georgian-English dictionary, because he soon will go to visit England.
13. When he will be in London he must telephone our good friends Michael and Vera.
14. Can I help you all? Yes, please. I have to buy a dress for my wife.
15. My wife bought me a necktie.
16. Whom do you see in the mirror? I see myself!
17. John is sending a gift to his good friend in Yerevan.
18. Hide the money from the thieves! Hide [yourself] from the thieves.
19. The man to whom I sent the letter was waiting for me at [in] the station.
20. The man who saw you at the station telephoned me yesterday.
21. The man whom you saw at the station will telephone you tomorrow.
22. My grandfather himself built his own house. He built the house where I was born for his son (id. o.).
23. Our parents sent us several interesting books and magazines. Then you must write your parents a long letter.
24. For whom are you all waiting? We are waiting for Elguǯa and Rusudan.
25. Where were you all? I was waiting for you all at the station.

26. When you will telephone me I shall describe myself to you so that when you see me at the station you will know [will know me] who I am.
27. My sister sent me this blue pen with which I am writing you. I must send her a gift, because soon it will be her birthday [birth's day].
28. I cannot help myself. Others must help that one who cannot help himself.
29. Did John telephone his brothers? No, he telephoned their neighbor, because they were not at home.
30. The general ordered his army to cross [go across] (use VN) the border (+ -*ze*).
31. I cannot see you all without glasses, my dear friends.
32. When I was at the embassy of the Soviet Union, I explained the matter to the ambassador. He wrote to his government in order to get more information.
33. Do you know each other? Of course, I know Vano and Vano knows me! We are very good friends and we often visit each other [are often at each other's place as guest (adv.)].
34. In order to read old Georgian texts knowledge of *xucuri* is necessary.
35. At the airport it is possible for you to buy presents for your grandchildren without duty.
36. At Tbilisi main station you can buy cigarettes very cheaply.
37. Don't wait for us any longer! I must go to the city in order to buy a new necktie.
38. Your cat frightened me when it suddenly entered the room. But now, nothing astonishes me any more.
39. When a border guard stopped us at the Turkish border [Turkey's border], this was surprising for us.
40. I shall stop this young man on the street. Perhaps he might define this Georgian word for me. But he is a foreigner and can't define the word.
41. Grandfather and grandmother will send you all a beautiful Georgian rug. (Note that there is no formal distinction between *they will send you* and *they will send you all*.)
42. Define the word grandfather for me! Grandfather means father's father or mother's father.
43. Describe your house to me! It is a small house in which there are four rooms: a kitchen, a living room (lit., guest, adj. form with *sa-.....-o*), a dining room and a bedroom.
44. For whom did Mr. Aḳaḳi build a house? He built

it for his children.

45. The general ordered us to cross the border at night in order to unexpectedly attack the enemy's army.
46. Read this letter to me please. I shall read it to you with great pleasure.
47. How many books did your uncle send you? He sent me six books. I must write him a letter now.
48. The shepherds hid from the enemy in the mountains during the war.
49. Professor: You all must prepare the third lesson's exercises for me. Students: Yes, sir [mister] we shall prepare these exercises for you.
50. In order to understand this question, you all must read my new book.
51. To whom will this letter be sent? This one will be sent to the city council.
52. This palace was built for the king.
53. Father will wash the child's (id.o.) face tomorrow, today however mother washed his [to him] (id.o.) face.
54. Whom did the priest praise? He praised his bishop. The bishop however praised the priest's (id. o.) sons.
55. For whom did you buy this bottle [of] vodka? I bought it for myself. The salesman sold it to me. He also sold John a [one] bottle [of] vodka. (In this construction ბოთლი is treated like an adjective modifying არაყი. The construction is somewhat reminiscent of German *eine Flasche Schnapps*.)
56. If you all will give me money, I shall buy you all this new record of Georgian popular [stage] music.
57. Don't buy (pl.) me the record of popular music. I will give you all the money; buy me a record of Georgian folk music. The salesman will sell it to me with great pleasure. In his store they sell popular and folk music records.
58. Don't give me the money now. When I give you all the record, then give me the money. So it will be easier [more easy].
59. Give Givi (dat.) the money! I already gave him 15 rubles. How much? Fifteen rubles and 20 copecks.
60. Let's give these poor people money! How much? You must give them as much as [that much as much] is possible.
61. Vano gave that student 9 rubles and 10 copecks. You must give this student money, too.
62. I must help my father; he will write his uncle,

who sent us a large package from Leningrad.

63. Georgia was united to tsarist Russia (id.o.) in 1801.
64. We shall see each other at the meeting tomorrow. At which meeting? At that meeting about which I wrote you.
65. Your trousers are too short; your legs have become longer.
66. The keys which your mother gave you, give to us please.
67. For whom (ვისთვის) was this banquet prepared? The students prepared it for their professor.
68. This chair was made for my grandmother in London.

Reading Passage

ქუთაისი

1 საქართველოს სს რესპუბლიკის მეორე ინდუსტრიულ ცენტრს წარმოადგენს ქალაქი ქ უ თ ა ი ს ი. იგი ერთ-ერთი უძველესი ქალაქია არა მარტო ამიერკავკასიაში, არამედ მთელ მსოფლიოშიც. ქალაქის წარმოშობის ისტორიის ზოგიერთი მკვლევარის აზრით, თანამედროვე ქუთაისის ქვეშ 3500 წლის წინათ არსებულ ქალაქს სძინავს.

2 ერთ-ერთი უძველესი წერილობითი ცნობა ქუთაისის შესახებ მოცემული აქვს ბიზანტიელ ისტორიკოს პროკოფი კესარიელს ახ. წ. VI ს. შუა წლებში. VII--VIII სს. ქუთაისში მოთავსებული ყოფილა მეფეთა განძთსაცავი. XI ს. დასაწყისიდან ქუთაისი საქართველოს სამეფო ქალაქს წარმოადგენდა. ქუთაისიდან სამეფო ტახტი ქალაქ თბილისში დავით აღმაშენებელმა გადმოიტანა. სამეფო ტახტის თბილისში გადმოტანა გამოწვეული იყო იმით, რომ ამ უკანასკნელს ახალი ვითარებისათვის უკეთესი სტრატეგიული მნიშვნელობა ჰქონდა, ვიდრე ქუთაისს.

3 XI—XII სს. პირველ მეოთხედში ქუთაისი წარმოადგენდა მძლავრი ფეოდალური სახელმწიფოს პოლიტიკურ-ეკონომიკურ და კულტურულ ცენტრს. ამ პერიოდში შეიქმნა აქ ქართული კლასიკური არქიტექტურის თვალწარმტაცი ძეგლი — ბაგრატის ტაძარი, რომელიც ამჟამად ნანგრევების სახით არსებობს; გელათის მონასტერი, რომელიც ასევე ქართული არქიტექტურისა და ხელოვნების უშესანიშნავესი ძეგლია, გელათის აკადემია და სხვ.

4 სამეფო ტახტის ქუთაისიდან თბილისში გადატანის შემდეგაც, ვაჭრობისა და ხელოსნობის განვითარების დონის მიხედვით, ქუთაისი მაინც ფეოდალური ეპოქის ერთ-ერთ უმნიშვნელოვანეს ქალაქად რჩება. ქ. ქუთაისის მნიშვნელობას ფეოდალური საქართველოსათვის აძლიერებდა, ჯერ ერთი, მისი ხელსაყრელი მდებარეობა დასავლეთ საქართველოს ცალკეული კუთხეებისადმი და, მეორეც, ის, რომ ქუთაისი შედარებით უკეთესად იყო დაცული აღმოსავლეთიდან შემოსეული მტრებისაგან. XV ს. 70 წლებში ვენეციის ელჩი ამბროზი კონტარინი წერდა: „9 ივლისს მივედი პატარა ქალაქ ქუთაისს. აქ მცირე გორაზე არის ციხე სულ ქვითკირისა. შიგ ციხეში ეკლესია არის, როგორც ეტყობა, ძლიერ ძველი“. ამ პერიოდისათვის ქუთაისი მცირე ქალაქს წარმოადგენდა, რადგან იგი მტრების გამუდმებულმა შემოსევებმა, განსაკუთრებით კი თემურლენგის ურდოებმა, დაქვეითების გზაზე დააყენეს.

5 რუსეთის ელჩების ს. ტოლოჩანოვისა და დ. იევლევის მიერ მოწოდებული ცნობებით, XVII ს. მეორე ნახევარში ქუთაისში 1000 კომლი ცხოვრობდა. მიუხედავად იმისა, რომ ამ დროს ქუთაისი ეკონომიკურად დაქვეითებული იყო, ადგილობრივი ვაჭრები ეკონომიკურ ურთიერთობას არ წყვეტდნენ საქართველოს დანარჩენ სამთავროებთან და მეზობელ ქვეყნებთანაც კი.

6 1668 წლიდან დაწყებული 1770 წლამდე ქუთაისის ერთი ნაწილი — ეგრეთ წოდებული „დიდი ქუთაისი“ („დიდი ქუთაისი“ ეწოდებოდა მაღალ გორაზე, მდ. რიონის მარჯვენა მხარეზე, გაშენებულ ქალაქს, ხოლო „პატარა ქუთაისი“ დაბლობ ვაკეზე, მდ. რიონის მარცხენა ნაპირზე, განლაგებულ ქალაქს) თურქების ბატონობის მძიმე უღლის ქვეშ გმინავდა. მათ გაანადგურეს ქალაქის მოსახლეობა, ეკონომიკა. ი. ა. გვილდენშტეტის ცნობით, 1772 წ. ქუთაისში 50 კომლიღა ცხოვრობდა.

Vocabulary

1

ქუთაისი	Kutaisi (city in Western Georgia)
სს	საბჭოთა სოციალისტური
წარმო+ადგენს	be; represent (present series only)
ერთ-ერთი	one (of several) (+ sing.)
უძველესი	very old; ancient; oldest
მარტო	only
მთელი	whole; entire [usually (E)]
მსოფლიო	world
წარმოშობა	origin
მკვლევარი	investigator (A)
აზრით	in the opinion of (pp) (cf. აზრი thought, idea, opinion)
თანამედროვე	contemporary
ქვეშ	under (pp)
3500	სამი ათას ხუთასი
არსებული	existing; here: 'a city which existed 3500 years ago'
[სძინავს]	it (dat.) sleeps

2

[ცნობა]	here: report
[მოცემული აქვს]	he (dat.) has given something (nom.)
ბიზანტიელი	Byzantine
პროკოპი-	Procopius
კესარიელი	from Caesaria
ახ. წ.	ახალი წელთაღრიცხვით,A.D.
ს.	საუკუნის
შუა	middle
VII-VIII სს.	მეშვიდე-მერვე საუკუნეების
[მოთავსებული ყოფილა]	had been located
განძთსაცავი	treasury

დასაწყისი	beginning
სამეფო	royal (cf. მეფე king)
ტახტი	throne
გადმოიტანს	move; transfer (present tense irregular; see 12.1.3)
გამოწვეული	caused
იმით რომ	here: by the fact that
უკანასკნელი	last; here: the latter
ვითარება	circumstance
უკეთესი	better
სტრატეგიული	strategic
მნიშვნელობა	significance
[ჰქონდა]	it (dat.) had it (nom.)
ვიდრე ქუთაისს	than Kutaisi (ქუთაისს is in the dative because the verb ჰქონდა [see above] is understood)

3

მეოთხედი	quarter
მძლავრი	powerful
ფეოდალური	feudal
შე=ქმნის	create (aor. შე(ვ)ქმენი(თ), შექმნა, შექმნეს, opt. შე(ვ)ქმნა(თ), შექმნას, შექმნან)
თვალწარმტაცი	beautiful, charming
ძეგლი	monument
ბაგრატი	(a king of Georgia)
ტაძარი	cathedral
ამჟამად	at present
ნანგრევები	ruins [pl.]
სახით	in the form of [pp.]
[არსებობს]	exists
გელათი	(town in Georgia)
ასევე	just such
უშესანიშნავესი	(a) most notable

და სხვ. = და სხვა etc.

4

გადატანა transfer [VN] **შემდეგაც** even after

ვაჭრობა trade

ხელოსნობა craft(s)

განვითარება development

დონე level

მაინც still

ეპოქა epoch

უმნიშვნელოვანესი most important

[რჩება] remains (+ adv.)

ქ. ქალაქ

მნიშვნელობას here: = d.o. of აძლიერებდა

გა=აძლიერებს strengthen (Note: subjects follow this verb; see below.)

ჯერ ერთი in the first place

ხელსაყრელი advantageous

მდებარეობა situation (NB: subject of აძლიერებდა)

დასავლეთ საქართველო Western Georgia (დასავლეთ is not declined)

ცალკეული separate, isolated; various (i.e., various other)

კუთხე region; district; corner

-დმი with relation to [pp.]

ის, რომ here: the fact that (NB: subject of აძლიერებდა)

შედარებით comparatively

დაცული defended

შემოსეული invading

70 სამოცდაათ(იან)

ვენეცია Venice

ქუთაისს ქუთაისში

პატარა little (nontruncating)

მცირე small

გორა	hill
ციხე	fortress
სულ	here: entirely; completely
ქვითკირი	stone-and-mortar
შიგ	inside
[როგორც ეტყობა]	to all appearances
ძლიერ	very
რადგან	because
იგი	it; here = d.o. of დააყენებს
გამუდმებული	constant
შემოსევა	invasion [VN]
განსაკუთრებით	particularly
თემურლენგი	Tamerlane
ურდო	horde
დაქვეითება	decline [VN]
და=აყენებს	here: bring to
5	
მოწოდებული	communicated (მიერ by)
ნახევარი	half (A)
1000	ათასი
კომლი	household; farm
[ცხოვრობდა]	was/were living
მიუხედავად ამისა	in spite of this (Note that მიუხედავად 'in spite of' occurs as both preposition and postposition.)
ამ დროს	at this time
[დაქვეითებული იყო]	had declined
ადგილობრივი	local
ვაჭარი	merchant (A)
ურთიერთობა	relation
გა=წყვეტს	interrupt; break off (aor. E → I)
დანარჩენი	remaining
სამთავრო	principality
მეზობელი	neighbor(ing) (E)

-ც კი — even ... too

6

1668 — ათას ექვსას სამოცდარვა

...-იდან დაწყებული — from ... on

1770 — ათას შვიდას სამოცდაათ

ეგრეთ წოდებული — so called

[ეწოდება] — s.o./sthg. (dat.) is named/called sthg. (nom.) (only present series)

მაღალი — high; tall (A)

მდ. — მდინარე river

რიონი — (river in West Georgia)

მარჯვენა — right (E) (as opposed to left)

მხარე — side

გაშენებული — built

ხოლო — but; while; and (ეწოდებოდა [see above] is the understood verb in this clause)

დაბლობი — lowland

ვაკე — plain

მარცხენა — left (as opposed to right)

ნაპირი — shore; bank

განლაგებული — laid out; placed

ბატონობა — domination

მძიმე — heavy; harsh

უღელი — yoke (E)

[გმინავს] — groan

მათ — they; them (erg., dat., gen. pl.)

გა=ანადგურებს — destroy

მოსახლეობა — population

ეკონომიკა — economy

ი. ა. გიულდენშტედტი — J.A. Güldenstädt (1745-1781)

ცნობით — by means of a report

1772 წ. — ათას შვიდას სამოცდათორმეტ წელს

50 — ორმოცდაათი

-ღა — only

LESSON 8

8.1. Third conjugation. The third conjugation[1] contains mainly intransitive verbs (although a not insignificant number can take direct objects) which denote *ongoing activities*.[2] Since the focus is on the activity itself and not on its start, end, or results, III. conjugation verbs do not distinguish aspect as do I. and II. conjugation verbs. III. conjugation verbs most commonly denote denominal activities (see sec. 8.3.1), motion, emission of light or noise, and phenomena of weather.

In their formation and in their syntax III. conjugation verbs pattern almost identically to I. conjugation verbs except that they do not form their future series screeves (and, consequently, their aorist series screeves, based, as in the I. and II. conjugations, on the future stem) by means of preverbs. They use rather a circumfix *i-.....-eb-*.

8.1.1. Formation of III. conjugation screeves. Unlike I. and II. conjugation verbs, where our dictionary entry form is the 3sg. *future* (from which the present series screeves are derived by dropping the preverb), the dictionary entry form for III. conjugation forms will be the 3sg. *present* tense. III. conjugation verbs can have no present stem formant (root verbs) or can have the PSFs *-i*, *-av*, *-eb*, or *-ob* (the last mentioned, *-ob*, is the most common; see sec. 8.3.1).

8.1.2. Present series screeves. The present, imperfect, and conjunctive present series screeves are formed identically to I. conjugation verbs for all III. conjugation verbs except those with PSF *-i*. This means that the screeve endings are:

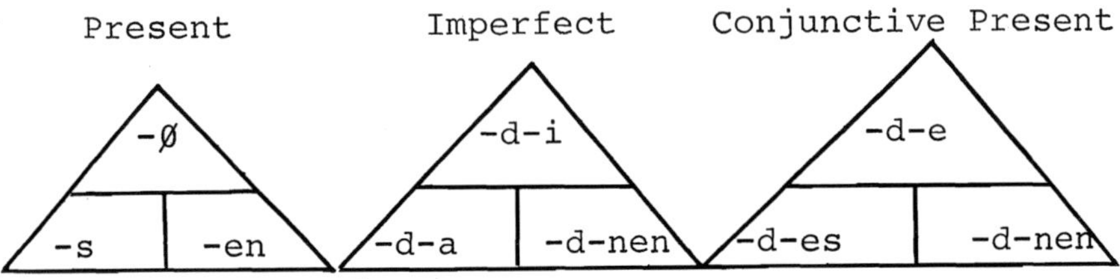

Verbs with PSF *-i* take the 3pl. ending *-an* in the present (just as in I. conjugation verbs). In the imperfect and conjunctive present these verbs (*unlike* I. conjugation verbs in *-i*) lose the PSF *-i* and take the II. conjugation screeve endings, i.e., with *-od-* instead of *-d-*. For examples, see sec. 8.1.6.

8.1.3. Future series screeves. The future, conditional, and conjunctive future are formed by:

(a) dropping any PSF,
(b) adding the circumfix *i-.....-eb*,
(c) adding the regular I. conjugation screeve endings.

The future screeve series of III. conjugation verbs are conjugated exactly as regular I. conjugation verbs in *-eb*. For examples, see below, sec. 8.1.6.[3]

8.1.4. Aorist series screeves. The aorist and optative of III. conjugation verbs are formed from the *future stem* according to exactly the same rules as for the formation of the aorist series screeves of regular I. conjugation verbs (with P/FSF *-eb*); these rules were given in sec. 5.3.1.

8.1.5. The subject case of III. conjugation verbs is the same as for I. conjugation verbs. In the present and future series the subject is in the *nominative* (and any direct object is in the dative); in the aorist series the subject is in the *ergative* (and any direct objects are in the nominative).

8.1.6. Examples. Forms given for each screeve are: (a) 1-2 sing. and pl., (b) 3 sing., and (c) 3 pl.

	Root	-*av*
Present	(ვ)ყეფ(თ)	(ვ)გორავ(თ)
	ყეფს ყეფენ	გორავს გორავენ
Imperfect	(ვ)ყეფდი(თ)	(ვ)გორავდი(თ)
	ყეფდა ყეფდნენ	გორავდა გორავდნენ
Conj. Pres	(ვ)ყეფდე(თ)	(ვ)გორავდე(თ)
	ყეფდეს ყეფდნენ	გორავდეს გორავდნენ
Future	(ვ)იყეფებ(თ)	(ვ)იგორებ(თ)
	იყეფებს იყეფებენ	იგორებს იგორებენ
Conditional	(ვ)იყეფებდი(თ)	(ვ)იგორებდი(თ)
	იყეფებდა იყეფებდნენ	იგორებდა იგორებდნენ
Conj. Fut.	(ვ)იყეფებდე(თ)	(ვ)იგორებდე(თ)
	იყეფებდეს იყეფებდნენ	იგორებდეს იგორებდნენ
Aorist	(ვ)იყეფე(თ)	(ვ)იგორე(თ)
	იყეფა იყეფეს	იგორა იგორეს
Optative	(ვ)იყეფო(თ)	(ვ)იგორო(თ)

	იყეფოს იყეფონ qep-s 'bark'	იგოროს იგორონ gor-av-s 'roll' intrans.
	-eb	*-i*
Present	(ვ)ტრიალებ(თ) ტრიალებს ტრიალებენ	(ვ)ტირი(თ) ტირის ტირიან
Imperfect	(ვ)ტრიალებდი(თ) ტრიალებდა ტრიალებდნენ	(ვ)ტიროდი(თ) ტიროდა ტიროდნენ
Conj. Pres.	(ვ)ტრიალებდე(თ) ტრიალებდეს ტრიალებდნენ	(ვ)ტიროდე(თ) ტიროდეს ტიროდნენ
Future	(ვ)იტრიალებ(თ) იტრიალებს იტრიალებენ	(ვ)იტირებ(თ) იტირებს იტირებენ
Conditional	(ვ)იტრიალებდი(თ) იტრიალებდა იტრიალებდნენ	(ვ)იტირებდი(თ) იტირებდა იტირებდნენ
Conj. Fut.	(ვ)იტრიალებდე(თ) იტრიალებდეს იტრიალებდნენ	(ვ)იტირებდე(თ) იტირებდეს იტირებდნენ
Aorist	(ვ)იტრიალე(თ) იტრიალა იტრიალეს	(ვ)იტირე(თ) იტირა იტირეს
Optative	(ვ)იტრიალო(თ) იტრიალოს იტრიალონ	(ვ)იტირო(თ) იტიროს იტირონ
	ṭrial-eb-s 'turn' intrans.	ṭir-i-s 'cry'

-ob

Present	(ვ)ცხოვრობ(თ) ცხოვრობს ცხოვრობენ

Imperfect	(ვ)ცხოვრობდი(თ)	
	ცხოვრობდა	ცხოვრობდნენ
Conj. Pres.	(ვ)ცხოვრობდე(თ)	
	ცხოვრობდეს	ცხოვრობდნენ
Future	(ვ)იცხოვრებ(თ)	
	იცხოვრებს	იცხოვრებენ
Conditional	(ვ)იცხოვრებდი(თ)	
	იცხოვრებდა	იცხოვრებდნენ
Conj. Fut.	(ვ)იცხოვრებდე(თ)	
	იცხოვრებდეს	იცხოვრებდნენ
Aorist	(ვ)იცხოვრე(თ)	
	იცხოვრა	იცხოვრეს
Optative	(ვ)იცხოვრო(თ)	
	იცხოვროს	იცხოვრონ

cxovr-ob-s
'live'

8.1.7. Verbal nouns of III. conjugation verbs. As a rule, most III. conjugation verbs in *-av*, *-ob*, and root verbs form the verbal noun regularly, as in sec. 2.5. But verbs of these classes may have irregular verbal nouns. Such irregular formations will be indicated in the vocabularies. Examples:

ცურავს	swim	ცურვა	swimming
ყეფს	bark	ყეფა	barking
მუშაობს	work	მუშაობა	work
მეფობს	reign	მეფობა	reign
ცეკვავს	dance	ცეკვა	dance; dancing (sec. 1.11.1)
ყარაულობს	stand watch	ყარაულობა	watch

Examples of irregular formations are:

დუღს	boil	დუღილი	boiling
ლაპარაკობს	speak	ლაპარაკი	speaking
თამაშობს	play	თამაში, თამაშობა	playing
ცხოვრობს	live	ცხოვრება	life

III. conjugation verbs with PSF *-i* are often irregular although there is a tendency to form the verbal noun with the suffix *-il-i* (or, less commonly, *-ol-a*). Some such verbs will take an *-l-* in the future; such verbs will be indicated in the vocabulary. Examples:

ტირის	cry	ტირილი	crying
ყვირის	shout	ყვირილი	shouting
მღერის	sing	მღერა	singing
იცინის	laugh	გაცინება or სიცილი	laughing
იბრძვის fut. იბრძოლებს	fight	ბრძოლა	battle; fighting
ყივის fut. იყივლებს	crow	ყივილი	crowing

III. conjugation verbs with PSF *-eb* (which usually denote movement or noises) generally form the verbal noun by dropping the PSF *-eb* and simply adding the regular case endings to the resultant stem. Examples are:

ტრიალებს	turn, whirl	ტრიალი
ზუზუნებს	hum, buzz	ზუზუნი
ხიხინებს	speak hoarsely	ხიხინი

8.2. Relative forms of III. conjugation verbs. Just as I. and II. conjugation verbs, so III. conjugation verbs can take indirect objects. Such will be called *relative III. conjugation verbs*. Generally, if the relative form is derived from an absolute (i.e., objectless) III. conjugation verb, the *u*-series object markers are used. Examples:

მეზობლის ძაღლი ყოველთვის ყეფს.	The neighbor's dog always barks.
მეზობლის ძაღლი ხშირად მიყეფს.	The neighbor's dog often barks at me.
სოპრანო მშვენივრად მღერის.	The soprano sings beautifully.
დედა ქალიშვილს უმღეროდა.	Mother was singing to her daughter.

In the future and aorist series the preradical vowel *i-* of the absolute forms is replaced by *u*-series object markers: მიყეფებს, მიყეფა; უმღერებს, უმღერა.

Another, smaller group of III. conjugation verbs

takes the *h*-series object markers in the present series and the *u*-series in the future and aorist series. Such verbs by their very meaning generally imply the presence of someone in addition to the subject and as a rule occur only rarely as absolute III. conjugation verbs (and then only in the present series). Examples:

მამაჩემს ყოველთვის თავაზიანად ვპასუხობ.	I always answer my father politely.
თავის მეგობარს უპასუხა.	He answered his friend.
გივი ციხეს პყარაულობს.	Givi is guarding the fortress.
გივი ციხეს უყარაულებს.	Givi will guard the fortress.

8.3.0. Wordbuilding. Derived III. conjugation forms and derivatives of III. conjugation verbs.

8.3.1. III. conjugation denominatives. Just as I. conjugation verbs can be derived from nouns and adjectives by means of the circumfix *a-.....-eb* (sec. 3.5), so III. conjugation verbs can be derived from nominal forms by means of the suffix (PSF) *-ob*. Such denominatives generally have the meaning of 'doing the activities of the noun', 'be doing the things that such a person normally does', 'be behaving like such a person', etc. In certain instances the meaning can be 'pretending to be such a person'. Examples are:

რეჟისორი	director	რეჟისორობს	work as a director
ექიმი	doctor (medical)	ექიმობს	work as a doctor
მეციჩარა	obnoxious (A)	მეციჩრობს	be acting obnoxiously
ფრთხილი	careful	ფრთხილობს	be careful
ფილოსოფოსი	philosopher	ფილოსოფოსობს	philosophize (derogatory)
ბიჭი	boy	ბიჭობს	be a tomboy

8.3.2. Causatives formed from III. conjugation verbs. Transitive I. conjugation verbs can be derived from III. conjugation verbs by changing the preradical vowel *i-* of the *future* tense of the III. conjugation to *a-*. This change will result in the *present and future* tenses of the I. conjugation verb, which does not normally have a preverb in the future.[4] These I. conjugation forms are conjugated exactly as regular I. conjugation verbs with circumfix *a-.....-eb*; i.e., they pattern exactly as denominatives (sec. 3.5). Examples:

III. conj.		I. conj. (Fut. and pres.)	
მღერის:	sing	ამღერებს	have s.o. sing
იმღერებს		a-mǧer-eb-s	
ლაპარაკობს:	speak	ალაპარაკებს	have, let s.o. speak
ილაპარაკებს			
დუღს:	boil	ადუღებს	boil sthg.
იდუღებს			
ტირის:	cry	ატირებს	make s.o. cry
იტირებს			

8.3.3. Causatives of I. conjugation verbs prefixed with *a+* (see note 4 above) can have II. conjugation derivatives (II. conjugation in *-d-*; see 3.1.2) which have the meaning of a change of state, normally equivalent to English 'begin to ...', 'start ...-ing'. The regular II. conjugation in *-d-* forms corresponding to the transitive I. conjugation forms above (8.3.2) are:

ამღერდება	will begin to sing (a+mǧer-d-eb-a)
ალაპარაკდება	will start speaking
ადუღდება	will start boiling
ატირდება	will start to cry; burst into tears

8.3.4. The comitative. A number of III. conjugation verbs have relative II. conjugation forms in *e-* (see sec. 7.3.1), where the indirect object generally corresponds to English prepositional phrases with 'with'. To form such comitatives:

1. Change the preradical vowel of the *future* of the III. conjugation verb from *i-* to *e-*;
2. Add the endings of the II. conjugation to the future stem of the III. conjugation verb;
3. Add the *h*-series indirect object markers.

Such derived relative II. conjugation forms have identical future and present series (i.e., they do not form the future from the present by means of a preverb).[5] The aorist series is formed from the future (=present) by the same rules as for any other II. conjugation verbs. Examples are:

ლაპარაკობს:	speak	ელაპარაკება	speak to s.o.
ილაპარაკებს			

ომობს: იომებს	war	ეომება	war with (against) s.o.
თამაშობს: ითამაშებს	play	ეთამაშება	play with (against) s.o.
მუსაიფობს: იმუსაიფებს	converse	ემუსაიფება	converse with s.o.
საუბრობს: ისაუბრებს	converse	ესაუბრება	converse with s.o.

8.4. Irregular verb *say* (verbal noun:) თქმა. The Georgian verb meaning *say* has different stems depending upon the series the verb is in. Present series forms are based on the present tense form ამბობს. Future series forms are based on the future იტყვის. (იტყვის is conjugated like ტირის; in the conditional the form is იტყოდა and in the conjunctive, იტყოდეს [see sec. 1.11.1]). The aorist series is based on the aorist form თქვა. The aorist endings, however, are

i.e., (ვ)თქვი(თ)

თქვა თქვეს

The optative has the endings

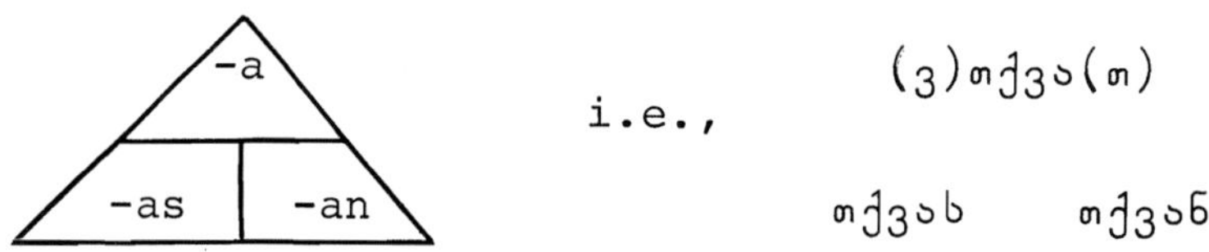

i.e., (ვ)თქვა(თ)

თქვას თქვან

Relative forms of this verb, with the meaning of 'say to someone', 'tell someone' also show irregularities. In addition to the expected უამბობს there is a present series based on the form ეუბნება (II. conjugation with *e*-series markers); the future series is based on ეტყვის (conjugated as იტყვის above, with *e*-series markers).

The aorist is: (ვ)უთხარი(თ)

უთხრა უთხრეს

The optative is: (ვ)უთხრა(თ)

უთხრას უთხრან

(The aorist series forms take *u*-series markers; note

the syncope in the third person aorist forms and throughout the optative.) The subject of aorist series forms of these verbs is in the ergative, the direct object in the nominative, and (for უთხრა) the indirect object in the dative.■[p. 215]

Summary of forms:	say	tell someone; say to someone
Present series	ამბობს	ეუბნება, უამბობს
Future series	იტყვის	ეტყვის
Aorist series	თქვა	უთხრა

8.5. Indirect speech. When someone's words are being reported in Georgian the tense of the original words is preserved *as well as the person markings*. Thus, if John says "I will come tomorrow" in English both the tense and the person are changed: John said that *he would* come tomorrow. In Georgian, however, the tense and person remain unchanged: John said that *I will* come tomorrow (*I* referring to John). The last word of the reported speech has the particle ო attached to it. So, if John says ხვალ მოვალ, then the reported sentence would be: ივანემ თქვა, ხვალ მოვალო. -ო is used with all persons except the first person singular, which uses the marker მეთქი, attached with a hyphen to the end of the reported sentence. Examples:

ილიკომ თქვა, სოსომ ყველაფერი გაიგოო.

Iliḳo said that Soso understood everything.

ხომ მითხარი, ხვალ წერილი გამოქვეყნდებაო?

You told me, didn't you, that the letter will be published tomorrow?

ვთქვი, ადრე მოვბრუნდები-მეთქი.

I said that I would return early.

ქალაქში მიდიხარ-მეთქი? არა, ახლა სოფელში მივდივარო.

Are you going to town? (said I); No, now I'm going to the country (said he).

The particle -ო is also used with printed reports, thoughts, and especially commonly, at the end of proverbs (and sections of proverbs). Examples:

ყველა საქმე ქვეყანაზე რიგდება, ცოლ-ქმრობა კი

ზეცაშიო.

All affairs are arranged on earth, marriage, however, in heaven.

სხვა გზებიც არსებობს.

Other ways also exist (literal), i.e., There's more than one way to skin a cat.

The conjunction რომ is usually not used with *-ო*. When it is used after verbs of speaking, there is often, as in English, both a change in pronouns and a change in tense *(sequence of tenses)*. (Sentences without sequence of tenses are also found.) Examples:

Direct speech:

მან თქვა, „ხვალ კინოში წავალ."

He said, "I shall go to the movies tomorrow."

Indirect speech:

a. with *-ო*

მან თქვა, ხვალ კინოში წავალო.

He said he (1st person) would go (future) to the movies tomorrow.

b. with რომ

მან თქვა, რომ მომდევნო დღეს კინოში წავიდოდა.

He said that he (3d person) would go (conditional) to the movies on the following day.

-ო can also be used to ask about or relate a third person's words. In such instances, the verb of saying (usually თქვა) is deleted but its subject (in the ergative) remains in the sentence. So, for example:

გულიამ რა მინდაო?	What did Gulia [say] she wants?
რეზომ აქედან არ წაიღოთ ეს წიგნიო?	[Did] Rezo [say] we shouldn't take this book from here?
მანანამ ჩემი წიგნი მომეციო.	Manana [said] you should give her her [sic!] book.

Note that in the above sentences the verb of saying is deleted but its subject in the ergative remains. Note that here, too, the pronouns that would occur in *direct* speech are used.

8.6. Derivative declension. Note the following: Givi painted Arčil's picture and Zurab painted Vano's picture გივიმ არჩილის სურათი დახატა და ზურაბმა ვანოს სურათი დახატა. But both in English and in Georgian it would be more natural to say 'Givi painted Arčil's picture and Zurab (painted) Vano's'. In the latter sentence the form *Vano's* serves a double function: it is both a possessive (Geo. gen. ვანოს) and the direct object of the verb *painted* (which in Georgian would be in the nominative, ვანო).[6] In such instances Georgian uses a declined form of the genitive, the so-called derivative declension. In the example above, the nominative of the genitive would be used: გივიმ არჩილის სურათი დახატა, ზურაბმა კი ვანოსი (დახატა). The derivative declension of the genitive varies according to whether the genitive is added to a truncating stem (ending *-is*) or a nontruncating stem (ending *-s*). The following cases are found:

	truncating stems			nontruncating	
Genitive	ბიჭის	მეფის	ფანჯრის	ბრბოს	ვერას
derived:					
nominative	ბიჭისა	მეფისა	ფანჯრისა	ბრბოსი	ვერასი
ergative	ბიჭისამ	მეფისამ	ფანჯრისამ	ბრბოსმა	ვერასმა
dative	ბიჭისას	მეფისას	ფანჯრისას	ბრბოსას	ვერასას
	ბიჭი	მეფე	ფანჯარა	ბრბო	ვერა
	boy	king	window	mob	Vera

Examples:

ჩვენმა პროფესორმა საქართველოს ისტორია განიხილა, დავითისამ კი პოლიტეკონომია განიხილა.

Our professor discussed Georgia's history and David's discussed political economy.

საქართველოს დედაქალაქი თბილისია, აზერბაიჯანისა კი ბაქო.

Georgia's capital is Tbilisi and Azerbaidjan's (is) Baku.

წიგნები ვის მშობლებს მიეცი? გივისასა და მარიამისასაც მივეცი.

To whose parents did you give the books? I gave them to Givi's and Mary's also.

With verbal nouns the derivative declension dative has the meaning of 'during', 'while'.[7] Examples are:

შესვლა: შესვლისას	while entering
ხატვა: ხატვისას	while painting

8.6.1. In a sentence such as 'Tbilisi is one of the oldest cities in Europe', *one of the oldest cities* will be expressed by the stylistically marked gen. pl. (sec. 5.6) with the postposition *-gan*; ქალაქთაგან. *One*, as the subject of the sentence, should be in the nominative, but, as an adjective it should be in agreement with the phrase it modifies. This dilemma is simply resolved by declining the whole postpositional phrase, in this instance by making it nominative: თბილისი ერთი უძველესი ქალაქთაგანია. Such phrases as ერთი ქალაქთაგანი are declined like any regular consonantal stem adjective plus noun. Examples:

ერთ თქვენს მეგობართაგანს გავუგზავნე.
I sent it to one of your friends.

ორმა მისმა ძმათაგანმა ის მშვენიერი ლექსი დაწერა.
Two of his brothers wrote that beautiful poem.

8.7. Wordbuilding.

8.7.1. Derivation of adjectives from expressions of time. The suffixes *-indel-*, *-(ev)andel-*, or (if the time expression ends in *in* or *an*) *-del-* are added to expressions of time (adverbs and nouns) to form adjectives. Examples:

ხვალ	tomorrow	ხვალინდელი	tomorrow's
ღამე	night	ღამინდელი	nocturnal
ზეგ	day after tomorrow	ზეგინდელი	pertaining to the day after tomorrow
დილა	morning	დილანდელი	morning's
კვირა	Sunday	კვირანდელი	pertaining to Sunday
დღეს	today (cf. დღე day	დღევანდელი	today's
წლეულს	this year (cf. წელი year)	წლევანდელი	this year's

გუშინ	yesterday	გუშინდელი	yesterday's
შარშან	last year	შარშანდელი	last year's

8.7.2. Derivation of adverbs from expressions of time. The suffix *-obit* added to nouns denoting periods of time forms adverbs. If the suffix is added to the days of the week, the resultant meaning is equivalent to English 'on Sundays', 'on Mondays', etc. Examples:

კვირა	Sunday	კვირაობით	on Sundays[8]
ორშაბათი	Monday	ორშაბათობით	on Mondays
სამშაბათი	Tuesday	სამშაბათობით	on Tuesdays
ოთხშაბათი	Wednesday	ოთხშაბათობით	on Wednesdays
ხუთშაბათი	Thursday	ხუთშაბათობით	on Thursdays
პარასკევი	Friday	პარასკეობით	on Fridays
შაბათი	Saturday	შაბათობით	on Saturdays

With other nouns denoting periods of time the meaning of the suffix *-obit* is similar, denoting a plurality of that period of time. Examples:

ზაფხული	summer	ზაფხულობით	in summer, summers
თვე	month	თვეობით	for months
საღამო	evening	საღამოობით	in the evening, every evening
წელი	year (E)	წლობით	for years, year after year
დღე	day	დღეობით	for days, several days

■ (From p. 211)

The II. conjugation form of this verb is: present and future ითქმება or ითქმის 'it is said,' aorist ითქვა.

LESSON 8: Notes

1. III. conjugation verbs are traditionally called middle verbs (Geo. საშუალი ზმნები) or (Vogt) "neuter verbs."

2. It should be noted that as a result of this basic meaning, III. conjugation verbs most commonly occur in the screeves of the present series; screeves of the future and aorist series occur less commonly.

3. Root III. conjugation verbs ending in *en* have a different pattern; these form the future series without the FSF *-eb*, taking only the preradical vowel *i-* (*u-* in relative forms). In the aorist series the *e* of the root alternates with *i*. Examples:

Present		Future	Aorist
ჰკბენს	bite s.o., sthg.	უკბენს	უკბინა
ფრენს	fly	იფრენს	იფრინა

(ფრენს also has the present series based on the form ფრინავს. The future and aorist series are as for ფრენს.)

სტკენს (s-ṭḳen-s)	hurt s.o.	ასტკენს	ასტკინა

(Future and aorist series take the preradical vowel *a-*.)

Note also:

დის	flow	იდენს	იდინა
ლხინობს	have a good time	ილხენს	ილხინა

Irregular is the verb 'to run' which patterns in the present series similarly to the verb 'to go'; like the verb 'to go', it occurs with the directional prefixes: present: 1. -ვრბივარ(-თ), 2. -რბიხარ(-თ), 3sg. -რბის, 3pl. -რბიან; imperfect: -რბოდა, etc. The future is -ირბენს and the aorist -ირბინა. The verbal noun is რბენა or სირბილი. Examples include: მორბის 'run here', მირბის 'run there', შერბის 'run into', გადარბის 'run across', დარბის 'run around', etc.

4. Causatives of III. conjugation verbs often may take a preverb (usually *a+*) in the future and in screeves derived from the future to mark the meaning of 'cause someone/something to begin to...'. Examples are:

მღერის: sing ამღერებს have s.o. sing (pr.
იმღერებს and fut.)

		აამღერებს a+a-mğer-eb-s	have s.o. start singing
დუღს: იდუღებს	boil	ადუღებს	boil sthg.
		აადუღებს a+a-duğ-eb-s	bring sthg. to a boil

(See also sec. 8.3.3)

5. In a few instances the comitative present series is formed by adding the preradical vowel *e-* to the present tense of the III. conjugation verb; the future and aorist series of the comitative are derived from the future of the III. conjugation verb:

pr. იბრძვის	fut. იბრძოლებს	fight
pr. ებრძვის	fut. ებრძოლება	fight with s.o.

6. Note how other languages cope with this problem:
French: Guivi a peint le tableau d'Artchil et Zourab (a peint) *celui* de Vano.
German: Giwi hat Artschils Bild gemalt und Surab (hat) *das von* Wano (gemalt).

7. These forms are to be interpreted as resulting from the deletion of the postposition დროს 'during' which is the dat. case of დრო 'time'. So შესვლისას 'while entering' can be explained as coming from შესვლ-ის დროს with deletion of დროს. It should be noted that adjectives modifying a noun in the derivative declension are treated as in agreement with a genitive; e.g. ჩვენი ლაპარაკისას გივი შემოვიდა: 'While we were talking Givi entered.'

8. კვირა (which comes from the Greek *kyrios* 'lord') also means 'week'. With this meaning the derivative კვირაობით means 'for weeks', 'week after week'.

LESSON 8: Exercises

1. მოხუცმა იტირა, როცა ვუთხარი, რომ თქვენი ვაჟიშვილი ჯარში უნდა წავიდეს-მეთქი.
2. რა თქვი? —არაფერი. ამ ახალგაზრდა ქალს ველაპარაკებოდი.
3. ხვალ არ ვიმუშავებთ, ვინაიდან დღესასწაულია.
4. სად ცხოვრობ? —ბათუმში ვცხოვრობდი, მაგრამ ახლა გორში ვცხოვრობ.
5. საწოლ ოთახში შესვლისას ძაღლმა ბავშვი ატირა. დიდხანს ტიროდა, რადგანაც დედამისი სახლში კი არ იყო, არამედ მაღაზიაში მუშაობდა.
6. როცა ძაღლი დაინახა, ბავშვი უცებ ატირდა.
7. წყალი აადუღეთ, გთხოვთ. მითხარით, როდესაც წყალი ადუღდება და ჩაის მოვამზადებ.
8. წყალი დუღს? დიახ, რამდენიმე წუთის წინ ადუღდა.
9. აფხაზეთში ქართულად უნდა ილაპარაკო. —ქართულად ვლაპარაკობ, მაგრამ აფხაზურად ვერ ვლაპარაკობ. —აფხაზურ ენას თუ ბეჯითად ისწავლი, უშეცდომოდ ილაპარაკებ.
10. როცა საქართველოში თამარი მეფობდა, ინგლისის მეფეები იყვნენ რიჩარდ პირველი და ჯონი, საფრანგეთისა კი—ფილიპე მეორე.
11. საქართველოს უკანასკნელი მეფე ვინ იყო? გიორგი მეთორმეტე, რომელმაც მარტო სამ წელს იმეფა.
12. საქართველოში რომ ვცხოვრობდე, ქართულად უფრო კარგად ვილაპარაკებდი.
13. რადგანაც ხვალ დღესასწაულია, მთელ დღეს კალათბურთს ვითამაშებ.
14. ფეხბურთი ვითამაშოთ! —ვის ვეთამაშოთ?
15. როცა ჭადრაკის თამაში დავიწყეთ, ყველა დუმდა, მაგრამ როცა ვთამაშობდით (= ჩვენი თამაშისას), ზოგიერთი ლაპარაკობდა.
16. არჩილმა მითხრა, ევროპის ყველაზე მაღალი მთა იალბუზიაო. —სად არის ეს მთა? —ჩრდილო

კავკასიაში.

17. კატები კნავიან და ძაღლები ყეფენ. რა უცნაური იქნებოდა, კატა რომ ყეფდეს და ძაღლი კნაოდეს (sec. 1.11.1)!

18. როცა ძაღლი აყეფდა, ბავშვი ატირდა. დედას ვეტყვი, ტირის-მეთქი.

19. როცა საჭმელი აღარ იქნება, კატა ხმამაღლა აკნავლდება.

20. როცა გუშინ გელაპარაკებოდი, მითხარი, თამარმა ოცდაცხრა წელიწადს იმეფაო. იმ დროს, როდესაც თამარი მეფობდა, შოთა რუსთაველმა „ვეფხისტყაოსანი" დაწერა.

21. ნუ იცინით, როცა ქართულად ვლაპარაკობ. შეუძლებელია ვილაპარაკო, როცა იცინით. —აღარ ვიცინებთ. სინამდვილეში ძალიან კარგად ლაპარაკობ!

22. ვიცურაოთ! —სამწუხაროდ აქ ვერ ვიცურავებთ. აქ ცურვა აკრძალულია, ვინაიდან ეს მდინარე ძალიან საშიშია.

23. იალბუზი ევროპის ყველაზე მაღალი მთაა. საქართველოსი რომელია? საქართველოს ყველაზე მაღალი მთა ყაზბეგია.

24. ბავშვებმა იცინეს და იყვირეს, როცა მასხარები ნახეს. ნახეს დათვებიც, რომლებიც ცეკვავდნენ.

25. „ცერულს" იცნობთ? —კი, ამ ცნობილ ქართულ ცეკვას ვიცნობ. ქართველები, რომლებიც მთაში ცხოვრობენ, ცერულს ცეკვავენ.

26. სამი ქართული ანდაზა:

ვინც „ანი" თქვა, იმან „ბანიც" უნდა თქვასო.
ძაღლი ყეფს, ქარავანი მიდისო.
კატისთვის თამაშობაა, თაგვისთვის სულთა ბრძოლააო.

27. ასე ნუ ყვირით! ასე თუ იყვირებთ, უთუოდ ბავშვს გამოაღვიძებთ.

28. დღეს კონცერტზე გუნდი ქართულ ხალხურ სიმღერებს

იმღერებს. სამწუხაროდ, ვერ წავალ, რადგანაც სხვა კონცერტზე უნდა წავიდე: იმღერებენ არიებს ფალიაშვილის ცნობილი ოპერა „აბესალომ და ეთერი"-დან.*

29. მითხარი, სიტყვა „ცერული" რას ნიშნავს? —განგიმარტავ. ეს სიტყვა „ცერი"-დან მოდის. „ცერი" ადამიანის ხელისა და ფეხის პირველი, ყველაზე მსხვილი თითია. ცერული სვანური ხალხური ცეკვაა ფეხის ცერებზე. მარტო მამაკაცები ცეკვავენ.

30. უცნაურია, რადგანაც ბალეტში ფეხის თითებზე შეიძლება იცეკვონ მარტო ქალებმა.

31. სამი ქართული ანდაზა:

> თეთრი ძაღლი და შავი ძაღლი ორივე ძაღლიაო.
>
> მამალმა თქვა: ყივილი ჩემი საქმეა და გათენება—ღვთისაო.
>
> კარგი დედა მომეციო, კარგი მამაც ვიქნებიო.

32. ივანე თუ მკითხავს, სად მიდიხარო, ვუპასუხებ, არსად არ მივდივარ-მეთქი.

33. არჩილს ვინ ელაპარაკებოდა? —რუსუდანს ვჰკითხავ, რადგანაც რუსუდანი კარგად იცნობს.

34. რუსუდანმა რა გიპასუხა? —მიპასუხა, ორშაბათს დაგირეკავო.

35. რომელი საათია? —როცა ზარი აწკრიალდება, ზუსტად სამი საათი იქნება.

36. საენათმეცნიერო წრის სხდომა როდის იქნება? —მითხრეს, ოთხშაბათს ოთხ საათზე იქნებაო.

37. აგვისტოში კვირაობით ამ მდინარეში ხშირად ვცურავთ.

38. უფრო ბეჯითად რომ მუშაობდე, მეტ ფულს მიიღებდი.

39. როგორც სხვა ქვეყნებში, საბჭოთა კავშირშიც შაბათობით და კვირაობით არ მუშაობენ.

40. ნუღარ ტყუი. მუდამ სიმართლე უნდა თქვა.

41. კავკასიაში ბევრი ლეგენდა არსებობს ამირანის შესახებ. ამბობენ, ბერძენი ლეგენდარული გმირი

პრომეთე კავკასიური წარმოშობისაა და მისი პროტოტიპი ამირანია.

42. 1921 წ. (ათას ცხრაას ოცდაერთ წელს) ბოლშევიკებმა საქართველოში საბჭოთა ხელისუფლება დაამყარეს.

43. როცა ტიკინა პინოკიო ტყუის, ცხვირი უგრძელდება.

44. ოცდახუთი მანეთი მომეცით, გთხოვთ. —აი ოცდახუთი მანეთი. გმადლობთ.

45. როცა ამბობენ, ქართველები საბჭოთა კავშირის ყველაზე ლამაზ რესპუბლიკაში ცხოვრობენო, არ ტყუიან!

46. გიორგი და ელენე პაპაშვილებს იცნობ? —დიახ, ვიცნობ. ამ მწერლებმა დაწერეს იუმორისტული რომანი „Anything Can Happen." ამ რომანში აღწერენ, როგორ ჩამოვიდა გიორგი პაპაშვილი საქართველოდან ამერიკაში და მის თავგადასავალს შეერთებულ შტატებში.

47. ამას წინათ გიორგი და ელენე პაპაშვილები საქართველოში დაბრუნდნენ. წიგნში „Home and Home Again" ეს ორი ავტორი გვიამბობს თავიანთ თავგადასავალს გიორგის სამშობლოში.

48. დღევანდელ გაზეთში რა წაიკითხე? —წავიკითხე, თვეობით იქნება წყლის ნაკლებობა.

49. ხვალინდელი ამინდი როგორი იქნება? —ამბობენ, ხვალ კვლავ იწვიმებსო. გუშინწინ და გუშინ მთელ დღეს წვიმდა. დღეს ათ საათზე უცებ გაწვიმდა.

50. როცა წვიმს, ხშირად ელავს და ქუხს.

51. შარშან ზამთარში ყოველდღე თოვდა.

52. ფრინველების უმრავლესობა ფრინავს, სირაქლემა კი არა.

53. მოსკოვიდან თბილისში ხვალ გავფრინდებით.

54. ფრინველები ფრთებით ფრინავენ.

55. მრავალი ფრინველი ზამთარში სამხრეთისაკენ გაფრინდება.

56. ეს თვითმფრინავი სად გაფრინდა? ლენინგრადისაკენ

გაფრინდა.

57. იმ კაცმა რატომ მიყვირა? ის გიჟი ყველას უყვირის.

58. ჩემი მეზობელი ყოველთვის ძალიან ხმამაღლა მღერის. ამ მღერას თუ გააგრძელებს მილიციაში ვუჩივლებ.

59. დიანა, ქართული სიმღერა მიმღერე, გთხოვ! აკაკი წერეთლის „სულიკოს" გიმღერებ.

60. როდესაც საქართველოში ვიყავით, საქართველოს მეცნიერებათა აკადემიამ გვიმასპინძლა. როცა ქართველი აკადემიკოსები ამერიკაში ჩამოვლენ, ჩვენი უნივერსიტეტი უმასპინძლებს. ახლა ათ რუს პროფესორს ვმასპინძლობთ.

*In this construction, ოპერა is declined like an adjective. In a title, such as აბესალომ და ეთერი, only the final member is declined.

Vocabulary

ადამიანი	human being; person
აი	here/there is/are (cf. Fr. *voici*, *voilà*; Rus. вот)
აკადემიკოსი	academician [member of an academy]
აკრძალული	forbidden
ამას წინათ	a short time ago; recently
ანი	name of the letter ა
ანდაზა	proverb
არია	aria
ბალეტი	ballet
ბანი	name of the letter ბ
ბოლშევიკი	Bolshevik
ბრძოლა	struggle; battle
გათენება	dawn(ing) (VN)
გიჟი	crazy
გუნდი	team; choir
გუშინწინ	day before yesterday
დათვი	bear
დიდხანს	for a long time
დღესასწაული	holiday
ზამთარი	winter (A)
ზარი	bell
ზუსტი	exact
თაგვი	mouse
თავგადასავალი	adventure (A)
თავიანთი	their own (reflexive; see sec. 7.4.2.)
თვითმფრინავი	airplane
თითი	finger (ფეხის თითი toe)
იუმორისტული	humorous
კალათბურთი	basketball
კი	yes; however; and
ლეგენდარული	legendary
ლეგენდა	legend
მამაკაცი	man (male human being)
მამალი	rooster (A)
მარტო	only; alone
მასხარა	clown
მაღალი	high; tall (A)
მდინარე	river
მეცნიერება	science
მილიცია	police
მოხუცი	old man
მრავალი	many (A)
მსხვილი	thick
ნაკლებობა	lack; shortage
ოთხშაბათი	Wednesday (ოთხშაბათს on Wednesday)
ორივე	both (+ sing.)

ორშაბათი Monday (ორშაბათს on Monday)
პროტოტიპი prototype
რადგანაც for; because
როგორ? how?
როგორი? of what kind? how? (adjective)
საათი hour; watch (ორ საათზე at 2 o'clock; ორ საათს for two hours)
სამშობლო homeland (cf. მშობლები parents)
სამხრეთი south; southern
საშიში dangerous
სიმართლე truth (cf. მართალი true [A])
სიმღერა song
სინამდვილე reality (cf. ნამდვილი real; true)
სირაქლემა ostrich
სული soul
ტიკინა puppet; doll
უთუო doubtless; sure
უკანასკნელი last; the latter
უმრავლესობა majority
უცნაური strange; unknown
ფეხბურთი soccer; football (cf. ფეხი foot, leg; ბურთი ball)
ფრთა wing
ფრინველი bird
ქალი woman
ქარავანი caravan (A)
ღმერთი God (irr.: see sec. 3.2.1.1)
ყველაზე most (see sec. 9.3.2)
ყოველდღე every day
შარშან last year
შეერთებული united
შეცდომა mistake
შტატი state (in USA)
ჩაი tea (dat.= ჩაის; see Lesson 5, note 2)
ჩრდილო north(ern)
ცერი thumb; big toe
ცერული Georgian folk dance
ცხვირი nose
ძაღლი dog
წარმოშობა origin
წელიწადი year (A)(French *année* cf. წელი [French *an*])
წუთი minute
წყალი water (A)
ჭადრაკი chess
ხელისუფლება power (political)
ხმამაღალი loud (A) (cf. ხმა voice); ad-

	verb = ხმამაღლა	ამირანი	[m.]
გორი	city in Eastern Georgia	პინოქიო	Pinocchio [m.]
		პრომეთე	Prometheus [m.]
იალბუზი	Mt. Elbrus	რიჩარდი	Richard [m.]
ყაზბეგი	Mt. Kazbek	ფილიპე	Philip [m.]

Verbs

დააარსებს	da=a-*ars*-eb-s	establish
არსებობს	*arseb*-ob-s	be; exist
მიბრუნდება	mi=*brun*-d-eb-a (II. conj.)	return (intrans.)
ჩამოდის	čamo+*d*-i-s (irr.: sec. 4.5, 5.4.3)	arrive; come down; come (from a distance)
დუღს	*duǧ*-s	boil (VN დუღილი)
დუმს	*dum*-s (irr. 1. ვდუმვარ(-თ), 2. დუმხარ(-თ), 3pl. დუმან; only present series forms)	be silent (VN დუმილი)
ელავს:იელვებს	*el*-av-s: fut. i-*elv*-eb-s	(be) lightning
თამაშობს	*tamaš*-ob-s	play [games; roles] (VN თამაში, თამაშობა)
თოვს	*tov*-s	snow
tkv	see *ṭqv*	
txr	see *ṭqv*	
ჰკითხავს	*Ø=h-*ḳitx*-av-s	ask s.o. sthg.
კნავის: იკნავლებს	*ḳnav*-i-s: fut. i-*ḳnavl*-eb-s	meow (VN კნავილი)
ლაპარაკობს	*lap̣araḳ*-ob-s	speak (VN ლაპარაკი) (+ adv.)
[მადლობს]	(H-)*madl*-ob-s used only in:	
	გმადლობ(-თ)	thank you
მასპინძლობს	*masp̣injl*-ob-s	act as host

(H-) მასპინძლობს: fut. უმასპინძლებს (sec. 8.2)		act as host to s.o.
mb	see *ṭqv*	
მეფობს	*mep*-ob-s	reign
მუშაობს	*muša(v)*-ob-s, fut. იმუშავებს	work (VN მუშაობა)
მღერის	*mğer*-i-s	sing
უმღერის		sing s.o. sthg.
დაამყარებს	da=a-*mqar*-eb-s	establish; found
დაინახავს	da+i-*nax*-av-s	catch sight of; see
ჰპასუხობს: უპასუხებს	h-*p̣asux*-ob-s: fut. u-*p̣asux*-eb-s	answer s.o. (dat.)
ტირის	*ṭir*-i-s	cry
იტყვის	i-*ṭqv*-i-s (irr.; sec. 8.4) pres. ამბობს (a-*mb*-ob-s), aor. თქვა (*tkv*-a)	say
ეტყვის	e-*ṭqv*-i-s (irr.; sec. 8.4) pres. ეუბნება (e-*ubn*-eb-a), aor. უთხრა (u-*txr*-a) **	say sthg. to s.o.
ტყუის	*ṭqu(v)*-i-s	lie (tell untruths) (VN ტყუილი)
ubn	see *ṭqv*	
ფრინავს, იფრენს, იფრინა	*prin*-av-s (irr.): fut. i-*pren*-s aor. i-*prin*-a (pres. also ფრენს [see note 3])	fly
გაფრინდება	ga+*prin*-d-eb-a	fly off
ჩაფრინდება	ča+*prin*-d-eb-a	fly down; fly to

ქუხს	*kux*-s	thunder (VN ქუხილი)
გამოაღვიძებს	gamo=a-*ǧvij*-eb-s	wake s.o. up
ყეფს	*qep*-s	bark
ყვირის	*qvir*-i-s	shout (VN ყვირილი)
უყვირის		scream at s.o.
ყივის: იყივლებს	*qiv*-i-s: fut. i-*qivl*-eb-s	crow (VN ყივილი)
შეაჩერებს	še=a-*čer*-eb-s	stop (for a moment)
ჩივის: იჩივლებს	*čiv*-i-s: fut. i-*čivl*-eb-s	make a complaint, complain (VN ჩივილი)
უჩივის: უჩივლებს		complain about s.o.
ცეკვავს	*ceḳv*-av-s	dance
იცინის	i-*cin*-i-s	laugh
ცურავს	*cur*-av-s	swim
ცურაობს: იცურავებს	*cura(v)*-ob-s: i-*curav*-eb-s	swim around
ცხოვრობს	*cxovr*-ob-s	live (VN ცხოვრება)
წვიმს	*c̣vim*-s (II. conj. derivative [sec. 8.3.3] has preverb *ga+*: გა+წვიმდება)	rain
წკრიალებს	*c̣ḳrial*-eb-s	ring (of bell) (VN წკრიალი)

*I. and II. conjugation verbs which do not have a preverb in the future series will be marked with Ø=. This symbol indicates that there is no preverb in the future and that consequently the present series forms are identical to those of the future series.

**Alongside these forms, the III. conj. verb უამბობს Ø=u-*amb*-ob-s 'tell s.o. sthg.' is also found. Note the aorist: უამბო.

Key to the Exercises

1. The old man cried when I told him that his son had to enter the army [that your son has to enter the army].
2. What did you say? Nothing. I was speaking with this young woman.
3. We shall not work tomorrow, because it is a holiday.
4. Where do you live? I was living in Batumi but now I live in Gori.
5. While entering into the bedroom the dog caused the baby to cry. It cried for a long time because its mother wasn't at home [in the house] but rather was working in the store.
6. When it caught sight of the dog, the baby suddenly began to cry.
7. Boil the water please. Tell me when the water will begin boiling and I will prepare tea.
8. Is the water boiling? Yes, it began boiling a few minutes ago [before a few minutes].
9. In Abkhazia you must speak Georgian (adv. case). I speak Georgian but I cannot speak Abkhaz. If you will study the Abkhaz language diligently you will speak it without mistake.
10. When Tamar was reigning in Georgia England's kings were Richard [the] first and John; France's, however -- Phillip [the] second.
11. Who was Georgia's last king? George XII, who reigned only three years (1798-1800).
12. If I were living in Georgia, I would speak Georgian better [more well].
13. Because tomorrow is a holiday, I shall play basketball the whole day.
14. Let's play football! With whom are we to play (opt.)?
15. When we began playing (use verbal noun) chess everybody was silent but when we were playing [during our playing] several [people] were speaking.
16. Arčil told me Europe's highest [most high] mountain is Elbrus. Where is this mountain? In the North Caucasus.
17. Cats meow and dogs bark. How [what?] strange it would be if a cat barked and a dog meowed.
18. When the dog began to bark, the baby began to cry. I will tell [his] mother he is crying.
19. When there will no longer be food the cat will loudly begin to meow.
20. When I was speaking with you yesterday you told me Tamar reigned twenty-nine years. In that time

(dat.) while Tamar was reigning Šota Rustaveli wrote "The Hero in the Tiger's Skin."

21. Don't [you all] laugh when I speak Georgian. It is impossible that I speak when you all laugh. We won't laugh any more. In fact [in reality] you speak very well!
22. Let's swim! Unfortunately here we can't swim. Swimming here is forbidden because this river is very dangerous.
23. Elbrus is Europe's highest [most high] mountain. What is Georgia's? Kazbek is Georgia's highest mountain.
24. The children laughed and shouted when they saw the clowns. They also saw bears which were dancing.
25. Are you acquainted with the *ceruli*? Yes, I am acquainted with this well-known Georgian dance. Georgians who live in the mountains dance the *ceruli*.
26. Three Georgian proverbs:
    Who said *A*, that one must say *B* also.
    The dog barks but the caravan goes [on anyway].
    For the cat it is play, for the mouse it is a struggle of souls (old gen. pl).
27. Don't shout so (pl.)! If you will shout so you all will surely wake the baby.
28. Today at the concert a choir will sing Georgian folk songs. Unfortunately I cannot go because I must go to another concert; they will sing arias from Paliašvili's well known opera *Abesalom and Eter* (ოპერა is declined adjectivally here; აბესალომი has no ending and is not declined).
29. Tell me: what does the word *ceruli* mean? I shall explain it to you. This word comes from *ceri*. *Ceri* is the first, most thick finger/toe of a human being's hand or foot. The *ceruli* is a Svan folk dance on the (big) toes. Only men dance it.
30. It is strange, because in ballet only women can dance on toes.
31. Three Georgian proverbs:
    A white dog and a black dog are both dogs.
    The rooster said: Crowing is my business and daybreak is God's.
    Give me a good mother, I will also be a good father.
32. If John will ask me where I'm going, I'll answer him [that] I'm not going anywhere.
33. Who was speaking with Arčil? I shall ask Rusudan, because Rusudan knows him well.
34. What did Rusudan answer you? She answered me

[that] she will call me Monday (dat.).

35. What time [which hour] is it? When the bell begins to ring it will be exactly three o'clock [three hour].
36. When will the session of the linguistic circle be? They told me [that] it will be Wednesday (dat.) at (+ postposition *-ze*) 4 o'clock.
37. In August on Sundays we often swim in this river.
38. If you were working more diligently, you would receive more money.
39. As in other countries, in the Soviet Union, too, they don't work on Saturdays and Sundays.
40. Don't lie anymore. You must always tell the truth.
41. In the Caucasus many legends exist about Amirani. They say the Greek legendary hero Prometheus is of Caucasian origin and his prototype is Amirani.
42. In 1921 the Bolsheviks established Soviet power in Georgia.
43. When the puppet Pinocchio lies, his (id.o.) nose becomes longer.
44. Give me 25 rubles, please. Here are 25 rubles. Thank you.
45. When they say Georgians live in the most beautiful republic of the Soviet Union, they are not lying.
46. Do you know George and Helen Papashvily (pl.)? Yes, I know them. These writers wrote the humorous novel *Anything Can Happen*. In this novel they describe how George Papashvily came from Georgia to America and his adventure(s) in the United States.
47. A short time ago George and Helen Papashvily returned to Georgia. In the book *Home and Home Again* these two authors tell us their adventure(s) in George's native land.
48. What did you read in today's paper? I read [that] for months there will be a shortage of water.
49. How [of what kind] will tomorrow's weather be? They say tomorrow it will rain again. The day before yesterday and yesterday it was raining all day long. Today at 10 o'clock it suddenly began raining.
50. When it rains it often lightnings and thunders.
51. Last year in winter it snowed every day.
52. Most birds [the majority of birds] fly; the ostrich however [does] not (არა).
53. We shall fly from Moscow to Tbilisi tomorrow.
54. Birds fly with wings (instr.).
55. Many birds fly off toward the south in winter.
56. Where did this airplane fly off to? If flew off

to (-*ḳen*) Leningrad.

57. Why did that man scream at me? That crazy [man] screams at everyone.

58. My neighbor always sings very loud. If he continues this singing, I shall complain about him to the police (pp. -*ši*).

59. Diana, sing me a Georgian song, please. I shall sing you Aḳaḳi Çereteli's (E) 'Suliḳo'.

60. When we were in Georgia, the Georgian Academy of Sciences hosted us. When the Georgian academicians will arrive in America, our university will host them. Now we are hosting ten Russian professors.

Georgian Folk Dancer

Reading Passage მოხევეების საოჯახო ყოფა

1 საოჯახო ურთიერთობის მეცნიერული შესწავლა, საზოგადოებრივი ყოფის სხვა ძირითად საკითხებთან ერთად, დაიწყო XIX საუკუნის მეორე ნახევრიდან, როდესაც დასავლეთის ქვეყნებსა და რუსეთში ეთნოგრაფია დამოუკიდებელ სამეცნიერო დისციპლინად ყალიბდებოდა.

2 ამავე პერიოდიდან მიიქცია მკვლევართა ყურადღება კავკასიელ ხალხთა საოჯახო ყოფამ. ოჯახის ფორმების შესწავლისადმი მკვლევართა ესოდენ დიდი ინტერესი განაპირობა აქ ხანგრძლივად შემონახულმა მდიდარმა ფაქტობრივმა მასალამ, რაც საფუძვლად დაედო არაერთ ეთნოგრაფიულ აღწერილობას და გამოკვლევას. ეს მასალა მისი გამომზეურებისთანავე გასცდა კავკასიის ფარგლებს და ზოგადი ეთნოგრაფიის კუთვნილებად იქცა.

3 საოჯახო ურთიერთობის შესწავლის თვალსაზრისით საქართველოს ერთ-ერთი საყურადღებო კუთხეა ხევი, სადაც დიდხანს იყო შემონახული ისტორიულად არსებული სოციალური ინსტიტუტების გადმონაშთები. XIX საუკუნის ბოლომდე გადმონაშთის სახით შემორჩენილ ერთ-ერთ ასეთ სოციალურ ერთეულს წარმოადგენდა საოჯახო თემი, ანუ დიდი ოჯახი, რომელიც არსებობას განაგრძობდა ოჯახის გაბატონებული ფორმის — ინდივიდუალური ოჯახის, ანუ პატარა ოჯახის გვერდით. მოხევურ დიდ ოჯახში რელიეფური სიცხადით იყო წარმოდგენილი გადმონაშთური ფორმით შემორჩენილი საოჯახო თემის ძირითადი კომპონენტები: რამდენიმე თაობისა და საქორწინო წყვილის ერთად ცხოვრება, ქონებაზე საერთო საკუთრება, კოლექტიური შრომის ორგანიზაცია, დოვლათის კოლექტიური მოხმარება და სოლიდარული მმართველობის სისტემა. ამ ნიშნების მიხედვით, მოხევური დიდი ოჯახი დემოკრატიული, ანუ სოლიდარული ბუნებისა იყო და არსებითად განსხვავდებოდა ქართველთა ყოფისათვის უცნობი და ზოგიერთი სხვა ხალხისათვის დამახასიათებელი დესპოტური ოჯახისაგან, რომლის ქონებაზე და მმართველობაში განუსაზღვრელი უფლებებით სარგებლობდა ოჯახის უფროსი მამაკაცი.

4 მოხევეების საოჯახო ყოფის შესწავლის ძირითად წყაროდ გამოვიყენეთ ჩვენ მიერ ხევში შეკრებილი ეთნოგრაფიული მასალები, XVIII—XIX სს. სტატისტიკური მონაცემები და სხვადასხვაგვარი ლიტერატურული წყაროები. წინასწარ გვინდა აღვნიშნოთ, რომ XIX საუკუნის ავტორთაგან მოხევეების საოჯახო ყოფას ყველაზე ახლოს იცნობდა ხევში აღზრდილი დიდი ქართველი მწერალი ალ. ყაზბეგი, ხოლო საბჭოთა მკვლევართაგან ამ საკითხის შესწავლაში განსაკუთრებით დიდი წვლილი შეიტანა რუსუდან ხარაძემ.

5 1960—1961 წლებში რუსულ ენაზე ორ წიგნად გამოქვეყნებულ მონოგრაფიაში — „ქართული საოჯახო თემი", რ. ხარაძემ, საქართველოს სხვა კუთხეებთან ერთად, მოგვცა ხევში გადმონაშთის სახით შემონახული საოჯახო თემის დახასიათებაც. მის მიერ გამომზეურებული მასალა ასახავს XIX საუკუნის ბოლოსა და XX საუკუნის დასაწყისის ვითარებას, როდესაც ხევში მეცხვარეობა უკვე მეურნეობის წამყვან დარგს წარმოადგენდა და, ამდენად, ის იყო საოჯახო თემის ძირითადი ეკონომიური საფუძველი. ამის გამო რ. ხარაძის მსჯელობა ეხება უმთავრესად მეცხვარეობაზე დამყარებული საოჯახო თემის სტრუქტურას, მის სპეციფიკას. ......

6 ეთნოგრაფიული ძიების შედეგად ხევში დადასტურდა ორი სხვადასხვა ტიპის ოჯახის თანაარსებობა; XIX საუკუნის ბოლომდე ინდივიდუალური ოჯახის გვერდით არსებობდა საოჯახო თემი. ფეოდალიზმისა და კაპიტალიზმის ხანაში ოჯახის ეს ფორმა განიცდიდა თვისებრივ ცვლილებებს და მისი ხვედრითი წონა თანდათანობით მცირდებოდა, ხოლო მათი რღვევის ბაზაზე იზრდებოდა ინდივიდუალური ოჯახების რიცხვი. XX საუკუნის კარიბჭესთან საბოლოოდ დაიმსხვრა საოჯახო თემის უკანასკნელი ნაშთები ხევში და სრული მონოპოლია მოიპოვა თანამედროვე ტიპის ინდივიდუალურმა ოჯახმა.

7 ეს პროცესი რომ თვალნათლივ წარმოვიდგინოთ და ოჯახის არსებულ ტიპებს შორის განსხვავება დავინახოთ, საჭიროა ვიცოდეთ, როგორი იყო ოჯახის შემადგენლობა, მისი ეკონომიური საფუძვლები, მმართველობის სისტემა, შრომის ორგანიზაცია და საკუთრების ხასიათი.

Vocabulary

1

მოხევე — Mokheve (s.o. from N. Georgian mountain valleys)
ოჯახი: საოჯახო — family: domestic
ყოფა — life(style) (Russ. быт)
ურთიერთობა — relation(ship)
საზოგადოებრივი — social
ძირითადი — fundamental
ნახევარი — half (A)
დამოუკიდებელი — independent (E)

2

ამავე — (this) same; nom. ეზევე; oblique (attributive) ამავე (used as N. ეს, oblique ამ, see sec. 5.5.)
[მი=იქცევს ყურადღებას] — draw (lit., turn) attention to oneself
მკვლევარი — investigator (A)
ხალხი — people
ფორმა — form; ფორმით in the form of
-დმი — [pp.] to(wards); here: in
ესოდენ — such
ინტერესი — interest
გან=აპირობებს — condition; cause (cf. პირობა condition)
ხანგრძლივი — long (of time)
შემონახული — preserved
ფაქტობრივი — factual
რაც — here: which
საფუძველი — basis; foundation (E)
[დაედო საფუძვლად] — served as the basis for (dat.)
არაერთი — more than one; many a
აღწერილობა — description
გამომზეურება — elucidation

-თანავე	[pp.] simultaneously with
[გასცდა]	went beyond sthg. (dat.)
ფარგალი	border (A)
ზოგადი	general
კუთვნილება	possession, property
[იქცა]	became (aor.) (II. conj. + adv.)

3

თვალსაზრისით	[pp.] from the point of view of
ერთ-ერთი	one (of several)
საყურადღებო	important
კუთხე	corner; here: region
ხევი	region of N. Georgia (see map, Lesson 6, fig. 6.1)
არსებული	existing
ინსტიტუტი	institution; institute
გადმონაშთი	remnant
სახით	[pp.] in the form of
შემორჩენილი	remaining
ერთეული	unit
თემი	clan
დიდი ოჯახი	extended family
გან+აგრძობს	continue
გაბატონებული	(pre)dominant
პატარა	small; little (nontruncating); here: nuclear
გვერდით	[pp.] alongside
რელიეფური	vivid; graphic (cf. რელიეფი relief)
სიცხადე	clarity
წარმოდგენილი	represented
თაობა	generation
საქორწინო	married; wedding (adj.)
წყვილი	pair; couple
ერთად	together (Note that VNs can be modified by adverbs; ერთად ცხოვრება = living to-

	gether)
ქონება	property; estate
საერთო	common
საკუთრება	ownership (-ზე of), property
კოლექტივი	collective
შრომა	work
დოვლათი	wealth
მოხმარება	use
სოლიდარული	solidary
მმართველობა	government
სისტემა	system
ნიშანი	sign; feature (A)
ბუნება	nature
არსებითი	essential
გან+ასხვავებს	distinguish (also გან=)
-თვის ... უცნობი	unknown to
დამახასიათებელი	characteristic (-თვის of) (E)
დესპოტი	despot
განუსაზღვრელი	unlimited
უფლება	power
სარგებლობს	(+inst.) profit from; make use of; take advantage of; enjoy
უფროსი	elder; chief

4

გამო=იყენებს	use
ჩვენ მიერ	by us
შეკრებილი	gathered
მონაცემი	datum
სხვადასხვაგვარი	of various sorts
წინასწარ	first (of all)
[გვინდა]	we (dat.) want
აღ=ნიშნავს	note; remark
იცნობს	know s.o. (pr. series only)
აღზრდილი	raised; educated

ალ. = ალექსანდრე

ხოლო	while; however
-გან	[pp.] here: by
განსაკუთრებით	particularly
წვლილი	contribution
შე+იტანს	bring in (pres. series irr.; see sec. 12.1.3)

5

1960-1961	ათას ცხრაას სამოც-ათას ცხრაას სამოცდაერთი
ორ წიგნად	in two volumes
გამოქვეყნებული	published
მონოგრაფია	monograph
და=ახასიათებს	characterize
გამომზეურებული	exposed; brought to light
ა+სახავს	represent; portray
დასაწყისი	beginning
ვითარება	circumstance; case
მეცხვარეობა	sheepherding
უკვე	already
მეურნეობა	agriculture
წამყვანი	leading
დარგი	branch
ამდენად	to this extent
მსჯელობს	discuss; consider
შე=ეხება	concern (+ dat.) (VN შეხება)
მთავარი	chief (A)
დამყარებული	based
სპეციფიკა	specific character

6

ძიება	investigation
შედეგი	result (შედეგად[pp.] as a result of)
და=ადასტურებს	confirm
სხვადასხვა	different

ტიპი type
თანაარსებობა coexistence
ფეოდალიზმი feudalism
ხანა period
გან+იცდის undergo (aor. irr.; see sec. 9.1.1)
თვისებრივი qualitative
ცვლილება change
ხვედრითი წონა specific weight; relative importance
თანდათანობით gradually
მცირე little
რღვევა disintegration
ბაზა base
გა=ზრდის grow; raise sthg.; გა=იზრდება (II.) grow (intransitive)
რიცხვი number
კარიბჭე threshold
საბოლოო final
და=ამსხვრევს destroy: II. conj. irr.: და=იმსხვრევა, aor. და(ვ)იმსხვერი(-თ), დაიმსხვრა.
უკანასკნელი last
ნაშთი remnant
სრული entire; complete
მო=იპოვებს achieve
თანამედროვე contemporary
7
პროცესი process
რომ here: in order to (+ opt.)
თვალნათლივ clearly
წარმო=იდგენს conceive of; imagine
განსხვავება difference
[ვიცოდეთ] here: to know (see sec. 9.1.4) (conj. pres. = opt.)
როგორი (of) what kind?
შემადგენლობა composition
ხასიათი character

LESSON 9

9.1. Irregularities in conjugation.

9.1.1. Irregularities in I. conjugation verbs. The number of *irregular* I. conjugation verbs is quite limited but some such roots are extremely common. (Irregular verbs are those verbs whose roots are vowelless; see sec. 5.0.)

Most irregular I. conjugation verbs take the so-called strong aorist series endings:[1]

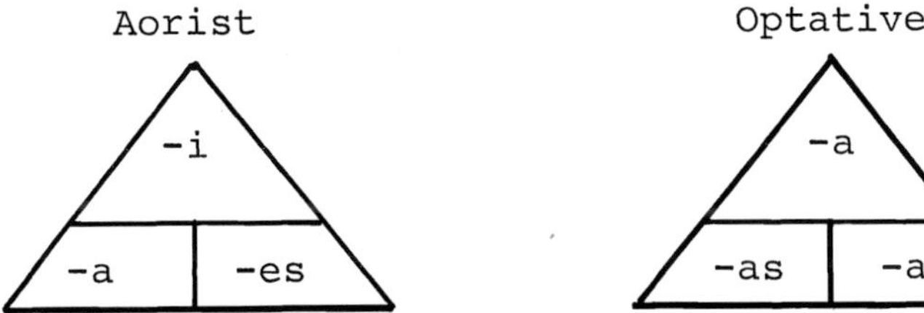

Verbs taking the strong aorist endings are those with present/future stem formant *-am*, *-av*, and some in *-i*.[2]

Verbs in *-am*. There are about nine such roots. These form the aorist as for regular I. conjugation verbs, except that they take the strong endings. Examples:

Future	Aorist		Optative		
მიაბამს	მი(ვ)აბი(თ)		მი(ვ)აბა(თ)		tie
	მიაბა	მიაბეს	მიაბას	მიაბან	
დადგამს	და(ვ)დგი(თ)		და(ვ)დგა(თ)		put
	დადგა	დადგეს	დადგას	დადგან	
დაასხამს	და(ვ)ასხი(თ)		და(ვ)ასხა(თ)		pour
	დაასხა	დაასხეს	დაასხას	დაასხან	
ჩაიცვამს	ჩა(ვ)იცვი(თ)		ჩა(ვ)იცვა(თ)		dress o.s.
	ჩაიცვა	ჩაიცვეს	ჩაიცვას	ჩაიცვან	

Verbs in *-av*. There are about twelve such roots. The majority of them form the aorist by dropping the present/future stem formant and inserting *-a-* in the first and second persons of the aorist. Strong endings are added. The optative is formed (with strong endings) from the stem of the 3sg. aorist (which does not have the inserted vowel). Examples:

Future	Aorist	Optative	
მოკლავს	მო(ვ)კალი(თ)	მო(ვ)კლა(თ)	kill

	მოკლა	მოკლეს	მოკლას	მოკლან	
ჩაფლავს	ჩა(ვ)ფალი(თ)		ჩა(ვ)ფლა(თ)		bury
	ჩაფლა	ჩაფლეს	ჩაფლას	ჩაფლან	

Verbs in -*i*. There are about fifteen irregular roots in -*i*, all but about three of which end in *n*, which take the *strong* endings in the aorist series. The aorist is formed by dropping the P/FSF and inserting -*e*- before the root final consonant in the first and second persons only. The optative is formed from the 3sg. aorist (which does not have the inserted -*e*-). Examples:

Future	Aorist		Optative		
შექმნის	შე(ვ)ქმენი(თ)		შე(ვ)ქმნა(თ)		create
	შექმნა	შექმნეს	შექმნას	შექმნან	
მოჭრის	მო(ვ)ჭერი(თ)		მო(ვ)ჭრა(თ)		cut
	მოჭრა	მოჭრეს	მოჭრას	მოჭრან	

(Note that მოჭრის is the only common root following this pattern which does not end in *n*.)

There are about twenty roots with present/future stem formant -*i* which take the *regular* aorist and optative endings. These forms are irregular in that the vowel -*a*- is inserted *after* the initial consonant, harmonic cluster, or consonant + *v* in all forms of both the aorist and the optative. An example would be:

Future	Aorist		Optative		
ჩათვლის	ჩა(ვ)თვალე(თ)		ჩა(ვ)თვალო(თ)		con-
	ჩათვალა	ჩათვალეს	ჩათვალოს	ჩათვალონ	sider
აღზრდის	აღ(ვ)ზარდე(თ)		აღ(ვ)ზარდო(თ)		edu-
	აღზარდა	აღზარდეს	აღზარდოს	აღზარდონ	cate, raise

Similarly,

დასჯის	punish
გაშლის	unwrap; spread out
გამოცდის	test
გამოცვლის	change
გადაიხდის	pay

9.1.2. Irregularities in II. conjugation verbs.

II. conjugation verbs derived from *irregular* I. conjugation verbs. II. conjugation verbs derived from irregular I. conjugation verbs form their aorist series screeves exactly as the corresponding I. conjugation verbs, except that they have the II. conjugation marker *i*- and in the 3pl. aorist have the ending -*nen* instead of -*es* (cf. sec. 5.4.1). Examples:

I. conj.

Aorist		Optative		
და(ვ)აბი(თ)		და(ვ)აბა(თ)		tie
დააბა	დააბეს	დააბას	დააბან	
ჩა(ვ)თვალე(თ)		ჩა(ვ)თვალო(თ)		consider
ჩათვალა	ჩათვალეს	ჩათვალოს	ჩათვალონ	

II. conj.

Aorist		Optative		
და(ვ)იბი(თ)		და(ვ)იბა(თ)		tie
დაიბა	დაიბნენ	დაიბას	დაიბან	
ჩა(ვ)ითვალე(თ)		ჩა(ვ)ითვალო(თ)		consider
ჩაითვალა	ჩაითვალნენ	ჩაითვალოს	ჩაითვალონ	

(The optative may also take the *e*-endings shown below.)

9.1.2.1. "Root" II. conj. verbs. This class of II. conjugation verbs is called "root" because in the aorist series there are no affixes marking the form as II. conjugation; i.e., there is neither a preradical vowel *i*- (see sec. 3.1.3) nor a suffix -*d*- (sec. 3.1.2). Most (a little over twenty) root II. conjugation verbs have no corresponding I. conjugation forms. Their vocabulary entry forms will be the 3sg. future. They are conjugated like all other II. conjugation verbs in all the screeves of the future and present series. In the aorist series they take the same endings as the II. conjugation verbs in -*d*-:

Aorist

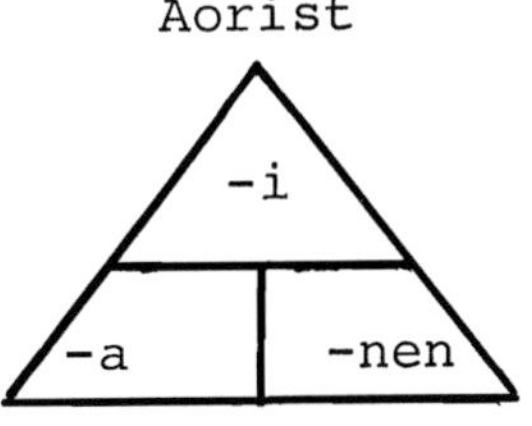

Optative

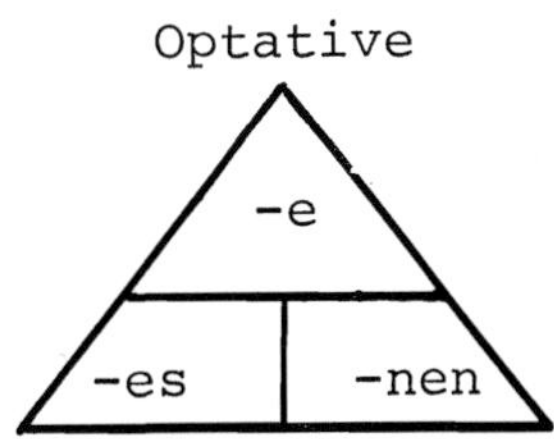

Examples of such verbs are: მოკვდება (mo=ḳvd-eb-a)[3] die; შეცდება (še=cd-eb-a) err, be mistaken; შეხვდება (še=xvd-eb-a) encounter, meet; გახდება (ga=xd-eb-a) become; დარჩება (da=rč-eb-a) remain. An example of the conjugation in the aorist and optative:

Aorist		Optative	
მო(ვ)კვდი(თ)		მო(ვ)კვდე(თ)	
მოკვდა	მოკვდნენ	მოკვდეს	მოკვდნენ

Such verbs usually form the verbal noun by adding *-oma* to the aorist stem: მოკვდომა, შეცდომა, გახდომა, but დარჩენა, შეხვედრა. To this class also belong the II. conjugation forms derived from some I. conjugation verbs with preradical vowel *a-* and P/FSF *-ob*. Examples:

I. conj.	II. conj.		
	Future (3sg.)	Aorist (3sg.)	
გაათბობს →	გათბება	გათბა	heat, warm
გააშრობს →	გაშრება	გაშრა	dry
გამოაცხობს →	გამოცხვება	გამოცხვა	bake (root *cxv-* [sec. 1.11.1])

Relative forms of root II. conjugation verbs. Relative forms of root II. conjugation verbs are infrequent and are generally formed from the absolute forms by means of the *u*-series indirect object markers. The meaning of such indirect objects often corresponds to the use of possessive adjectives in English. Examples:

გასულ წელს ბებია მოკვდა.

Last year grandmother died.

გასულ წელს ბებია მომიკვდა.

Last year my grandmother died (lit.: grandmother died to/on me)

Verbs denoting *change* of position. Four verbs denoting change of position follow the root II. conjugation in all forms except for the first and second persons in the aorist. These are

დადგება	da=dg-eb-a	stand up
დაწვება	da=c̣v-eb-a	lie down
დაჯდება	da=ǰd-eb-a	sit down (sg.)
დასხდებიან	da=sxd-eb-ian	sit down (pl.)

1, 2 aorist	aorist 3sg.	optative 3sg.
და(ვ)დექი(თ)[4]	დადგა	დადგეს
და(ვ)წექი(თ)	დაწვა	დაწვეს
და(ვ)ჯექი	დაჯდა	დაჯდეს
და(ვ)სხედით	დასხდნენ (pl.)	

Note that the verb დაჯდება normally takes only a singular subject referring to only one person. When the subject of the verb is plural, დასხდებიან must be used.[5] When a grammatically singular third person subject refers to more than one being (i.e., the subject noun is a collective or is modified by a quantifier) then a special third person singular form დასხდება is used. Examples:

ივანე შემოვიდა და დაჯდა.

John came in and sat down.

ივანე და მარიამი შემოვიდნენ და დასხდნენ.

John and Mary came in and sat down.

ჩემი მშობლები შემოვიდნენ და დასხდნენ.

My parents came in and sat down.

ჩემი სამი მეგობარი შემოვიდა და დასხდა.

My three friends came in and sat down.

ახალგაზრდა წყვილი შემოვიდა და დასხდა.

The young couple came in and sat down.

These four verbs form the verbal noun in *-oma* (ადგომა, დაჯდომა, დასხდომა) or *-ola* (დაწოლა; sec. 1.11.1).

9.1.3. Verbs denoting *position*. Corresponding to the four verbs denoting *change of position* there are four verbs denoting *position*. These verbs show considerable irregularity. In the present tense the endings of the first and second persons are the corresponding forms of the verb 'be'; in the third plural present the ending is *-an* or *-anan*. These verbs lack both the imperfect and the present stem conjunctive, substituting the aorist and optative for these. The present tense forms are:

	be standing	be lying down
1.	ვდგავარ(თ)	ვწევარ(თ)
2.	დგახარ(თ)	წევხარ(თ)

3.	დგას დგანან	წევს წვანან
	be sitting[6]	
	sing.	pl.
1.	ვზივარ	ვსხედვართ
2.	ზიხარ	სხედხართ
3.	ზის (სხედს)	სხედან

In the future and aorist series these verbs are conjugated like *root II. conjugation forms* except that they do not take any preverbs and they have the preradical vowel *i-*. In the aorist screeve they have the same alternations as the verbs of change of position. Examples:[7]

Future	იდგება	იწვება
Aorist	(ვ)იდექი(თ)	(ვ)იწექი(თ)
	იდგა იდგნენ	იწვა იწვნენ
Future	იჯდება	ისხდებიან
Aorist	(ვ)იჯექი	(ვ)ისხედით
	იჯდა (ისხდა)	ისხდნენ

These verbs pattern syntactically as II. conjugation forms; i.e., the grammatical subject is always in the nominative case. The verbal nouns are the same as for the corresponding verbs of change of position.

9.1.4. Irregular verb იცის. The verb იცის, verbal noun ცოდნა, means 'know something', 'know how'. It corresponds in meaning to French *savoir* or German *wissen*. In the present series იცის is conjugated like ტირის (see sec. 8.1.6). This verb's irregularity lies in the fact that the subject is in the ergative case in the present series and any direct object is in the nominative. This is the only verb in modern Georgian with such syntax in the present series. For the future series of this verb, see sec. 12.1.3e. This verb has no aorist series; in place of the aorist the imperfect (იცოდა) is used and in place of the optative the conjunctive present (იცოდეს) is used.

9.2. Personal pronouns. As a general rule personal pronouns are used in Georgian only for emphasis or contrast; otherwise the verbal form itself is generally capable of marking person. The pronouns of the first and second persons are:

N.E.D.	მე }	1sg.	I, me	ჩვენ	1pl. we, us
G.	ჩემ }				

შენ 2sg. you[8] თქვენ 2pl. you all[8]

Note that with the exception of the personal pronoun of the first person singular, these are not declined; instr. and adv. forms do not occur.

In the third person singular and plural the demonstrative pronoun ის or იგი, pl. ისინი is used (see sec. 5.5.2). In cases other than the nominative the initial *i-* is lost:

3sg.	he, she, it	3pl.	they
N.	ის, იგი	N.	ისინი, იგინი
E.	მან	E.D.G.	მათ
D.	მას		
G.	მის		
I.	მით		

When the postpositions *-ši* and *-ze* are added to the dative form of the personal pronoun the final *s* of მას is not lost; i.e., the rule given in sec. 4.4.1 does not apply to მას. Compare the personal pronouns მასში 'in it', მასზე 'on it' with the demonstrative pronouns იმაში 'in that', იმაზე 'on that'. Other examples of personal pronouns with postpositions are:

-tvis ჩემთვის, შენთვის, მისთვის; ჩვენთვის, თქვენთვის, მათთვის

-gan ჩემგან, შენგან, მისგან; ჩვენგან, თქვენგან, მათგან

-tan ჩემთან, შენთან, მასთან; ჩვენთან, თქვენთან, მათთან

etc. [■ p. 247]

As in Russian, the third person plural *without personal pronoun* is often used to give an indefinite meaning, e.g., ამბობენ 'they (without antecedent) say'. This function is similar to that of French *on* or German *man*.

9.3. Comparison of adjectives and adverbs.

9.3.1. Comparative. The comparative is formed either (a) with უფრო 'more' followed by the adjective or adverb; 'than' is expressed by the conjunction ვიდრე; or (b) a noun + postposition *-ze*, corresponding to English 'than' clauses, followed by the adjective or adverb in the positive degree. Examples:

The Georgian alphabet is older than the Slavic.

(a) ქართული ანბანი უფრო ძველია, ვიდრე სლავური.

(b) ქართული ანბანი სლავურზე ძველია.

9.3.2. Superlative. The superlative is generally formed by ყველაზე 'most' (= ყველა 'all' + *-ze*, i.e., 'than all') followed by the positive degree of the adjective or adverb:

ყველაზე დიდი მთა ევროპაში იალბუზია.

The highest mountain in Europe is Elbrus.

A few adjectives and adverbs can also have simple forms for the comparative and superlative. These include:

	Positive		Comparative	
(a)	კარგი	good	უკეთესი	better
(b)	ცუდი	bad	უარესი	worse
(c)	ცოტა	a little	ნაკლები	less
(d)	ბევრი	much, many	მეტი	more

	Superlative	
(a)	საუკეთესო	best
(b)	ყველაზე ცუდი, ყველაზე უარესი	worst
(c)	ყველაზე ცოტა, ყველაზე ნაკლები	least
(d)	ყველაზე ბევრი, ყველაზე მეტი	most

9.4. Wordbuilding.

9.4.1. The intensive circumfix *u-.....-es*. The circumfix *u-.....-es* added to adjectives gives the meaning 'very', 'exceedingly', 'a most'. In addition, it can serve to form a simple superlative ('the most'). Examples:

ლამაზი	beautiful	ულამაზესი
ულამაზესი სურათი	= {a very / an exceedingly / a/the most} beautiful picture	
ძველი	old	უძველესი
ახალი	new (A)	უახლესი
მოკლე	short	უმოკლესი
ღრმა	deep	უღრმესი
ფართო	wide	უფართოესი

9.4.2. The circumfix *mo-.....-o*. This circumfix is added to adjectives and corresponds in meaning to the

English suffix -*ish*:

ლურჯი	blue	მოლურჯო	bluish
დიდი	large	მოდიდო	largish

Many adjectives ending in -*el*- or -*il*- drop the -*el*-, -*il*- when adding the circumfix *mo*-.....-*o*. Examples:

გრძელი	long	მოგრძო	longish
ტკბილი	sweet	მოტკბო	sweetish

Irregular forms are:

წითელი	red (E)	მოწითა̲ლო	reddish
ყვითელი	yellow (E)	მოყვითა̲ლო	yellowish

■(to sec. 9.2, p. 245.) With masdars (sec. 3.3. 1.2) (and the present active participle; see sec. 5.7.2; 11.5) the *possessive adjective* replaces the genitive of the personal pronouns:

თქვენ გნახეთ 'I saw you' > თქვენი ნახვა 'seeing you'
ის ნახე 'you saw her' > მისი ნახვა 'seeing her'

LESSON 9: Notes

1. Note that these endings are the same as those of the aorist series screeves of თქმა 'say, tell' (sec. 8.4) and the aorist endings of ცემა 'give' (sec. 7.4). This latter verb is the only I. conjugation verb in Georgian which takes the *-e*, *-es*, *-en* endings in the optative. Note too, that the strong aorist endings are identical to the endings of the aorist of the II. conjugation in *-d-* except for the 3pl.

2. Two irregular verbs in *-av* form the aorist series with the strong aorist endings, but without the insertion of a vowel: დაფქვავს 'mill, grind', aor. და(ვ)-ფქვი(თ), დაფქვა, and დაწვავს.'burn', aor. და(ვ)წვი(თ), დაწვა.

Note also that the verb დაიცავს 'defend' which has *c* as its root in the present and future series (*da=i-c-av-s*) but has the root *cav* (alternating with *cv*) in the aorist: და(ვ)იცავი(თ); დაიცვა.

3. Note that although many of these verbs have a *d* before the P/FSF, this is part of the root and not a marker of the II. conjugation.

4. Originally the strong aorist had no ending in the first and second persons and thus the aorist 2sg. of დადგება was დადეგ. The final *g* was devoiced to *k* resulting in დადექ, to which the ending *-i* was added. და(ვ)წექი(თ) and და(ვ)ჯექი have been explained as due to analogy with და(ვ)დექი(თ).

5. A formal imperative to *one* person uses the form დაჯექით.

6. The distribution of ზის and სხედან is the same as for დაჯდება and დასხდებიან; see sec. 9.1.2. above. With a quantified singular subject or with a collective subject the 3sg. forms present სხედს, future ისხდება, aorist ისხდა are found.

There is a strong tendency in the spoken language to use ზის in the plural also: ვზივართ, ზიხართ, ზიან, etc.

7. Note that the verbs of position differ from the corresponding verbs of change of position in the future and aorist screeves only by the absence of a preverb and by the presence of the preradical vowel *i-*.

8. შენ and თქვენ normally serve also in a vocative function. When followed immediately by a noun or ad-

jective in the vocative, however, the special forms შე and თქვე occur; e.g., შე გიჟო! 'you lunatic you!', თქვე სულელებო! 'you fools you!'.

Remember that თქვენ is used speaking to more than one person or to a single person with whom one is on formal terms. შენ is used speaking to a single person with whom one is on familiar terms. თქვენ and შენ pattern analogously to French *vous* and *tu* or Russian вы and ты.

Illustration from Vepxisṭqaosani
(Artist: Iraḳli Toije)

LESSON 9: Exercises

1. ვინ იცის, როგორ გახდა თბილისი საქართველოს დედაქალაქი? ილიკომ იცის. გვითხარი, ილიკო!
2. ძველი ლეგენდა არსებობს, რომლის მიხედვითაც მეფე ვახტანგ გორგასალი ერთ დღეს ნადირობდა. ირემი დაინახა და სცადა მისი მოკვლა.
3. მან ირემი ვერ მოკლა, არამედ მარტო დაჭრა. ირემმა ტყეში შეირბინა. იმ ტყეში ირემმა იპოვა თბილი წყარო და იქ მორჩა. იმ წყაროს თბილმა წყლებმა ირემი მოარჩინა.
4. როცა ვახტანგ გორგასალმა ნახა, რომ ირემი ჯერ კიდევ ცოცხალია, მან ეს სასწაულად ჩათვალა და გადაწყვიტა თავისი ახალი დედაქალაქის იქ აშენება.
5. თუმცა ამბავი ირმის შესახებ ალბათ ლეგენდაა, ვახტანგ გორგასალი ნამდვილად არსებობდა (446-510) და უნდა ჩავთვალოთ სიტყვა „თბილისი" „თბობა" ზმნის ნაწარმოებად.
6. იმის შემდეგ, როცა ანგარიში გადავიხადეთ, რესტორნიდან გავედით და ქუჩაზე შენ მოულოდნელად შეგხვდით.
7. ოქტომბრის რევოლუციის შემდეგ (1917) რამდენიმე თვეში თბილისში შეიქმნა ამიერკავკასიური სეიმი (ანუ პარლამენტი). მასში ქართველი, აზერბაიჯანელი და სომეხი წარმომადგენლები მონაწილეობდნენ.
8. 28 აპრილს 1918 წ. (ათას ცხრაას თვრამეტ წელს) სეიმმა ამიერკავკასიის დემოკრატიული ფედერაციული რესპუბლიკა გამოაცხადა, მაგრამ ერთი თვის შემდეგ ეს ამიერკავკასიური კავშირი დაიშალა.
9. საბჭოთა ხელისუფლება საქართველოში 1921 (ათას ცხრაას ოცდაერთ) წელს დამყარდა. საქართველო ამიერკავკასიის საბჭოთა ფედერაციული სოციალისტური რესპუბლიკის ნაწილი გახდა. ის ამ ფედერაციულ რესპუბლიკაში დარჩა 1936 (ათას ცხრაას ოცდათექვსმეტ) წლამდე, როცა საქართველოს საბჭოთა

სოციალისტური რესპუბლიკა შეიქმნა.

10. შოთა რუსთაველი იერუსალიმში გარდაიცვალა. ის ალბათ იერუსალიმის ჯვრის მონასტერში დამარხეს.

11. ვენერა ურუშაძემ შოთა რუსთაველის „ვეფხისტყაოსანი" ინგლისურად გადათარგმნა და თავისი თარგმანი მარჯორი უორდროპის ხსოვნას მიუძღვნა.

12. ხვალ სადოქტორო დისერტაცია უნდა დავიცვა. პროფესორების კომისიის წინაშე უნდა წარვდგე და ამ პროფესორებმა უნდა გამომცადონ.

13. საქართველოში ბევრი ხილი და მწვანილი იზრდება. საქართველოს ჰავა ისეთია, რომ კოლმეურნეობებში შეიძლება წლიდან წლამდე გაიზარდოს ციტრუსების, ყურძნის, ჩაის, კომბოსტოსა და მწვანე ლობიოს მოსავალი.

14. შენი ქალიშვილი და ვაჟიშვილი ისე უნდა აღზარდო, რომ თავაზიანები გამოვიდნენ.

15. კომბოსტო და ლობიო ან მაგიდაზე დადგი და დაჯექი!

16. უძველესი ქართული წარწერები მოიპოვება ქართულ მონასტერში ბეთლემის ახლოს ისრაელში. ისინი ბოლნისის ტაძრის წარწერებზე ძველია.

17. კონცერტზე სად ისხედით? მე სცენის ახლოს, მესამე რიგში ვიჯექი, ხოლო გივი და მისი ცოლი აივნის უკანასკნელ რიგში ისხდნენ.

18. ჩვეულებრივ, ჩემსძმაზე ადრე ვწვები, მაგრამ გუშინ მასზე გვიან დავწექი.

19. გუშინ ორი უცნობი კაცი ჩემს კანტორაში შემოვიდა და დასხდა. ერთი მეორეზე სქელი და მაღალი იყო.

20. სასამართლოში დღეს იყავით? დიახ, სასამართლოში ვისხედით, როცა მოსამართლემ ბრძანა, რომ ბრალდებული სიკვდილით დაისაჯოს.

21. ეს ანგარიში სად გადავიხადო? —იქ გადაიხადე, სალაროში.

22. თქვენ რევაზ ჯაფარიძე უნდა იყოთ! —არა ბატონო, მას არ ვიცნობ. —ბოდიშს ვიხდი! შევცდი! რევაზ

ჯაფარიძეს მარტო ერთხელ შევხვდი, და თქვენ და მას შორის დიდი მსგავსებაა.

23. საზოგადოებრივი პირობები საქართველოში მნიშვნელოვნად შეიცვალა კოლექტივიზაციის შემდეგ.

24. პოლიტიკაზე თუ ილაპარაკებენ, შენ საუბრის საგანი უნდა შეცვალო.

25. საქართველო ერთ-ერთი უძველესი ქრისტიანული სახელმწიფოთაგანია. ქართველი მეფე მირიანი 330 წ. (სამას ოცდაათ წელს) გაქრისტიანდა, ე.ი., ქრისტიანი გახდა.

26. ყველამ იცის, რომ რუსებისა და ბერძნების მსგავსად, ქართველებიც მართლმადიდებლები არიან.

27. წყალი ჩვენი ქალაქის მდინარეში გაზაფხულობით მოთბოა, შემოდგომობით კი მოცივოა.

28. რიგში რატომ დგახარ? რიგში ვდგავარ ხილის საყიდლად. ხილს აქ ნუ ყიდულობ! საუკეთესო ხილს საკოლმეურნეო ბაზარში ყიდიან.

29. თუ უნდა მოვკვდეთ, სამშობლოსათვის მოვკვდეთ!

30. დეკემბერში დისერტაცია დავიცავი. ხუთმა პროფესორმა გამომცადა.

31. სამწუხაროდ, როცა მკითხეს, ილია ჭავჭავაძე როდის დაიბადა და როდის გარდაიცვალაო, პასუხი არ ვიცოდი.

32. ახლა უნდა ჩავიცვა, რადგანაც სტუმრები მალე მოვლენ. ოთარ, თუ შეიძლება, ღვინო დაასხი! ჩვენს სუფრაზე ყველამ ბევრი უნდა დალიოს.

33. თქვენს სუფრაზე თამადა ვინ იქნება? —ბოდიშს ვიხდი, ვერ გავიგე. „თამადა" რას ნიშნავს?

34. სუფრის თამადა ისაა, ვინც სადღეგრძელოები უნდა წარმოთქვას. ის არის სუფრის ხელმძღვანელი, მაგრამ ის მასპინძელი ყოველთვის არ არის.

35. იცით, საიდან მოდის სიტყვა „სადღეგრძელო"? —დიახ, ეს სიტყვა მოდის სურვილიდან, რომ თქვენი დღეები გრძელი იყოს.

36. ეს ქართული წინადადება წარმოთქვი! „ბაყაყი წყალში ყიყინებს." ვცდილობ, რომ წარმოვთქვა, მაგრამ ვერ წარმოვთქვამ.
37. თამარ, გთხოვ, აქ დაჯექი! პავლე და მედეა აქ დასხდებიან, ამ რიგში, სადაც ჩვენ ვსხედვართ.
38. როცა თეატრში მოხვალთ, ჩვენ მეხუთე რიგში ვისხდებით.
39. მე ალბათ ვიწექი, როდესაც შენ შინ დაბრუნდი.
40. ჩემი მეგობრები აივანზე სხედან, მაგრამ არ ვიცი, სად ზის ნოე.

State Seal of the Georgian SSR

Vocabulary

აივანი balcony (A)
ამბავი story; news; information; thing; (gen. ამბის; sec. 1.11.1)
ანგარიში bill; account; calculation (A)
აპრილი April
ახლოს near [pp.]
ბაზარი market (A)
ბაყაყი frog
ბოდიში excuse; apology (ბოდიშს ვიხდი excuse me)
ბრალდებული accused
გაზაფხული spring
გრძელი long (adv. irr.: გრძლად)
დეკემბერი December (E)
დემოკრატიული democratic
დისერტაცია dissertation
დოქტორი doctor (Ph.D.)
ე.ი. = ესე იგი i.e., that is
ერთ-ერთი one (of several) (see sec. 10.4.3)
ერთხელ one time; once
თავაზიანი polite
თამადა toastmaster (especially at Georgian banquet)
თბილი warm
თვე month
თუ შეიძლება if possible (= please)
ირემი deer (E)
ისე so, thus; ისე ... რომ so ... that
კანტორა office
კოლექტივიზაცია collectivization
კოლმეურნე collective farmer (kolkhoznik)
კოლმეურნეობა collective farm (kolkhoz)
კომბოსტო cabbage
კომისია commission
ლობიო beans (collective)
მაინც still; however; at least
მაისი May
მართლმადიდებელი Orthodox (person) (cf. მართალი (A) true and დიდება glory, praise) (E)
მასპინძელი host (E)

მოსავალი	harvest, yield
მოსამართლე	judge
მსგავსი	similar; მსგავსად [pp.] similar to, like; მსგავსება similarity, resemblance
მწვანილი	greens (vegetables)
ნამდვილი	real; actual
ნაწარმოები	derivative; work
ოქტომბერი	October (E)
პარლამენტი	parliament
პირობა	condition
პოლიტიკა	politics
რევოლუცია	revolution
რიგი	row; order; series; line
საგანი	subject; object (= Ger. *Gegenstand*, Russ. предмет) (A)
სადღეგრძელო	toast
საზოგადოებრივი	social
საიდან	whence
სალარო	cashier's [booth]
სასამართლო	court
სასწაული	miracle
საუბარი	conversation (A)
სეიმი	diet (= parliament); seim
სიკვდილი	death
სურვილი	wish
სქელი	fat
სცენა	stage
ტაძარი	cathedral; temple (A)
ტყე	forest
უცნობი	unknown
ფედერაციული	federated
ყურძენი	grape(s) (collective) (E)
შემოდგომა	autumn
ცივი	cold (adj.)
ციტრუსი	citrus fruit
წინადადება	sentence; clause
ცოცხალი	living; alive, lively (A)
წარმომადგენელი	representative (E)
წარწერა	inscription
წინაშე	[pp.] in front of; opposite
ხელმძღვანელი	leader

ხილი	fruit	ვახტანგ	[m.]
ხოლო	and; but; however (cf. Russ. *a*)	გორგასალი	
		ვენერა	[f.]
ხსოვნა	memory	ურუშაძე	
ჯვარი	cross (A)	ილიკო	[m.; from ილია]
ჰავა	climate	მირიანი	[m.]
ბეთლემი	Bethlehem	ნოე	Noah [m.]
ბოლნისი		ოთარი	[m.]
ისრაელი	Israel	ჯაფარიძე	(surname)

Verbs

იდგება:დგას	i-*dg*-eb-a: pr. dga-s	be standing (see sec. 9.1.3)
დადგება	da=*dg*-eb-a	stand up (sec. 9.1.2)
წარდგება	ċar+*dg*-eb-a	appear before (+წინაშე) (sec. 9.1.2)
დადგამს	da=*dg*-am-s	put down
dga-, dek-	see *dg-*	
zi-	see *ǯd-*	
აღზრდის	ağ=*zrd*-i-s	raise; bring (s.o.) up
გაზრდის	ga=*zrd*-i-s	raise (s.o., sthg.); grow (sthg.)
მოკვდება	mo=*ḳvd*-eb-a (VN მოკვდომა)	die
მოკლავს	mo=*ḳl*-av-s	kill
დამარხავს	da=*marx*-avs	bury
მონაწილეობს	*monaċile*-ob-s	participate (only pres. series)
ნადირობს	*nadir*-ob-s	hunt
იპოვ(ნ)ის: პოულობს	i=*ṗov(n)*-i-s; pres. ṗoulobs (VN პოვნა)	find
მოიპოვება	mo+i-*ṗov*-eb-a	be found (only pres. series)
შერბის: შეირბენს	še+*rb*-i-s: fut. še+i-*rben*-s	run into (see Lesson 8, note 3)

დარჩება	da=*rč*-eb-a (VN დარჩენა)	remain
მორჩება	mo=*rč*-eb-a (VN მორჩენა)	be healed
მოარჩენს	mo=a-*rčen*-s (aor. E → I)	heal, cure
დაასხამს	da=a-*sx*-am-s	pour
ისხდებიან: სხედან	i-*sxd*-eb-ian: pr. *sxed*-an	be sitting (of more than one) (see sec. 9.1.3)
დასხდებიან	da=*sxd*-eb-ian	sit down (of more than one) (for aorist see sec. 9.1.2)
sxed-	see *sxd-*	
დასჯის	da=*sǯ*-i-s	punish; condemn
შექმნის	še+*kmn*-i-s	create
ყიყინებს	*qiqin*-eb-s (VN ყიყინი)	croak
დაშლის	da=*šl*-i-s	dissolve; take apart; dissect
იცის	i-*c*-i-s	know (sthg.) (see sec. 9.1.4)
დაიცავს	da=i-*c*-av-s (aor. და(ვ)იცავი(თ), დაიცვა)	defend; protect
გამოცდის	gamo=*cd*-i-s	test, examine (s.o.)
შეცდება	še=*cd*-eb-a	err, make a mistake
ცდილობს	*cdil*-ob-s: (a) imperfective: fut. ეცდება e-*cd*-eb-a, aorist (ვ)ეცადე(თ), ეცადა; (b.) perfective: fut. (ს)ცდის (s-)*cd*-i-s, aor. (ვ)(ს)ცადე(თ), (ს)ცადა (may take id.o. marker *s-* without any id.o.)	try
ჩაიცვამს	ča=i-*cv*-am-s	(get) dress(ed); dress (o.s.)
შეცვლის	še=*cvl*-i-s	change
გარდაიცვლება	garda+i-*cvl*-eb-a	pass away (=die)

	aor. -(ვ)იცვალე(თ), -იცვალა	
გამოაცხადებს	gamo=a-*cxad*-eb-s	proclaim
მიუძღვნის	mi-u-*jǧvn*-i-s	dedicate sthg. to s.o./sthg.
ç̣ev	see *ç̣v*-	
ç̣ek-	see *ç̣v*-	
იწვება:წევს	i-*ç̣v*-eba: pr. *ç̣ev*-s	be lying down (see sec. 9.1.3)
დაწვება	da=*ç̣v*-eb-a	lie down; go to bed (see sec. 9.1.2)
გადაწყვეტს	gada=*ç̣qveṭ*-s (aor. E → I)	decide
დაჭრის	da=*č̣r*-i-s	wound; cut (bread, etc.) (aor. irr.: see sec. 9.1.1)
გახდება	ga=*xd*-eb-a	become (+ Nom.); be transformed into (+ Adv.)
გადაიხდის	gada=i-*xd*-i-s	pay
შეხვდება	še=(H-)*xvd*-eb-a	encounter, meet (s.o.)
იჯდება:ზის	i-*ǯd*-eb-a: pr. zi-s	be sitting (of one) (see sec. 9.1.3)
დაჯდება	da=*ǯd*-eb-a	sit down (of one) (see sec. 9.1.2)
ǯek-	see *ǯd*-	

Key to the Exercises

1. Who knows how Tbilisi became Georgia's capital? Iliḳo knows. Tell us, Iliḳo!
2. An old legend exists, according to which King Vaxṭang Gorgasali was hunting one day. He saw a deer and tried to kill it [its killing].
3. He couldn't kill the deer, but rather only wounded it. The deer ran into the forest. In that forest the deer found a warm spring, and there it was healed. The warm waters of that spring cured the deer.
4. When Vaxṭang Gorgasali saw that the deer still is alive, he considered it a miracle and decided to build (VN) his new capital there.
5. Although the story about the deer probably is a legend, Vaxṭang Gorgasali really existed, and we must consider the word 'Tbilisi' as a derivative of the verb *tboba*.
6. After [after that, when] we paid the bill we went out of the restaurant and we unexpectedly encountered you on the street.
7. [In] several months after the October Revoluation (1917), the Transcaucasian Diet [seim] (or Parliament) was created in Tbilisi. In it Georgian, Azerbaijani, and Armenian representatives participated.
8. On 28 April 1918 the Diet proclaimed the Transcaucasian [Transcaucasus's] Democratic Federative Republic, but after one month this Transcaucasian union was dissolved.
9. Soviet power was established in Georgia in 1921. Georgia became a part of the Transcaucasian Soviet Federated Socialist Republic. It remained in this federated republic until 1936 when the Georgian SSR was created.
10. Šota Rustaveli passed away in Jerusalem. They probably buried him there in Jerusalem's Monastery of the Cross.
11. Venera Urušaje translated Šota Rustaveli's *Vepxisṭqaosani* into English (adv.), and she dedicated her translation to Marjory Wardrop's memory.
12. I must defend (my) doctoral dissertation tomorrow. I must appear before a commission of professors and these professors must examine me.
13. In Georgia many fruits and greens grow. Georgia's climate is such that in collective farms the harvest of citrus fruits, grapes, tea, cabbage and green beans can grow from year to year (*-mde*).
14. You must raise your daughter and son so that they grow up [come out] polite (nom.).

15. Put down the cabbage and beans on this table and sit down.
16. The oldest Georgian inscriptions are found in a Georgian monastery in Israel near Bethlehem. They are older than the inscriptions of the Bolnisi cathedral.
17. Where were you sitting at (-*ze*) the concert? I was sitting near the stage, in the third row, and Givi and his wife were sitting in the last row of the balcony.
18. Ordinarily I go to bed earlier than my brother, but yesterday I went to bed later than he.
19. Yesterday two unknown men came into my office and sat down. One was fatter and taller than the other [the second].
20. Were you all in the court today? Yes, we were sitting in court when the judge ordered that the accused be executed [punished by death].
21. Where am I to pay this bill? Pay it there, at the cashier's.
22. You must be Revaz J̌aparije! -No, sir, I don't k̦now him. -Excuse me! I erred! I met Revaz J̌aparije only once, and between you and him there is a great resemblance.
23. Social conditions in Georgia significantly changed after collectivization.
24. If they will speak about (-*ze*) politics, you must change the subject of the conversation.
25. Georgia is one of the oldest Christian states. The Georgian king Mirian was Christianized, i.e., became a Christian, in 330.
26. Everybody knows that, similar to the Russians and the Greeks, the Georgians, too, are Orthodox.
27. The water in our city's river is warmish in the spring; in the autumn, however, it is coldish.
28. Why are you standing in line? I am standing in line to buy [some] fruit. Don't buy fruit here! They sell the best fruit at the collective farmers' market.
29. If we must die, let us die for (our) native land!
30. In December I defended my dissertation. Five professors examined me.
31. Unfortunately, when they asked me when Ilia Č̣avčavaje was born and when he passed away, I didn't k̦now the answer.
32. I must get dressed now, because the guests will soon come. Otar, if possible, pour the wine. At (-*ze*) our banquet everyone must drink a lot.
33. Who will be *tamada* at your banquet? Excuse me, I couldn't understand. What does *tamada* mean?
34. The *tamada* [toastmaster] of a banquet is that one

who must propose [pronounce] the toasts. He is the leader of the banquet, but he is not always the host.

35. Do you know whence the word *sadğegrjelo* [toast] comes? Yes, this word comes from the wish that your days may be long.
36. Pronounce this Georgian sentence! 'The frog croaks in the water.' I am trying to pronounce it [that I pronounce it], but I can't pronounce it.
37. Tamara, please sit down here. Paul and Medea will sit down here in this row where we are sitting.
38. When you will come to the theater, we will be sitting in the fifth row.
39. I probably was in bed [was lying down] when you returned home.
40. My friends are sitting in (*-ze*) the balcony, but I do not know where Noah is sitting.

Reading Passage

საქართველოს სსრ მოსახლეობა

1 საქართველოს სს რესპუბლიკა დასავლეთით შავ ზღვას ესაზღვრება, ჩრდილოეთით — რუსეთის სფს რესპუბლიკას (კრასნოდარის მხარე, ყარაჩაი-ჩერქეზეთის ა. ო., ყაბარდო-ბალყარეთის ასსრ, ჩრდილოეთ ოსეთის ასსრ, ჩაჩნეთ-ინგუშეთის ასსრ და დაღისტნის ასს), აღმოსავლეთით და აღმოსავლეთ-სამხრეთით — აზერბაიჯანის სსრ, ხოლო სამხრეთით — სომხეთის სსრ და თურქეთს.

2 საქართველოს სსრ ტერიტორიის ფართობი 1911 წ. იანვრისათვის 70 ათ. კვ. კილომეტრს უდრიდა.

3 საქართველოს სსრ ტერიტორიის საზღვრების მეხუთედამდე შავი ზღვის ნაპირებს გასდევს, ხოლო ოთხ მეხუთედამდე — ხმელეთს.

4 საქართველოს რუსეთთან შეერთებამდე ჩვენი ქვეყნის მტრებთან სამშობლოს დამოუკიდებლობისათვის წარმოებული თავდადებული ბრძოლები ქართველ ხალხში დიდ მსხვერპლს იწვევდა და ოდესღაც მრავალრიცხოვანი მოსახლეობა თანდათან მცირდებოდა ხალხის ხშირი დარბევის, გასახლებისა და სახელმწიფოს ტერიტორიის ნაწილის მტრის მიერ მიტაცების შედეგად.

5 XIII საუკუნის პირველ ნახევარში საქართველოს მოსახლეობას მილიონობით ითვლიდნენ, ხოლო XIX საუკუნის დამდეგს, ე. ი. საქართველოს რუსეთთან შეერთების მომენტისათვის, იგი ექვსასი ათას სულს ოდნავ აღემატებოდა.

6 საქართველოს რუსეთთან შეერთებამ იხსნა ქართველი ხალხი ფიზიკური მოსპობისაგან, უზრუნველყო მტრის მიერ მიტაცებული ტერიტორიების ნაწილის უკან დაბრუნება, ხელი შეუწყო ეკონომიკისა და კულტურის განვითარებას, მოსახლეობის რიცხვის ზრდას.

7 საბჭოთა ხელისუფლების დამყარების შემდეგ ქვეყნის ეკონომიური და კულტურული აღმავლობა სწრაფად გაძლიერდა და მოსახლეობის რაოდენობაც მნიშვნელოვნად გაიზარდა.

8 საქართველოს სსრ მოსახლეობას საბჭოთა ხელისუფლების დამყარების დროს 2,4 მილიონი სულის რაოდენობით ანგარიშობდნენ, ხოლო 1959 წლის 15 იანვრისათვის 4 მილიონ სულს აღემატებოდა, ე. ი. 67% გაიზარდა. მოსახლეობის ზრდა მოხდა როგორც მისი ბუნებრივი მატების, ისე მექანიკური ზრდის შედეგად.

9 მოკავშირე რესპუბლიკებს შორის საქართველო ერთ-ერთი ყველაზე მჭიდროდ დასახლებული ქვეყანაა. ერთ კვადრატულ კილომეტრზე საქართველოში საშუალოდ 6-ჯერ მეტი მცხოვრები მოდის (58 სული), ვიდრე სსრ კავშირში მთლიანად.

Vocabulary

1

სსრ	= საბჭოთა სოციალისტური რესპუბლიკის
მოსახლეობა	population
დასავლეთით	on the west (cf. დასავლეთი 'west')
ზღვა	sea
ესაზღვრება	(sthg.) adjoins/borders on (sthg.) (dat.)
ჩრდილოეთით	on the north (cf. ჩრდილოეთი 'north')
სფს	= საბჭოთა ფედერაციული სოციალისტური
კრასნოდარი	Krasnodar
მხარე	region, area; side (A) (Russ. *krai*)
ჩერქეზეთი	Circassia
ა.ო.	= ავტონომიური ოლქი
ყაბარდო-ბალყარეთი	Kabardo-Balkaria
ასსრ	= ავტონომიური საბჭოთა სოციალისტური რესპუბლიკა
ჩაჩნეთ-ინგუშეთი	land of Chechens and Ingush
დაღისტანი	Daghestan (A); ასს, misprint, =ასსრ
სამხრეთი	south

2

ფართობი	area
1911 წ.	= ათას ცხრაას თერთმეტი წლის
იანვარი	January (A)
70 ათ.	= სამოცდაათ ათას (70,000)
კვ.	= კვადრატული square
უდრის imperf. უდრიდა	is equal to (dat.) (Pres. ser. only)

3

მეხუთედი	fifth (fraction)
ნაპირი	shore
გასდევს [ga+s-*dev*-s]	follow; run along (sthg.) (dat.) (only pres.)
ხმელეთი	dry land

4

მტრებთან ... ბრძოლები	struggles with the enemies
დამოუკიდებლობა	independence
წარმოებული	here: undertaken
თავდადებული	self-sacrificing
ხალხი	people
მსხვერპლი	sacrifice
გამო=იწვევს	evoke; cause
ოდესღაც	at one time; once
მრავალრიცხოვანი	numerous (cf. მრავალი 'many', რიცხვი 'number')
თანდათან	gradually; by degrees
მცირე	small
ხშირი	frequent
და=არბევს	destroy; devastate
გა=ასახლებს	expel
მი=იტაცებს	capture
შედეგად [pp.]	as a result (cf. შედეგი 'result, consequence')

5

XIII	= მეცამეტე
ნახევარი	half (A)
მილიონობით	in millions
და=ითვლის	count
XIX	= მეცხრამეტე
დამდეგი	beginning (of a time-period); დამდეგს at the beginning
მომენტი	moment
ექვსასი ათასი	[600,000]
სული	soul (here: person; cf. Russian душа)
ოდნავ	hardly; scarcely
აღ+ემატება	surpass; excede [rel. II. conj.]

6

Ø=იხსნის	set free; save
მო=სპობს	annihilate; destroy
უზრუნველყო	[secured (3sg. aor.)](see sec. 15.1.6)
მიტაცებული	captured
და=უბრუნებს	return (sthg.) to (s.o.) (უკან დაბრუნება 'return' VN)
შე=უწყობს ხელს	help (s.o.) (dat.); give (s.o.) a hand
განვითარება	development
რიცხვი	number; amount; quantity

7

აღმავლობა	rise; progress
სწრაფი	fast; quick
გა=აძლიერებს	make strong; increase
რაოდენობა	quantity; amount
მნიშვნელოვნად	considerably

8

დროს	here: at the time (of)
2,4 მილიონი	= ორი მილიონი ოთხასი ათასი
რაოდენობით	here: at (a quantity)
ანგარიშობს	*angariš-ob-s* count; here: reckon
	= ათას ცხრაას ორმოცდაცხრამეტი
აღ=ემატება	exceed
67%	სამოცდაშვიდი პროცენტით
მო=ხდება	occur (root II. conj.)
როგორც ... ისე ...	both ... and ...
ბუნებრივი	natural
მატება	addition; increase
მექანიკური	mechanical

9

მოკავშირე	here: Union (i.e., of the Soviet Union)
ერთ-ერთი	one (among a number)
მჭიდრო	compact; dense

დასახლებული	settled
საშუალო	mean; average
ექვსჯერ	6 times
მცხოვრები	inhabitant; dweller
მოდის	here: there are
58	= ორმოცდათვრამეტი
ვიდრე	than
მთლიანი	entire, მთლიანად as a whole

REGIONS OF THE GEORGIAN SSR

1. ქართლი
2. კახეთი
3. მესხეთი-ჯავახეთი
4. იმერეთი
5. გურია-სამეგრელო

6/6a. დიდი კავკასიონი
7. აფხაზეთი
8. აჭარა
9. სამხრეთ-ოსეთი

LESSON 10

10.1 The perfect series of I. and III. conjugation verbs. The third series of Georgian verbs is traditionally called the *perfect* series in Western grammatical literature. This name, unfortunately, is not very appropriate since there is not much equivalence between the Georgian perfect series screeves and English forms with similar names, such as the present perfect and pluperfect (or past perfect). As will be seen below (sec. 10.1.3), the main nuance of the present perfect is the inference of an event having occurred in the past, while the pluperfect is used mainly to denote unreal (counter-factual) events in the past.

The perfect series of I. and III. conjugation verbs is characterized by a phenomenon called *inversion*, in which the grammatical subject is in the dative case (and marked in the verb by formants which mark indirect objects in the other series of the verb). Direct objects (mainly with I. conjugation verbs) are in the nominative case. Unlike the present-future and aorist series, the verb by itself *cannot* mark an indirect object: indirect objects are paraphrased, generally by a noun in the genitive plus the postposition *-tvis*.

In contemporary Georgian only two screeves are generally encountered in the perfect series. These are called the present perfect and the pluperfect.[1] The present perfect is based upon a stem generally derived from the future stem, while the stem of the pluperfect is identical to the stem of the aorist.

Since perfect series forms occur most commonly with a third person direct object, we shall present the conjugation of perfect series forms first with such an object (or, as in the case of most III. conjugation verbs, with no direct object at all).

10.1.1. Perfect series with third person direct object or with no direct object. The *subject* markers of the *present perfect* are:

	sing.	pl.
1.	mi-	gvi-
2.	gi-	gi-.....-t
3.	u-	u-.....-t

Note that these are identical to the *u*-series indirect object markers of present, future, and aorist series forms, except that there is a formal difference between the third person singular (*u*-) and the third person plural (*u*-.....-*t*), a distinction not found in the *u*-series indirect object markers (cf. sec. 7.2.2).

If the *subject* in the *dative* shows number agreement in the 3d person, the *direct object* in the *nominative* does not show 3d person number agreement.

The marker of a third person *direct object* (singular or plural) is: -i-a, consisting of a suffix -*i*- and the short form of the 3sg. of the verb 'be': -*a*. With verbs with P/FSF -*am* or -*av*, the marker is officially -s, although colloquially other forms (e.g., with loss of P/FSF and object ending -*i*-*a*) are also found. The ending -*i*-*a* also occurs with all III. conjugation verbs in the present perfect; i.e., all I. and III. conjugation verbs have such a marker if there is *no* direct object or if there is a third person direct object.

10.1.1.1. The present perfect stem. The stem of the present perfect is based on the future stem for both I. and III. conjugation verbs. All preradical vowels and all person and number markers are dropped. The P/FSF is dropped in the following verb types:

a. All III. conj. verbs[2]
b. Verbs with both P/FSF -*eb* or -*ob* and nonsyllabic (vowelless) roots
c. Verbs with P/FSF -*i*.

The direct object marker -*s* is added to I. conjugation verbs with P/FSF -*av* or -*am*. To all other verbs the ending -*i*-*a* (-*n*-*i*-*a* with some III. conjugation verbs[3]) is added. The subject markers appear immediately before the root. Examples:

I. conj.

Future		Present perfect (subj. = 1sg.)
დაწერს	write	დამიწერია
აღმოაჩენს	discover	აღმომიჩენია
მოჭრის	cut	მომიჭრია
გაგზავნის	send	გამიგზავნია
გაიმეორებს	repeat	გამიმეორებია
დაიწყებს	begin	დამიწყია
გააღებს	open	გამიღია
ნახავს	see	მინახავს, მინახია
დახატავს	paint	დამიხატავს
დადგამს	put	დამიდგამს
ჩათვლის	consider	ჩამითვლია

მოამზადებს	prepare	მომიმზადებია	
III. conj.			
Present	(3sg.)	Future	Present Perfect (subj. = 1sg.)
ყეფს	bark	იყეფებს	მიყეფ(ნ)ია
კივის	scream	იკივლებს	მიკივლია
გორავს	roll	იგორებს	მიგორია
თამაშობს	play	ითამაშებს	მითამაშ(ნ)ია
ტრიალებს	turn	იტრიალებს	მიტრიალ(ნ)ია

Note: The irregular verb მისცემს 'give' (sec. 7.4) forms the perfect with the root *c* instead of the future stem in *cem*:

1. მიმიცია 2. მიგიცია 3. მიუცია

Examples of the conjugation of present perfect forms with third person direct object:

I. conj.

ამიშენებია მინახავს

I have built, seen it/them

აგიშენებია გინახავს

You have built, seen it/them

აუშენებია უნახავს

He, she, it has built, seen it/them

აგვიშენებია გვინახავს

We have built, seen it/them

აგიშენებიათ გინახავთ

You all have built,seen it/them

აუშენებიათ უნახავთ

They have built, seen it/them

III. conj.

მიტირია	I have cried
გიტირია	You have cried
უტირია	He, she, it has cried
გვიტირია	We have cried
გიტირიათ	You all have cried
უტირიათ	They have cried

10.1.1.2. The pluperfect with third person direct object or without direct object. All III. conjugation verbs and all I. conjugation verbs (except those with preradical vowel *a-* and P/FSF *-eb*) have as the stem of the pluperfect the *3sg. aorist* minus any preradical vowel and/or person markers. When the direct object is third person or when there is no direct object, the marker is the same as the 3sg. *subject* marker of the (corresponding) aorist. Some III. conjugation verbs (in general, those inserting *-n-* in the perfect) insert *-n-* before the *-a.*[4]

I. conjugation verbs with preradical vowel *a-* and P/FSF *-eb*[5] form the pluperfect stem from the future stem by dropping the preradical vowel and any person markers, but keeping the P/FSF *-eb* and adding *-in-* to the stem before the object marker:

-in-a

The *subject* markers of the pluperfect are the *e*-series markers; note the contrast between 3sg. and 3pl.:

	Singular	Plural
1.	me-	gve-
2.	ge-	ge-.....-t
3.	e-	e-.....-t

Examples: (Objects in all forms are third person.)[6]

I. conj.

Future (subject 3sg.)		Aorist (subject 3sg.)	Pluperfect (subject 1sg.)
დაწერს	write	დაწერა	დამეწერა
აღმოაჩენს	discover	აღმოაჩინა	აღმომეჩინა
მოჭრის	cut	მოჭრა	მომეჭრა
დაიწყებს	begin	დაიწყო	დამეწყო
გააღებს	open	გააღო	გამეღო
ნახავს	see	ნახა	მენახა
დახატავს	paint	დახატა	დამეხატა
დადგამს	put	დადგა	დამედგა
ჩათვლის	consider	ჩათვალა	ჩამეთვალა
გაამზადებს	prepare	(გაამზადა)	გამემზადებინა
გააგრძელებს	continue	(გააგრძელა)	გამეგრძელებინა

III. conj.

Present (3sg.)		Future (3sg.)	Aorist (3sg.)	Pluperfect (1sg.)
ყეფს	bark	იყეფებს	იყეფა	მეყეფ(ნ)ა
კივის	scream	იკივლებს	იკივლა	მეკივლა
გორავს	roll	იგორებს	იგორა	მეგორა
თამაშობს	play	ითამაშებს	ითამაშა	მეთამაშ(ნ)ა
ტრიალებს	turn	იტრიალებს	იტრიალა	მეტრიალ(ნ)ა

Examples of the conjugation of pluperfect forms with third person direct objects:

I. conj.

	had sent it/them		had prepared it/them
1.	გამეგზავნა	1.	გამემზადებინა
2.	გაგეგზავნა	2.	გაგემზადებინა
3.	გაეგზავნა	3.	გაემზადებინა
1.	გაგვეგზავნა	1.	გაგვემზადებინა
2.	გაგეგზავნათ	2.	გაგემზადებინათ
3.	გაეგზავნათ	3.	გაემზადებინათ

III. conj.

	had played		
1.	მეთამაშა	1.	გვეთამაშა
2.	გეთამაშა	2.	გეთამაშათ
3.	ეთამაშა	3.	ეთამაშათ

10.1.2. Perfect series with first or second person direct object.

10.1.2.1. Present perfect with direct object in the first or second person. The number of verbs which can normally take a direct object in the first or second person is limited. In these forms the direct object is marked by the vowel *-i-* following the perfect stem and followed by the appropriate present tense form of the verb 'be' marking the direct object. In the first person the form of the verb 'be', *-var*, occurs with the first person prefix, *v-*. According to the norm, verbs with P/FSF *-av* and *-am* add the forms of the verb 'be' directly to the perfect stem. But one also finds the perfect screeve of such verbs formed with either complete loss of the P/FSF or with syncope of the P/FSF and with regular formation (i.e., with the vowel *-i-*

following the perfect stem). Examples:

მიქიხარ(თ) mi-k-i-xar(-t)

I (*mi-*) have praised you (*-xar*)/you all (*-xart*)

გიქივარ(თ)[7] gi-k-i-var(-t)

You (*gi-*) have praised me (*-var*)/us (*-vart*)

ვუქივარ(თ) v-u-k-i-var(-t)

He (*u-*) has praised me (*v-.....-var*)/us (*v-.....-vart*)

უქიხარ(თ) u-k-i-xar(-t)

He (*u-*) has praised you (*-xar*)/you all (*-xart*)

გვიქიხარ(თ) gvi-k-i-xar(-t)

We (*gvi-*) have praised you (*-xar*)/you all (*-xart*)

გიქივართ[7] gi-k-i-var-t

You all (*gi-.....-t*) have praised me (*-var*)/us (*-vart*)

When the subject is third person *plural* and the direct object is first or second person *singular* the verb takes no plural marker:

ვუქივარ They (*u-*) have praised me (*v-..... -var*) (= also 'He has praised me.')

უქიხარ They (*u-*) have praised you (*-xar*) (= also 'He has praised you.')

When both the subject and the direct object are plural the plural marker *-t* occurs:

ვუქივართ They (*u-.....-t*) have praised us (*v-.. ...-var-t*) (= also 'He (*u-*) has praised us.')

უქიხართ They (*u-.....-t*) have praised you all (*-xar-t*) (= also 'He (*u-*) has praised you all.')

Examples with a verb in *-av*: *nax-av-s* 'see'

Standard	Nonstandard
მინახავხარ(-თ)	მინახ(ვ)იხარ(-თ)
I have seen you/you all	
გინახავვარ(-თ)[7]	გინახ(ვ)ივარ(-თ)[7]
You have seen me/us	
ვუნახავვარ(-თ)	ვუნახ(ვ)ივარ(-თ)
He has seen me/us	

უნახავხარ(-თ) უნახ(ვ)იხარ(-თ)
He has seen you/you all

გვინახავხარ(-თ) გვინახ(ვ)იხარ(-თ)
We have seen you/you all

გინახავვარ(-თ)[7] გინახ(ვ)ივარ(-თ)[7]
You have seen me/us

ვუნახავვარ ვუნახ(ვ)ივარ
They have seen me (see above)

ვუნახავვართ ვუნახ(ვ)ივართ
They have seen us

უნახავხარ უნახ(ვ)იხარ
They have seen you (see above)

უნახავხართ უნახ(ვ)იხართ
They have seen you all

10.1.2.2. Pluperfect with direct object in the first or second persons. In the formation of the pluperfect the direct object markers are identical to the *subject* markers of the aorist of the verb. If the aorist takes the regular ending -*e* in the first and second persons, so does the pluperfect; if the aorist takes the strong ending -*i*, so does the pluperfect.

Examples:

(a) regular endings

I had seen you/you all მენახე(-თ)
You had seen me/us გენახე(-თ)[7]
He had seen me/us ვენახე(-თ)
He had seen you/you all ენახე(-თ)
We had seen you/you all გვენახე(-თ)
You all had seen me/us გენახეთ[7]
They had seen me ვენახე
They had seen us ვენახეთ
They had seen you ენახე
They had seen you all ენახეთ

(b) strong endings

I had killed you/you all მომეკალი(-თ)
You had killed me/us მოგეკალი(-თ)[7]

He had killed me/us	მოვეკალი(-თ)
He had killed you/you all	მოეკალი(-თ)
We had killed you/you all	მოგვეკალი(-თ)
You all had killed me/us	მოგეკალით[7]
They had killed me	მოვეკალი
They had killed us	მოვეკალით
They had killed you	მოეკალი
They had killed you all	მოეკალით

10.1.3. Function of the perfect series screeves.[8]

10.1.3.1. Present perfect. Of the present perfect's wide range of meanings, perhaps the two most important are its use to mark "inferred actions" and its use in negation.

a. Inferred action. The speaker may deduce or infer the occurrence in the past of a given action on the basis of its results. In such uses the Georgian present perfect often can be paraphrased in English by constructions containing *must have* or *apparently* (თურმე in Georgian; this adverb occurs commonly with the present perfect)[9]. Compare the following two sentences:

ვანომ წერილი მიიღო.

Vano received the letter. (simple statement)

ვანოს მოსაწვევი ბარათი მიუღია; ლექციაზე მოვიდა.

Vano received [must have received] the invitation; he came to the lecture.

Note also:

ეს სურათი დაუხატავს ლადო გუდიაშვილს; მის სტილს ვიცნობ.

Lado Gudiašvili painted [i.e., must have painted] this picture; I recognize his style.

თუ არ ვცდები, მე თქვენ სადღაც მინახავხართ.

If I am not mistaken, I have seen [i.e., must have, apparently have] seen you all somewhere.

The use of the aorist in such sentences might imply that the speaker actually saw the event being narrated; e.g., ლადო გუდიაშვილმა ეს სურათი დახატა; see c. below. Most commonly, though, the aorist in affirmative sentences simply states a fact while the present perfect will have the nuance of supposition, deduction, inference.

Fig. 10.1. Formation of the Perfect and the Pluperfect

Perfect

Direct Object (nominative)	Subject (dative) 1sg	2sg	3sg
1sg	---	gi-...-var	v-u-...-var
2sg	mi-...-xar	---	u-...-xar
1pl	---	gi-...-var-t	v-u-...-var-t
2pl	mi-...-xar-t	---	u-...-xar-t
3^{sg}_{pl}	mi-...-a*	gi-...-a*	u-...-a*

	1pl	2pl	3pl
1sg	---	gi-...-var-t	v-u-...-var(!)
2sg	gvi-..-xar	---	u-...-xar(!)
1pl	---	gi-...-var-t	v-u-...-var-t
2pl	gvi-..-xar-t	---	u-...-xar-t
3^{sg}_{pl}	gvi-...-a*	gi-...-a*-t	{u-...-a-t u-...-t}

Pluperfect

	1sg	2sg	3sg
1sg	---	ge-...-e**	v-e-...-e**
2sg	me-...-e**	---	e-...-e**
1pl	---	ge-...-e**-t	v-e-...-e**-t
2pl	me-...-e**-t	---	e-...-e**-t
3^{sg}_{pl}	me-...-a***	ge-...-a***	e-...-a***

	1pl	2pl	3pl
1sg	---	ge-...-e**-t	v-e-...-e**(!)
2sg	gve-..-e**	---	e-...-e**(!)
1pl	---	ge-...-e**-t	v-e-...-e**-t
2pl	gve-..-e**-t	---	e-...-e**-t
3^{sg}_{pl}	gve-...-a***	ge-...-a***-t	e-...-a***-t

*Or -*s* with verbs with P/FSF -*av*, -*am*.
**Or -*i* (sec. 9.1.1).
***Or -*o* (sec. 5.4.1).

b. The perfect with negation. The use of the perfect is particularly common with negation in the past.[10] The negated present perfect differs in meaning from the negated aorist in that the latter generally connotes an unwillingness to perform the action while the former does not; compare:

Perfect: ის პერანგი არ მიყიდია.

I didn't buy that shirt.

Aorist: ის პერანგი არ ვიყიდე.

I didn't buy that shirt [because I didn't feel like it].

c. Reported action. The present perfect is often used instead of the aorist when the action described was not witnessed by the speaker but rather the speaker learned of it from someone else's words. Examples:

ვიღაცამ მეფე მოკლა! ქუჩაში ვიდექი და ვნახე.

Someone killed [aorist] the king! I was standing in the street and saw it!

ვიღაცას მეფე მოუკლავს! საიდან იცით? ვიღაცამ მითხრა.

"Someone killed [present perfect] the king!" "From where do you know?" "Someone told me."

d. The present perfect with present meaning. In a limited number of instances, the present perfect can have a present meaning.

ეს არ შეიძლება, გალაქტიონ, არ შეიძლება, მითქვამს შენთვის.

This isn't possible, Galakṭion, it isn't possible, *I tell you.*

e. Questions in the present perfect. Some questions referring to the past can be put in the present perfect; the response can be in the perfect or in the aorist. Examples:

ეს ფილმი გინახავს?	Have you seen this film?
ვნახე.	I have seen it.
იას ხომ არ გამოუგზავნია თქვენთვის წერილი?	Didn't Violet send the letter to you?
(a) (ჩვენთვის) გამოუგზავნია	She sent it to us. (present perfect)

(b) გამოგვიგზავნა. She sent it to us. (aorist)

(For the difference in meaning between the present perfect and the aorist in the reply, see a. and c. above.)

10.1.3.2. Pluperfect. The major function of the pluperfect is to denote past modality.[11] It serves as a *past tense* to both the conjunctive (present and future) and the optative. In conditional sentences the past condition is pluperfect, the result clause conditional. Compare:

Conjunctive present:

ახლა რომ საქართველოში ვცხოვრობდე, ქართულად უფრო კარგად ვილაპარაკებდი.

If I were living in Georgia now, I would speak Georgian better.

Pluperfect:

საქართველოში დიდხანს რომ მეცხოვრა, ქართულად უფრო კარგად ვილაპარაკებდი.

If I had lived in Georgia for a long time, I would speak Georgian better.

Optative:

გამოცდა კალმით უნდა დაწერო, ფანქრით კი არა!

You must write the examination with a pen, not with pencil!

Pluperfect:

გამოცდა კალმით უნდა დაგეწერა, და არა ფანქრით!

You should have written the examination with a pen, not with pencil!

As can be seen from the examples, the pluperfect is used to express *past* conditions which are counter to fact.

Expressions of past anteriority in Georgian. The English past perfect is often used to denote an action which occurred prior to another past action, e.g., 'John *had* (already) *spoken* to his lawyer when he sent me the letter.' In Georgian, such past anteriority is usually expressed not by the pluperfect but rather by the aorist or present perfect, often with the adverb უკვე 'already'. Examples:

ივანეს თავის ადვოკატთან უკვე ულაპარაკია, როცა წერილი გამომიგზავნა.

John [apparently] had already spoken to his lawyer when he sent me the letter.

თქვენ უკვე გნახეთ, როცა ადვოკატი მოვიდა.

I had already seen you all when the lawyer came.

(The resultative past can also be used in this function; see sec. 13.5.)

10.1.4. Expression of indirect objects in the perfect series. Since a I. or III. conjugation verb in the perfect series cannot express an indirect object by itself, what were indirect objects (in the dative) in the present, future, and aorist series are usually marked in the perfect series with the postposition -*tvis* (+ genitive). Examples:

Future:	ლიდას მივწერ
	I shall write to Lida.
Pres. perf.:	ლიდასათვის მიმიწერია
	I have written to Lida.
Aorist:	ფული გამომიგზავნა
	He sent me money.
Pluperfect:	ფული ჩემთვის გამოეგზავნა
	He had sent me money.
Future:	სახლს აგიშენებთ
	We will build you a house.
Pres. perf.:	სახლი შენთვის აგვიშენებია
	We have built you a house.

The absence of marking for indirect objects in the perfect series means that there is no contrast between verbs which in other series have a formal distinction between absolute and relative forms:

absolute:	ააშენებს	
	he will build it	perfect:
relative:	ამიშენებს	აუშენებია
	he will build it for me	

Verbs which take *mo-* with first and second person indirect objects keep this *mo-* in the perfect series:

absolute:	გაგზავნის	
	He will send it	perfect:
relative:	გაუგზავნის	გაუგზავნია

	He will send it to him	
relative:	გამომიგზავნის	
	He will send it to me	Perfect:
relative:	გამოგიგზავნის	გამოუგზავნია
	He will send it to you	

Note that verbs which regularly have markings for indirect objects in the future, present, and aorist series lose that marking in the perfect series:

მომწერს	he will write me	perfect: მოუწერია
მისცემ	you will give him	perfect: მიგიცია

Since there is no marking of indirect objects in the perfect series, there is no opposition between relative and absolute forms of the verb 'say', 'tell' in that series. Note that the perfect is irregular, based on the absolute aorist stem:

	Absolute	Relative
Pres.	ამბობს	ეუბნება
Fut.	იტყვის	ეტყვის
Aor.	თქვა	უთხრა
Perfect	უთქვამს	

10.2. Summary of case markings for I. and III. conjugation verbs:

Series	Subject	Direct Object	Indirect Object
Present, Future	Nominative	Dative	
Aorist	Ergative	Nominative	Dative
Perfect	Dative	Nominative	---

10.3. Numerals. From 30 to 99 Georgian numerals are based on the vigesimal system, i.e., a system to base 20, unlike our decimal system to base 10. This system is similar to the French system from 80 to 99. Compare:

	Georgian	*French*
80	otx-m-oc-i	quatre-vingts
	4 X 20	4 20's

81	otx-m-oc-da-ert-i	quatre-vingt-et-un
	4 X 20 & 1	4 20 & 1
82	otx-m-oc-da-or-i	quatre-vingt-deux
	4 X 20 & 2	4 20 2
90	otx-m-oc-da-at-i	quatre-vingt-dix
	4 X 20 & 10	4 20 10
99	otx-m-oc-da-cxrameṭ-i	quatre-vingt-dix-neuf
	4 X 20 & 19	4 20 19

Examples:

30 ოცდაათი (= 20 + 10)
31 ოცდათერთმეტი
32 ოცდათორმეტი
33 ოცდაცამეტი
34 ოცდათოთხმეტი
35 ოცდათხუთმეტი
36 ოცდათექვსმეტი
37 ოცდაჩვიდმეტი
38 ოცდათვრამეტი
39 ოცდაცხრამეტი
40 ორმოცი (= 2 X 20)
50 ორმოცდაათი
60 სამოცი (<sam-m-oc-i)
70 სამოცდაათი
80 ოთხმოცი
90 ოთხმოცდაათი

The hundreds are:
100 ასი
200 ორასი
300 სამასი, etc.

The thousands are:
1000 ათასი
2000 ორი ათასი
3000 სამი ათასი, etc.

1,000,000 is ერთი მილიონი. In numbers below 2000 only the last number is declined. So: 1979 = ათას ცხრაას სამოცდაცხრამეტი. In the thousands and millions any numeral modifying the words ათასი or მილიონი is declined, for example, 25,657 = ოცდახუთი ათას ექვსას ორმოცდაჩვიდმეტი.

10.3.1. Ordinals. The ordinal circumfix *me-.....-e* is added immediately after the *-da-* in numerals containing this form, for example:

1347th, 347th, 47th:
(ათას) (სამას) ორმოცდამეშვიდე

1357th, 357th, 57th:
(ათას) (სამას) ორმოცდამეჩვიდმეტე

Note:

61st: სამოცდამეერთე (rare: სამოცდაპირველი)

101st: ასმეერთე or ასპირველი

Elsewhere the circumfix is placed around the last full numeral, for example, 40th მეორმოცე; 840th რვაას მეორმოცე; 100th მეასე; 1000th მეათასე.

10.4. Wordbuilding: Derivatives from numerals.

10.4.1. Fractions. Fractional numerals are derived from the adverbial case of the ordinals. This adverbial form is the base to which case endings are added, for example, 1/3 მესამედი, 1/4 მეოთხედი, 1/5 მეხუთედი, 1/10 მეათედი, etc. 1/2 is ნახევარი (A).

10.4.2. Approximatives. The suffix *-iode* is added to the stem of numerals. These derivatives have the meaning 'approximately'; for example, ორიოდე 'approximately two', სამიოდე 'about three', ათიოდე 'about ten', ასიოდე 'about one hundred', etc. Note that the final *e* is nontruncating: ოციოდე 'about twenty', gen. ოციოდეს.

10.4.3. Distributives. When the stem of a numeral is reduplicated, the resultant meaning is equivalent to English 'apiece', for example, ორ-ორი 'two apiece', ექვს-ექვსი 'six apiece'. Compare თავის შვილებს ას-ასი მანეთი გაუგზავნა. 'He sent his children one hundred rubles apiece; he sent each of his children one hundred rubles.' Note however the adjective ერთ-ერთი 'one of two', 'one of many'; compare პრესის თავისუფლება ერთ-ერთი ჩვენი ძირითადი თავისუფლებათაგანი. 'Freedom of the press is one of our basic freedoms.'

10.4.4. Derivatives with *-ive*. Note the following: ორივე 'both', სამივე 'all three', ათივე 'all ten', etc. Note that the final *e* of this suffix is nontruncating, for example ოცივე 'all twenty', gen. ოცივეს.[12]

10.4.5. Derivatives with *-eul-*. The suffix *-eul-* added to numerals results in the meaning 'a unit composed of the given number of individual members'. Examples: სამეული 'a commission consisting of three members'; ოთხეული 'a team of four members', etc. In many instances these forms take on an unpredictable meaning, for example, ორეული 'double (someone resembling someone else completely)', რვეული 'notebook' (originally consisting of eight pages), etc. Note particularly ერთეული 'unit'.

10.4.6. Suffix *-ǰer*. This suffix added to the stem of the numeral corresponds to English 'times' (French *fois*, German *-mal*, Russian *раз*); for example, ორჯერ 'twice', სამჯერ 'three times', ათჯერ 'ten times'. 'Once' is normally ერთხელ. The suffix *-xel* can also be found from time to time with the meaning of *-ǰer*.

Monument to Vaxtang Gorgasali (l.) and Meṭexi Fortress (r.) in Tbilisi

LESSON 10: Notes

1. The functions of a third screeve of the perfect series, the conjunctive perfect, obsolescent in the contemporary language, have been taken over by the pluperfect. For the forms of the conjunctive perfect, see below, note 11.

2. Since the present perfect of III. conjugation verbs is based on the future stem, the FSF that is dropped is always -*eb*.

3. There is much oscillation as to which III. conjugation verbs take -*n*-*i*-*a* instead of -*i*-*a* in the perfect. So, from ყეფს 'bark' the present perfect is according to some sources უყეფნია while other sources give the form უყეფია without *n*. The 1970 თანამედროვე ქართული სალიტერატურო ენის ნორმები, vol. I [Norms of the contemporary Georgian literary language, vol. I] recognizes only the forms without *n*. Nonetheless, the student should be prepared to recognize forms with *n* encountered in contemporary Georgian texts. In the exercises, forms with and without *n* will be given.

4. Verbs of the III. conjugation taking -*n*- in the perfect tend also to take infixed -*n*- before the final -*a* of the pluperfect. Thus, both ეთამაშა and ეთამაშნა can be found. The თანამედროვე ქართული სალიტერატურო ენის ნორმები, vol I, 1970, recognizes only the forms without *n*. Nonetheless, the student should be prepared to encounter the forms with *n* in contemporary Georgian writing.

5. This is the productive group of denominatives (see sec. 3.5), verbs which form the II. conjugation in -*d*- (sec. 3.1.2).

6. For many I. conjugation verbs the pluperfect is formally identical to the corresponding II. conjugation *relative* aorist forms, although, generally speaking, the pluperfect is encountered more commonly than relative II. conjugation aorists. Compare:

> ივანეს წერილი უნდა გაეგზავნა.
>
> John should have sent the letter.
> (I. conj. pluperfect)
>
> წერილი ივანეს გაეგზავნა.
>
> The letter was sent to John.
> (relative II. conj. aorist)

Note the differences in person marked by the various verbal affixes:

I. conj. pluperfect:

ga= [e] -gzavn- [a]

subject (3d person) — [e]; direct object (3d person) — [a]

Relative II. conj. aorist:

ga= [e] -gzavn- [a]

indirect object (3d person) — [e]; subject (3 sing.) — [a]

7. For the loss of the *-v-* (i.e., why the form is not **v*-gi-k-i-*var(-t)*, etc., see sec. 7.1.2, rule 2.

8. The various descriptions of the functions of the Georgian perfect series do not fully explain why in one given context a Georgian speaker will use a perfect series form while in a superficially analogous context he will choose an aorist or other form. Unfortunately, our presentation must share this shortcoming.

9. The Georgian name of the perfect series, თურმეობითი, comes from the common occurrence of the adverb თურმე with these forms.

10. Note that some instances of the use of the aorist with negation in the exercises to past lessons would have indicated an unwillingness by the subject to perform the action. In such instances the use of the present perfect would often have been more appropriate.

11. In its modal uses, the pluperfect replaces the now obsolescent *conjunctive perfect*, a screeve formed on the same stem as the pluperfect. As in the pluperfect, the grammatical subject is marked by *e*-series markers, but the direct object is marked by the endings of the optative of the given verb. Examples (subject 1sg., object 3d person) corresponding to the pluperfect forms given in sec. 10.1.1.2:

დამეწეროს, აღმომეჩინოს, მომეჭრას, გამეგზავნოს,
დამეწყოს, გამეღოს, მომეკლას, დამეხატოს,
დამედგას, ჩამეთვალოს გამემზადებინოს,
გამეგრძელებინოს, მეყეფოს, მეკივლოს, მეგოროს,

მეცრიალოს.

Important! The pluperfect in its modal use replaces the optative after a main verb that is in a past screeve (imperfect, conditional, aorist). This is because the optative cannot occur after such screeves; it occurs after non-past screeves (present, future).

12. The eight volume ქართული ენის განმარტებითი ლექსიკონი does not attest such forms for რვა 'eight' and ცხრა 'nine'. In older styles, the case endings can precede the *-ve*: N. ორივე, E. ორმავე, D. ორსავე, G. ორისავე, etc.

LESSON 10: Exercises

1. პეტრე თუ გინახავს დღეს? —დიახ, ვნახე.
2. ქართული ენა თურმე მრავალი წლის განმავლობაში გისწავლია, რადგანაც ქართულად უშეცდომოდ ლაპარაკობ. —დიახ, ექვსი წელი ვსწავლობდი.
3. პროფესორს მეცხრამეტე საუკუნის ქართული ლიტერატურის განვითარება განუხილავს? —დიახ, განუხილავს. მე კი არ ვიყავი კლასში, მაგრამ თამაზმა მითხრა.
4. გივისათვის ანგარიში ხომ არ გაგიგზავნია? არა, ჯერ კიდევ არ გამიგზავნია.
5. პეტრესათვის თქვენი ოქროს საათი არ მიგიყიდიათ? არა, ვინაიდან მას საათი უკვე ეყიდა, მისთვის არ მიმიყიდია.
6. ფეხბურთი გუშინ არ გითამაშნია (გითამაშია)? არა, არ ვითამაშე, ვინაიდან სპორტსმენი არა ვარ. (არ becomes არა before monosyllables.)
7. (a) ახლა რომ საქართველოში ვცხოვრობდე, ქართულად უფრო კარგად ვილაპარაკებდი. (b) საქართველოში რომ მესწავლა, ახლა ქართულად უფრო კარგად ვილაპარაკებდი.
8. (a) ხვალ თუ არ იწვიმებს, სოფელში წავალთ.
   (b) ახლა რომ არ წვიმდეს, სოფელში წავიდოდით.
   (c) გუშინ რომ არ ეწვიმა, სოფელში წავიდოდით.
9. თქვენთან უფრო კარგად რომ მელაპარაკა ქართულად, გამიგებდით!
10. ივანეს თქვენთვის არ უთქვამს, რაც მოხდა? დიახ, მითხრა.
11. ოთარს ახალი სახლი თავისთვის აუშენებია. საიდან იცი? მისმა ძმამ მითხრა.
12. ექიმისათვის ფული არ მიგიცია? დიახ, მივეცი.
13. ფული რომ ჩემთვის მოგეცა, წიგნს გიყიდდი.
14. (a) ივანეს თუ ნახავ, უთხარი, რომ წერილს მალე გავუგზავნი. (b) ივანე რომ მენახა, წერილს

გავუგზავნიდი.

15. (a) ეს წიგნი უნდა წაიკითხო, ძალიან საინტერესოა.
(b) ეს წიგნი ალბათ წაგიკითხავს, ვინაიდან მთელი მასალა უკვე იცი.

16. როცა უნივერსიტეტში სტუდენტები ვიყავით, პოლიტეკონომია უნდა შეგვესწავლა.

17. თამარ მეფემ უკვე ოცდაათი წელი იმეფა, როცა ათას ორას ცამეტ წელს გარდაიცვალა.

18. ძაღლს არ უყეფნია? დიახ, მან იყეფა, მე თვითონ მოვისმინე მისი ყეფა.

19. ლობიოს რომ საკმარისად ედუღნა, სადილს დავამზადებდით.

20. მათ სიმინდი და ბრინჯი ამ წელს არ დაუთესავთ? არა, არც სიმინდი და არც ბრინჯი არ დაუთესავთ. ამ წელს მხოლოდ ხორბალი დათესეს.

21. საქართველოში გიცხოვრიათ? სამიოდე წელი თბილისში ვიცხოვრე (ვცხოვრობდი); ოთარს კი იქ არასოდეს არ უცხოვრია.

22. (a) ვინაიდან მეტისმეტად ბევრი ვჭამე სადილობისას, ვახშმად არაფერს (არ) ვჭამ.
(b) როცა რესტორანში მივედით, უკვე დახურული იყო და ამიტომ არაფერი (არ) მიჭამია.

23. ჩემთვის რომ უფრო ადრე მოგეწერათ, მე თქვენ სადგურში დაგხვდებოდით.

24. მსახიობებს რომ პიესა უფრო ხშირად გაემეორებინათ, წარმოდგენა უფრო კარგი იქნებოდა.

25. რუსუდანს ჯერ კიდევ არ უპასუხნია შენთვის? დიახ, მან მიპასუხა. შენთვის უნდა ეპასუხნა, როცა შინ არ ვიყავი.

26. (a) როგორც ჩანს, მკვლელს თავისი მსხვერპლი დანით მოუკლავს. (b) მოწმეებმა თქვეს, რომ მკვლელმა თავისი მსხვერპლი დანით მოკლა.

27. მათ ცნობები უკვე მიეღოთ, როცა მათ წერილი გაეგზავნა.

28. ექიმს რომ უფრო ადრე მივედე, დროზე შეგხვდებოდი.
29. გუშინ თეატრში არ მინახავხარ. იქ რომ მენახე, ამ საქმეზე გელაპარაკებოდი.
30. მას რომ შენ მოეკალი, მე მას მოვკლავდი!
31. როსტომს მე ქუჩაში უკვე შევუჩერებივარ, როცა დაგინახე.
32. კრებაზე რომ არ მენახე, სუფრის შესახებ არ გეტყოდი.
33. მწყემსებს ომის დროს დაუმალავხარ (დაუმალიხარ)? კი, დამმალეს.
34. კბილის ექიმმა დღეს მიგიღო? არა, დღეს არ მივუღივარ, რადგანაც ოთხშაბათობით საზოგადოდ ავადმყოფებს არ ღებულობს.
35. პეტრესათვის რომ უფრო კარგად დაგეხასიათებინე, ფულს დროზე მომცემდა.
36. როგორც ვხედავ, ილიკოს გამოუგზავნიხარ, რადგანაც აქ მის ძმასთან ერთად მოხვედი.
37. მტრისაგან რომ არ დაგეცავი, მოვკვდებოდი.
38. პროფესორის ახსნა-განმარტებას ხომ არ დაუბნევიხართ? არა, არ დავუბნევივართ. ყველაფერი გავიგეთ, რადგანაც სწავლის დაწყების წინ სახელმძღვანელო წავიკითხეთ.
39. თქვენს მეგობარს რომ ისე არ დავებნიე, ადგილს უფრო ადრე ვიპოვნიდი.
40. შენს დას ხომ არ უპოვნიხარ? პარკში ამას წინათ გეძებდა.
41. თქვენი სიტყვებიდან ვხედავ, რომ ჩემთვის გიღალატნიათ; მტრისათვის გაგიცივართ.
42. ექიმს რომ მაშინ არ მივედე, მოვკვდებოდი.
43. დავით მესამე აღმაშენებელი ტახტზე ავიდა ათას ოთხმოცდაცხრა წელს, როცა თექვსმეტი წლის იყო. ოცდათექვსმეტი წელი იმეფა. ათას ას ოცდახუთ წელს მოკვდა. მისი სიკვდილის შემდეგ ტახტზე ავიდა მისი ვაჟიშვილი დიმიტრი პირველი და ათას ას

ორმოცდათექვსმეტ წლამდე იმეფა.

44. საქართველოს საბჭოთა სოციალისტური რესპუბლიკის მოსახლეობის ორი მესამედი ქართველები არიან. დაახლოებით ერთი მეცხრედი სომხები არიან. რუსებიც მოსახლეობის დაახლოებით ერთ მეცხრედს წარმოადგენენ.

45. ათას ცხრაას სამოცდაათ წელს თბილისის მოსახლეობა რვაას ოთხმოცდაცხრა ათასი სული იყო. ის სიდიდით საბჭოთა სოციალისტური რესპუბლიკების კავშირის მეცამეტე ქალაქია.

46. გერმანულ და ბერძნულ ენებში ოთხ-ოთხ ბრუნვას ვპოულობთ; ქართულსა და რუსულში კი — ექვს-ექვსს.

47. სექტემბერში, ნოემბერში, აპრილსა და ივნისში ოცდაათ-ოცდაათი დღეა.

48. წელიწადში სამას სამოცდახუთი დღეა.

49. ბრალდებული სიკვდილით ხომ არ დაუსჯიათ? არა, ბატონო, სასამართლოში ვიყავი, როცა მოსამართლემ გაათავისუფლა იგი.

50. ბრალდებული თურმე გაუთავისუფლებიათ. ეს გაზეთში წავიკითხე.

51. მთელი ბოთლი ღვინო დაგვილევია? არა, მხოლოდ ნახევარი ბოთლი დავლიეთ.

52. თქვენ წერილი ჩემთვის ხომ არ გამოგიგზავნიათ? კი, ბატონო, მე გამოგიგზავნეთ წერილი.

53. წინათ გინახავვარ (გინახივარ)? დიახ, გუშინ გნახე.

54. (a) შენი ფული რომ დაგემალა, ვერავინ (ვერ) მოგპარავდა. (b) ოთარი რატომ დაგემალა?

55. საბჭოთა კავშირში გიცხოვრია? დიახ, ორჯერ, ერთხელ ათას ცხრაას ორმოცდაცხრა წელს და მეორედ ათას ცხრაას სამოცდარვა წელს.

56. ეს კინოფილმი გინახავს? დიახ, სამჯერ ვნახე.

Vocabulary

ავადმყოფი	patient; sick person
ამიტომ	therefore
არასოდეს	never
არც ... არც ...	neither... nor...
ახსნა-განმარტება	explanation
ბრინჯი	rice
ბრუნვა	case (grammatical)
განვითარება	development; education
განმავლობაში	in the course of; during (pp.)
დახურული	closed
დროზე	on time
ვახშამი	supper (A)
თავისუფალი	free (A)
თუ	interrogative particle that here intensifies a question; somewhat equivalent to Eng. 'by any chance.'
თურმე	apparently
ივნისი	June
კბილი	tooth
მკვლელი	murderer; killer (cf. კლავს)
მოსახლეობა	population
მოწმე	witness
მსახიობი	actor
მსხვერპლი	victim
მწყემსი	shepherd
ნახევარი	half (A)
ნოემბერი	November (E)
ოქრო	gold
პარკი	park
პოლიტეკონომია	political economy
როგორც	as
სადილი	dinner
სადილობა	dinnertime
სადილობისას	during, at dinnertime
საზოგადო	general
სახელმძღვანელო	textbook
საკმარისი	sufficient, satisfactory
სექტემბერი	September (E)
სიდიდე	bigness; size
სიმინდი	corn (maize)
სოფელი	village (E) სოფელში: to, in the country
სპორტსმენი	sportsman
ტახტი	throne
წინათ	before; pre-

viously; ago

ხომ interrogative particle that with a negative sentence expects the answer 'no', with an affirmative sentence, the answer 'yes' (cf. French *n'est-ce pas*)

ხორბალი wheat (A)

როსტომი [m.]

Verbs

დააბნევს	da=a-*bnev*-s (see sec. 5.3.2.2)	confuse
ჩადის, ჩამოდის	(irr., sec. 4.5., 5.4.3)	arrive; go; come down
წარმოადგენს	ç̣armo+a-*dgen*-s (only pres. series)	represents; is (= Russian является)
დათესავს	da=*tes*-av-s	sow
მოჰპარავს	mo=h-*p̣ar*-av-s	steal (sthg. from s.o.)
ღალატობს: უღალატებს	(H-)*ğalaṭ*-ob-s; fut. u-*ğalaṭ*-eb-s	betray (s.o.)
ღებულობს	ğebul-ob-s (only present series)	alternate present series form of მი=იღებს; see sec. 15.1.5
ჩანს	*čan*-s (only pres. series) (pres. ვჩანვარ(თ), ჩანხარ(თ), ჩანს, ჩანან (impf.reg.)	seem; appear
გასცემს	ga+s-*cem*-s (conjugated as *cem*; aorist, sec. 7.3.4.) perf. გაუცია, plup. გაეცა	betray (to s.o.)
ეძებს	e-*jeb*-s: fut. irr. = pres. (III. rel. with *e*-series id.o. markers) (VN ძებნა)	look for s.o./sthg.
ჭამს	Ø=*č̣am*-s	eat
დაახასიათებს	da=a-*xasiat*-eb-s	characterize
მოხდება	mo=*xd*-eb-a	happen; occur
დახვდება	da=H-*xvd*-eb-a	meet (s.o.) (e.g., at a station)

Key to the Exercises

1. Have you seen Peter today? Yes, I saw him.
2. You apparently have studied Georgian in the course of many years, because you speak Georgian without mistake. Yes, I was studying it six years.
3. Has the professor discussed the development of nineteenth century Georgian literature? Yes, he has discussed it. I, however, wasn't in class, but Tamaz told me.
4. Haven't you sent the bill to Givi? No, I still haven't sent it.
5. Haven't you sold your (pl.) gold watch to Peter? No, because he had already bought a watch, I haven't sold it to him.
6. Didn't you play soccer yesterday? No, I didn't play because I am not a sportsman. (I.e., I didn't want to play.)
7. (a) If I were living in Georgia now, I would speak Georgian better. (b) If I had studied in Georgia, now I would speak Georgian better.
8. (a) If it doesn't rain tomorrow, we will go to the village. (b) If it weren't raining now, we would go to the village. (c) If it hadn't rained yesterday, we would have gone to the village.
9. If I had spoken Georgian with (-*tan*) you better, you would have understood me.
10. Hasn't John told you what happened? Yes, he told me.
11. Otar has built a new house for himself. From where do you know? His brother told me.
12. Haven't you given the money to the doctor? Yes, I gave it [to him].
13. If you had given me the money, I would have bought you the book.
14. (a) If you [will] see John, tell him that I will send him the letter soon. (b) If I had seen John, I would have sent him the letter.
15. (a) You must read this book, it is very interesting. (b) You probably have read this book, because you already know the whole material.
16. When we were students in the university we had to study political economy.
17. Queen Tamara had already reigned thirty years when in 1213 she passed away.
18. Hasn't the dog barked? Yes, it barked. I myself listened to its barking.
19. If the beans had boiled sufficiently, we would have prepared dinner.
20. Haven't they planted [sown] corn and rice this year? No, they have sown neither corn (and) nor

rice; this year they sowed only wheat.

21. Have you all lived in Georgia? I lived in Tbilisi about three years (nom.); Otar, however, never has lived there.
22. (a) Because I ate too much at dinner(time) I will eat nothing for supper (adv.). (b) When we went to the restaurant it was already closed, and therefore I didn't eat anything.
23. If you all had written me earlier, I would have met you all at the station.
24. If the actors had rehearsed [repeated] the play more often, the performance would have been better.
25. Hasn't Rusudan answered you yet? Yes, she answered me. She must have answered you when I was not at home.
26. (a) As it appears, the murderer must have [has] killed his victim with a knife. (b) The witnesses said that the murderer killed his victim with a knife.
27. They had already received the information when the letter was sent to them.
28. If the doctor had received me earlier, I would have met you on time.
29. I didn't see you at the theater yesterday. If I had seen you there I would have talked with you on this matter.
30. If he had killed you, I would have killed him.
31. Rostom had already stopped me in the street when I caught sight of you.
32. If I hadn't seen you at the meeting, I wouldn't have told you about the banquet.
33. Did the shepherds hide you during the war? Yes, they hid me.
34. Did the dentist [tooth doctor] receive you today? No, he didn't receive me today because in general on Wednesdays he doesn't receive patients.
35. If you had described [characterized] me better to Peter, he would have given me the money on time.
36. As I see, Iliko must have [has] sent you, because you came here with his brother.
37. If you had not defended me from the enemy, I would have died.
38. Hasn't the professor's explanation confused you all? No, it hasn't confused us. We understand everything because before the beginning of learning we read the textbook.
39. If your friend hadn't confused me so, I would have found the place earlier.
40. Hasn't your sister found you? She was looking for you in the park a little while ago.

41. From your words I see that you all have betrayed me; you all have betrayed me to the enemy.
42. If the doctor had not received me then, I would have died.
43. David III the Builder ascended [went up on] the throne in 1089 when he was 16 years old [was of 16 year]. He reigned thirty-six years. In 1125 he died. After his death his son Dimitri I ascended the throne and reigned until 1156.
44. Two thirds of the population of the Georgian SSR are Georgians. Approximately one ninth are Armenians. Russians too represent approximately one ninth of the population.
45. In 1970 Tbilisi's population was 889,000 [souls]. It is the thirteenth biggest [bigness (instr.)] city of the USSR.
46. In the German and Greek languages we find four cases apiece; in Georgian and Russian, however, six apiece.
47. In September, November, April, and June there are thirty days apiece.
48. In a year there are 365 days.
49. Haven't they condemned the accused to death (instr.)? No, sir, I was in court when the judge freed him.
50. They apparently have freed the accused. I read this in the newspaper.
51. Have we drunk the whole bottle [of] wine? No, we only drank a half bottle.
52. Didn't you all send me the letter? Yes, sir, I sent a letter to you.
53. Have you seen me before? Yes, I saw you yesterday.
54. (a) If you had hidden your money, no one could have stolen it from you. (b) Why did Otar hide from you? (aorist)
55. Have you lived in the Soviet Union? Yes, twice, once in 1949 and secondly in 1968.
56. Have you seen this movie? Yes, I saw it three times.

ზ. პ. ფალიაშვილი

1 ზაქარია პეტრეს ძე ფალიაშვილი დაიბადა 1871 წლის 4 (16) აგვისტოს ქუთაისში. იგი იზრდებოდა და განვითარებას ღებულობდა მუსიკალურ ოჯახში. მომავალი კომპოზიტორის პირველი აღმზრდელი და დამრიგებელი იყო მისი უფროსი ძმა, შემდეგში გამოჩენილი დირიჟორი ივანე პეტრეს ძე ფალიაშვილი. ნორჩი მუსიკოსის განვითარება სწრაფად მიმდინარეობდა. რვა წლის ასაკში იგი უკვე ეკლესიის გუნდში მღეროდა, პატარაობიდანვე შეისწავლა ორღანზე დაკვრაც. 1887 წელს ფალიაშვილი გადადის თბილისში და შედის ქართულ გუნდში, რომელიც ჩამოაყალიბა ხალხური მუსიკის ენთუზიასტმა ლ. ტ. აღნიაშვილმა. რამდენიმე წლის შემდეგ ახალგაზრდა მუსიკოსი შედის თბილისის მუსიკალურ სასწავლებელში — ვალტორნის კლასში. იქვე სწავლობს კომპოზიციის თეორიას. სასწავლებელში ყოფნის დროს ფალიაშვილი წერს სონატას ფორტეპიანოსათვის, მესას, რომანსებს და ამავე დროს აწარმოებს ხალხური სიმღერების გადამუშავებას. 1900—1903 წლებში იგი სწავლობს მოსკოვის კონსერვატორიაში ს. ი. ტანეევთან. ამ პერიოდში ფალიაშვილი მჭიდროდ უკავშირდება რუსულ მუსიკალურ კულტურას, რომლის ტრადიციებმა დიდი გავლენა მოახდინეს ქართველი კომპოზიტორის შემოქმედებაზე.

2 საქართველოში დაბრუნების შემდეგ ფალიაშვილმა მონაწილეობა მიიღო ფართო მოძრაობაში, რომელიც მიზნად ისახავდა ეროვნული ხელოვნების შექმნას და რომელშიც ჩაბმული იყო მრავალი ხელოვნების მოღვაწე. ფალიაშვილი იყო საქართველოს ფილარმონიული საზოგადოების ერთ-ერთი ფუძემდებელთაგანი და მასთან არსებულ გუნდისა და ორკესტრის ხელმძღვანელი. იგი ბევრ დროს უთმობდა აგრეთვე პედაგოგიურ მოღვაწეობასაც.

3 1910 წლის დასაწყისში დამთავრდა ფალიაშვილის შემოქმედების ადრინდელი პერიოდი. დიდი აზრებით იყო გატაცებული კომპოზიტორი, იგი მრავალი წლის მანძილზე მუშაობდა „აბესალომ და ეთერზე" (1918), რომელიც მიეკუთვნება ქართული მუსიკის უმაღლეს მიღწევას. საქართველოში საბჭოთა ხელისუფლების დამყარების შემდეგ ფალიაშვილის საკომპოზიტორო და საზოგადოებრივი მოღვაწეობა უფრო მეტი ნაყოფიერებით ხასიათდება. ფალიაშვილი დიდი ხნის განმავლობაში ხელმძღვანელობს თბილისის კონსერვატორიას. სიცოცხლის უკანასკნელ ათწლეულში შექმნა მან ოპერები: „დაისი" (1923) და „ლატავრა" (1927), საზეიმო კანტატა, მიძღვნილი ოქტომბრის რევოლუციის 10 წლისთავისადმი (1927), საორკესტრო სუიტა, გუნდები და რომანსები.

4 ფალიაშვილი გარდაიცვალა 1933 წლის 6 ოქტომბერს თბილისში.

Vocabulary

1

ძე	son (used in formation of patronymics)
4 (16)	date according to Julian calendar (4) and corresponding Gregorian date (16) (such dates are cardinals)
ოჯახი	family
მომავალი	future (A)
აღმზრდელი	tutor; educator
დამრიგებელი	adviser (E)
უფროსი	elder
შემდეგში	later (adv.)
გამოჩენილი	outstanding
დირიჟორი	conductor (orchestral)
ნორჩი	tender; young
მუსიკოსი	musician
სწრაფი	quick; rapid
მი+მდინარეობს	proceed (only present series)
ასაკი	age
პატარაობიდანვე	from childhood on
ორღანი	organ
და=უკრავს	play (a musical instrument) (only id.o., no d.o.)
სასწავლებელი	school; college (E)
ვალტორნა	French horn
იქვე	there in the same place; ibid.
მესა	mass (Catholic)
ამავე [nom. ესევე]	the same
Ø+აწარმოებს (aor. Ø+აწარმოვა)	carry out
გადა+ამუშავებს	revise; rework; adapt
ტანეევი	Sergei Taneyev (1856-1915) Russian composer

მჭიდრო	close; compact; tight
და=აკავშირებს	connect; link
გავლენა	influence
მო=ახდენს	make; effect (E → I); მოახდენს გავლენას have influence
შემოქმედება	creation; creative work
2	
მონაწილეობა	participation; მონაწილეობას მიიღებს participate
ფართო	broad; wide
მოძრაობა	movement
მიზანი	aim; goal (A)
და=ისახავს მიზნად	to set as one's goal
ეროვნული	national
ჩაბმული	involved
ხელოვნების მოღვაწე	figure in the world of art
ფუძემდებელი	founder (E)
არსებული	existing (მასთან = as a part of it, i.e., the Philharmonic Society; არსებული would be expected.)
და=თმობს	give over
აგრეთვე	too, also
მოღვაწეობა	activity
3	
დასაწყისი	beginning
ადრინდელი	early
აზრი	idea; opinion; thought
გატაცებული	inspired (here = predicate nominative; does not modify კომპოზიტორი)
მანძილზე	in the course of (pp.)
აბესალომ და ეთერი	Abesalom and Ether
მი+ეკუთვნება	belong to
უმაღლესი	highest; supreme
მიღწევა	achievement

და=ამყარებს	establish
უფრო მეტი	even more
ნაყოფიერება	fruitfulness
ხანი	time (A)
სიცოცხლე	life
ათწლეული (<ათი წელი)	decade
დაისი, ლატავრა	(f.pr. names)
ზეიმი	festival
მიძღვნილი	dedicated
წლისთავი	anniversary
-დმი	to (pp.)

Z. Paliašvili Theatre of Opera and Ballet
(Tbilisi)

LESSON 11

11.1. The perfect participle. The Georgian perfect participle generally corresponds in meaning to the English past participle and is formed from I. and II. conjugation verbs. The normal markers of the participle are:

-il- This suffix occurs with:
a. root verbs (except those in *ev*);
b. verbs with P/FSF *-i*, which is lost before this suffix;
c. verbs with root vowel *e* or *o* and P/FSF *-av*, which is lost before this suffix;
d. certain verbs with P/FSF in *-ob*.[1]

m-...-ar- This circumfix occurs with:
a. root II. conj. verbs which have no regularly corresponding I. conj. forms;
b. verbs with P/FSF *-ob* which have root II. conj. forms (see sec. 9.1.2).

In verbs whose roots contain an *r* the circumfix is *m-...-al-*. Any P/FSF is lost with this marker.

-ul- This suffix occurs with all remaining verb classes:
a. I. conj. verbs in *-eb*;
b. remaining verbs with P/FSF *-av* which is lost before this suffix;[2]
c. verbs with P/FSF *-am*, which undergoes syncope before this suffix, losing the *a*;
d. root verbs in *ev*; the *v* of the P/FSF is lost before the *u* of the suffix (sec. 1.11.1).

In the formation of the perfect participles all preradical vowels and person/number markers are dropped from the I. conjugation future. The suffixes are added to the resulting stem. With root II. conjugation verbs the prefix *m-* follows the preverb, coming immediately before the root. The perfect participle, being a nominal form, has regular nominal declension. Examples:

	I. conj.	II. conj.	Perfect participle	
-il-				
	დაწერს	დაიწერება	დაწერილი	written
	დაიჭერს	დაიჭირება	დაჭერილი	caught
	გაგზავნის	გაიგზავნება	გაგზავნილი	sent
	მოჭრის	მოიჭრება	მოჭრილი	cut off
	დაბეჭდავს	დაიბეჭდება	დაბეჭდილი	printed
	გაზომავს	გაიზომება	გაზომილი[3]	measured
	მოსპობს	მოისპობა	მოსპობილი	destroyed
-ul-	წარმოთქვამს	{ წარმოითქმის / წარმოითქმება	წარმოთქმული (1.11.1)	pronounced
	დახატავს	დაიხატება	დახატული	painted
	მოკლავს	მოიკვლება	მოკლული	killed
	მიიღებს	მიიღება	მიღებული	received
	გააგრძელებს	გაგრძელდება	გაგრძელებული	continued
m-...-ar-, m-...-al-				
	გაათბობს	გათბება	გამთბარი	warmed
	გააშრობს	გაშრება	გამშრალი	dried
		შეცდება	შემცდარი	mistaken

Note the following irregular formation of a perfect participle from a root II. conjugation verb. (Other irregular formations of this participle can be found in dictionaries.)

დარჩება	დარჩენილი	remained

The perfect participles of the irregular verbs are:

Verbal noun	Present	Future	Perfect participle	
დგომა	დგება	დადგება	დამდგარი	stood up
ყოფნა	არის	იქნება	ყოფილი	been; former
მოსვლა	მოდის	მოვა	მოსული	come

(and similarly for all prefixed forms of სვლა.)

ჯდომა	ჯდება	დაჯდება	დამჯდარი	sat down
სხდომა	სხდებიან	დასხდებიან	დამსხდარი	sat down
წოლა	წვება	დაწვება	დაწოლილი	lain down

The perfect participle is used similarly to the

English past participle, for example:

ასო არის დაწერილი (ან დაბეჭდილი) ნიშანი ბგერისა.

A letter is a written (or printed) sign of a sound.

რუსეთის ელჩების მიერ მოწოდებული ცნობებით, იმ დროს ქუთაისში ათასი კომლი ცხოვრობდა.

According to information communicated by the Russian ambassadors, at that time in Kutaisi 1000 households lived.

11.2. Perfect series of II. conjugation verbs. II. conjugation verbs have the subject in the nominative case *in all series*. Indirect objects, if present, will be in the dative case in all series. (Note that unlike I. and III. conjugation verbs, II. conjugation verbs can mark an indirect object in the perfect series.) The perfect series forms of II. conjugation verbs vary widely between *absolute* forms (i.e., without indirect object) and relative forms (with indirect object).

11.2.1. Perfect series of absolute II. conjugation verbs. The present perfect is formed by adding the auxiliary verb 'be' to the stem of the perfect participle. In the first person the first person marker *v-* occurs immediately before the root. The 3sg. ending is *-a*, the 3pl. is *-an*. (Since most II. conjugation verbs are passive in meaning, the third person is the most common.) Examples:

1.		2.
დავჭერილვარ(-თ)	catch	დაჭერილხარ(-თ)
მოვჭრილვარ(-თ)	cut	მოჭრილხარ(-თ)
მოვკლულვარ(-თ)	kill	მოკლულხარ(-თ)
შევმცდარვარ(-თ)	err	შემცდარხარ(-თ)
დავრჩენილვარ(-თ)	remain	დარჩენილხარ(-თ)
ვყოფილვარ(-თ)	be	ყოფილხარ(-თ)
მოვსულვარ(-თ)	come	მოსულხარ(-თ)
3sg.		3pl.
დაჭერილა		დაჭერილან
მოჭრილა		მოჭრილან
მოკლულა		მოკლულან

შემცდარა	შემცდარან
დარჩენილა	დარჩენილან
ყოფილა	ყოფილან
მოსულა	მოსულან

The pluperfect is formed by adding the aorist of 'be' (sec. 5.4.2) to the perfect participle stem.[4] In the first person the marker is *-v-....-iqavi(-t)*. Examples:

1., 2.	3sg.	3pl.
და(ვ)ჭერილიყავი(-თ)	დაჭერილიყო	დაჭერილიყვნენ
მო(ვ)ჭრილიყავი(-თ)	მოჭრილიყო	მოჭრილიყვნენ
მო(ვ)კლულიყავი(-თ)	მოკლულიყო	მოკლულიყვნენ
შე(ვ)მცდარიყავი(-თ)	შემცდარიყო	შემცდარიყვნენ
და(ვ)რჩენილიყავი(-თ)	დარჩენილიყო	დარჩენილიყვნენ
(ვ)ყოფილიყავი(-თ)	ყოფილიყო	ყოფილიყვნენ
მო(ვ)სულიყავი(-თ)	მოსულიყო	მოსულიყვნენ

11.2.2. Perfect series of relative II. conjugation verbs. The stem of the perfect series (both present perfect and pluperfect) of relative II. conjugation verbs bears little resemblance to the stem of the corresponding absolute forms; it is the same as the stem of the corresponding *verbal noun* minus the final *-a* of such verbal nouns.[5] The indirect object is marked both in the present perfect and in the pluperfect by the *h*-series object markers (see sec. 7.2.4 and the rules in 7.1.2).[6]

Remember that the subject of these verbs is in the nominative case and the indirect object is in the dative!

The present perfect is marked by the suffix *-i-* followed by the present tense of the verb 'be' which marks the grammatical subject:

1.	-v-....-i-var(-t)		
2.	....-i-xar(-t)		
3sg.	....-i-a	3pl.	....-i-an

Examples (only singular objects are illustrated):

დაემალება (VN: დამალვა) he will hide from someone

დაგმალვივარ(-თ)	I/we hid from you
დავმალვივარ(-თ)	I/we hid from him

დამმალვიხარ(-თ)	you/you all hid from me
დამალვიხარ(-თ)	you/you all hid from him

დამმალვია	დამმალვიან	he/they hid from me
დაგმალვია	დაგმალვიან	he/they hid from you
დამალვია	დამალვიან	he/they hid from him

Similarly:

Verbal noun		Rel. II. conj. Future	Rel. II. conj. Present perfect
დაწერა	write	დაეწერება	დასწერია
შეკითხვა	ask	შეეკითხება	შეჰკითხვია
დახმარება	help	დაეხმარება	დახმარებია
აშენება	build	აუშენდება	აშენებია
შეერთება	unite	შეუერთდება	შეერთებია
შეხება	concern	შეეხება	შეხებია

The relative pluperfect has the II. conjugation imperfect/conditional marker *-od-* followed by the subject markers of the imperfect/conditional:

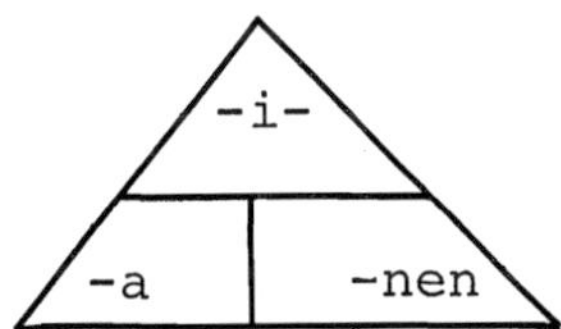

Example (only singular objects are illustrated):

დაემალება	he will hide from someone
დაგმალოდი(-თ)[7]	I/we had hidden from you
დავმალოდი(-თ)	I/we had hidden from him
დამმალოდი(-თ)	you/you all had hidden from me
დამალოდი(-თ)	you/you all had hidden from him

დამმალოდა	დამმალოდნენ	he/they had hidden from me
დაგმალოდა	დაგმალოდნენ	he/they had hidden from you
დამალოდა	დამალოდნენ	he/they had hidden from him

Similarly:

დასწეროდა
შეჰკითხოდა (sec. 1.11.1)
დახმარებოდა
აშენებოდა
შეერთებოდა
შეხებოდა

Note: The relative forms of II. conjugation perfects and pluperfects can be easily distinguished from the corresponding II. conjugation futures and conditionals by:

(a) the absence of the II. conjugation markers *i-* or *-d-*;
(b) the absence of the P/FSF *-eb-* in verbs derived from I. conj. forms in *-am*, *-av*, *-i* and root verbs;
(c) in the present perfect by the 3sg. ending *-i-a* instead of *-a* alone.

11.3. The periphrastic passive. The perfect participle (in the nominative singular) is used with the present, aorist, and optative of the verb 'be' to denote a passive of state, i.e., a passive which can correspond to the English simple passive (as opposed to the progressive passive of action, which generally corresponds to the Georgian II. conjugation). Examples are:

Simple passive	Periphrastic passive
იწერება	დაწერილია
it is being written	it is written
იწერებოდა	დაწერილი იყო
it was being written	it was written
უნდა დაიწეროს	უნდა დაწერილი იყოს
it should be written	it should have been written[8]

Examples:

თბილისი განლაგებულია მდინარე მტკვარის ნაპირებზე.

Tbilisi is located on the banks of the river Kura (Geo. Mṭḳvari).

ეს შრომა ჯაფარიძის მიერ იყო დაწერილი.

This work was written by J̌aparije.

A second type of periphrastic passive is formed with the perfect participle and the auxiliary იქნება/იქნა 'become', 'be'. This passive form is used basically with those I. conjugation verbs which cannot form a II. conjugation (passive) paradigm,[9] but its use is being extended to other verbs which do have their own II. conjugation forms. When the participle precedes the auxiliary, the participle has no case ending; if the auxiliary comes first, the participle is in the nom. sg. The auxiliary იქნება is identical in form to the future tense of არის 'be', while the past tense (aorist) has the following conjugation:

1. ვიქენი(-თ)
2. იქენი(-თ)

3sg. იქნა 3pl. იქნენ

The optative is either the expected (ვ)იქნა(-თ); იქნას, იქნან or the preferred (ვ)იქნე(-თ); იქნეს, იქნნენ. Examples of this construction are:

მიღებულ იქნა ახალი ბრძანება.

A new order was received (cf. მიიღებს)

ეს უნდა გარჩეულ იქნეს მარტივი ვნებითისაგან.

This must be distinguished from the simple passive.

საჭირო ზომები იქნება მიღებული.

Necessary measures will be taken.

ბრალდებული იქნა დასჯილი.

The accused was sentenced.

The periphrastic passive with the verb 'be' is by far more common in Georgian than the periphrastic passive with იქნება/იქნა, which is literary.

11.4. Causative of I. conjugation verbs. Regular I. conjugation (transitive) verbs and irregular verbs in *-eb*, *-ob* can take on a causative meaning by the addition of a circumfix *a-...in-eb-* which is added to the present or future stem minus any preradical vowels and with loss of P/FSF *-i-* and syncope of the P/FSF *-av-*. These causatives can have a variety of translations into English, including: to cause/have someone do something, to let/permit someone do something, to make/help someone do something, etc. In these constructions, the causer (permitter, forcer, etc.) is the grammatical subject and the person caused (permitted, forced, etc.) to perform the given action is the indirect object and marked by the *h*-series of object markers (see sec. 7.2.4 and the rules in 7.1.2).

Causatives of I. conjugation verbs are themselves I. conjugation verbs and are conjugated as any regular I. conjugation verb with P/FSF -*eb*[10], with the same case syntax, i.e., with the subject, direct and indirect objects marked as in sec. 10.2. Examples of formation of the causative are:

მოისმენს	მოასმენინებს
listen to	have s.o. listen to
დაწერს	დააწერინებს
write	have s.o. write
გაგზავნის	გააგზავნინებს
send	have s.o. send
დახატავს	დაახატვინებს
paint	have s.o. paint
გაიგებს	გააგებინებს
understand	make s.o. understand
გაიმეორებს	გაამეორებინებს
repeat	have s.o. repeat
გაათბობს	გაათბობინებს
warm	have s.o. warm

Irregular verbs (those with no root vowel) with P/FSF -*i*, -*av*, -*am* take the circumfix -*a*-...-*evin*-*eb*. The P/FSF -*i* is lost and the P/FSFs -*av* and -*am* undergo syncope. Examples are:

დასჯის	punish	დაასჯევინებს
მოკლავს	kill	მოაკვლევინებს (see sec. 1.11.2)
გამოთქვამს	pronounce	გამოათქმევინებს (see sec. 1.11.1)
დადგამს (da=dg-am-s)	stand (sthg.) up	დაადგმევინებს

The verbs Ø=ჭამს 'eat' and დალევს (pr. სვამს) 'drink' have irregular causatives:

Future	Present	Causative future	Causative present
ჭამს		აჭმევს	
დალევს	სვამს	დაალევინებს	ასმევს

Causative aorist	Causative perfect
(ვ)აჭამე(-თ) აჭამა; აჭამეს	უჭმევია
(ვ)ასვი(-თ) ასვა; ასვეს	უსმევია

დალევს also forms the aorist and perfect series regularly: aorist: დაალევინა; perfect: დაულევინებია. Note the translations of these causatives, including for აჭმევს 'feed', and for დაალევინებს 'water' (e.g., animals). Examples of the use of causative forms:

კიტას ამ წერილს მის ჟურნალში გამოვაქვეყნებინებ.

I will have Ḳiṭa (dat.) publish this letter (dat.) in his magazine. (Future)

რედაქტორმა კიტას ეს წერილი თავის ჟურნალში გამოაქვეყნებინა.

The editor (erg.) had Ḳiṭa (dat.) publish this letter (nom.) in his magazine. (Aorist)

რედაქტორს კიტასათვის ეს წერილი თურმე თავის ჟურნალში გამოუქვეყნებინებია.

The editor (dat.) has apparently had Ḳiṭa (postpositional phrase with *-tvis*) publish this letter in his magazine. (Present perfect)

11.5. Wordbuilding: participles. Georgian has four so-called participles: the (present) active, the (future) passive, the negative, and the perfect. The perfect participle has been discussed above in section 11.1.

11.5.1. The (present) active participle. The (present) active participle of I. conjugation verbs was discussed in section 5.7.2. III. conjugation verbs form this participle with the prefix *m-* and no suffix or the suffixes *-are* or *-ar-*(*-ale* or *-al-*respectively if the root contains *r*), or with the circumfix *mo-...-e*.[11] Examples: [■ see p. 314.]

ცურავს	swim	მცურავი

ფრინავს	fly	მფრინავი
ლაპარაკობს	speak	მოლაპარაკე
მუშაობს	work	მომუშავე
დუღს	boil	მდუღარე
ტირის	cry	მტირალი

The active participles of the irregular verbs are:

	Active participle		
არის be	მყოფი	cf. verbal noun	ყოფნა
(მო)დის come	(მო)მავალი	cf. future (1sg.)	(მო)ვალ
დგას stand	მდგომარე	cf. verbal noun	დგომა
ზის sit (sg.)	მჯდომარე		ჯდომა
სხედან sit (pl.)	მსხდომარე		სხდომა
წევს lie down	მწოლარე		წოლა

11.5.2. The future (passive) participle of I. conjugation verbs was discussed above in section 7.6.3.[12] As a rule, III. conjugation verbs do not form this participle.[13] The future (passive) participles of the irregular verbs are:

			also means:
არის	be	სამყოფი	dwelling; sufficient
(მო)დის	come	(მო)სავალი	harvest
დგას	stand	სადგომი	dwelling, abode
დაჯდება	sit down	დასაჯდომი	
წევს	lie down	საწოლი	bed

11.5.3. The negative participle. I. conjugation verbs form this participle with either the prefix *u*- or the circumfix *u*-...-*el*-. (The latter often, though not always, has syncope.) The prefix *u*- alone is most commonly found with regular verbs with P/FSF -*av*; elsewhere the circumfix is found. The markers of the negative participle are added to the future stem (minus person/number markers and preradical vowels); the P/FSF -*i* is dropped and the P/FSFs -*am* and -*av* undergo syncope before the suffix -*el*. Examples:

დაწერს	write	დაუწერელი	unwritten
მოჭრის	cut	მოუჭრელი	uncut
წარმოთქვამს	pronounce	წარმოუთქმელი (sec. 1.11.1)	unpronounced
ნახავს	see	უნახავი	unseen
დახატავს	paint	დაუხატავი	unpainted
მოკლავს	kill	მოუკვლელი (sec. 1.11.2) or მოუკლავი	not killed
გაიმეორებს	repeat	გაუმეორებელი (E)	unrepeated
მოსპობს	destroy	მოუსპობელი (E)	undestroyed

Verbs which form the perfect participle with the circumfix *m-...-ar-* (*m-...-al-*) can form the negative participle by prefixing the *m-* of the perfect participle with *u-* or with the circumfix *u-...-el-*. Examples:

გაათბობს	heat
გამთბარი	heated
გაუმთბარი	unheated
გაუთბობელი (E)	
შეცდება	be mistaken
შემცდარი	mistaken
შეუმცდარი	unmistaken
შეუცდომელი (E)	

The negative participles of the irregular verbs are (less common forms are given in parentheses):

მოდის	come
მოუსვლელი	having not come
დადგება	stand
დაუდგომელი (დაუმდგარი)	having not stood
დაჯდება	sit down (sg.)

დაუჯდომელი (E) (დაუმჯდარი)	having not sat down (sg.)
დასხდებიან	sit down (pl.)
დაუსხდომელი (E) (დაუმსხდარი)	having not sat down (pl.)
დაწვება	lie down
დაუწოლელი	having not lain down

As can be seen from the above glosses, the negative participle can be translated into English as a negative past (passive) participle. They also often have the meaning 'unable to be', for example, წარმოუთქმელი 'unpronounceable'. The negative participle in the adverbial case corresponds to English 'without having ...'. Example:

მისი წერილის წაუკითხავად მე შენ ვერ გიპასუხებ.

Without having read his letter I will not be able to answer you.

11.5.4. Perfect participle in *na*-. In addition to the formation described in sec. 11.1 above, the perfect participle can be formed by adding the prefix *na*- to the future stem immediately before the root.[14] The P/FSF -*i* is dropped and the P/FSF -*av* is dropped in regular verbs. Examples (glosses as in sec. 11.1):

დანაწერი	მინაღები
დანაჭერი	განაგრძელები
განაგზავნი	განათბობი
მონაჭერი	განაშრობი
დანაბეჭდი	etc.
განაზომი	
მონასპობი	
გამონათქვამი	
დანახატი	
მონაკლავი	

This participle in *na*- is typical of the older Georgian literary language and is less common in the modern language than the suffixed perfect participle. It is not used to form the perfect series of II. conjugation verbs.

11.5.5. Many Georgian participial forms are used

both as nouns and as participles. Examples have been given in sections 5.7.2 and 7.6.3. Here we shall give a few examples of such uses of *na-* perfect participles and the participles derived from III. conjugation verbs.

ყინავს	freeze	ნაყინი	ice cream
აწარმოებს	produce, work	ნაწარმოები	product, work
იცნობს	know s.o.	ნაცნობი	acquaintance
წერს	write	ხელნაწერი	manuscript (ხელი 'hand')
თამაშობს	play	სათამაშო	toy
		მოთამაშე	player
ჩივის	complain	საჩივარი	complaint
ლაპარაკობს	speak	მოლაპარაკე	speaker
ფრინავს	fly	მფრინავი	pilot

Reference Chart for Participles

	Prefix	Suffix
Present active	m-	-
	m-	-el
	m-	-ar(e) (-al(e))
	mo-	-e
Future passive	sa-	-
	sa-	-el
	sa-	-o
Perfect	-	-il
	-	-ul
	m-	-ar (-al)
	na-	-
Negative	u-	-
	u-	-el
	u-	-ar

LESSON 11: Notes

1. Verbs in *-ob* which form their II. conjugation forms with prefixed *i-* (and not with root II. conjugation forms) also form their perfect participle in *-il-*; e.g.: მოსპობს 'destroy', passive მოისპობა, perfect participle მოსპობილი.

2. More accurately, the P/FSF *-av* undergoes syncope, losing the *a*, and the *v* is then lost before the *u* of the suffix.

3. Some verbs with root vowel *o* syncopate the P/FSF before the suffix, keeping the *v*; e.g., I. conj. დალოცავს, perf. part. დალოცვილი.

4. In older texts one might find examples of the perfect conjunctive, which is formed similarly to the pluperfect, except that the endings are the corresponding optative forms of the verb 'be' (sec. 6.1).

5. It should be remembered that I. and II. conjugation verbs have the same verbal nouns and that there is no difference in verbal nouns between those derived from absolute and those derived from relative verbs. It should also be noted that the perfect series is almost always formed from the perfective, i.e., prefixed, stem.

6. There is a tendency in these forms to use the indirect object marker *h-* before many consonants which according to the norm (see sec. 7.2.4) should have no such marker. This *h-* is found before such consonants as *p*, *š*, *x*, etc. So, alongside such forms as შეხებია, დახმარებია we can find forms such as შეჰხებია, დაჰხმარებია. A similar phenomenon is found in IV. conjugation verbs (sec. 12.1) and passives of state (sec. 13.4).

7. In accord with rule 1.11.1, the final *v* of the verbal noun *da-mal-v-a* is lost before the *o* of the suffix *-od-*.

8. There is very little difference in meaning between the II. conjugation aorist series forms and the periphrastic passive forms. So, both დაიწერა and დაწერილი იყო correspond to English 'it is written'. Similarly, there is little difference in meaning between the optatives დაიწეროს and დაწერილი იყოს.

9. Many I. conjugation verbs with preradical vowel

i- cannot form derived II. conjugation forms and so use the periphrastic passive with იქნება/იქნა. Examples of such verbs are:

> გადასახადს გადაიხდის.
>
> He will pay the tax.
>
> Passive: გადასახადი გადახდილ იქნება.
>
> The tax will be paid.
>
> საბჭოთა ჯარებმა ბერლინი აიღეს.
>
> The Soviet armies took Berlin.
>
> Passive: ბერლინი აღებულ იქნა.
>
> Berlin was taken.

See also Lesson 12, note 7.

10. As a consequence of this, these verbs have in the pluperfect two occurrences of the suffix -*in*-: first as the marker of the causative and second as a marker of the pluperfect of regular verbs in -*eb*; cf. *še-a-ḳer-v-in-eb-s* 'she will have him sew something', pluperfect: *še-e-ḳer-v-in-eb-in-a*. With causatives derived from verbs in -*eb*- both the -*eb*- and -*in*- are repeated; e.g., *da-a-grjel-eb-s* 'he will lengthen something', pluperfect *da-e-grjel-eb-in-a*; causative: *da-a-grjel-eb-in-eb-s* 'he will have someone lengthen it', pluperfect *da-e-grjel-eb-in-eb-in-a*.

11. With the exception of the perfect participle, there is a great deal of variation in the formation of the various participles. Some verbs have more than one possible form accepted for a given participle, whereas from other verbs (particularly III. conjugation verbs) certain participles cannot be formed at all. The examples given here are meant to be illustrative and do not permit the prediction of how other, similar verbs might form their participles.

12. This participle (generally from verbs of motion) can also be used to indicate someone (or something) that is to do something, that should or ought to do something. Examples:

> სახლში იყავი, ბავშვი სკოლიდან არის მოსასვლელი.
>
> Be at home, the child should be coming from school.
>
> ორ საათზე ექიმთან ვარ წასასვლელი.
>
> I am [supposed] to go to the doctor's at two

o'clock.

იჩქარე, დროზე ვართ წასასვლელი!

Hurry up, we should leave on time!

13. So, according to A. Šanije, ქართული გრამატიკის საფუძვლები (Tbilisi, 1973), p. 579. Other sources recognize such forms, including Tschenkéli's *Einführung* (pp. 549-52) and the eight volume ქართული ენის განმარტებითი ლექსიკონი. For these latter, the future participle of III. conjugation verbs always has the prefix *sa-* with no suffix or with the suffixes *-o* (mainly with verbs in *-ob*, with loss of this PSF), *-ar-* (mainly with verbs in *-i*, which lose this PSF; the suffix is *-al-* if the root contains an *r*), or *-el-* (mainly with verbs in *-eb*). Examples are:

თამაშობს	play	სათამაშო
ვარჯიშობს	exercise	სავარჯიშო

14. In some verbs this particple can also be formed from the present stem; e.g., ნაწერი 'written', ნახატი 'drawn', 'drawing', ნაბეჭდი 'printed'.

(■ to sec. 11.5.1, p. 307.) With the present active participle, the object of the corresponding I. conj. verb is marked by the genitive of nouns and by the possessive adjective of personal pronouns; e.g.:

ის ჩხუბს უყურებს 'He sees the quarrel.' >

ჩხუბის მაყურებელი '[the one] seeing the quarrel'

პოეტი გხატავს. 'The poet paints you.' >

შენი მხატავი პოეტი 'the poet painting you'

LESSON 11: Exercises

1. წერილი რომ უფრო ადრე გამოგზავნილიყო, მაშინ გუშინ მივიღებდით.
2. ივანე თურმე დაგხმარებიათ. ვიცი, რომ ამ სავარჯიშოს თქვენ თვითონ ვერ გააკეთებდით.
3. ბევრი ქართველი მეცნიერი ამბობს, რომ „ვეფხისტყაოსანი" უნდა დაწერილიყო თამარ მეფის ქმრის დავით სოსლანის სიკვდილამდე. ის თურმე ათას ორას შვიდ წელს მომკვდარა.
4. ვახტანგი გუშინ ხომ არ გინახავს? არა, არ მინახავს. ის თურმე დაგვმალვია.
5. სუფრასთან რატომ არ დამჯდარხარ? იმიტომ, რომ მოსაწვევი ბარათი არ მიმიღია.
6. პროფესორმა ამირანაშვილმა წაგვაკითხა ნიკო ფიროსმანიშვილის (1860-1918) შესახებ. ვინ იყო ფიროსმანიშვილი? ეს იყო სახელოვანი ქართველი მხატვარი; ღარიბი გლეხის ოჯახიდან იყო გამოსული. მას არავითარი პროფესიული განათლება არ მიუღია.
7. მან არ იცოდა ფერწერის ტექნიკა, არ იცნობდა არც წარსულ, არც მის თანამედროვე ქართულ ხელოვნებას.
8. ცნობილია, რომ მხატვარი იცნობდა მხოლოდ კახეთსა და თბილისს. საქართველოს სხვა კუთხეებში ის არ ყოფილა.
9. ფიროსმანიშვილი ფრანგი მხატვრისათვის რუსოსთვის ხომ არ შეუდარებიათ? კი, შეადარეს!
10. პროფესორმა დაგვაწერინა მოკლე თხზულება ფიროსმანიშვილის მიერ დახატული სურათების შესახებ.
11. ეს წერილი ივანესთვის რატომ არ გაგიგზავნინებია? მისთვის რომ გამეგზავნინებინა, ლიდა მას დროზე არ მიიღებდა.
12. ამ ახალგაზრდა მხატვარს ჩემს პორტრეტს დავახატვინებ. პეტრეს პორტრეტიც თურმე მის მიერ დახატულა.
13. შენ უნდა შემცდარიყავი, როცა თქვი, ლიდა ზეგ მოვაო.

14. ქართული ანბანი ქართველთა მოქცევის შემდეგ უნდა შექმნილიყო.
15. ასოთა რიგიდან ჩანს, რომ ქართული ანბანი ბერძნულს უნდა დაფუძნებოდა.
16. სომხები ამტკიცებენ, რომ ქართველებისათვის ანბანი შეუქმნია სომხური ანბანის შემქმნელს, მესროპ მაშტოცს.
17. სომხეთის ერთ-ერთ ძველ ისტორიაში დაწერილია, მესროპ მაშტოცმა სომხებს, კავკასიის ალბანელებსა და ქართველებს ანბანები შეუქმნაო.
18. სომხეთის ეს ისტორია დაწერილია მეხუთე საუკუნეში სომეხი ისტორიკოსი კორიუნის მიერ. მისი თავდაპირველი რედაქცია არ **შემონახულა.**
19. არსებობს მხოლოდ მომდევნო საუკუნეებში გადაწერილი და გადაკეთებული რედაქ[illegible]ე
20. მაგრამ მეხუთე საუკუნისავ [illegible]ვა სომეხი ისტორიკოსის თხზულებაში ნა[illegible]ვამია, რომ მესროპ მაშტოცმა დამწერლობა მხოლოდ სომხებს შეუქმნაო.
21. როგორც ჩანს, ცნობები ქართული და კავკასიის ალბანური ანბანების გამოგონების შესახებ კორიუნის ისტორიის ტექსტს სხვისი ხელით დამატებია.
22. ცხადია, რომ მესროპ მაშტო[illegible] ქართული ანბანი არ შეუქმნია. ეს ანბანი უნდა შექმნილიყო საქართველოში მეოთხე ან მეხუთე საუკუნეში. მისი გამომგონებელი ქართველი უნდა ყოფილიყო.
23. კავკასიის ალბანეთი ქრისტიანული სახელმწიფო იყო აღმოსავლეთ ამიერკავკასიაში, სადაც ახლანდელი აზერბაიჯანია განლაგებული.
24. ალბანური დამწერლობის ძალიან ცოტა ნიმუში **შე-მონახულა.** . არსებობს ერთადერთი მაგალითი ალბანური ანბანისა, რომელიც გადაწერილა შუა საუკუნეების სომხურ ხელნაწერში.
25. ეს ხელნაწერი გამოკვლეულ იქნა პროფესორი აკაკი შანიძის მიერ.

26. ამ ანბანში ასოთა რიცხვიდან ჩანს, რომ ალბანური ენა ჩრდილო-აღმოსავლეთის კავკასიის ენების მონათესავე ყოფილა.
27. ჩანს, რომ ალბანური ენა ახლანდელი უდური ენის წინაპარი ყოფილა.
28. გაამეორებინეთ ვიქტორს პროფესორის ნათქვამი! როცა ლაპარაკობდა, არ ვუსმენდი.
29. ნესტორი ძაღლებს ნუღარ აჭმევს! მე უკვე ვაჭამე.
30. ეს ცნობა მიღებულ იქნა ვახტანგის გასვლის შემდეგ.
31. თუმცა ქართული ენის ბრუნვათა რიგი ტრადიციითაა დადგენილი, ეს ბრუნვები თეორიულად შეიძლება სხვადასხვა რიგით იქნეს დალაგებული.
32. ანდაზა: უთქმელის მთქმელი თქმულმა შეჭამაო.
33. ქართული ენის დამწერლობაში წარმოუთქმელი ასოები არ არსებობს.
34. ბასკური ენის შეუსწავლელად ვერ გეტყვი, ქართული და ბასკური ერთმანეთს ენათესავება თუ არა.
35. ცხადია კი, რომ ასეთი გენეტიკური ნათესაობა ჯერ კიდევ დაუმტკიცებელია. ესე იგი, ეს გენეტიკური ნათესაობა აქამდის არ დამტკიცებულა.
36. სამწუხაროდ, თანამედროვე ქართული ლიტერატურული ნაწარმოებების უმრავლესობა ინგლისურ ენაზე ჯერ კიდევ გადაუთარგმნელია, ე.ი., ისინი ჯერ კიდევ არ გადათარგმნილა.
37. ფული უკვე ხომ არ გაგზავნილა? არ ვიცი; ვაჟას უნდა გაჰგზავნოდა. მას კი თურმე არ მიუღია.
38. მელქისედეკ კათალიკოსმა ოსტატ კონსტანტინე არსუკიძეს მცხეთის სვეტიცხოვლის ტაძარი ააშენებინა.
39. ჩანს, რომ ამ ოსტატისათვის მარჯვენა მოუჭრიათ. ლეგენდის მიხედვით, მეფე გიორგი პირველმა თავის ჯალათს არსუკიძისათვის მარჯვენა მოაჭრევინა.
40. ეს თურმე იმიტომ მომხდარა, რომ მეფე გიორგის შეყვარებულმა, მშვენიერმა შორენამ, მეფეს კონსტანტინე არსუკიძე ამჯობინა.

Vocabulary

ან	or (noninterrogative; cf. თუ)
არავითარი	no (kind of)
ასო	letter
აქამდის	up to now
ახლანდელი	present(-day) (E)
გამოგონება	invention
გამომგონებელი	inventor (E)
განათლება	education; instruction
გლეხი	peasant
დამწერლობა	writing system; writing
ერთადერთი	only one; the only; a single; unique
-ვე	same (particle indicating identity)
თავდაპირველი	original; initial; first
თანამედროვე	contemporary
თეორიული	theoretical
კუთხე	corner; angle; region
მარჯვენა	right (as opposed to left); right hand
მომდევნო	following
მონათესავე	related

მოსაწვევი ბარათი	invitation
მოქცევა	conversion
მშვენიერი [G. მშვენივრის]	beautiful
მხატვარი	artist; painter (A)
ნათესაობა	relationship
ოჯახი	family
პროფესიული	professional
რედაქცია	edition
რიცხვი	number
სახელოვანი	famous (A)
სხვადასხვა	different
სხვისი	someone else's (cf. სხვა)
ტექნიკა	technique
ტრადიცია	tradition
უდური	Udi (NE Caucasian language)
ფერწერა	painting
ქმარი	husband (A)
ღარიბი	poor (= not rich)
შემქმნელი	creator
შეყვარებული	beloved (person)
შუა საუკუნეები	Middle Ages
ცხადი	clear
წარსული	past

წინაპარი	ancestor (A)	დავით სოსლანი	(d. 1207)
ჯალათი	executioner	ვაჟა	(m. pr. n.)
ალბანეთი	Albania (both Caucasus and Balkan)	კორიუნი	(V. cent.)
		მელქისედეკი	Melchizedek
		მესროპ მაშტოცი	(361-440)
კახეთი	Kakhetia (province in East Georgia)	ნესტორი	Nestor
		რუსო	Rousseau
		ფიროსმანიშვილი ნიკო	(1860-1918)
ამირანაშვილი	(surname)	შანიძე აკაკი-	(1887-)
არსუკიძე კონსტანტინე	(XI. cent.)	მორენა	(f. pr. n.)

Verbs

დაადგენს	da=a-*dgen*-s (aor. E → I)	fix; determine
გადააკეთებს	gada+a-*ḳet*-eb-s	remake; alter
(წა)აკითხებს	(c̣a=)a-*ḳitx*-eb-s	cause to read (causative of (წა)იკითხავს 'read')
გა(ნ)ალაგებს	ga(n)=a-*lag*-eb-s	locate
დაალაგებს	da=a-*lag*-eb-s	arrange, order
დაუმატებს	da=u-*maṭ*-eb-s II. conj. = დაემატება	add (sthg.) to (sthg.)
ამჯობინებს	Ø=H-a-*mǯobin*-eb-s	prefer (sthg./s.o.) to (sthg./s.o.)
დაენათესავება	da=e-*natesav*-eb-a	be related to
შემოინახავს	šemo=i-*nax*-av-s	preserve; keep; save (e.g., money)
დაეფუძნება	da=e-*pujn*-eb-a II. conj.	be based on (sthg.)
შეჭამს	še+*č̣am*-s	eat up; consume
აჭმევს	Ø=a-*č̣mev*-s aor. = აჭამა	feed (animals; children)
მოაჭრევინებს	mo=a-*č̣rev*-in-eb-s	cause to cut off

დახატავს da=*xaṭ*-av-s draw; paint

ახსნის a=*xsn*-i-s solve; explain

Šota Rustaveli
(From an XVII. Century ms. of
Vepxisṭqaosani)
შოთა რუსთაველი

Key to the Exercises

1. If the letter had been sent earlier, then we would have received it yesterday.
2. John apparently has helped you all. I know that you weren't able to do this exercise (by) yourselves.
3. Many Georgian scientists say that *The Knight in the Tiger's Skin* must have been written before (= up to) the death of King Tamara's husband David Soslani. He apparently died in 1207.
4. Didn't you see Vaxṭang yesterday? No, I didn't see him. He apparently was hiding from us.
5. Why didn't you go to (= sit down at) the banquet? Because I didn't receive an invitation.
6. Professor Amiranašvili had us read about Niḳo Pirosmanišvili (1860-1918). Who was Pirosmanišvili? This was a famous Georgian painter. He had (= was) come [out] from a poor peasant's family. He received no (kind of) professional education.
7. He did not know the technique of painting, was not acquainted with either past or contemporary to him (= his contemporary) Georgian art.
8. It is known that the artist was acquainted with only Kakhetia and Tbilisi. He was not in other regions of Georgia.
9. Haven't they compared Pirosmanišvili to the French artist Rousseau? Yes, they compared him to him.
10. The professor had us write a short composition about the pictures painted by Pirosmanišvili.
11. Why didn't you have John send this letter? If I had had him send it, Lida wouldn't have received it in time.
12. I shall have this young artist paint my portrait. Peter's portrait too has apparently been painted by him.
13. You must have been mistaken when you said Lida was coming (= will come) the day after tomorrow.
14. The Georgian alphabet must have been created after the conversion of the Georgians.
15. From the order of letters it appears that the Georgian alphabet must have been based upon the Greek.
16. The Armenians maintain that the creator of the Armenian alphabet, Mesrop̣ Maštoc, created the alphabet for the Georgians (id.o.).
17. In one old history of Armenia it is written that Mesrop̣ Maštoc created alphabets for the Armenians, the Albanians of the Caucasus, and the Georgians.

18. This history of Armenia was (= is) written in the fifth century by the Armenian historian (declined adjectivally) Ḳoriun. His original redaction has not been preserved.
19. There exist only redactions copied and altered in following centuries.
20. But in the [literary] work of another Armenian historian of the [same] fifth century it is said that Mesrop̣ Mašṭoc created a writing system only for the Armenians.
21. As it appears, the information about the invention of the Georgian and Caucasus Albanian alphabets was added to the text of Ḳoriun's history by someone else's hand.
22. It is clear that Mesrop̣ Mašṭoc did not create the Georgian alphabet. This alphabet must have been created in Georgia in the fourth or fifth century. Its inventor must have been a Georgian.
23. Caucasus Albania was a Christian state in the Eastern Transcaucasus, where present day Azerbaijan is located.
24. Very few examples of the Albanian writing system have been preserved. There exists only one example of the Albanian alphabet, which has been copied into a medieval (= of the middle centuries) Armenian manuscript.
25. This manuscript was investigated by Professor (declines like ბატონი, see Lesson 6, note 9) Aḳaḳi Šanije.
26. From the number of letters in this alphabet it appears that the Albanian language was related to the languages (gen.) of the northeast Caucasus.
27. It appears that the Albanian language was the ancestor of the contemporary Udi language.
28. Have Victor repeat what the professor said (= the professor's said; use prefixed participle). When he was speaking, I wasn't listening to him.
29. Don't let Nestor feed the dogs any more! I already fed them.
30. This news was received after Vaxṭang left (use VN).
31. Although the order of the cases of the Georgian language is fixed by tradition, these cases can theoretically be arranged in (use instr.) a different order.
32. Proverb: [That which was] spoken consumed [ate up] the speaker of the unspoken.
33. In the writing system of the Georgian language, unpronounced letters do not exist.
34. Without learning Basque I will not be able to tell you [whether] Georgian and Basque are relat-

ed to each other or not.

35. It is clear, however, that such a genetic relationship still is unproven. I.e., this genetic relationship has not been proven up to now.

36. Unfortunately, most (= the majority of) contemporary Georgian literary works still are untranslated into English, i.e., these works have not yet been translated.

37. Hasn't the money been sent yet? I don't know; it was supposed to have been sent to Važa. He, however, apparently hasn't received it.

38. The catholicos Melkizedeḳ [Melkizedeḳ Catholicos] had the master Ḳonsṭanṭine Arsuḳije build Mtskheta's Cathedral of the Living Pillar [SveṭicxovEli] (1010).

39. It seems that they cut off this master's right hand. According to legend, King George I had his executioner cut off Arsuḳije's (-*tvis*)* right hand.

40. This apparently happened for that reason that King (not declined) George's beloved, the beautiful Šorena, preferred Ḳonsṭanṭine Arsuḳije to the king.

*As a rule in Georgian the relationship between a person and a part of that person's body is marked by an indirect object (and not by a possessive construction as in English); e.g.,: ამ ოსტატს მარჯვენა მოუჭრეს 'They cut off this master's right hand (dat., id.o.)'. In this sentence with the causative verb (მოაჭრევინა) there is already an indirect object (ჯალათს) so, as in the perfect series, what elsewhere would be an indirect object in the dative case is changed to a postpositional phrase with -*tvis*.

Reading Passage „რეპორტაჟი საქართველოდან"

1 საქართველოს წარსული ლეგენდების ბურუსშია გახვეული. კავკასიის მთებში იტანჯებოდა მიჯაჭვული ამირანი, კავკასიის კლდეს მიაჯაჭვა ზევსმაც ბერძენთა ტიტანი პრომეთე, რომელმაც ღმერთებს გამოსტაცა ცეცხლი და ადამიანებს ჩამოუტანა. კოლხეთის ნაპირებს მოადგა გმირი იაზონი, არგონავტების წინამძღოლი. კავკასიის შავი ზღვის სანაპიროებზე დაეხეტებოდა ქარიშხლებში გზადაკარგული ოდისევსის გემი. ბრინჯაოს საუკუნის საფლავის ძეგლები — ქვის დოლმენები, ზეპირი გადმოცემები, სამარხებში მიგნებული ნივთები, წერილობითი ძეგლები ინახავენ ცნობებს გარდასულ საუკუნეებზე, მსოფლიოს ერთ-ერთი უძველესი სახელმწიფოს — საქართველოს ისტორიულ წარსულზე.

2 ჩვენი სამშობლოს ბუნებრივი სიმდიდრეები, საამო ჰავა, სტრატეგიული მდებარეობა თავიდანვე იზიდავდნენ უცხოელ დამპყრობლებს. საქართველოსაკენ ეჭირათ თვალი აღმოსავლეთის მრისხანე მბრძანებლებს. VII—VIII საუკუნეებში საქართველოს არაბები ჯიჯგნიდნენ, XI საუკუნიდან ქვეყნის დაპყრობა თურქ-სელჯუკებმა მოიწადინეს. XIII—XIV საუკუნეებში საქართველოს თათარ-მონღოლები აოხრებენ. XIV—XV საუკუნეების მიჯნაზე საქართველოში რვაჯერ შემოიჭრა თემურ-ლენგი, რომელმაც გააჩანაგა სოფლები, დააქცია ქალაქები და გაჟლიტა უთვალავი ადამიანი. იმ შავბნელ ჟამს გაჩნდა საქართველოში საყოველთაო ნგრევისა და გაპარტახების გამომხატველი სახელწოდებები, ჟამთა სიავემ რომ დაანათლა ჩვენს მიწა-წყალს: ნაქალაქევი, ნასოფლარი, ნასახლარი, პარტახი, ნაბეღლარი...

3 XVI—XVIII საუკუნეებში საქართველო გააფთრებულ წინააღმდეგობას უწევდა თურქ-ოსმალთა ურდოებს. ეკონომიურად ჩამორჩენილი ქვეყანა, ფეოდალურ სამთავროებად დაქუცმაცებული საქართველო, რომლის მწარმოებელი ძალა მტერთან უთანასწორო ბრძოლაში წყდებოდა, რა წინააღმდეგობას გაუწევდა კბილებამდე შეიარაღებულ ფანატიკოს გადამთიელთა ათჯერ მრავალრიცხოვანი არმიების მოძალებას?! საქართველოს წინაშე ისტორიამ სასტიკი დილემა დასვა. არჩევანი ასეთი იყო: ან მტრის უღელქვეშ უნდა მოდრეკილიყო ან დახმარება უნდა ეთხოვა ერთმორწმუნე რუსეთისათვის.

4 კიევის რუსეთი და საქართველო ჯერ კიდევ XI—XII საუკუნეებში იცნობდნენ ერთმანეთს. ამაზე დამაჯერებლად მეტყველებს ქართული სტილი რუსული ხუროთმოძღვრების ძეგლებში, ქართველთა ხსენება რუსეთის მატიანეებში და რუსეთისა — ქართულ მატიანეში. ქართველთა დედოფლის თამარ მეფის პირველი ქმარი — იური — რუსი მთავრის, ანდრია ბოგოლუბსკის შვილი იყო.

5 მაგრამ ადრინდელი კავშირის ძაფი გაწყვიტა საქართველოსა და რუსეთის მიწა-წყალზე მონღოლების შემოჭრამ. მოგვიანებით, XVI საუკუნეში, საქართველოში მონღოლთა უღელი თურქთა და სპარსთა უღლით შეიცვალა.

6 ქართველი ხალხის მოწინავე შვილებმა კარგად იცოდნენ, რომ მხოლოდ რუსეთთან კავშირით შეიძლებოდა ქვეყნის დამოუკიდებლობის შენარჩუნება, ხალხის ხსნა. გამოჩენილმა ქართველმა სარდალმა და პოლიტიკოსმა მეფე ერეკლე II, პატარა კახმა XVIII საუკუნის ბოლოს ეკატერინე მეორეს სთხოვა, საქართველო რუსეთის იმპერიის მფარველობაში მიეღო. 1783 წელს გეორგიევსკში (ჩრდილოეთ კავკასიაში) ხელმოწერილ იქნა ტრაქტატი, რომლის ძალითაც საქართველო რუსეთის მფარველობაში შედიოდა, მაგრამ ამ ფორმალურმა აქტმა დიდი შვება ვერ მისცა მრავალტანჯულ ქართველ ხალხს. რუსეთის მეფეები ყოყმანობდნენ, მათი სარდლები კი, მაგალითად, გენერალი ტოტლებენი, უაღრესად ორჭოფულ, თითქმის ვერაგულ როლს თამაშობდა.

7 1801 წელს გამოიცა მანიფესტი საქართველოს რუსეთთან შეერთების შესახებ. ამან იხსნა ჩვენი ქვეყანა თურქთა და სპარსთა დაუსრულებელი თარეშისაგან.

8 რუსეთის შემწეობით მოხდა ქართველთა მიწების გაერთიანება. 1824 წელს თურქეთთან ომის შემდეგ მშობლიურ წიაღს დაუბრუნდა მესხეთ-ჯავახეთი, ქართული კულტურის უძველესი კერა, 1878 წელს კი — აჭარა და მისი მთავარი ქალაქი ბათუმი. ქართველი ხალხი მუდამ გულწრფელი მადლიერების გრძნობით იყო გამსჭვალული რუსი ხალხის მიმართ, რომელმაც მის ცხოვრებაში უდიდესი პროგრესული როლი შეასრულა.

—მიხეილ დავითაშვილი

Vocabulary

1

ბურუსი	fog; mist
გა=ხვევს	wrap up; envelope
და=ტანჯავს	torment; torture
მი=აჯაჭვავს ●	fetter; chain (sthg.) onto (sthg.) (dat., *H*- series markers). N.B. rule 1.11.1 doesn't apply in forming the perfect participle.
კლდე	rock
ზევსი	Zeus
ღმერთებს	(see sec. 3.2.1.1)
გამო=ს-ტაცებს	tear (sthg.) away from (s.o.) (dat., *H*-series markers)
ცეცხლი	fire
ჩამო+იტანს	bring down (pres. series irregular)
ნაპირი	border; edge; bank
ნაპირს მო=ადგება	land (from a boat)
წინამძღოლი	leader
ზღვა	sea
სანაპირო	coastline; borderland
და+ე-ხეტება	wander around (no id.o.)
ქარიშხალი	gale; storm (A)
გზადაკარგული	having lost one's way
ოდისევსი	Odysseus; Ulysses
გემი	ship; boat
ბრინჯაო	bronze
საუკუნე	here: age
საფლავი ძეგლი	gravestone, (ძეგლი = monument)
ქვა	stone
დოლმენი	dolmen
ზეპირი	oral
გადმოცემა	tradition; legend
სამარხი	burial place

მი=აგნებს	discover (aor. -(ვ)აგენი(-თ), -აგნო)
ნივთი	material
გარდასული	which have passed by
მსოფლიო	world

2

ბუნებრივი	natural
სიმდიდრე	here: resource
საამო	pleasant
მდებარეობა	situation; position
თავიდანვე	from the very beginning on
მი=/მო=იზიდავს	attract
და=იპყრობს	conquer (aor. irr. -(ვ)იპყარი(-თ), -იპყრო)
[ეჭირათ თვალი]	they (dat.) directed their gaze
მრისხანე	wrathful
და=ჯიჯგნის	tear to pieces
სელჯუკები	Seljuks (Turkish dynasty, XI-XIIIcc.)
მო+იწადინებს	wish; desire
მიჯნა	border (here: on the border between)
-ჯერ	times
შემო+იჭრება	invade (II. conj., + -*ši*)
თემურ-ლენგი	Tamerlaine
გა=ავერანებს	lay waste; devastate
და=აქცევს	destroy
გა=ჟლეტს	kill; crush (E → I)
უთვალავი	countless (+ sing.)
შავბნელი	dark; evil; unbearable
ჟამი	time; ... ჟამს at, in ... time
გა=ჩნდება (ga=čn-d-eb-a)	appear
საყოველთაო	general; common; universal
ნგრევა	destruction
გა=აპარტახებს	lay waste; devastate
გამო+ხატავს	depict

სახელწოდება	name
ავი	bad; evil
რომ	here: which (= სახელწოდებები)
და=ანათლებს	present; give (lit. s.o. gives s.o. being baptized some gift)
მიწა-წყალი	territory
ნა-...-ევი / ნა-...-არი	circumfix indicating the ruins or former site of sthg.
პარცახი	forsaken; destitute (here: name of a village)
ბეღელი	granary (E)
	(These forms in *na*- are the names of Geo. villages.)

3

გა=ა-აფთრებს	infuriate; enrage
წინააღმდეგობა	opposition
გა=უწევს წინააღმდეგობას	offer resistance to (s.o.)
ოსმალი	Ottoman
ურდო	horde
ჩამორჩენილი	backward
სამთავრო	principality
და=აქუცმაცებს	cut up; splinter (here: Adv. = into)
მწარმოებელი	productive (E)
ძალა	energy; force; power
თანასწორი	equal
გა=წყდება (ga=c̣qd-eb-a)	break; destroy (II. conj. form of გა=წყვეტს; VN გაწყდომა)
რა წინააღმდეგობას გაუწევდა	here: what opposition could (Georgia) show against (dat.)...? (Subject = the two phrases ending in საქართველო above.)
შე=ა-იარაღებს	arm
ფანატიკოსი	fanatic(al)

გადამთიელი	foreigner
მრავალრიცხოვანი	numerous; ათჯერ მრავალრიცხოვანი ten times more numerous
მოძალება	attack
წინაშე	before (pp.)
სასტიკი	cruel
და=სვამს	put; place; set (d.o. in sing.)
არჩევანი	choice; election (A)
ან...ან...	either ... or ...
უღელი	yoke (E)
-ქვეშ	under (pp. with Dat. without -s)
მო=დრეკს	bend down (E → I)
Ø=ს-თხოვს	ask s.o. (id.o.) for sthg. (d.o.)
ერთმორწმუნე	someone of the same religion
4	
კიევი	Kiev
დამაჯერებელი	convincing (E)
მეტყველებს	speak (III. conj.)
სტილი	style
ხუროთმოძღვრება	architecture
ხსენება	mention
მატიანე	chronicle
დედოფალი	queen (A) (i.e., თამარ მეფე)
იური	(Russian name: Jurij, Yuri)
მთავარი	prince (of a principality) (A)
ანდრია ბოგოლუბსკი-	Andrej Bogoljubskij (ca. 1111-1174)
შვილი	child; son
5	
ძაფი	thread
გა=წყვეტს	break; rupture (E → I)
შემოჭრა	invasion
კავშირი	here: connection; link
მოგვიანებით	later [on]

შე=ცვლის change; replace

6

მოწინავე progressive

დამოუკიდებლობა independence

შენარჩუნება retention; preservation

ხსნა here: deliverance; salvation

გამოჩენილი famous; outstanding

სარდალი commander (A)

პოლიტიკოსი political figure

პატარა კახი "The Little Kakhetian," nickname of Erekle II

ეკატერინე II Catherine the Great

იმპერია empire

მფარველობა protection

გეორგიევსკი Georgievsk (town)

ხელმოწერილი signed

ტრაქტატი treaty

შვება joy; solace; relief

და=ტანჯავს torment; torture

ყოყმანობს hesitate; waver

უაღრესად extremely

ორჭოფული ambiguous; unclear

ვერაგული treacherous; disloyal

7

გამო+სცემს publish (no id.o.; sec. 7.4)

Ø=იხსნის save

დაუსრულებელი endless (E)

თარეში raid

8

შემწეობა help

მიწა land; earth; ground

მშობლიური native

წიაღი womb

კერა hearth

გულწრფელი	sincere
მადლიერება	gratitude
გრძნობა	feeling; sense
გამსჭვალული	filled
მიმართ	toward; to (pp.)
შე=ასრულებს	fulfill; accomplish

•ADDENDUM TO VOCABULARY

1

ამირანი	Caucasian folk hero; similar to the Greek Prometheus in many respects

Tbilisi University
(Original Building)

თბილისის უნივერსიტეტი

LESSON 12

12.1 The IV. conjugation, indirect verbs. The IV. conjugation consists of the so-called *indirect verbs*, primarily *verba sentiendi*, i.e., verbs denoting emotions or sensations felt or experienced by a person. In many languages such verbs take "dative constructions." Compare:

English:	It seems *to me*	
	(archaic:) *Methinks*	
	Something pleases *me*, is pleasing *to me*	
French:	Il me plaît	I like
	Il me faut	I need
German:	Mir gefällt	I like
	Mir ist kalt	I am cold
Russian:	Мне нравится	I like
	Мне холодно	I am cold
	Мне нужно	I need
	Мне кажется	It seems to me

The Georgian IV. conjugation verbs pattern somewhat similarly to the above constructions. In the IV. conjugation the grammatical subject is in the *dative* case and denotes the person *affected* by the emotion or sensation, while the source of the emotion or sensation is in the nominative case. Compare the following:

German:	Mir ist Hannah lieb.	I love Ann
Georgian:	Me Ana mi-qvar-s.	
German:	Mir sind Hannah und Edward lieb.	I love Ann and Edward
Georgian:	Me Ana da Eduardi mi-qvar-s.	

Note that in German, the source of the emotion (Hannah or Hannah and Edward) is the grammatical subject and the verb agrees in number with that source. ('I love Hannah' can be viewed as meaning something like 'Hannah turns me on'.)

In Georgian the source of the emotion (Anna or Anna and Edward) usually does not have number agreement with the verb; in this respect it patterns somewhat similarly to the objects of I. conjugation verbs, which do not have number agreement in the third person. In the Georgian IV. conjugation the number agreement is for the experiencer of the sensation. Compare:

German:	Ihm ist Hannah lieb.	He loves Ann
Georgian:	Mas Ana u-qvar-s.	
German:	Ihm sind Hannah und Edward lieb.	He loves Ann and Edward
Georgian:	Mas Ana da Eduardi u-qvar-s.	
German:	Ihnen ist Hannah lieb.	They love Ann
Georgian:	Mat Ana u-qvar-t.	
German:	Ihnen sind Hannah und Edward lieb.	They love A & E
Georgian:	Mat Ana da Eduard-i u-qvar-t.	

As can be seen from the examples, the grammatical subject (the experiencer of the feeling) is in the *dative* case while the source of the emotion is treated as an object in the *nominative* case. The IV. conjugation, like the perfect series of I. and III. conjugation verbs, is characterized by this *inversion*. Unlike the I. and III. conjugation verbs, however, IV. conjugation verbs have the subject in the dative and the object in the nominative *in all three series*. It should be noted that, like III. conjugation verbs, IV. conjugation verbs occur most commonly in the present series.

The majority of IV. conjugation verbs denote *states*. As a general rule, they do not occur in the imperative, either affirmative or negative, since commands generally imply a *change of state*, rather than a state. But a meaning similar to that of the imperative can be conveyed by the use of (არ)უნდა + optative. IV. conjugation verbs also generally do not take the negation ვერ; they generally take only არ.

To denote changes of state, rather than the states themselves, II. conjugation verbs in *-d-* can be derived from IV. conjugation verbs. For examples, see sec. 12.3.3.

12.1.2. Formation of IV. conjugation verbs. The vocabulary entry form for IV. conjugation verbs will be the *present tense* with *1sg. subject* and third person object.

12.1.2.1. Present series. In the present series the *grammatical subject* (in the dative case) is marked in the verb by either:

a. the *u*-series of (object) markers; or
b. the *h*-series of object markers with:
   i. no preradical vowel,
   ii. preradical vowel *a*-, or
   iii. preradical vowel *e*-.

In the present tense a third person *grammatical object*[1] (in the nominative case) is normally marked in the verb by the suffix *-s* or *-a*. Grammatical objects of the first and second persons are marked by the corresponding suffixed forms of the verb 'be'.

Subject markers
(Present series)

	sing.		pl.
1.	m-, mi-, ma-, me-	1.	gv-, gvi-, gva-, gve-
2.	g-, gi-, ga-, ge-	2.	g-, gi-, ga-, ge-....-t
3.	ø- / h- / s-, u-, a-, e-	3.	ø- / h- / s-, u-, a-, e-....-t

Object markers
(Present tense)

1.	v-....-var	1.	v-....-vart
2.	-xar	2.	-xart
3.	-s or -a		

In the *imperfect* and *conjunctive* present the subject markers are as above while the object markers are the corresponding subject markers of the imperfect and conjunctive present of I. or II. conjugation verbs. The PSF *-i* is dropped before these endings.

Object markers Imperfect		Object markers Conjunctive present	
1.	v-...-(o)d-i(-t)	1.	v-....-(o)d-e(-t)
2.	-(o)d-i(-t)	2.	-(o)d-e(-t)
3.	-(o)d-a	3.	-(o)d-e-s

IV. conjugation verbs which have the third person object marker *-a* in the present take the object markers *-od-* while those with *-s* in the present take the object markers with *-d-*.

The subject and object markers generally combine according to the rules given in sec. 7.1.2, but see Lesson 11, note 6. When the subject is third person *plural* and the object is first or second person *singular*, the plurality of the subject might not be marked; compare the similar pattern found in the perfect series of I. and III. conjugation verbs. In general, though, the tendency is to mark the plurality of the subject with the marker -*t*. Examples:

Present:

მიყვარხარ(-თ) I love you (all)	გვიყვარხარ(-თ) We love you (all)
მიყვარს I love her/them	გვიყვარს We love her/them
გიყვარვარ(-თ) You love me (us)	გიყვარვართ You all love me/us
გიყვარს You love her/them	გიყვართ You all love her/them
ვუყვარვარ(-თ) He loves me (us)	ვუყვარვარ They love me ვუყვარვართ They love us
უყვარხარ(-თ) He loves you (all)	უყვარხარ(თ) They love you უყვარხართ They love you (all)
უყვარს He loves her/them	უყვართ They love her/them

Imperfect:

მიყვარდი(-თ) I loved you (all)	გვიყვარდი(-თ) We loved you (all)
მიყვარდა I loved her/them	გვიყვარდა We loved her/them
გიყვარდი(-თ) You loved me (us)	გიყვარდით You all loved me/us
გიყვარდა You love her/them	გიყვარდათ You all loved her/them
ვუყვარდი(-თ) He loved me (us)	ვუყვარდი They loved me

	ვეყვარდით They loved us
ეყვარდი(-თ) He loved you (all)	ეყვარდი They loved you
	ეყვარდით They loved you (all)
ეყვარდა He loved her/them	ეყვარდათ They loved her/them

The conjunctive present is formed similarly.

12.1.2.2. Future, aorist, and perfect series. In the future series IV. conjugation verbs are conjugated according to the pattern of relative II. conjugation verbs with object marker *e*- (sec. 7.3.1). To form the future, any PSF is dropped and the suffix -*eb* is added to the root. An example of the conjugation of a IV. conjugation verb in the future:

მეყვარები(-თ)	I shall love you (all)
მეყვარება	I shall love her/them
გეყვარები(-თ)	You will love me (us)
გეყვარება	You will love her/them
ვეყვარები(-თ)	He will love me (us)
ეყვარები(-თ)	He will love you (all)
ეყვარება	He will love her/them
გვეყვარები(-თ)	We shall love you (all)
გვეყვარება	We shall love her/them
გეყვარებით	You all will love me/us
გეყვარებათ	You all will love her/them
ვეყვარები	They will love me
ვეყვარებით	They will love us
ეყვარები	They will love you
ეყვარებით	They will love you (all)
ეყვარებათ	They will love her/them

The following are similarly conjugated; future

forms in parentheses are rare.

Present	Future
მნებავს	(მენებება)
(would) like[2]	
მღვიძავს	მეღვიძება
be awake	
მძაგს	(მეძაგება)
be disgusted by	
მძინავს	მეძინება
sleep	
მძულს	(მეძულება)
hate	
მჭყინს	მეჭყინება
find unpleasant	
მგონია	მეგონება
think	
მშია	მეშიება
be hungry	(imperfect: მშიოდა)
მეშინია[3]	---
fear; be afraid of	(imperfect: მეშინოდა)
მწადია	(მეწადება)
desire	(imperfect: მწადდა)
შემიძლია	შემეძლება
be able	

With some IV. conjugation verbs a slightly different root is used in the formation of the future:

Present		Future
მსურს	wish	(მესურვება)
მახსოვს	remember	მეხსომება
მტკივა	hurt	მეტკინება
მინდა[4]	want	მენდომება

In the following verb the future may take the preverb *mo*-:

მესმის[5]	hear	მომესმება, ([მო]მესმის)

The remaining screeves of the future series, the

aorist and optative (aorist series), and the screeves of the perfect series of IV. conjugation verbs are formed generally as for other relative II. conjugation forms with preradical vowel *e*-. The rules for combination of person markers are as for the present series and future tense of IV. conjugation verbs. (For the missing aorist series of მიყვარს, the aorist series of მძინავს 'sleep' has been substituted.)

Conditional: მეყვარებოდა

Conjunctive future: მეყვარებოდეს

Aorist: მეძინა Optative: მეძინოს

Present perfect: მყვარებია (cf. sec. 11.2.2)

Pluperfect: მყვარებოდა (cf. sec. 11.2.2)

The verbs მწყინს (fut. მეწყინება) 'find unpleasant', მტკივა (fut. მეტკინება) 'hurt', and მესმის (fut. (მო)მესმება) have the vowel *e* in the perfect series: მწყენია, მტკენია, (მო)მსმენია.

Many IV. conjugation verbs are *defective*, i.e., they lack one or more series of screeves. Of the verbs listed above, the following lack the aorist series of screeves:

მძაგს, მძულს, მინდა

In such verbs, the missing aorist and optative are replaced by the imperfect and conjunctive respectively.

The following verbs lack both the aorist and perfect series of screeves:

მახსოვს, მშია

Some IV. conjugation verbs lack in addition the future series. These verbs have only present series screeves. Examples are მცივა 'be cold', მწყურია 'be thirsty', მჭირია 'need'. (This last verb is synonymous with the present series of დასჭირდება; see below, sec. 12.1.2.4.)

12.1.2.3. Expression of 'can' in Georgian. One must distinguish between the IV. conjugation verb შემიძლია 'can', 'be able', Russian мочь and შეიძლება 'be permitted', 'possible', Russian (воз)можно. Compare the following:

შეიძლება შემოვიდე?

Can I (= Is it permitted that I) come in?

აქ თამბაქოს მოწევა შეიძლება.

Here one can (= it is permitted to) smoke.

შეიძლება ეს გავაკეთოთ?

Can we (= are we allowed to) do this?

But:

შემიძლია ინგლისურად ლაპარაკი.

I can speak English.

შემიძლია ამის გაკეთება.

I can (am able to) do this.

არ შემიძლია დაგეხმაროთ.

I cannot help you.

The negative of შემიძლია can often be expressed simply by ვერ; so the last sentence above can also be expressed: ვერ დაგეხმარებით.

In impersonal constructions შეიძლება can be used to denote physical ability. Example:

ეს ორ დღეში შეიძლება გაკეთდეს.

This can be done in two days.

12.1.2.4. There is a strong tendency for the subjects of II. conjugation verbs to be inanimate, i.e., third person. Many such verbs occur with indirect objects referring to animate beings. Examples are:

a. II. conj. in *e*-:

შეექმნება	(sthg.) is created for him
გაეგზავნება	(sthg.) is sent to him
მოერგება	(sthg.) fits (s.o.) (dat.); cf. მოარგებს fit (s.o.)

b. II. conj. in -*d*-:

და+ა-ვიწყდება	(sthg.) is forgotten by him; i.e., he forgets (sthg.)
დაუმძიმდება	(sthg.) becomes hard(er) for him
მოუმზადდება	(sthg.) is prepared for him
და=ს-ჭირდება	(sthg.) is necessary for him; i.e., he needs something

Such verbal forms are said to have *objective conjugation* in that the grammatical subject can only be third person while the person of the (indirect) object changes in conjugation. Examples are:

obj. 1.	დამჭირდება	I will need (sthg.)
obj. 2.	დაგჭირდება	You will need (sthg.)
obj. 3.	დასჭირდება	He will need (sthg.)

Note that such forms pattern similarly to indirect verbs, but are distinct from them because they have in the present (and future and aorist) series the II. conjugation markers *e*- or -*d*-. [■ p. 345]

Very often a II. conjugation verb with objective conjugation contrasts in meaning with a corresponding I. conjugation verb. In such contrasts the I. conjugation verb often denotes a *voluntary, deliberate* action while the II. conjugation form denotes an involuntary, even accidental action. Compare the following:

a. ფული დავკარგე.
   I lost the money.

b. ფული დამეკარგა.
   I lost the money.

a. მისი მისამართი არ დაივიწყო!
   Don't forget his address!

b. მისი მისამართი დამავიწყდა.
   I forgot his address.

a. ჭიქა გატეხა.
   He broke the glass.

b. ჭიქა გაუტყდა.
   The glass broke on him; i.e., he broke the glass. (გა(უ)ტყდება is the II. conj. form of გატეხს.)

In each of the pairs above the *b* sentence indicates that the action was not voluntary, while the *a* sentence can indicate a deliberate action or (as in the first sentence above) be neutral in meaning.

12.1.3. Irregular IV. conjugation verbs.

a. მაქვს 'have something' (the thing possessed [in the nominative case] is inanimate, i.e., neither a person nor an animal).

Present	მაქვს	Future	მექნება[6]
Imperfect	მქონდა		
Conj. pres.	მქონდეს		

Perfect მქონია

Pluperfect მქონოდა

This verb has no aorist or optative; for these the imperfect and conjunctive present are used. The verbal noun is ქონა or ქონება.

b. მყავს 'have someone' (the possessed [in the nominative] is a person or an animal).

Present series: მყავს[7]

Future series: მეყოლება

All remaining series are formed regularly from the future. The verbal noun is ყოლა.

c. Verbs meaning 'to carry something', 'bring, take something'. The thing carried, brought, or taken is inanimate. In the present series of screeves these are IV. conjugation verbs, consisting of a preverb of direction (see sec. 2.2.1) plus the verb მაქვს. Examples:

მომაქვს I am bringing it, carrying it here.

მიმაქვს I am taking it, carrying it there.

შემომაქვს I am bringing it, carrying it in (here).

შემაქვს I am taking it, carrying it in (there), etc.

In the future, aorist, and perfect series, these are regular I. conjugation verbs with the root *-ṭan* and in the future and aorist series the preradical vowel *i-*. The future forms are:

მოვიტან I shall bring, carry it here.

3sg. subj. მოიტანს

{ მივიტან (წავიღებ)[8] I shall take, carry it there

3sg. subj. მიიტანს (წაიღებს) }

შემოვიტან I shall bring, carry it in (here).

3sg. subj. შემოიტანს

შევიტან I shall take, carry it in (there).

3sg. subj. შეიტანს

In the future series the subject is in the nominative and the direct object in the dative; in the aorist series the subject is ergative and the direct object, nominative; and in the perfect series, the subject is dative and the direct object nominative. The verbal nouns of these verbs are formed with the root *-ṭan-*, for example, მოტანა, მიტანა, შემოტანა, შეტანა, etc.

d. Verbs meaning 'to lead someone', 'bring, take someone'. The object of these verbs is animate, i.e., human or animal. In the present series these are IV. conjugation verbs, consisting of a preverb of direction (see sec. 2.2.1) plus the verb მყავს. In the future, aorist, and perfect series these are regular I. conjugation verbs with the root -*qvan*- and, in the future and aorist series, the preradical vowel *i*-. Examples:

Present (subject 1sg.)		Future (subject 3sg.)
მომყავს	lead, bring (s.o.)	მოიყვანს
მიმყავს	lead, take (s.o.)	მიიყვანს
შემომყავს	lead, bring (s.o.) in	შემოიყვანს
შემყავს	lead, take (s.o.) in	შეიყვანს

The case syntax of these verbs is as in *c* above.[9] The verbal noun of these verbs is formed with the root -*qvan*-: მოყვანა, მიყვანა, შემოყვანა, შეყვანა.

e. Future series of the verb იცის 'know'. The future and perfect series of the irregular verb იცის (sec. 9.1.4) are formed according to the IV. conjugation:

Future:	მეცოდინება	I shall know
Perfect:	მცოდნია	I have known

12.2. *Have* plus future participle. The verb 'have' plus the future participle (sec. 11.5.2) is used to express obligation, the equivalent of the English *have to* construction. Examples:

წერილი აქვს დასაწერი.

He has to write a letter.

ეს წიგნი წასაკითხავი გაქვთ.

You have to read this book.

ეს წერილი გასაგზავნი მაქვს.

I have to send this letter.

(Passive versions of this construction can be formed with the verb არის:

წერილი დასაწერია; ეს წიგნი წასაკითხავია; ეს წერილი გასაგზავნია.

12.3. Wordbuilding.

12.3.1. Nominal forms of IV. conjugation verbs. The verbal nouns of IV. conjugation verbs tend to be irregular in formation and not all such verbs have verbal nouns. The participles, when they can be formed, generally have the usual prefixes: *m-* (or *mo-*) for the present participle and *sa-* for the future participle, although there is great variation in the suffixes. Examples are:

IV. conj.	Verbal noun	Present part.	Future part.
მიყვარს	სიყვარული	მოყვარული	საყვარელი (E)
მძინავს	ძილი	მძინარი, მძინარე	საძილე
მსურს	სურვილი	მსურველი	სასურველი
მძულს	სიძულვილი	მოძულე	საძულველი
მცივა	ცივილი	მცივანი	საცივარი (A)

Other examples of verbal nouns are:

IV. conj.	Verbal noun	IV. conj.	Verbal noun
მნებავს	ნება	მწყურია	წყურვილი
მშია	შიმშილი	მახსოვს	ხსოვნა
მღვიძავს	ღვიძილი	მინდა	ნდომა
მწადია	წადილი	მესმის	სმენა

The nominal forms of the irregular verbs are:

მაქვს	ქონ(ებ)ა	მქონე, მქონებელი (E)	საქონელი (E)[10]
მყავს	ყოლა	----	საყოლი

12.3.2. 'Modal' II. conjugation forms in *e-*. There is a special category of II. conjugation verbs, usually derived from III. and IV. conjugation verbs, which take the preradical vowel *e-* with *h*-series object markers. These verbs (which usually occur only in the present series) have objective conjugation (see above, 12.1.2.4) and are modal in meaning. They denote an urge on the part of a person (marked by the dative) to perform a given action. This urge is often involuntary. The usual English translation is 'feel like doing something'.[11] Examples:

Base form		Modal II. conj.	
მძინავს (IV)	sleep	ეძინება	feel like sleeping, be tired

მღერის	(III)	sing	ემღერება	feel like singing
თამაშობს	(III)	play	ეთამაშება	feel like playing
იცინის	(III)	laugh	ეცინება	feel like laughing
ცეკვავს	(III)	dance	ეცეკვება	feel like dancing

12.3.3. Derivatives of IV. conjugation verbs denoting change of state. To denote *changes of state*, rather than the states themselves, II. conjugation verbs can be derived from IV. conjugation verbs. Examples include:

მწყინს	მომწყინდება
I find unpleasant	Sthg. will become unpleasant to me
მშია	მომშივდება
I am hungry	I will become hungry
მწყურია	მომწყურდება
I am thirsty	I will become thirsty
მცივა	შემცივდება
I am cold	I will become cold
მტკივა	ამტკივდება
Sthg. hurts me	Sthg. will begin to hurt me
მიყვარს	შემიყვარდება
I love	I will fall in love
მეშინია	შემეშინდება
I am afraid of	I will become afraid
მღვიძავს	გამეღვიძება
I am awake	I will wake up
მწადია	მომეწადება
I desire	I will come to desire

12.4. Summary Chart of Subject and Object Cases.

CONJUGATION	I. III.			II.		IV.	
SERIES	Subj.	D.O.	Id.O.	Subj.	Obj.	Subj.	Obj.
Present, Future	Nom	Dat	Dat				
Aorist	Erg	Nom	Dat	Nom	Dat	Dat	Nom
Perfect	Dat	Nom	*				

*Postpositional phrase with -*tvis*.

Summary of Vocabulary Entry forms for Verbs:

In this textbook the particular conjugation that a given verb belongs to should be readily recognizable on the basis of the form of that verb given in the vocabulary:

I. Conj. 3sg. subject, future; relative forms: 3d person id.o.
II. Conj. 3sg. subject, future; relative forms: 3d person id.o.
III. Conj. 3sg. subject, present; relative forms: 3d person id.o.
IV. Conj. 1sg. subject, present; object in 3d person.

■(to §12.1.2.4, p. 340.) There is a strong tendency for such verbs to have number agreement with a third-person dative indirect object and no number agreement with a nominative third-person subject. This is the same pattern as found with third-person dative *subjects* and nominative *objects* in the perfect series of I. conjugation verbs and in all series of IV. conjugation verbs. Example:

მას ის/ისინი დაჭირდებათ.	He will need it/them.
მათ ის/ისინი დაჭირდებათ.	They will need it/them.

[Under similar circumstances, a similar phenomenon can be found with the *direct* object of some I. conjugation verbs; cf.

ეს თეორია ‖ ეს თეორიები მას აინტერესებს.
This theory ‖ these theories interest him.
ეს თეორია ‖ ეს თეორიები მათ აინტერესებ**თ**.
This theory ‖ these theories interest them.]

CHAPTER 12: Notes

1. The 3d person grammatical object marker is also used in impersonal constructions, where it often corresponds to English 'it', as in მგონია 'it (*-a*) seems to me (*m-*)', as well as constructions which in English have no object, e.g. მძინავს 'I (*m-*) am sleeping', where the final *-s* serves much the same function as the 3d person suffix in the perfect series of III. conj. verbs, cf. *mi-ṭir-i-a* 'I have cried'.

2. This "verb of politeness" is generally not used in the first person. It is commonly used in expressions such as რა გნებავთ? "What would you like?" i.e., "What can I do for you?", რამდენიც გნებავთ "as much as you'd like", etc. There is a I. conj. derivative of this verb, ინებე(თ) 'please', which is used when offering someone something. It is similar in usage to the Russian пожалуйста.

3. The person or thing feared is in the extended form of the genitive case (see sec. 4.3). If the person or thing feared is represented in the sentence by a personal pronoun, the *possessive* (adjective) form is used in the nominative case. These genitive or possessive "objects" are treated as third person in terms of verb agreement. Examples:

მე ძაღლისა მეშინია.	I am afraid of the dog.
შენ ჩემი გეშინია.	You are afraid of me.
მას შენი ეშინოდა.	He was afraid of you.

(The same is true of მრცხვენია 'be ashamed'.)

4. The third person of this verb, უნდა 'he wants', is homonymous with the modal form უნდა 'must'. With the modal however, the subject is always in the case determined by the syntax of the main verb (which is usually in the optative). With the IV. conj. form უნდა (from მინდა) the subject is in the dative. Compare:

ივანემ ეს წიგნი უნდა წაიკითხოს.
John has to read this book.

ივანე უნდა დარჩეს.
John has to remain.

ივანეს უნდა ეს წიგნი წაიკითხოს.
John wants to read this book.

ივანეს უნდა დარჩეს.

John wants to remain.

5. The verb მესმის is historically a relative II. conjugation form with objective conjugation (see below, sec. 12.1.2.3). Consequently the imperfect and conjunctive present are formed with the suffix *-od-*: მესმოდა, მესმოდეს. In the aorist series, alongside aorist **მომესმა**, opt. **მომესმეს**, additionally forms of the verb გაიგებს are used: aorist გაიგო, optative გაიგოს. The present perfect is მსმენია.

6. Note that the future series screeves of this verb are formally the relative forms of the future series screeves of არის 'be'. Compare იქნება 'it will be', მექნება 'it will be to me', i.e., 'I shall have'.

7. This verb has a special form for the third *plural* object: მყვანან 'I have them'. The imperfect and conjunctive present can also be formed from this root: მყვანდა, მყვანდეს.

8. The expected წაიტანს is usually replaced by წაიღებს with root *-ǧ-*.

9. These verbs do not form II. conj. passives. Rather, they form their passives periphrastically with იქნა, e.g., მოტანილ იქნა 'was brought'; see sec. 11.3.

10. More commonly this word has the meanings 'cattle', 'goods'.

11. A close correspondence is the Russian dative + reflexive construction: мне спится 'I am tired', мне не пишется 'I don't feel like writing', мне не работается 'I don't feel like working'.

LESSON 12: Exercises

1. ჩემს სტუდენტს არ უნდა მათემატიკა ისწავლოს, მაგრამ მან ის უნდა ისწავლოს!
2. რამდენი და-ძმა გყავს? ერთი უფროსი და და ერთი უმცროსი ძმა მყავს.
3. არ გსმენია, რომ ძველ ქართულ ლიტერატურაში მალე ახალი პროფესორი გვეყოლება?
4. უკვე გავიგე. აი აქ მაქვს მისი ახალი ნარკვევები „შუშანიკის წამების" შესახებ.
5. არ მახსოვს, ვინ დაწერა ძველი ქართული ენის ეს ძეგლი.
6. მგონია, მისი ავტორი იაკობ ცურტაველია.
7. დიახ, მისი გვარი რომ მესწავლა, მეხსომებოდა.
8. როცა საქართველოში ვიქნები, ყოველდღე მენდომება ქართული ღვინის დალევა!
9. როცა მოგვშივდება, მწვადს, ხარჩოსა და მაწონს შევჭამთ.
10. როცა მოგვწყურდება, კარგ კახურ ღვინოებს დავლევთ.
11. თქვენ ქართული ღვინო გნებავთ? რასაკვირველია, იგი ყველას უყვარს.
12. თუ გწყურია, კარგი ქართული მინერალური წყალი დალიე! ამ მინერალურ წყალს „ბორჯომი" ჰქვია.
13. არაყი არ მომწონს. ასე მგონია, რომ იმათ, რომლებსაც არაყი მოსწონთ, პირში გემო არა აქვთ.
14. მათ ღვინის სიყვარული აკლიათ.
15. ზამთარში კი, როცა მცივა კონიაკი მირჩევნია.
16. უთხარი ექიმს, რა გტკიოდა? დიახ, ვუთხარი, ყელი მტკივა-მეთქი.
17. ჩვენს სუფრაზე არავის არასოდეს არც შია და არც სწყურია.
18. რა გჭირდებათ? —არაფერი არ გვჭირდება! ყველაფერი გვაქვს, რაც საჭიროა.
19. კარგი ქართულ-ინგლისური ლექსიკონი გაქვს? არა, მქონდა, მაგრამ ჩემს უფროს ძმას მივეცი. —არ

ვიცოდი, რომ შენ ძმა გყავს! კი, ორი ძმა და ერთი და მყავს.

20. არ დაგავიწყდეს ამ ნარკვევის წაკითხვა! —არ დამავიწყდება, მეხსომება.
21. შეგიძლიათ ქართულად კითხვა? რასაკვირველია, ქართულად შემიძლია კითხვა და სომხურადაც.
22. იცით თუ არა, რომ კავკასიას „ენათა მთა" ჰქვია?
23. მგონი, ეს თქვა არაბმა გეოგრაფმა იბნ-ხაუკალმა.
24. როცა საქართველოში ვიყავით, გვინდოდა სვანეთში წავსულიყავით, მაგრამ, სამწუხაროდ, დრო არ გვქონდა.
25. არ გახსოვთ, რომ მასწავლებელი სტუდენტებს მუზეუმში წაიყვანს?
26. ეს პაკეტი სად მიგაქვს? ფოსტაში მიმაქვს გასაგზავნად.
27. არ შეიძლება ითქვას, რომ საქართველოს ბუნებრივი სიმდიდრეები აკლია. მას აქვს ნახშირი და ნავთობი და განსაკუთრებით მდიდარია მარგანეცით.
28. გუშინ არ მეძინა. მთელი ღამე მეღვიძა, და ამიტომ ახლა მეძინება.
29. პიანინოზე უკრავ? —არა, როცა უფრო ახალგაზრდა ვიყავი, შემეძლო, მაგრამ ახლა ვეღარ ვუკრავ.
30. თქვენ ჩემი სახელი თურმე დაგვიწყებიათ. კონსტანტინე მქვია. —არა, თქვენი სახელი არ დამვიწყებია. ყველაფერი მახსოვს. კარგი მეხსიერება მაქვს.
31. ჩვენს ინგლისელ სტუმარს სუფრას ვუმზადებთ. საჭმელს ვინ მოიტანს? —რა უნდა მოვიტანო? —რაც გინდა, ის მოიტანე. —ბევრ ღვინოს მოვიტან, ვინაიდან ყველას ძალიან სწყურია.
32. მეძინება, აღარ მეთამაშება.
33. შენ თურმე არ გცოდნია, რომ საქართველოში ჩაი იყო შემოტანილი მეცხრამეტე საუკუნის მეორე მეოთხედში.
34. მოსკოვში და ლენინგრადში ზამთარში ცივა. ზაფხულში

თბილისში ძალიან ცხელა. როცა გასულ გაზაფხულზე ლენინგრადში ვიყავი, ყოველდღე მციოდა.

35. ამბობენ, ხვალ ეცხელებათ. გუშინაც ცხელოდა. მე კი არ მცხელოდა, რადგანაც ჩვენთან ჰაერი ყოველთვის გრილია.

36. რუსთაველის „ვეფხისტყაოსან"-ში ავთანდილს უყვარს არაბეთის მეფე, თინათინი, ხოლო ინდოეთის ადმირალს (ამირბარს) ტარიელს უყვარს მშვენიერი ნესტან-დარეჯანი.

37. ამბობენ, თვითონ რუსთაველს თამარ მეფე უყვარდა და მეფე თინათინის პროტოტიპი თამარ მეფე ყოფილა.

38. პიანინოზე დაკვრა შეგიძლიათ? —კი, შემიძლია, მაგრამ ახლა არ შეიძლება დაკვრა ვინაიდან გვიანაა და მეზობლებს ეწყინებათ, რომ დავუკრა.

39. ცურვა შეგიძლიათ? დიახ, შემიძლია, მაგრამ აქ ცურვა არ შეიძლება, აკრძალულია.

40. რაც მეტს ისწავლი, მით მეტი გეცოდინება!

41. არ იცოდი, რომ თბილისის უნივერსიტეტის პირველი რექტორი პეტრე მელიქიშვილი იყო?! —არ მცოდნია. მრცხვენია, რომ არ ვიცოდი. მე ივანე ჯავახიშვილი მეგონა.

42. მე რომ მცოდნოდა, რაც გინდოდა, ახლავე მოგცემდი.

43. გაიგეთ, რას ამბობს პროფესორი? —დიახ, ის ლაპარაკობს საქართველოს ექსპორტის შესახებ. საქართველოდან გააქვთ ჩაი, მარგანეცი და ღვინო. მთელ მსოფლიოს შეაქვს საქართველოს ნაწარმი.

44. ჩაის გარდა, საქართველოს გააქვს ციტრუსები: ლიმონი და ფორთოხალი.

45. რაც მეტს ვკითხულობ საქართველოზე, მით უფრო მწადია იქ წავიდე. საქართველოს გარდა, მინდა ვნახო სომხეთიც და აზერბაიჯანიც.

46. უნდა გრცხვენოდეს, რომ ქართულად უფრო ჩქარა ვერ ლაპარაკობ. —ეს იმიტომ, რომ ბევრი ქართული სიტყვა მაკლია, შენ ჩემზე ჩქარა შეგიძლია

ილაპარაკო.

47. მტერს ეშინოდა ქართველების შეერთებული ძალისა.

48. შენი არ მეშინია. პეტრესი და დავითისა მეშინია.

49. ჩემი არავის არ ეშინია და არავის არ ვ(ს)ძულვარ; ყველას ვუყვარვარ.

50. გეშინოდა ჩემი, როცა პატარა იყავი? არა, შენი არ მეშინოდა; მიყვარდი!

VI. Century Mosaic Inscription from a Georgian Monastery in Palestine

Vocabulary ●356

ადმირალი	admiral
ამირბარი	(older word for *admiral*)
არაბი	Arab
აუცილებლად	certainly; without fail
ბუნება	nature
ბუნებრივი	natural
განსაკუთრებით	particularly; especially
გარდა (pp.)	in addition to; except for; besides (also used as a *preposition*, with the genitive or dative)
გემო	taste
გეოგრაფი ●	geographer
გრილი	cool
გრძნობა	feeling; sense
და-ძმა	brother(s) and sister(s); siblings
ექსპორტი	export
ზაფხული	summer
თვითონ	[one]self
კონიაკი	(grape) brandy; cognac
ლიმონი	lemon
მარგანეცი	manganese
მაწონი (G. მაწვნის)	yogurt
-მეთქი	(see sec. 8.5)
მეხსიერება	memory
მინერალი	mineral
მსოფლიო	world
მუზეუმი	museum
მწვადი	shish-kebab; shashlik
ნავთობი	oil; petroleum
ნარკვევი	essay; study (= Russ. очерк)
ნაწარმი	product
ნახშირი	coal
პიანინო	piano
რაც მეტი... მით მეტი	the more... the more
რექტორი	rector (= head of a university)
სიყვარული	love
უმცროსი	younger; junior
უფროსი	elder
ფორთოხალი	orange (A)
ფოსტა	post-office; mail
ყელი	throat
ჩქარი	fast; quick
ჩქარა ●	quickly
ძეგლი	monument
წამება	martyrdom; torment; torture

ხარჩო	(Geo. soup made with mutton, rice, and sour plums)
ჰაერი	air
ავთანდილი	m. pr. n.
თინათინი	f. pr. n.
იბნ-ხაუკალი	(X century)
კონსტანტინე	Constantine
ნესტან-დარეჯანი	f. pr. n.
ცარიელი	m. pr. n.
შუშანიკი	f. pr. n. (V century Geo. saint)
იაკობ ცურტაველი	flourished second half of the V century
ბორჯომი	health resort town in Inner Kartli
ინდოეთი	India

Verbs

(Note that IV. conj. verbs will be listed in the present tense with subject in first person singular and object, if any, in the third person.)

მგონია	m-*gon*-i-a [1.sg. pres. also = მგონი]	think; seem
დაავიწყდება	da=a-*viç̣q*-d-eb-a (with H-series id.o. markers; see sec. 12.1.2.4)	forget
მაკლია, მაკლდება	m-a-*ḳl*-i-a, fut. m-a-*ḳl*-d-eb-a, perfect m-*ḳl*-eb-i-a	lack
დაუკრავს	da=u-*ḳr*-av-s (always takes *u*-series id.o. markers but has no id.o.)	play (a musical instrument)
მინდა, მენდომება	mi-*nd*-a, fut. m-e-*ndom*-eb-a (no aorist series)	want
მნებავს	m-*neb*-av-s (polite, see note 2)	(would) like
მირჩევნია, მერჩივნება	mi-*rčevn*-i-a, fut. m-e-*rčivn*-eb-a	prefer
მრცხვენია, შემრცხვება	m-*rcxven*-i-a, fut. še+m-*rcxv*-eb-a (see	be ashamed

	note 3; no perfect)	
მესმის, მომესმება	m-e-*sm*-i-s (imperf. m-e-*sm*-od-a), fut. mo+m-e-*sm*-eb-a: for aorist გაიგო is also used, see note 6.	hear; understand
მსურს, მომესურვება	m-*sur*-s, fut. mo=m-e-*surv*-eb-a	wish
მტკივა, მეტკინება, მტკენია	m-*ṭḳiv*-a, fut. m-e-*ṭḳin*-eb-a, perf. m-*ṭḳen*-i-a	s.o.'s (dat.) sthg. (nom.) hurts
მქვია, მერქმევა, მერქვა	m-*kv*-i-a, fut. m-e-*rkmev*-a, aor. m-e-*rkv*-a, perf. m-*rkmev*-i-a	be named; called; s.o.'s name is
მაქვს	m-a-*kv*-s, irr. see sec. 12.1.3.a.	have sthg.
გა(მო)მაქვს, გა(მო)იტანს	ga(mo)+m-a-*kv*-s fut. ga(mo)+i-*ṭan*-s, irr., see sec. 12.1.3.c.	bring; carry sthg. out, export
მიმაქვს, მომაქვს	mi+/mo+m-a-*kv*-s, irr. see sec. 12.1.3.c.	take, bring sthg.
შე(მო)მაქვს	še(mo)+m-a-*kv*-s, irr., see sec. 12.1.3.c.	bring; carry sthg. in; import; introduce
მღვიძავს	m-*ǧvij*-av-s	be awake
მყავს	m-*qav*-s, irr., see sec. 12.1.3.b.	have s.o.
მიმყავს, მიიყვანს	mi+m-*qav*-s, fut. mi+i-*qvan*-s, irr., see sec. 12.1.3.d.	lead s.o.
მიყვარს	mi-*qvar*-s	love
მშია	m-*ši*-a, imperf.	be hungry

	m-*ši*-od-a (no aor. or perf. series)	
მოშივდება	mo+H-*šiv*-d-eb-a (sec. 12.1.2.4.)	become hungry
მეშინია	m-e-*šin*-i-a (only present series)*	be afraid of; fear
მეცოდინება, მცოდნია	fut. m-e-*codin*-eb-a, perf. m-*codn*-i-a (from i-*c*-i-s); see sec. 12.1.3.e.	know
ცივა	*civ*-a, imperf. *ci*-od-a (only pres. series)	it is cold
მცივა	m-*civ*-a, imperf. m-*ci*-od-a (only pres. series)	s.o. is cold
ცხელა	*cxel*-a (only present series)	it is hot
მცხელა	m-*cxel*-a (only present series)	s.o. is hot
მძინავს	m-*jin*-av-s	sleep
შემიძლია, შემეძლო	še+mi-*jl*-i-a (aor. še+m-e-*jl*-o)	can, be (physically) able
მძულს	m-*jul*-s (no aor. series)	hate
მწადია	m-*c̣ad*-i-a, imperf. m-*c̣ad*-d-a	desire
მომწონს	mo+m-*c̣on*-s	like
მწყინს, მწყენია	m-*c̣qin*-s, perf. m-*c̣qen*-i-a	be annoyed; find unpleasant
მწყურია	m-*c̣qur*-i-a (only present series)	be thirsty
მოსწყურდება	mo+s-*c̣qur*-d-eb-a	become thirsty
დასჭირდება	da=s-*č̣ir*-d-eb-a (sec. 12.1.4.)	need
მახსოვს, მეხსომება	m-a-*xsov*-s, fut. m-e-*xsom*-eb-a (no aor. or perf. series)	remember

*The object of this verb is in the genitive with derived declension nominative ending; see derivative declension, sec. 8.6.

•ADDENDA TO VOCABULARY

გვარი	last name, family name
ძალა	force, strength
ითქმის, ითქმება	i-*tkm*-i-s, i-*tkm*-eb-a (II. conjugation of see note to p. 211.)

Key to the Exercises

1. My student doesn't want to study mathematics, but he must study it!
2. How many brothers and sisters (lit. sister-brother) do you have? I have one older sister and one younger brother.
3. Haven't you heard that we shall soon have a new professor in Old Georgian literature?
4. I have already heard it. Here, here I have his new essays about the "Martyrdom of Šušaniķ."
5. I don't remember who wrote this monument of Old Georgian language.
6. It seems to me, its author is Jacob Curṭaveli.
7. Yes, if I had learned his (last) name, I would have remembered it.
8. When I shall be in Georgia I shall want to drink [VN] Georgian wine everyday!
9. When we will become hungry we will eat shashlik, xarčo (soup), and yogurt.
10. When we'll become thirsty we'll drink good Kakhetian wines.
11. Would you (pl.) like (pres. tense) (some) Georgian wine? Of course, everyone likes it.
12. If you are thirsty, drink (some) good Georgian mineral water. This mineral water is called "Borǯomi".
13. I don't like vodka. It seems to me so that those who like vodka don't taste in the mouth.
14. They lack the love of wine.
15. In winter, however, when I am cold I prefer brandy.
16. Did you tell the doctor what was hurting you? Yes, I told him that my throat hurts.
17. At our banquet no one is ever hungry or thirsty.
18. What do you need? We don't need anything. We have everything that (= what) is necessary.
19. Do you have a good Georgian-English dictionary? No, I had one, but I gave it to my older brother. --I didn't know that you had (= have) a brother. --Yes, I have two brothers and a sister.
20. Don't forget to read (= the reading of) this essay. I shall not forget, I shall remember.
21. Can you read (VN) Georgian? --Of course, I can read (VN) Georgian and Armenian, too.
22. Do you know or not that the Caucasus is called the "mountain of languages"?
23. It seems to me the Arab geographer Ibn-Ḥawḳal said this.
24. When we were in Georgia we wanted to go to Svane-

tia, but, unfortunately, we didn't have time.

25. Don't you all remember that the teacher will take (= lead) the students to the museum?
26. Where are you carrying this package? I am carrying it to the post office to mail (=send) it.
27. It is impossible to say (= to be said, opt.) that Georgia lacks natural resources (= richnesses). It has coal and oil and is particularly rich in manganese (instr.).
28. Yesterday I didn't sleep. I was awake all night (nom.) and therefore now I am sleepy (= I feel like sleeping).
29. Do you play on the piano? --No, when I was younger I could, but now I can no longer play it.
30. You apparently have forgotten my name. My name is Constantine. --No, I haven't forgotten your name. I remember everything. I have a good memory.
31. We are preparing a banquet for our English guest. Who will bring the food? --What should I bring? --Bring what (= that, what) you want. --I shall bring a lot of wine because everyone is very thirsty.
32. I am sleepy, I no longer feel like playing.
33. You apparently didn't know that tea was introduced into Georgia in the second quarter of the nineteenth century.
34. In Moscow and Leningrad in winter it is cold. In Tbilisi in the summer it is very hot. When I was in Leningrad last spring (-*ze*) I was cold every day.
35. They say it will be hot tomorrow. Yesterday, too, it was hot. I, however, wasn't hot because the air is always cool at our place.
36. In Rustaveli's *Knight in the Tiger Skin* Avṭandil loves the Queen (= king) of Arabia Tinatin, and the admiral (*amirbari*) of India Ṭariel loves the beautiful Nesṭan-Darej̆an.
37. They say that Rustaveli himself loved Queen Tamara and that Queen Tamara was the model of Queen Tinatin.
38. Can you all play (VN) on the piano? Yes, I can, but now I cannot play (VN) because it is late and the neighbors will be annoyed if I were to play (opt.).
39. Can you swim? --Yes, I can, but here one cannot swim (use VN); it is forbidden.
40. The more you study, the more you will know.
41. Didn't you know that Peter Melikišvili was Tbilisi University's first rector? --I didn't know. I am ashamed that I didn't know. I

thought that [it was] Ivane J̌avaxišvili.

42. If I knew what you wanted, I would have given it to you immediately.

43. Did you understand what the professor is saying? Yes, he is talking about Georgia's export[s]. From Georgia they export tea, manganese, and wine. The whole world imports Georgia's product[s].

44. In addition to tea, Georgia exports citrus (products): lemon and orange (use sing.).

45. The more I read about (= on) Georgia, the more I desire to go there. In addition to Georgia, I want to see both Armenia and Azerbaijan.

46. You should be ashamed that you cannot speak Georgian more rapidly. --This [is] for the reason that I lack many Georgian words, you can speak better than [-*ze*] I.

47. The enemy was afraid of the united force of the Georgians.

48. I am not afraid of you (= შენი). I am afraid of Peter and David.

49. No one is afraid of me (= ჩემი) and no one hates me; everyone loves me.

50. Were you afraid of me when you were little? No, I wasn't afraid of you; I loved you.

Reading Passage ძველი ქართული თარიღები*

1 ძველ ქართულ ძეგლებში დამოწმებული თარიღების სწორად გაშიფვრისათვის საჭიროა წინასწარი მომზადება. უნდა გვახსოვდეს, რომ ძველ საქართველოში წელთაღრიცხვის რამდენიმე სისტემას იყენებდნენ. მწიგნობრობის ცალკეულ ცენტრებში დროის სხვადასხვა გამოთვლა იყო მიღებული და ერთიანი, საყოველთაოდ აღიარებული, წელთაღრიცხვა, როგორიც დღესა გვაქვს, არ ყოფილა. მეცნიერებმა (ნ. მარი, ივ. ჯავახიშვილი, ე. თაყაიშვილი, კ. კეკელიძე, ა. შანიძე და სხვ.) შეისწავლეს ეგ დასახელებული სისტემები და დაადგინეს მათი ტრადიციები კულტურის კერათა მიხედვით, საგულისხმოა იმის აღნიშვნაც, რომ adრინდელ ხელნაწერებში ხშირად ერთსა და იმავე დროს ორ ან სამნაირი თარიღია აღნიშნული ერთი მნიშვნელობით, რაც იმის მაჩვენებელია, რომ ავტორები ცდილობდნენ ყველასათვის ხელმისაწვდომად გაეხადათ თავიანთ თხზულებებში აღწერილი მოვლენები და ფაქტები, მათი დრო ეჩვენებინათ ყველასათვის გასაგებად. ეს პირველ რიგში ითქმის „ქართლის ცხოვრებაში" შესულ მემატიანეთა თხზულებებსა და იმ ძეგლებზე, რომლებშიაც თარიღები ორი ან სამი სისტემითაა წარმოდგენილი.

2 იმისათვის, რომ გავშიფროთ ძველი თარიღები, უწინარეს ყოვლისა, უნდა გვახსოვდეს ჩვენი ანბანის (ასოების) რიცხობრივი მნიშვნელობა, შემდეგ კი წელთაღრიცხვის ძველად გავრცელებული სისტემები. ორივე მათგანი ერთმანეთთან მჭიდროდაა დაკავშირებული.

3 ქართული ანბანის (ასოების) რიცხობრივი მნიშვნელობა, როგორც ვიცით, ასეთია: ა) **ერთეულებია:** ა (1), ბ (2), გ (3), დ (4), ე (5), ვ (6), ზ (7), ჱ (8), თ (9); ბ) **ათეულებია:** ი (10), კ (20), ლ (30), მ (40), ნ (50), ჲ (60), ო (70), პ (80), ჟ (90); გ) **ასეულებია:** რ (100), ს (200), ტ (300), უ(ჳ) (400), ფ (500), ქ (600), ღ (700), · (800), შ (900); დ) **ათასეულებია:** ჩ (1000), ც (2000), ძ (3000), წ (4000), ჭ (5000), ხ (6000), ჴ (7000), ჯ (8000), ჰ (9000), ჵ (10.000).

4 ძველ საქართველოში ყველაზე მეტად გავრცელებული იყო წელთაღრიცხვა დასაბამიდან, ანუ ქვეყნის გაჩენიდან, ქართული ქრონიკონითა და ქრისტიანული წესით (ახალი ერა). ზოგჯერ მაჰმადიანური (თათრული) სისტემაც იხმარებოდა. ყველა სისტემას დროის თავისი სათვალავი ჰქონდა.

1. დასაბამიდან წელთაღრიცხვა გულისხმობს, რომ ქვეყნის გაჩენიდან ახალი ერის დაწყებამდის გასულია 5.604 წელი (ასე ანგარიშობდნენ მხოლოდ ქართველები. ევსევი კესარიელის მიხედვით კი დასაბამიდან ახალი წელთაღრიცხვის დაწყებამდის გასულია 5.198 წელი, პანოდორე ალექსანდრიელის ანგარიშით — 5.492 წ., ანიანე ალექსანდრიელსა და იულიუს აფრიკელის გამოთვლით — 5.500 წ., ბიზანტიური სისტემით — 5.508 წ.). ამ გამოთვლების ახალ ერაზე გადმოსაყვანად საჭიროა დასაბამიდან გასულ წელთა ჯამს გამოვაკლოთ დასაბამიდან ჩვენი ერის დაწყებამდის გასული წლების ჯამი (ქართულით 5.604) და მივიღებთ ჩვენთვის საჭირო თარიღს დღევანდელი ანგარიშით.

2. ქართული ქრონიკონი ანუ ქორონიკონი ეყრდნობა 532 წლიანი მოქცევის ციკლებს და, როგორც ცნობილია, საფუძვლად იღებს მზის 28 წლიან და მთავარის 19 წლიან მოქცევას. ამ ორი რიცხვის ნამრავლი (28 × 19) სწორედ 532 წელს გვაძლევს. 532 წელიწადი კი პერიოდულად მეორდება, ე. ი. ყოველი 532 წლის შემდეგ მეორდება დღეთა და თვეთა ანგარიში.

5 .... გამოთვლით, დასაბამიდან ვიდრე 1844 წლამდის, 532 წლიანი ციკლის შესაბამისად, გასულა 14 მოქცევა, 1845 წელს დაწყებულა მე-15 მოქცევა და, მაშასადამე, ამჟამად მეთხუთმეტე მოქცევის 133-ე წელი დგას. ძველი ქართული ძეგლები, რომელთა დათარიღებას მეცნიერება ახერხებს, შექმნილია მეთორმეტე (დაიწყო 248 წ.), მეცამეტე (დაიწყო 780 წ.) და მეთოთხმეტე (დაიწყო 1312 წ.) მოქცევათა შუალედებში. X-XII სს. ძეგლების უდიდეს უმეტესობაზე ჩვეულებრივ აღნიშნული არ არის მოქცევა, რადგან თავისთავად იგულისხმება მეცამეტე მოქცევა. ამიტომ თუ გვინდა, ძველი თარიღი გადმოვიტანოთ ახალ ერაზე, მეცამეტე მოქცევის წლებს უნდა მივუმატოთ ამ მოქცევის დასაწყისი (780).

3. ქრისტიანული წელთაღრიცხვა ჩვენში VIII ს. დასტურდება. ევროპის ქვეყნებში კი გავრცელდა 525 წლიდან. მისი შემოღება დიონისეს სახელთანაა დაკავშირებული. კ. კეკელიძის ცნობით, იგი „ოფიციალურ დოკუმენტებში პირველად 742 წელს ჩანს, მუდმივს ხასიათს კი მხოლოდ მეათე საუკუნეში ღებულობს". მის დასაწყისად ზოგი ავტორი „ქრისტეს დაბადებას" თვლის, ზოგი „ვნებას, ჯვარცმასა და აღდგომას", ზოგიც „ამაღლებას" მიიჩნევს.

6 წელთაღრიცხვის ჩამოთვლილი სისტემები მეტნაკლებად გავრცელებული იყო ჩვენშიაც, ამ სისტემებითაა დათარიღებული ძველ საისტორიო

ძეგლებში აღწერილი ბევრი ღირსშესანიშნავი მოვლენა. ზოგჯერ ერთსა და იმავე დროს გამოყენებულია ორი ან სამი სისტემით მიღებული ანგარიში.

7 სუმბატ დავითის ძის ქრონიკაში, მაგალითად, აღნიშნულია: „მოიკლა ესე აშოტ კურაპალატი დასაბამითგან წელთა **ხჳლ**. ქრონიკონსა მეათცამეტედ მოქცეულსა შინა **მვ**“ („ქართლის ცხოვრება“, I, ს. ყაუხჩიშვილის რედ., 1955, გვ. 377). აქ ორი სისტემით დამოწმებულია ერთი და იგივე თარიღი, რაც ასე გაიშიფრება: დასაბამიდან **ხჳლ** წელი = 6430 წ., რასაც უნდა გამოაკლდეს ქვეყნის გაჩენიდან ჩვენი ერის დასაწყისამდის გასული 5.604 წ. (6.430- 5.604) და მივიღებთ აშოტ კურაპალატის გარდაცვალების თარიღს — 826 წ. ამავე თარიღს ადასტურებს აქვე დამოწმებული მეორე ანგარიშიც. მეცამეტე მოქცევის დასაწყისს — 780 წ. უნდა მივუმატოთ ამ მოქცევის დასაწყისიდან გასული **მვ** (46) წელი (780 + 46 =) და მივიღებთ იმავე 826 წელს. ე. ი. ორივე სისტემით (დასაბამით და ქრონიკონით) დამოწმებულია ერთი თარიღი.

8 იმავე წყაროში ბაგრატ კურაპალატის გარდაცვალების შესახებ ნათქვამია: „გარდაიცვალა ესე ბაგრატ ქრონიკონსა **სლდ**“ (იქვე, გვ. 383). აქ დასახელებულია ერთი თარიღი: ქრონიკონი **სლდ** = 234, რასაც უნდა მივუმატოთ 780 (მეცამეტე მოქცევის დასაწყისის მაჩვენებელი წელი) და მივიღებთ 1014 წ. (234 + 780 = 1014). ე. ი. ამ წელს გარდაცვლილა ბაგრატ მეფე.

9 ძველი ქართულის შესანიშნავი ძეგლის - სინური მრავალთავის ანდერძში ვკითხულობთ: „დაიწერა წმიდაჲ ესე წიგნი დასაბამითგან წელთა **ხუჲჱ**, ქრონიკონი იყო **პდ**“ (სინური მრავალთავი 864 წლისა, ა. შანიძის რედ., 1959, გვ. 280). დასაბამით **ხუჲჱ** = 6.468 წ., ამას უნდა გამოაკლდეს ჩვენი ერის დაწყებამდის გასული 5.604 წ. (6.468 5.604 = 864) და მივიღებთ ძეგლის გადაწერის თარიღს 864 წ ამავე თარიღს გვაძლევს ქრონიკონი **პდ**: 84 + 780 = 864 წ. ორივე თარიღის ჩვენებით, ძეგლი 864 წელსაა გადაწერილი....

10 თამარ მეფის ერთი ლაშქრობის შესახებ აგარიანთა წინააღმდეგ ვახუშტი ამბობს ეს მოხდა „ქრონიკონსა **ჩრჟგ**, ქართულსა **უიგ**-სა“ („აღწერა სამეფოსა საქართველოსა“, ს. ყაუხჩიშვილის რედ., 1973, გვ. 183). ქრონიკონი **ჩრჟგ** = 1193 წ.; ასევე ქართული ანგარიშით **უიგ** = 413 + 780 = 1193 წ., ე. ი. თამარის ლაშქრობა აგარიანთა წინააღმდეგ 1193 წ. მომხდარა.

11 ვახუშტისავე ცნობით, გიორგი სააკაძემ ყიზილბაშნი შემუსრა ქრონიკონსა **ჩქკგ**. ქართული ანგარიშით **ტია** (იქვე. გვ. 590), რაც ასე გამოითვლება: **ჩქკგ** = 1623; **ტია** = 311 + 1312 = 1623 წ. ე. ი. გიორგი სააკაძეს ყიზილბაშნი 1.623 წ. შეუმუსრავს.

12 დავიმოწმებ, ბოლოს, გვიანდელი, XVIII საუკუნის, ძეგლის თარიღსაც. სულხან-საბა ორბელიანის „სიტყვის კონის" ერთ ნუსხას ახლავს გადამწერის ასეთი ანდერძი:

სჯობს, განვაცხადო, ეს წიგნი
როს დაიწერა, ან სადა,
ქართულსა ქორონიკონსა
უნსა, **ო**ნსა და **ა**ნსადა,
თელავის სემინარიის
წარჩინებულსა სტილსადა...

13 როგორც ვხედავთ, აქ „სიტყვის კონის" გადანუსხვის თარიღი ზუსტადაა მითითებული: **უოა** = 471, ამას უნდა მივუმატოთ მეცამეტე მოქცევის დასასრულის აღმნიშვნელი 1312 წ. და მივიღებთ 1783 წ. (471 + 1312 = 1783).

14 წელთაღრიცხვა დასაბამიდან და ქრონიკონი ამჟამად აღარ იხმარება. ცივილიზებულ ქვეყნებში დიდი ხანია დამკვიდრებულია ახალი ერა დაზუსტებული ახალი სტილით (ქრისტიანული წელთაღრიცხვა). ზოგიერთ ქვეყანაში მოქმედებს წელთაღრიცხვის სხვა სისტემაც. მაჰმადიანური სამყარო, მაგალითად, წელთაღრიცხვას ითვლის ჰიჯრით, ე. ი. მუჰამედის მექიდან წასვლის დღით, რაც 622 წლის 16 ივლისს მომხდარა.

15 1977 წელი ძველი სისტემებით შეიძლება ასე აღინიშნოს: ა) დასაბამით 7.581 წ. (5.604 + 1977): **ჴფპა**; ბ) ქრონიკონით 133 წ.: **რლგ**.

ალ. ღლონტი,
პროფესორი.

---

* Note: This reading deals with the methods by which dates were indicated in Old Georgian manuscripts. Reference to the numerical values of the letters of the Georgian alphabets (given in the Appendix to Lesson One) should be helpful.

Vocabulary

1

ძეგლი	monument
სწორად	(note that adverbs can modify verbal nouns)
გა=შიფრავს	decipher
წინასწარი	preliminary
გვახსოვდეს	(Since this verb has no aorist series, the conjunctive is used to replace the lacking optative)
წელთაღრიცხვა	chronology
გამო=იყენებს	use
მწიგნობრობა	literature; erudition
ცალკეული	individual
გამო=თვლის	calculate
მიღებული	here: accepted
ერთიანი	single; standard
საყოველთაო	general
Ø=ა-ღიარებს	recognize (disregard following comma)
და სხვ. = და სხვები	etc.
ეს (nom.); E-D-G-I-Adv = ამ	this (adj.)
და=ასახელებს	name, mention
კერა	hearth; here: place of origin
საგულისხმო	important; noteworthy
ის..., რომ	that; the fact that (cf. Russ. то, что)
აღნიშვნა	(VN) here: to note, cf. აღ=ნიშნავს note
-ნაირი	of .... kinds
Ø=აჩვენებს	show; indicate (sthg.) to (s.o.) (*H*-series)
მაჩვენებელი (E)	indicative

ცდილობს: fut: ეცდება, aor: (ვ)ეცადე(თ), ეცადა — try (+ optative [pluperfect after past screeves])

ხელმისაწვდომი — accessible; available

გა=ხდის — make (sthg. sthg.) (adv.)

მოვლენა — phenomenon; appearance

პირველ რიგში — first of all

ითქმის (II. conj.) — be said; here: can be said

„ქართლის ცხოვრება" = Georgian historical chronicles

მემატიანე — chronicler

2

უწინარეს ყოვლისა — first of all

რიცხობრივი — numerical

გა=ავრცელებს — spread; გავრცელებული widespread

მჭიდრო — tight; compact, close

და=აკავშირებს — tie up; connect

3

ერთეული, ათეული — units; tens, etc.

8, 60, 7000, 10,000 (see alphabet table, appendix to Lesson 1.)

4

დასაბამი — beginning; origin (i.e., creation of the universe)

ქვეყანა — here: world

გაჩენა — creation

ქრონიკონი = ქორონიკონი = a cycle of 532 years used in a perpetual calendar for the determination of the date of Easter

წესი — law; custom; usage (instr. = according to...)

ზოგჯერ — sometimes

მაჰმადიანი — Mohammedan

თათარი (A) — Tatar; Mongol; Persian; Arab; Muslim

იხმარება — be used (only pres. series)

სათვალავი	reckoning; counting
გულისხმობს	mean
ანგარიშობს ●	reckon; count
გადმო+იყვანს	translate; transfer (sec. 12.1.3)
ჯამი	sum
გამო=აკლებს	subtract (sthg.) (d.o.) from (sthg.) (id.o.)
და=აყრდნობს	base; lean (sthg.) on (sthg.)
მოქცევა	here: *mokceva*, cycle (technical term)
საფუძველი (E)	base
მთავარის misprint, = მთვარის	from მთვარე moon
ნამრავლი	product (multiplication)
ანგარიში	here: the [same sequence of] counting

5

ვიდრე ....-მდის	up until; up to
შესაბამისად (pp.)	corresponding to
მაშასადამე	consequently
ამჟამად	now (= 1977)
დგას	here: it is
მო=ახერხებს	contrive; manage
შუალედი	interval; space; timespan
უმეტესობა	majority
რადგან = რადგანაც	
თავისთავად	by itself
იგულისხმება (only pres. series)	be understood
მი=უმატებს	add (sthg.) to (sthg.)
დასაწყისი	beginning
ჩვენში	among us; in our country
და=ადასტურებს	attest; confirm
შემო+იღებს	introduce

ცნობით	here: according to information
მუდმივს = მუდმივ (from მუდმივი)	permanent
ხასიათი	character
ქრისტე	Christ
ვნება	passion
ჯვარცმა	crucifixion
აღდგომა	resurrection; Easter
ამაღლება •	Ascension

6

ჩამო=თვლის	enumerate
მეტ-ნაკლებად	more or less
ღირსშესანიშნავი •	notable; remarkable

7

ძე	son (used to form patronymics)
ქრონიკა	chronicle

Old Georgian: "This Ašoṭ the Kuropalatēs [Byzantine title used by old Georgian kings and princes] was killed 6430 years from the beginning, the 46th year in the 13th *koronikon* cycle."

რედ. = რედაქციით	under the editorship of
გვ. = გვერდი	page

8 •

და=ადასტურებს	confirm
ეხე (archaic)	= ეს
იქვე	ibid.

9

შე=ნიშნავს	note; notice
სინა	Sinai (here: Mt. Sinai)
მრავალთავი	collection of lives of saints and martyrs
ანდერძი	signature, date and location at the end of a will or other document; colophon

Old Georgian: "This holy book was written in the year

6468 from the beginning; the *koroniḳon* was 84."

გამო=ა-კლდება sthg. is subtracted from sthg.

10

ლაშქრობა war, (military) campaign

აგარიანი (archaic) Arab; Moslem

წინააღმდეგ (pp.) against

ვახუშტი (ბაგრატიონი) Georgian historian (1695-1772)

ქრონიკონსა in the *koroniḳon*

სამეფო ● kingdom

11

-ვე the same

ყიზილბაში Persian (of the XVI-XVIII centuries)

შე=მუსრავს destroy; smash

12

და=იმოწმებს bring in as evidence

ბოლოს finally

სულხან-საბა ორბელიანი Georgian writer and lexicographer (1658-1725)

კონა bundle

სიტყვის კონა dictionary (archaic)

ნუსხა list

[ახლავს] s.o. (dat.) has sthg. (nom.)

სჯობს...: It is proper that I declare when this book was written or where; in the Georgian *koroniḳon uni, oni, ani* (names of the letters უ, ო, ა) in Telavi Seminary's outstanding style.

13

გადანუსხვა compilation

მი=უთითებს indicate (sthg.) to (s.o.)

დასასრული end

14

იხმარება (only pres. series) be used

დიდი ხანია for a long time

და=ამკვიდრებს introduce; install; consolidate
მოქმედებს (III. conj.) be active; work; function; be operative
სამყარო world
ითვლის = თვლის
ჰიჯრა Hegira (flight of Mohammed from Mecca (მექა) in 622)

15

აღ=ნიშნავს note; denote; mark

ADDENDA TO VOCABULARY

4 გასულია have, has passed
5 მი=იჩნევს consider
6 ერთსა და იმავე დროს at one and the same time
8 იმავე the (that) same
10 ამავე the (this) same

Museum of the Arts of Georgia, Tbilisi

LESSON 13

13.1. Reflexive indirect objects. In sec. 7.1.2, the marking of indirect objects for I. conjugation verbs was discussed. It was pointed out that such indirect objects cannot refer to the subject of the verb. When the indirect object refers to the same person as the subject of a I. conjugation verb, a special marker is used in the present, future, and aorist series. This marker is the preradical vowel *i*-, which is added to the base form immediately before the root, replacing the preradical vowel *a*- if present. The meaning of this form is similar to some of the meanings of the indirect objects marked by the *u*- or *h*-series of object markers and can generally be translated into English 'for one's...' or by a possessive pronoun. We shall call this use of the preradical vowel *i*- the *reflexive indirect object* or simply the *reflexive*; traditionally it is known as the *subjective version*. Examples:

Base form	Reflexive[1]
დაჭრის	დაიჭრის
slice sthg.	slice one's sthg.
გაჭრის	გაიჭრის
cut sthg.	cut sthg. for o.s.
აარჩევს	აირჩევს
elect s.o.	elect s.o. for o.s.; elect one's s.o.
დაბანს	დაიბანს
wash s.o.; wash part of body	wash one's sthg. (e.g., face)
ააშენებს	აიშენებს
build sthg.	build sthg. for o.s.
აადუღებს	აიდუღებს
bring sthg. to a boil	bring sthg. to a boil for o.s.[2]

Unlike the nonreflexive indirect object markers, the reflexive indirect object cannot be correlated with any pronoun. Compare:

id.o. ქეთევანმა საუზმე გაუმზადა.

ქეთევანმა <u>მათ</u> საუზმე გაუმზადა.

Ketevan prepared breakfast for

them.

reflexive id.o. ქეთევანმა საუზმე გაიმზადა.

Ketevan prepared breakfast for herself.

Examples of the use of the reflexive indirect object:

ბავშვმა ხელი გაიჭრა.

The child cut *his* (own) hand.

პირი უნდა დაიბანო!

You must wash *your* face.

მან ეს სახლი აიშენა.

He built this house *for himself*.

ახალი კაბა უნდა შევიკერო.

I must sew *myself* a new dress.

The reflexive indirect object is often used when an action directly affects the subject of the sentence or when the direct object is a reflexive form with თავი. Compare:

მტერი მოკლა. He killed the enemy.

თავი მოიკლა. He killed himself; committed suicide.

მეფე აქო. He praised the king.

თავი იქო. He praised himself.

In this course a form will be judged as reflexive only if it is derived from a nonreflexive form with the same preverb and with the same basic lexical meaning. So დაიჭრის 'cut sthg. for o.s.' will be regarded as the reflexive of დაჭრის 'cut sthg.', but მიიღებს 'receive' will not be regarded as a reflexive of გააღებს 'open', and დაინახავს 'catch sight of' will not be regarded as the reflexive of ნახავს (fut.) 'see'. Rather the forms with preradical vowel *i-* will be regarded as base forms, i.e., vocabulary entry forms.[3]

13.2. Though rare, at times one might encounter sequences of the type *mi-*, *gi-*, *gvi-* which represent not the *u*-series of indirect object markers, but rather verbs with the preradical vowel *i-*, marking the base form.

Examples of such forms are:

მიიღებს receive:

ექიმი მალე მიგიღებს.

The doctor will receive you soon.

დაივიწყებს forget:

შენ არასოდეს არ დაგივიწყებ.

I shall never forget you.

შემოიყვანს (pres. შემოჰყავს) bring, lead into:

ამ ოთახში შემომიყვანა.

He led me into this room.

It must be emphasized that instances are quite rare when *mi-*, *gi-*, *gvi-* represent a *direct* object marker plus a preradical vowel; the overwhelming majority of such sequences are *u*-series indirect object markers.

13.3. The superessive. The *superessive*[4] is a special verbal marker indicating the surface upon which the action of the verb occurs. The marker of the superessive in the verb is the preradical vowel *a-*. The noun denoting the surface on which the action occurs is either an indirect object in the dative case or is followed by the postposition *-ze* 'on'. The superessive most commonly occurs with I. conjugation verbs.[5] Examples:

ხატავს paint sthg.

ახატავს paint sthg. on sthg.

ეს მხატვარი ჩემს პორტრეტს ხატავს.

This artist is painting my portrait.

პირველყოფილი ადამიანი ხშირად გამოქვაბულის კედლებს ნადირებს ახატავდა.

Primitive man often painted wild animals *on the walls* of a cave.

დაწერს write sthg.

დააწერს write sthg. on sthg.

ეს რომანი ვინ დაწერა?

Who wrote this novel?

პროფესორმა ახალი სიტყვები დაფას დააწერა.

The professor wrote the new words *on the blackboard*.

Since the *a-* of the superessive is a preradical vowel, it is not found in the perfect series and the indirect object generally is replaced by a postpositional phrase with *-ze* for inanimate objects and by a postpositional phrase with *-tvis* for animates, for example,

პროფესორს ახალი სიტყვები <u>დაფაზე</u> დაუწერია.

The professor has [apparently] written the words *on the blackboard*.

In some verbs with the preradical vowel *a-* this vowel can function as both the marker of the base form and the superessive. (The semantics of such verbs is often such that the action denoted by the verb implies some surface for its occurrence.) Examples:

მიაბამს	tie, bind (base form; absolute, no id.o.)
ცხენი იქ მიაბი!	Tie the horse there!
მიაბამს	tie, bind sthg. on sthg. (superessive; relative, has id.o.)
ცხენი ხეს მიაბეს.	They tied the horse (on) to the tree (id.o.).

13.4. Passive of state. A *limited* number of verbs can form a special *passive of state*, a simple form corresponding in meaning to the periphrastic passive (sec. 11.3). The passive of state is formed from only about eighty verbal roots. All passives of state share the following peculiarities:

a. passives of state *never* have preverbs;
b. passives of state may have an indirect object marker *even when there is no indirect object.*[6]

In the present series of screeves only the present screeve occurs. It can be:

a. without indirect object; in this case the verb may take the *h*-series 3d person object marker (*h-*, *s-*, *Ø-*); see also Lesson 11, note 6.
b. with indirect object; in this case the verb will take the *u*-series object markers (*mi-*, *gi-*, *gvi-*, *u-*).
c. in the superessive, with the superessive marker, the preradical vowel *a-* (with id.o. markers).

The stem of the present tense is the root of the verb to which is added the third person subject marker *-i-a*.[7] Examples:

გაფენს, დაფენს spread out; lay out

ფენია	it is spread out
უფენია	his ... is spread out
აფენია	it is spread out on it
დათესავს	sow; plant
თესია	it is planted
უთესია	his ... is planted
დააკერებს	sew (sthg. on sthg.)
აკერია	it is sewn on sthg.
უკერია	it is sewn on his sthg.
დაკიდებს	hang
ჰკიდია	it is hanging
უკიდია	his ... is hanging; it is hanging in his house
დაწერს	write
სწერია	it is written
უწერია	it is written in his sthg.
აწერია	it is written on it
გადააფარებს	spread (e.g., tablecloth)
აფარია	it is spread on sthg.

The future series screeves are, in form, II. conjugation verbs with *e*-series object markers, i.e., with the preradical vowel *e*- and FSF -*eb*-.[8] There is never any preverb and there is always an indirect object marker (*e*-), whether or not there is an id.o. in the sentence. This indirect object marker corresponds in function to the *h*-series, *u*-series, and superessive markers of the present tense. Examples:

Present	Future	
ფენია		it will be spread
უფენია	ეფინება	his ... will be spread
აფენია		it will be spread on it

The aorist series is formed regularly according to the rules for relative II. conjugation verbs. The perfect series, too, is formed according to the rules for II. conjugation verbs; if there is *no indirect object* in the sentence, according to the rules for absolute II. conjugation verbs in sec. 11.2.1; if there is an indirect object (*u*-series or superessive in the present tense), then according to the rules for relative II. conjugation verbs, sec. 11.2.2. Examples are:

Present	Future	Aorist	Perfect	
ფენია	ეფინება	ეფინა	ფენილა	(abs.)
უფენია, აფენია			ფენია	(rel.)
ხთესია, უთესია	ეთესება	ეთესა	—	(abs.)
აკერია, უკერია	ეკერება	ეკერა	ჰკერებია	(rel.)
ჰკიდია	ეკიდება	ეკიდა	კიდებულა	(abs.)
უკიდია			ჰკიდებია	(rel.)
სწერია	ეწერება	ეწერა	წერილა	(abs.)
უწერია, აწერია			სწერებია	(rel.)

An example of the use of the passive of state would be:

მაგიდაზე ახალი სუფრა ფენია.

A new tablecloth is spread on the table.

სუფრა მაგიდაზე გვიფენია.

The table cloth is spread on *our* table.

მაგიდას ახალი სუფრა აფენია.

A new tablecloth is spread *on the table*.

მაგიდაზე ახალი სუფრა ეფინა.

A new tablecloth was spread on the table.

სუფრა მაგიდაზე გვეფინა.

The new tablecloth was spread on *our* table.

მაგიდას ახალი სუფრა ეფინა.

A new tablecloth was spread *on the table*.

Note: Although most grammars and dictionaries list perfect screeve forms for passives of state, in actual usage such forms do not occur and are generally replaced by the corresponding aorist of the passive of state. (The pluperfect, however, does occur in past counterfactual clauses.)

13.5. The Resultative. The Georgian resultative is formed from transitive verbs with the auxiliary verbs მაქვს (with inanimate objects) and მყავს (with animate objects) plus the perfect participle. Both the perfect participle with suffix (sec. 11.1) and the participle with prefix *na*- (sec. 11.5.4) are used.

The resultative can occur in all the screeve forms of the auxiliary verbs. Since the auxiliary verbs are IV. conjugation, the subject of the auxiliary is always in the dative while the object is in the nominative.

The resultative emphasizes the *result* of an action. For example, წერილი აქვს დაწერილი is somewhat equivalent to English "He got the letter written." Compare this with the present perfect წერილი დაუწერია which does not focus on the result of the action so much as deduce the occurrence of the action from its result, for example, [I see the letter, so] he must have written it.

In general the Georgian resultative screeves can often be translated by the corresponding English *perfect* tenses. The past resultative corresponds to the English past perfect in denoting an event that occurred in the past before another event. The forms are:

Pres. result.	დაწერილი მაქვს	ნანახი მყავს
Past result.	დაწერილი მქონდა	ნანახი მყავდა
Conj. result.	დაწერილი მქონდეს	ნანახი მყავდეს
Fut. result.	დაწერილი მექნება	ნანახი მეყოლება
Cond. result.	დაწერილი მექნებოდა	ნანახი მეყოლებოდა
Conj. result.	დაწერილი მექნებოდეს	ნანახი მეყოლებოდეს
Perf. result.	დაწერილი მქონია	ნანახი მყოლია
Pluperf. result.	დაწერილი მქონოდა	ნანახი მყოლოდა

(The above can be translated 'I got it written', 'I have written it'; 'I had written it'; 'Were I to have written it'; etc.) Examples:

მას წერილი უკვე გაგზავნილი აქვს.

He has already sent the letter.

დედას შვილი მაღაზიაში ჰყავს გაგზავნილი.

Mother has sent [her] son to the store.

ეს წიგნი წაკითხული რომ მქონდეს, შევძლებდი თქვენთან ამ საკითხზე საუბარს.

If I had read this book, I could have talked (VN) with you about this question.

A small number of *intransitive* verbs (mainly verbs of motion and some root II. conjugation verbs) can form a resultative series with the auxiliary არის. (The subject is in the nominative case.) Examples:

ის მოსულია.

He has come.

ისინი მოსული იქნებიან.

They will have come.

სასწაული მომხდარია.

A miracle has occurred

13.6. Review: Functions of the preradical vowels. The preradical vowels in Georgian (*a*-, *i*-, [*u*-], and *e*-) have various functions depending upon the type of verb with which they occur and the particular series (present, future, aorist, perfect) that a given verb is in. These functions will be presented below, beginning with the most common functions of each vowel and proceeding to the least common.

13.6.1.1. The preradical vowel *i*- (without object marker).

a. absolute forms of II. conj. verbs derived from I. conj. verbs (other than those regular verbs with circumfix *a*-....-*eb*). See sec. 3.1.3. Examples:

დაიწერება	from დაწერს	write
დაიხატება	from დახატავს	paint
გაიგზავნება	from გაგზავნის	send

b. (without preverb) future and aorist series of absolute III. conj. verbs.[9] See secs. 8.1.4-5. Examples:

Pres. დუღს	Fut. იდუღებს	boil
Pres. ლაპარაკობს	Fut. ილაპარაკებს	speak
Pres. თამაშობს	Fut. ითამაშებს	play

c. the reflexive indirect object form of a I. conj. verb. See above, sec. 13.1.

d. the base form (i.e., the vocabulary entry form from which the other forms are derived) of a I. conj. verb.[10] Examples:

დაიწყებს	begin	ისწავლის	learn (cf.
მიიღებს	receive	ასწავლის	teach)
გაიმეორებს	repeat		

13.6.1.2. The preradical vowel *i*- with object marker.

The preradical vowel *i*- can occur with the first and second person object markers in the *u*-series of markers:

mi-	gvi-
gi-	gi-....-t
u-	[u-....-t]

The function of these markers will be discussed below in the section dealing with the preradical vowel *u*-. See also sec. 13.2 above.

13.6.2. The preradical vowel *u*-.

a. indirect objects in I., II., III. conjugation verbs. See secs. 7.2.2, 7.3.2, 8.2. Examples:

I. conj.

გაგზავნის	send	გაუგზავნის	send to s.o.
ააშენებს	build	აუშენებს	build for s.o.

II. conj. (in -*d*- or root II. conj.)

აშენდება	be built	აუშენდება	be built for s.o.
მოკვდება	die	მოუკვდება	one's ... die

III. conj.

მღერის	sing	უმღერის	sing to s.o.
ყეფს	bark	უყეფს	bark at s.o.

It can also mark the indirect object in the present tense of passives of state; see above, sec. 13.4.

b. the grammatical *subject* in the present perfect of I. and III. conj. verbs. See secs. 10.1.1, 10.1.2. Examples:

I. conj.

გაგზავნის	pres. perf.	გაუგზავნია	send
ააშენებს	pres. perf.	აუშენებია	build

III. conj.

იმღერის	pres. perf.	უმღერია	sing
ყეფს	pres. perf.	უყეფია	bark

c. the grammatical subject in the present series of a few IV. conjugation verbs. See sec. 12.1.2. Examples:

მიყვარს	3sg.	უყვარს	love
მინდა	3sg.	უნდა	want

13.6.3. The preradical vowel *a*-.

a. The most common function of the preradical

vowel *a*- is to mark (in all series but the perfect) I. conjugation denominal verbs (see sec. 3.5) and causatives, derived both from III. conjugation verbs (sec. 8.3.2) and from other I. conjugation verbs (sec. 11.4). It is also found with many I. conjugation verbs with P/FSF -*ob* and with many I. conjugation root verbs ending in -*ev*.[11] Examples:

გაათეთრებს	cf. თეთრი
whiten	white
დააინტერესებს	cf. ინტერესი
interest	interest
∅=ადუღებს	cf. დუღს
boil sthg.	boil (intr.)
∅=ატირებს	cf. ტირის
make s.o. cry	cry
დააწერინებს	cf. დაწერს
have s.o. write	write
ააშენებინებს	cf. ააშენებს
have s.o. build	build
გაათბობინებს	cf. გაათბობს
have s.o. heat	heat sthg.
დაანგრევინებს	cf. დაანგრევს
have s.o. destroy	destroy

The preradical vowel with I. conjugation verbs has as its major function the marking of such verbs as transitive, especially as opposed to the preradical vowel *i*-. Compare the following aorist forms:

მან წყალი ადუღა.

He boiled (trans.) the water (for a long time).

წყალმა იდუღა.

The water boiled (intrans.).

ბავშვმა ის ატირა.

The child made him cry (trans.).

ბავშვმა იტირა.

The child cried (intrans.).

b. *a*- is also the marker of the superessive; see above, sec. 13.3.

c. *a*- occurs in the present series of a few IV. conjugation verbs. Examples:

მაქვს	have
მახსოვს	remember

13.6.4. The preradical vowel *e*-.

a. marks the grammatical *subject* in the pluperfect of I. and III. conjugation verbs; see sec. 10.1.1.2. Examples:

I. conj.

გაგზავნის	pluperf.	გაეგზავნა	send
ააშენებს	pluperf.	აეშენებინა	build

III. conj.

მღერის	pluperf.	ემღერა	sing
ყეფს	pluperf.	ეყეფა	bark

b. marks the indirect object in relative II. conjugation verbs derived from II. conjugation verbs in *i*-; see sec. 7.3.1. Examples:

დამალავს: დაემალება

hide from s.o., cf. დაიმალება hide o.s.

დაჭრის: დაეჭრება

s.o.'s sthg. is wounded, cf. დაიჭრება be wounded

გაგზავნის: გაეგზავნება

be sent to s.o., cf. გაიგზავნება be sent

c. marks the subject of IV. conjugation verbs in the future and aorist series. See sec. 12.1.1.2. Examples:

მგონია	fut.	მეგონება	seem; think
მძინავს	fut.	მეძინება	sleep
მიყვარს	fut.	მეყვარება	love

d. marks passives of state in the future and aorist series; see above, sec. 13.4.

LESSON 13: Notes

1. Compare these forms with id.o. markers: დაუჭრის 'cut sthg. for s.o.', აურჩევს 'elect s.o. for s.o.', დაბანს (with *h*-series markers) 'wash s.o.'s sthg. (e.g., face)', აუშენებს 'build sthg. for s.o.', აუდუღებს 'boil sthg. for s.o.'.

2. As a rule the marking of reflexive indirect objects with denominal verbs (verbs with preradical vowel *a*- and P/FSF -*eb*) is relatively rare; without preverb such forms would be homonymous with the future and aorist series of III. conjugation verbs.

3. At times a given verb can occur with both preradical vowel *a*- and preradical vowel *i*- with the difference being lexical rather than the difference between the base form and the reflexive derived from it. Examples include:

წარმოადგენს present, represent, perform

წარმოიდგენს imagine

(cf. German *vorstellen* and *sich vorstellen*, Russian представлять and представлять себе.)

4. From Latin *super* 'on top of' and *esse* 'to be'.

5. The superessive is also found with a few II. conjugation verbs (both in -*d*- and root) and with some irregular verbs of change of position and of position.

II. conj.

ახტება	აახტება
jump up	jump up onto sthg.
(no absolute form)	დააკვირდება
	stare at [on] s.o.

Irregular

დაჯდება	დააჯდება
sit down (sing.)	sit down on sthg.
დასხდებიან	დაასხდებიან
sit down (pl.)	sit down on sthg.
დადგება	დაადგება
stand up	stand up on sthg.

დაწვება	დააწვება
lie down	lie down on sthg.
დგას	ადგას
be standing	be standing on sthg.

In the modern language the superessive now tends to occur more commonly with the postposition -*ze* rather than with the dative.

6. Remember that in the *h*-series of object markers the third person marker has the shape *h*- before *k*, *ḳ*, *g*, *q*, and *p̣* and the shape *s* before *t*, *ṭ*, *d*, *c*, *c̣*, *ʒ*, *č*, *č̣*, *ǯ* (sec. 7.2.4) but many writers will omit *h* or *s* in these contexts so that the passive of state may not, in such writers, have any such marker.

7. The subject of a passive of state is in the majority of instances inanimate and hence third person. In those instances when the subject is a human being, first and second person forms can also occur. These are marked by the suffix -*i*- followed by the appropriate form of the verb 'be': 1. *v-....-i-var(-t)*; 2. *-i-xar(-t)*. With a third person plural subject the ending is -*i-an*.

8. The future stem is identical to the stem of the corresponding relative II. conj. verb in the present tense if the relative form is formed with *e*-. If the alternation *e* → *i* occurs in the formation of the II. conj. from the I. conj., this same alternation will occur in the formation of the future of the passive of state. Examples:

I. conj.	II. conj. absolute	II. conj. relative	*Passive of state:* present	future
დაწერს	დაიწერება	დაეწერება	სწერია	ეწერება
დათესს	დაითესება	დაეთესება	თესია	ეთესება

9. A limited number of III. conj. verbs have the preradical vowel *i*- in the present series also. Examples are: იმღერის 'sing', იცინის 'laugh'.

10. Very often such verbs will contain in their meaning the notion that the action is performed for the benefit of the grammatical subject or otherwise directly affects him. Compare for example the following:

Ø=იყიდის	buy
გაყიდის	sell

Ø=ისწავლის	learn; study
Ø=ასწავლის	teach
Ø=ისესხებ	borrow
გა=ასესხებ	lend

Verbs with base form in *i*- with such meaning include: დაიჭერს 'catch', მიიღებს 'receive', იპოვნის 'find', შეინახავს 'keep', etc.

11. *a*- is also found with other I. conj. verbs whose meanings are either (a) causative or (b) strongly imply the presence of a surface upon which the verbal action takes place. Examples of the first type include: მიაფრენს 'have someone fly', მოარჩენს 'cure', 'heal' (i.e., cause to recover). An example of the second type is დაასხამს 'pour'; see also sec. 13.3 above.

LESSON 13: Exercises

1. მე ხელები და პირი უკვე დავიბანე; ახლა შენ უნდა დაგბანო პირი.
2. ეს კაცი კედელს რას აწერს? ლოზუნგს აწერს.
3. ამ კარს რა აწერია? აწერია „შესავალი".
4. პირველ ყოვლისა მე ტანთ ჩავიცვამ, შემდეგ კი პატარა შვილს ჩავაცვამ.
5. ამ საღამოს რა გეცმევა? --ის მეცმევა, რაც ახლა მაცვია.
6. ამდენ მარილს ხორცს ნუ აყრი!
7. მამათქვენს ეს სახლი თავისთვის ხომ არ აუშენებია? --დიახ, ეს სახლი მამაჩემმა აიშენა, როცა ოცდახუთი წლისა იყო.
8. ჩვენი თვითმფრინავებიდან მტერს ბომბები დავაყარეთ. უფრო ადრე რომ დაგვეყარა ბომბები მათთვის, ომიც უფრო ადრე დამთავრდებოდა.
9. ხვალ პერანგები უნდა გავირეცხო.
10. რა მოხდა? რატომ შეყვირე? თითი გავიჭერი.
11. ის, ვინც თავის შვილებს აქებს, თავს იქებსო.
12. ჩანს, რომ პატიმარს თავი მოუკლავს. დიახ, მან თავი მოიკლა.
13. ცეცხლი დაანთე! --ცეცხლი უკვე ანთია, ბატონო.
14. როცა ოთახში შევედით, სინათლე ენთო.
15. წიგნები მაგიდაზე ელაგა.
16. წიგნები იქ არ ელაგა, სადაც მე დავდევი.
17. ფირფიტა მაგიდაზე რატომ სდევს? მე კი ფონოგრაფს დავადევი.
18. (a) ზოგი დედალი კვერცხებს დიდხანს აზის.
    (b) კატა გოგონას მუხლზე აჯდება.
19. ექიმი როდის მიგიღებს? --ხვალ მიმიღებს.
20. ეს ახალი სუფრა მაგიდას გადააფარე! --სუფრა უკვე აფარია მაგიდაზე.
21. შვილებისათვის რატომ არ ჩაგიცმევია? --მათ ტანთ უკვე აცვიათ. ახლა მე ტანთ ვიცვამ.

22. საქართველოს ყველაზე სახელოვანი მხატვრების სურათები საქართველოს სსრ ხელოვნების სახელმწიფო მუზეუმში ჰკიდია. იქ ნიკო ფიროსმანიშვილის, დავით კაკაბაძისა და ლადო გუდიაშვილის სურათები ჰკიდია.
23. 1184 წელს თამარს გვირგვინი დაადგეს.
24. საქართველოს უდიდესი კულტურული მოღვაწეები მთაწმინდის პანთეონში მარხიან.
25. აქვე დიდი რუსი მწერალი ა. ს. გრიბოედოვიც მარხია.
26. მითხრეს, რომ შენი საბეჭდი მანქანა გაგიყიდია. ვის მიჰყიდე? უნივერსიტეტის სტუდენტმა იყიდა.
27. ქართულად ლაპარაკი სად ისწავლე? --ქალბატონმა შუქიამ მასწავლა, როცა თბილისში ვსწავლობდი.
28. „ლოკომოტივმა" ფეხბურთის მატჩი მოიგო? --არა, სამწუხაროდ წააგო; „დინამომ" მოიგო.
29. ყავას მოვიმზადებ. თუ გინდა, შენც მოგიმზადებ. --არა, არ მწყურია. ყავას ნუ მომიმზადებ.
30. ბავშვს სძინავს. შენ თუ ასე ხმამაღლა ილაპარაკებ, მას აატირებ. --ვილაპარაკებ ხმადაბლა, რომ არ იტიროს.
31. ქართულ ორთოგრაფიას ფონეტიკური პრინციპი უდევს საფუძვლად.
32. გუშინ მთაწმინდის რესტორანში ავედით. მთაწმინდიდან დავინახეთ მთელი თბილისი, რომელიც ჩვენ წინ იდო.
33. მისი სიტყვები მუდამ მძიმედ მადევს გულზე.
34. მთავრობამ მძიმე გადასახადები დაგვადო.
35. ძაღლს წინ ხორცი დაუდევს.
36. როცა ჯარისკაცს ეს სიტყვები მოესმა, მან ხანჯალზე დაიდო ხელი.
37. ვახტანგმა მითხრა, სოსომ ხელი მოიტეხაო. --არა, ხელი არ მოუტეხია. ფეხბურთის თამაშისას ფეხი მოიტეხა.
38. პატიმარმა მარჯვენა ხელის თითი მოიტეხა, როცა საპატიმროდან გარბოდა.

39. საწერი მაგიდა გამიტყდა. -ახალს იყიდი? --არა, ახალს გავიკეთებ.
40. ფიროსმანიშვილის საუკეთესო სურათთაგან მრავალი თბილისის სამიკიტნოების კედლებზე ეხატა.
41. პური მოიჭერით და ღვინო დაისხით! თქვენს ცოლსაც დაუსხით!
42. ბოდიშს ვიხდი! a. ჩემმა გოგონამ წყალი იატაკს დაასხა. b. ჩემს გოგონას იატაკზე წყალი დაესხა. --არაფერია, დღესვე უნდა გავრეცხო იატაკი.
43. როცა შევედით, ღვინო ჯერ კიდევ არ ესხა. ღვინო რომ სხმულიყო, დავლევდი.
44. ღვინო ყველას ესხა გარდა მასპინძლისა; მას არ ესხა. მას რომ სხმოდა, დალევდა.
45. ხელები რატომ არ დაიბანე, სანამ მაგიდას მოუჯდებოდი? --დავიბანე!
46. შვილო, ვინ დაგბანა? მამამ დამბანა. დას ხომ არ დაუბანიხარ? არა, მას არ დავუბანივარ.
47. მტერმა ბრძოლა მოიგო, ომი კი წააგო. ჩვენ რომ ბრძოლა არ წაგვეგო, მტერი ომს უფრო მალე წააგებდა.
48. ვერ გავიგე, რა აწერია დაფას. --დაფას არაფერი აწერია. --როცა შევედი, დაფაზე რამდენიმე სიტყვა ეწერა, მაგრამ ვერ გავიგე. ეს სიტყვები ხუცურად ეწერა.
49. გაიგეთ, რაც ეწერა დაფაზე, როცა ოთახში შეხვედით? დაფაზე არაფერი არ ეწერა. არსად არაფერი ეწერა!
50. არავის გაუგია, რატომ მოიკლა თავი პატიმარმა.
51. გუშინ კინოში რომ არ წავსულიყავი, ეს წერილი დამთავრებული მექნებოდა.
52. **მომავალი** წლისთვის ეს სახლი დამთავრებული გვექნება.
53. ასეთი კარგი მოლაპარაკე არასოდეს მყოლია ნანახი!
54. სანამ ფიროსმანიშვილი გარდაიცვლებოდა, მას თბილისის ასამდე სურათი ჰქონდა დახატული.
55. სტუმრები დაპატიჟებული რომ გვყოლოდა, კარგ სადილს გავაკეთებდით.

56. სანამ შენ ჩამოხვალ, ექიმი ნანახი მეყოლება.
57. ლადო არ წამოვიდა ჩვენთან ერთად კინოში, მას ეს ფილმი ნანახი ჰქონია.
58. მასწავლებელმა მითხრა, რომ შენ დღეს გაკვეთილი არ გქონია მომზადებული. ეს მართალია?
59. უფრო მეტი ფული რომ მქონოდა შენახული, უკეთეს საბეჭდ მანქანას ვიყიდდი.
60. მას პატიმარი რომ ჰყოლოდა ნანახი, ეს ამბავი არ მოხდებოდა.

Vocabulary

ამდენი	this much, many; so much, many
არავინ	no one (declined like ვინ, Lesson 5, note 3)
არაფერი	nothing (E)
არსად	nowhere
ბომბა	bomb
გადასახადი	tax
გვირგვინი	crown; wreath; garland
გოგონა	(little) girl (nontruncating)
გული	heart
დაფა	blackboard
დედალი	hen; female (of animals) (A)
იატაკი	floor (not story of a building)
კედელი	wall (E)
კვერცხი	egg
ლოზუნგი	slogan
მართალი	true (A) (adverb =მართლა)
მარილი	salt
მატჩი	(sporting) match; game
მოღვაწე	(public) figure (= Russian деятель)
მუხლი	knee; lap
მძიმე	heavy
ორთოგრაფია	orthography, spelling
პანთეონი	Pantheon; cemetery where famous people are buried
პატიმარი	prisoner (A)
პირველ ყოვლისა	first of all
პრინციპი	principle
საბეჭდი მანქანა	typewriter (lit. machine for printing)
სანამ	until; before (conjunction) (+ conditional for English past)
სამიკიტნო	inn; tavern
საპატიმრო	prison
საუკეთესო	best
საფუძველი	basis; base; foundation (E)
საწერი	for writing; writing-
სახე	face; image; form
სინათლე	light
ტანი	body (see *-cv-* below, in verbs)
ფონოგრაფი	phonograph
ყავა	coffee
შესავალი	entrance (A)
შვილი	child (= son or

	daughter)	ხორცი	meat
ცეცხლი	fire	ხმადაბალი	soft, low (of voice) (A); ხმადაბლა softly
ხანჯალი	dagger (A)		

ა. ს. გრიბოედოვი (1795-1829)

ლადო გუდიაშვილი (1896-1980)

დავით კაკაბაძე (1889-1952)

ნიკო ფიროსმანიშვილი (1860-1918; also ფიროსმანაშვილი)

დინამო	"Dynamo" (name of a sports team)
ლოკომოტივი	"Locomotive" (name of a sports team)
მუქია	(f. pr. n.)
მთაწმინდა	lit. "Holy Mountain," (mountain overlooking Tbilisi)

Verbs

მოიგებს	mo=i-*g*-eb-s	win
წააგებს	ç̣a=a-*g*-eb-s	lose
დადებს	da=*d*-eb-s aor.: და(ვ)დევი(თ), 3sg. დადო or დადვა; perf. დაუდვია	put (down)
დევს	(irr. passive of state) fut. იდება, aor. იდო or იდვა, perfect დებულა; relative: pres. ადევს, fut. ედება	be lying
ჩამოკიდებს	čamo=*ḳid*-eb-s	hang
ალაგია	Passive of state of განალაგებს	be arranged
დაანთებს	da=a-*nt*-eb-s	light (a fire)
დაპატიჟებს	da=*p̣aṭiž*-eb-s	invite
გარბის	ga+*rb*-i-s; fut. გაირბენს (see Lesson 8, note 3)	run away
გარეცხავს	ga=*recx*-av-s	wash sthg. (not s.o.!)
გატეხს	ga=*ṭex*-s	break (into pieces)

მოტეხს	mo=ṭ*ex*-s	break (off)
გატყდება	ga=*ṭqd*-eb-a (II. conj. form of გატეხს) perfect (absolute) გამტყდარა (relative: გასტეხია)	break (intr.)
გადააფარებს	gada=a-*par*-eb-s	spread (e.g., tablecloth)
შეუყვირებს	še+*qvir*-eb-s	shout out
დაყრის	da=*qr*-i-s	scatter, throw down (d.o. is plural or a collective)
ჩაიცვამს, ჩაიცვამს(ტანთ)	ča=i-*cv*-am-s	put sthg. on, dress o.s.
	Passive of state: pres. აცვია, fut. ეცმევა, aor. ეცვა, perf. სცმია	s.o. (*H*-series id.o.) is dressed
ჩააცმევს, ჩააცმევს(ტანს, ტანზე)	ča=H-a-*cmev*-s (aorist irr.: ჩა(ვ)აცვი(თ), ჩააცვა) Passive of state as for ჩაიცვამს above.	put sthg. on s.o.; dress s.o.
გაიჭრის	ga=i-*č̣r*-i-s	cut one's (e.g., finger)
მიუჯდება (მო-, see sec. 7.2.4)	(for forms see sec. 9.1.2)	sit near
მიუჯდება მაგიდას		sit down at the table

Key to the Exercises

1. I already washed my (refl.) hands and face (= mouth); now I must wash your face.
2. What is this man writing on the wall? He is writing a slogan on it.
3. What is written on this door? *Entrance* is written on it.
4. First of all I shall dress myself, and then I shall dress the small child.
5. What will you be wearing this evening? I shall be wearing what (= that, what) I'm wearing now.
6. Don't pour (= scatter) so much salt on the meat.
7. Didn't your father build this house for himself? Yes, my father built this house when he was twenty-five years old (= of twenty-five years).
8. From our airplanes we scattered bombs on the enemy. If we had scattered bombs on them earlier, the war, too, would have ended earlier.
9. I must wash the shirts for myself tomorrow.
10. What happened? Why did you shout out? I cut my finger.
11. He who praises his own children praises himself. (proverb)
12. It appears that the prisoner killed himself. Yes, he killed himself.
13. Light the fire! The fire is already lit, sir.
14. When we entered into the room the light was lit.
15. The books were arranged on the table.
16. The books were not arranged where I set them up.
17. Why is the record lying on the table? I (however) put it on the phonograph.
18. (a) Some (= several) hens sit on eggs for a long time. (b) The cat will sit on the girl's lap (= knee).
19. When will the doctor receive you? He will receive me tomorrow.
20. Spread this new tablecloth on the table. The tablecloth is already spread on the table.
21. Why haven't you dressed the children? They are already dressed. Now I am dressing myself.
22. The pictures of Georgia's most famous artists are hanging in the State Museum of Art of the Georgian SSR. There the pictures of Niḳo Pirosmanišvili, David Ḳaḳabaje, and Lado Gudiašvili are hanging.
23. In 1184 they crowned (= set the crown on) Tamara.
24. Georgia's greatest cultural figures are buried in the Mtaçminda Pantheon.
25. Here too (= -*ve*) is buried the great Russian writer A.S. Griboyedov also.

26. They told me that you sold your typewriter. To whom did you sell it? A university student bought it.
27. Where did you learn to speak Georgian (= Georgian [adv.] speaking)? Ms. Šukia taught me when I was studying in Tbilisi.
28. Did "Locomotive" win the football (soccer) match? No, unfortunately it lost; "Dynamo" won.
29. I will prepare coffee for myself. If you want, I will prepare (some) for you too. No, I am not thirsty. Don't prepare coffee for me.
30. The child is sleeping. If you will speak so loudly, you'll make him start to cry. I will speak softly [so] that he will not cry.
31. The phonetic principle lies at the basis (= as the basis [adv.]) of Georgian orthography (id.o.).
32. Yesterday we went up to the Mtaçminda restaurant. From Mtacminda we caught sight of all of (= the whole) Tbilisi, which was lying before us.
33. His words always lie heavily on my (id.o.) heart.
34. The government imposed (= set) heavy taxes on us.
35. They put (some) meat in front of the dog (id.o.).
36. When the soldier heard these words he put his hand on his dagger.
37. Vaxṭang told me that Soso broke his hand. No, he did not break (his) hand. While playing football (soccer) he broke his foot.
38. The prisoner broke (his) right hand finger when he was running away from the prison.
39. My (id.o.) writing table broke. Will you buy a new one? No, I will make a new one for myself.
40. Of Pirosmanišvili's best pictures many were painted (i.e., were to be found painted) on the walls of Tbilisi taverns.
41. Cut (slice) yourself (some) bread and pour yourself (some) wine. Pour your wife (some), too!
42. Excuse me! My girl poured water on the floor [(a), deliberately; (b), accidentally]. --It is nothing, this very day ('today' + *-ve*) I have to wash the floor.
43. When we entered, the wine had not yet been poured. If the wine had been poured, I would have drunk it.
44. The wine was poured for everyone except the host; for him it was not poured. If it had been poured for him he would have drunk it.
45. Why didn't you wash your (id.o.) hands before you sat down (cond.) at the table? I did wash.
46. Child, who washed you? Father washed me. Didn't sister wash you? No, she didn't wash me.

47. The enemy won the battle; the war, however, it lost. If we hadn't lost the battle, the enemy would have lost the war sooner.
48. I couldn't understand what is written on the blackboard. Nothing is written on the blackboard. When I entered, several words were written on the blackboard, but I couldn't understand them. These words were written in *xucuri* (adv.).
49. Did you understand what was written on the blackboard when you all entered the room? Nothing was written on the blackboard. Nothing was written anywhere (= nowhere)!
50. No one understood why the prisoner killed himself.
51. If I hadn't gone to the movies yesterday, I would have finished the letter (i.e., got the letter finished).
52. By next year (= for the coming [pres. part.] year) we will have finished this house.
53. I have never seen such a good speaker!
54. Before Pirosmanišvili died, he had painted up to a hundred pictures of Tbilisi.
55. If we had invited guests, we would have made a good dinner.
56. Before you will arrive I will have seen the doctor.
57. Lado did not come with us to the movies; he (probably) has seen this film.
58. The teacher told me that you haven't prepared the lesson today. Is this true?
59. If I had saved more (lit., more more) money, I would have bought a better typewriter.
60. If he had seen the prisoner, this thing wouldn't have happened.

Reading Passage ნიკო ფიროსმანაშვილი

1 ნიკო ფიროსმანაშვილი ღარიბი გლეხის შვილი იყო. დაიბადა 1860 წელს კახეთში. მშობლები ადრე დაეხოცა; ჭაბუკმა თბილისს მოაშურა და აქ თექვსმეტ წელიწადს ემსახურა ვიღაც სირაჯს, სოვდაგარს.

2 ნიკოს ჯერ კიდევ ბავშვობაში გამოაჩნდა ხატვის მიდრეკილება, მაგრამ მისი მშობლები იმდენად უსახსრონი იყვნენ, რომ შვილისთვის რაიმე საერთო, მით უფრო პროფესიული განათლება მიეცათ, ამაზე ფიქრი და ოცნებაც ზედმეტი იყო. ნიჭით დაჯილდოებულმა ნიკომ სხვების დაუხმარებლად, თავად ისწავლა წერა-კითხვა არა მარტო ქართულ, რუსულ ენაზედაც, და ერთხანს ძალიან გაიტაცა ლიტერატურის კითხვამ, მაგრამ მძიმე ფიზიკურმა შრომამ, ხვალინდელ დღეზე რწმენის უქონლობამ გზა გადაუღობა შემდგომი თვითგანვითარებისა და იდეურ-ინტელექტუალური ზრდისაკენ. ბავშვობიდანვე ფერწერისადმი განწყობილი ნიკო მუდამ თვალყურს ადევნებდა და გულდასმით უკვირდებოდა, თუ როგორ მუშაობდნენ მღებავები, განსაკუთრებით ფერმწერები, რომლებიც აბრებს წერდნენ, რესტორნებისა და სარდაფების კედლების მოხატვას აწარმოებდნენ. ისწავლა რა თვითონ, სხვების დაუხმარებლად აბრების წერა-მოხატვა, ნიკო შეუდგა შეკვეთით მიღებულ სამუშაოებს: მალე თვითონ ნასწავლ ფერმწერ გიგო ზაზიაშვილთან ერთად სამღებრო-საფერმწერლო სახელოსნოც კი დააარსა (1882 წ.).

3 მაგრამ ამ წამოწყებამ სრული მარცხი განიცადა და ფიროსმანაშვილი საარსებო სახსრების საშოვრად ერთხანს რკინიგზაზე მუშაობდა. მაგრამ იქ სამსახური და ის საქმე, რომელსაც იგი აკეთებდა, სულიერად ვერ აკმაყოფილებდა ნ. ფიროსმანაშვილს, ამიტომ მიატოვა რკინიგზაზე სამსახური და დაუბრუნდა თავის საყვარელ საქმეს — ფერწერას, რომელსაც სიკვდილამდე არ მოშორებია და თავის სიცოცხლეც კი მსხვერპლად მიუტანა.

4 უკიდურესად გულჩათხრობილი, უსაზღვრო ავადმყოფური თავმოყვარეობით შეპყრობილი ნიკო ფიროსმანაშვილი მარტოხელა კაცის კარჩაკეტილ ცხოვრებას ეწეოდა, არავის არ ეკარებოდა დახმარების გამოსათხოვადაც კი, თუმცა მუდამ დღე მწვავე გაჭირვებას განიცდიდა. უოჯახომ, უამხანაგომ, ყველასაგან განდეგილმა და განმარტოებულმა ფიროსმანაშვილმა მოხეტიალე კაცის ცხოვრება დაიწყო. ერთადერთი წრე, სადაც იგი ტრიალებდა, ეს იყო მიკიტნების, სირაჯების და ხელოსან-შინამრეწველების წრე... ისინი იყვნენ მისი შემკვეთელნი და მისი ნიჭის დამფასებელნი. ფუნჯებით და საღებავებით დახეტიალობს იგი სარდაფიდან სარდაფში, დუქნიდან დუქანში, რესტორნიდან რესტორანში, წერს სურათებს და აბრებს, ხოლო ზოგჯერ კედლებსაც ხატავს. სარდაფ-რესტორნების მეპატრონეები და მათი მუდმივი სტუმრები სასტიკ ექსპლოატაციას უწევდნენ თვითნასწავლ მხატვარს, არ იმეტებდნენ გასამრჯელოს შესრულებული სამუშაოსათვის, ზოგჯერ კი ერთ ჭიქა ღვინოს ან ერთ თეფშ კერძს მისცემდნენ ხოლმე.

5 ხმებმა და მითქმა-მოთქმამ ფიროსმანის ნიჭიერების შესახებ ქართველ მხატვართა წრემდეც მიაღწია. ეს მოხდა 1912 წელს.

6 პირველ ხანებში პროფესიონალი მხატვრები დაინტერესდნენ ნ. ფიროსმანაშვილით. ქართულ პრესაში მის შესახებ წერილი და მისი პორტრეტიც კი დაიბეჭდა, ნაბიჯიც კი გადაიდგა მისთვის ნივთიერი დახმარების აღმოსაჩენად. მაგრამ ამ კეთილი განზრახვის განხორციელების ნაყოფი ნიკო ფიროსმანაშვილს ვეღარ ეღირსა; პირიქით, იმავე გაზეთმა, რომელმაც ცოტა ხნის წინათ მისი ნიჭის საქებარი წერილი მოათავსა, ახლა მისი გამაბიაბრუებელი კარიკატურა დაბეჭდა. თავისი სისასტიკით ამ ულმობელმა დაცინვამ ღრმა შეურაცხყოფა, დიდი სულიერი ტრავმა მიაყენა ნ. ფიროსმანაშვილს. ამის შემდეგ იგი ახლო არ გაკარებია და სრულიად ჩამოშორდა ქართველ მხატვართა საზოგადოებას. უკიდურესად გამძაფრებული მისი თავმოყვარეობა გააღიზიანა იმ ფაქტმა, რომ მხატვრე-

ზმა მისდამი ნამდვილი ინტერესი არ გამოიჩინეს, არ ჩათვალეს იგი თავის თანასწორ და თავის ღირს კოლეგად.

7 შემდგომში ნ. ფიროსმანაშვილი ყოველთვის გაურბოდა პროფესიონალ მხატვრებთან შეხვედრას, რაიმე ურთიერთობას რომელიმე მათგანთან, და 1918 წელს ყველასაგან განკერძოებული გარდაიცვალა სრულ მარტოობაში.

"Cook"
Artist: N. Pirosmanašvili

„მზარეულუი“
ნ. ფიროსმანაშვილი

Vocabulary

1

და=ხოცავს	kill (d.o. is plural)
და=ეხოცება	s.o.'s ... are killed, die, perish (subject is always plural)
ჭაბუკი	youth (young person)
მო=აშურებს	hurry; run away (here) (*H*-series id.o.; no d.o.)
Ø=ემსახურება	serve s.o., sthg. (id.o.)
ვიღაც(ა)	some (indefinite pronoun, adjective referring to persons); not declined when modifying nouns; when used as a pronoun: Erg. ვიღაცამ, Dat. ვიღაცას, Gen. ვიღაცის or ვიღაცას(ი).
სირაჯი	wine-merchant
ხოვდაგარი	wholesaler (A)

2

გამო=აჩნდება	come to light; emerge in s.o., appear (*H*-series id.o.) (gamo=a-č*n*-d-eb-a)
მიდრეკილება ●	bent; tendency
სახსარი	resources (A)
რაიმე (= რამე)	(truncating or nontruncating) something; some, any
საერთო	general; common
მით უფრო	all the more; particularly; let alone
რომ ... მიეცათ	here: to give (lit. that they give [pluperf.])
ფიქრი	thought
ოცნება	dream; vision
ზედმეტი	superfluous
ნიჭი	talent; gift
და=აჯილდო(ვ)ებს	reward; endow
თავად	himself; by himself
-ზედაც	= -ზე + -ც

ერთხანს	for a time
გაიტაცებს	inspire; inspire enthusiasm in s.o.
შრომა	labor
რწმენა	belief; faith (-*ze* in)
უქონლობა	lack
გადა=ღობავს გზას	bar the way
შემდგომი	following, continuing
თვითგანვითარება	self-education
იდეური	(from იდეა)
-დმი (pp.)	to; toward
განწყობილი	disposed; predisposed
თვალყური	attention
Ø=ადევნებს თვალყურს	pay attention to; observe; follow
გულდასმით	attentively; assiduously
და=უკვირდება	look at; observe; consider sthg. (id.o.)
თუ	(interrogative pronouns in indirect questions and introducing subordinate clauses are often preceded by **თუ**.)
შე=ღებავს	paint
ფერმწერი	painter (artist)
აბრა	sign; signboard
და=წერს	here: paint
სარდაფი	cellar (here: wine-cellar)
მო=ხატავს	paint (e.g., house; walls; etc.)
Ø=აწარმოებს	(Ø=a-*ċarmo(v)*-eb-s) carry out
ისწავლა რა თვითონ	having learned himself
შე=უდგება	begin (see sec. 9.1.2. ff.)
შე=უკვეთს	order; commission
სამუშაო	work
ფერწერ	(here declined adjectivally)
მღებარი	painter (A)
სახელოსნო	workshop (cf. ხელოსანი (A) craftsman)

3

წამო=იწყებს	begin; undertake
სრული	complete
მარცხი	defeat; failure
გან+იცდის	experience; undergo
საარსებო	vital; necessary for existence
საშოვრად	in order to find
რკინიგზა	railroad (cf. რკინა 'iron', გზა 'road')
სამსახური	service; position; work; working
სულიერი	spiritual
და=აკმაყოფილებს	satisfy
მი=ატოვებს ●	leave; abandon
მო=შორდება ●	distance o.s. from sthg. (id.o.)
მსხვერპლად მიმაქვს	sacrifice (lit. bring as a sacrifice)

4

უკიდურესი	extreme
გულჩათხრობილი	reserved; reticent
ავადმყოფური	unhealthy; sickly
თავმოყვარეობა	self-respect; ambition
შე=იპყრობს	seize, capture [aor.: შე(ვ)იპყარი(თ), შეიპყრო]
მარტოხელა	single; unmarried; solitary (nontrunc.)
კარჩაკეტილი	isolated
ეწევა	lead sthg. (id.o.) (II. conj.; only present series)
გა=ეკარება	come into contact with s.o., here: turn to s.o.
გამო=ითხოვს	request sthg. from s.o.
მუდამ დღე	every day
მწვავე	burning; sharp; acute
გაჭირვება	need; poverty
განდეგილი	hermit; s.o. living in isolation

გა(ნ)=ამარტო(ვ)ებს	isolate; exclude from society
მოხეტიალე	vagabond; vagrant
ტრიალებს	turn; circulate
მიკიტანი	inkeeper; bartender (A)
ხელოსანი	craftsman; artisan (A)
შინამრეწველი	home worker
შემკვეთელი	customer (E)
და=აფასებს	value; evaluate; appreciate
ფუნჯი	brush
საღებავი	paint
და+ხეტიალობს	wander around (III. conj.)
დუქანი	(private) shop (A)
ზოგჯერ	sometimes
მეპატრონე	owner
მუდმივი	constant; continual; here: regular
სასტიკი	cruel (here translate as "cruelly")
ექსპლოატაციას გა=უწევს	exploit s.o. (id.o.)
თვითნასწავლი	self-taught
გა=იმეტებს	part with; give up
გასამრჯელო	recompense; reward
შე=ასრულებს	fulfill; execute
ერთ ჭიქა ღვინოს	a glass of wine (dat.); note that in this construction ჭიქა 'glass' is treated as an adjective
თეფში	plate (see note above)
კერძი	food; course; portion; part
5	
ხმები	rumour(s) (plural of ხმა 'voice')
მითქმა-მოთქმა	gossip; talk
ფიროსმანი	= ფიროსმანიშვილი, ფიროსმანაშვილი
ნიჭიერება	talent; creativity
მი=აღწევს	reach (no d.o.)

6

პირველ ხანებში	at the start
ნაბიჯი	step; pace
ნაბიჯს გადა=დგამს	stride; ნაბიჯი გადა=იდგმება (aor. გადაიდგა) (II. conj.) steps are taken
ნივთიერი	material
აღმო+აჩენს	here: find
კეთილი	kind; nice
განზრახვა	plan; intention; design
გან+ახორციელებს	realize (= make real)
ნაყოფი	fruit
Ø= ეღირსება	s.o. (dat.) is considered worthy of sthg. (nom.)
პირიქით	on the contrary
იმავე	(oblique form of იგივე) the same
ხანი	time (A)
საქებარი	of praise; praiseworthy; laudable (A)
მო=ათავსებს	locate; here: publish
გა=აბიაბრუებს	dishonor; besmirch •[see note]
ულმობელი	ruthless (A)
დაცინვა	derision; mockery
ღრმა	deep
შეურაცხყოფა	insult; offense
ტრავმა	trauma
მი=აყენებს	do; cause sthg. to s.o.
ახლო	near; nearby (adj. and adverb)
გაკარებია (= გაჰკარებია)	perf. of გაეკარება; come into contact with s.o.
სრულიად	completely
ჩამო=აშორებს	distance, separate s.o. from s.o.
გამძაფრებული	stubborn; embittered
გა=აღიზიანებს	irritate; provoke; incite; excite
-დამი (pp.)	to, toward (used with personal pronouns instead of -დმი)

გამო=იჩენს (E → I) pay attention, show interest (in)
 ინტერესს
თავისი here: = თავიანთი
თანასწორი equal
ღირსი worthy
კოლეგა colleague
7
შემდგომში later
შეხვედრა meeting; encounter
რაიმე any (nontrunc.)
რომელიმე some; any (indefinite pronoun and adj.) gen. = რომელიმეს or რომლისამე.
მათგანთან see sec. 8.6.1
გან=აკერძოებს isolate

•ADDENDA TO VOCABULARY

2 იმდენად to such an extent
3 საყვარელი beloved, favorite (E)
 სიცოცხლე life
 -ც კი even
6 მისი გამაბიაბრუებელი კაიკატურა: 'a caricature dishonoring *him*'; with participles (as with masdars) the possessive adjective replaces the corresponding direct object of a transitive verb.

LESSON 14

14.0. Peculiarities in the verbal system. A limited number of common Georgian verbs show peculiarities (from the point of view of English and many other Western European languages) either in meaning (semantic) or conjugation (formal). In this and the following lesson a limited number of such "peculiar" verbs will be discussed so that we might gain an idea of how they behave.

14.1. Semantic peculiarities.

14.1.1. Verbs of politeness. In polite speech certain verbs are replaced by others that are felt to be more polite. Such verbs are most common in the second person (including imperative). As a rule they are not used in the first person. In the third person, the subject is often a respected figure.

14.1.1.1. Prefixed II. conjugation verbs with the root *brjan-* 'command' are used as respectful, polite counterparts of the correspondingly prefixed forms of the verb ხვლა 'go':

Normal	Respectful	
შე(მო)ვა	შე(მო)ბრძანდება	go/come in
გა(მო)ვა	გა(მო)ბრძანდება	go/come out
ა(მო)ვა	ა(მო)ბრძანდება	go/come up

and similarly with other prefixed forms of ხვლა.[1] The same verb is used with the preverb *a+* also to mean 'stand up':

ადგება	აბრძანდება	stand up

With the preverbs *da+* and *gada+* (*gadmo+*) it can have the meaning of 'sit':

დაჯდება	დაბრძანდება	sit down
დასხდებიან	დაბრძანდებიან	
გადაჯდება	გადაბრძანდება	sit on that side
გადასხდებიან	გადაბრძანდებიან	
გადმოჯდება	გადმობრძანდება	sit on this side
გადმოსხდებიან	გადმობრძანდებიან	

Note also the following idiomatic uses of this verb

without preverb:

როგორა ხარ(თ)?	როგორ ბრძანდებით?	How are you?
ვინა ხარ(თ)?	ვინ ბრძანდებით?	With whom do I have the honor of speaking?

As can be seen, in these uses the verb ბრძანდება serves as a replacement of ხარ, არის (see below, sec. 14.1.1.2).

The I. conjugation form of this verb is used with the meaning 'say', 'tell':

იტყვის	(pres. ამბობს)	ბრძანებს	say
ეტყვის	(pres. ეუბნება)	უბრძანებს	tell s.o.

14.1.1.2. The root *xl-/xel-* occurs with the meaning of 'be'. In these uses the verb always contains a marker of a second person plural indirect object, although there is no indirect object in the sentence. Unlike the forms discussed above, this verb has forms for the first and third persons, but no second person forms. With the meaning of 'be' the conjugation is as follows:

ვარ(თ)	გახლავართ	I am/we are
არის	გახლავთ	He is
არიან	გახლავან	they are
ვიყავი(თ)	გახლდით	I was/we were
იყო	გახლდათ	He was
იყვნენ	გახლდნენ	They were

(The conjunctive forms of the polite verb correspond to the optative of ყოფნა.) The future tense (first person) is გეახლებით (g-e-*axl*-eb-i-t). For the missing second person of this verb (in the meaning 'you [all] are') the second person forms pres. ბრძანდები(თ), past ბრძანდებოდი(თ), etc. are used. The third person of this verb can also be used. As a result there are three possible forms for the third person: არის, გახლავთ, ბრძანდება.[2]

The polite form corresponding to 'come' has no present series. There are no forms for the second person.

მოვალ(თ)	გეახლები(თ)	g-e-*axl*-eb-i	I/we will come
მოვა	გეახლება		He will come

მოვლენ გეახლებიან They will come

The aorist is irregular: first person: გეახელი(თ) g-e-*axel*-i(-t). Third person sg. გეახლა, pl. გეახლნენ. This II. conjugation verb can also be used with the meanings of 'eat' and 'drink', although the preradical vowel -*i*- is found too: გიახლებით.

14.1.1.3. The root *rtmev-/rtv-* is used as a polite replacement in the second (and at times third) persons in the following instances:

Normal	Respectful	
ჭამს	მიირთმევს	eat
მიუტანს წაუღებს მისცემს	მიართმევს	bring, give sthg. to s.o.

This verb is irregular in the aorist series: second person -რთვი(თ), third person sg. -რთვა, third person pl. -რთვეს.

14.1.2. Personal vs. nonpersonal verbs. A limited number of Georgian verbs occur in pairs, one member of which is used to refer to human beings (personal), the other to nonhuman beings (animals, things; i.e., nonpersonal). As a rule, if the verb is transitive (generally I. conjugation), the *direct object* of the personal verb must be personal, while if the verb is intransitive, the *subject* of the personal verb must be personal (i.e., in the II. and III. conjugation verbs). With IV. conjugation verbs, it is the noun in the nominative case that must be personal if the verb is personal.

An example of a nonpersonal verb would be the IV. conjugation verb მაქვს 'have sthg.', while მყავს 'have s.o.' is an example of a personal verb (see sec. 12.1.3.a., b.). Verbs such as მოიტანს 'bring','carry sthg.' are non-personal and verbs such as მოიყვანს 'bring','lead s.o.' are personal (sec. 12.1.3.c.,d.). Examples:

Transitive

დაბანს	wash s.o.	გარეცხავს	wash sthg.
იცნობს	know s.o., be acquainted with s.o.	იცის	know sthg.

Intransitive

წევს	s.o. is lying (down)	დევს	sthg. is lying

14.1.3. "Singular" and "plural" verbs. A small number of verbs occur in pairs, one member of which is used with plural referents, the other with singular referents. With I. conjugation verbs, one verb form is used when the *direct object* is either plural or denotes more than one person or object (e.g., a collective noun or a noun modified by a numeral or quantifier) and the other is used with a singular object. With other verbs the "plural" verb is used with a plural *grammatical subject* or when the grammatical subject denotes more than one person or object while the "singular" verb is used with a singular subject denoting only one person or object. We have already seen examples of such verbs in: singular დაჯდება; იჯდება (pres. ზის); plural დასხდებიან; ისხდნენ (pres. სხედან) (sec. 9.1.2.2, 9.1.3). Examples of I. conjugation pairs are:

Singular object		Plural object	
გადააგდებს	throw sthg.	გადაყრის	throw, scatter things
დასვამს	set, put down sthg.	დასხამს	set things down
დაკლავს	slaughter (e.g., a chicken)	დახოცავს	slaughter (e.g., chickens)
დადებს	put sthg. down	დააწყობს	put things down
გატეხს	break sthg. (e.g., dish)	დაამტვრევს	break (e.g., dishes)

Examples of II. conjugation pairs are:

Singular subject		Plural subject	
ჩა(მო)ვარდება	sthg. falls down	ჩა(მო)ცვივ(დებ)ა	things fall down
დაეცემა თავს	attack	დაესხმება თავს	attack
მოკვდება	s.o. dies	დაიხოცებიან	they die

The II. conjugation forms of I. conjugation verbs show a similar pattern. Note, for example, the II. conjugation forms of დაკლავს, დახოცავს:

დაიკვლება	დაიხოცება
s.o. is killed	some are killed; some die

Many verbs with preverbs other than *da-* can change the preverb to *da-* when an object, direct or indirect, depending on the verb, is plural or collective. Some examples from verbs already introduced are:

შეჭამს	eat sthg. up	დაჭამს	eat things up
გააფრენს	have sthg. fly	დააფრენს	have things fly
გაუგზავნის	send sthg. to s.o.	დაუგზავნის	send sthg. to people (id.o.)
გარეცხავს	wash sthg.	დარეცხავს	wash things
გაათბობს	warm sthg.	დაათბობს	warm things
გამოაცხობს	bake sthg.	დააცხობს	bake things

14.1.4. Conjugation and voice. The vast majority of I. conjugation verbs are transitive, that is, they have direct objects. Nonetheless, there is a small number of I. conjugation verbs which are intransitive, i.e., they occur without a direct object. In some instances such verbs may have an indirect object corresponding to a direct object in other languages. Examples of such verbs include:

დაიგვიანებს	be late
დაახველებს	cough
დააფურთხებს	spit
Ø= ს-ცემს	hit s.o. (id.o.)
დაურეკავს	telephone s.o. (id.o.)
Ø= უყურებს	look at sthg., s.o. (id.o.)
მიაღწევს	reach s.o., sthg. (id.o., H-series)
მიაშურებს	hurry someplace (i.do., H-series)
დახედავს	look at s.o. (id.o., H-series)

Similarly, there are some verbs which always will have an indirect object marker of the third person (*h*-, *s*-, *u*-, *e*-) but which may have no indirect object.

დაუკრავს	play (musical instrument)
გაუშვებს	let sthg. out, release s.o., sthg.
გაემგზავრება	travel (intrans.)
გაემართება	move, make one's way
გაებმება	become entangled (in sthg.)
დაეცემა	fall (down)
დაეხეტება	wander around

14.1.5. II. conjugation verbs with two indirect objects. A limited number of II. conjugation verbs can take two indirect objects. One of these indirect objects generally corresponds to a direct object in English. Such verbs often have only present series forms; when they do have other series, both indirect objects remain in the dative case.[3] Examples:

ეუბნება	tell s.o. sthg.
დაჰპირდება (also შე-)	promise s.o. sthg.
მოუყვება	tell. s.o. sthg.
დაემუქრება	threaten s.o. with sthg.

Examples:

ლევანი ჩემს დას საჩუქარს შეჰპირდა.

Levan promised my sister a gift.

მასწავლებელი ბავშვებს საინტერესო ზღაპარს უყვებოდა.

The teacher was telling the children an interesting fairy tale.

In some instances, the present series forms of II. conjugation verbs can be used with a transitive meaning, taking, at times, an object in the dative. Example: გაზეთები ერთ ამისთანა ამბავს იწერებიან, რომელსაც ადამიანი გვერდს ვერ აუქცევს. 'The newspapers are writing such a story that a man can't avoid it' (lit.: turn one's side away from it).

14.1.6. Note. It is important to keep in mind the fact that irregularities of the types described above are relatively rare in Georgian. Further, in many instances such distinctions as outlined above are no longer observed by many speakers and writers of Georgian and are more typical of an older stage of the language.

14.2. Wordbuilding: Suffixed pronouns and adjectives.

14.2.1. The suffix *-ğac(a)*. The suffix *-ğac(a)* added to pronominal or adverbial forms yields the meaning of a certain specific but unspecified person, place, time, etc., that is usually, though not necessarily, known to the speaker. It often corresponds in meaning to Russian -то as in кто-то, что-то, где-то, как-то, etc. Examples include:

ვიღაც(ა) (ვინღაც) someone (specific)

რაღაც(ა)	something
რატომღაც	for some reason
სადღაც	somewhere
როგორღაც	somehow, in some way

14.2.2. The suffix *-me*. Contrasting with *-ǧac(a)* is the suffix *-me*, which, when added to pronominal forms, gives the meaning of an indefinite, nonspecific, unknown person, place, time, etc. It is close in meaning to Russian -нибудь, as in кто-нибудь, что-нибудь, где-нибудь, как-нибудь, etc. Examples include:

ვინმე	anyone, someone (indefinite)
რამე	anything, something
რომელიმე	any, some
რამდენიმე	some (indefinite quantity)
როდისმე	anytime, at sometime
როგორმე	in some manner (or other)

Compare the following examples, which contrast the suffixes *-ǧac(a)* and *-me*:

ვიღაც მოვიდა.
Someone (a known person) came.

იქნებ ვინმე მოვიდეს.
Perhaps someone (not known who) will come.

რაღაც გაგიყიდე.
I sold something (known, specific) for you.

რამე იყიდე!
Buy something (anything) for yourself!

სადღაც ვნახე.
I saw him somewhere (specific).

ხვალ სადმე წავიდეთ!
Let's go somewhere (not specific) tomorrow.

Note that the suffix *-me* tends to occur most commonly with modal forms of the verb such as imperatives, optatives, conditionals; it is also extremely common in questions and with the future screeve.

Pronouns ending in *-ǧac(a)* in the nominative have the stem *-ǧaca-* in all remaining cases and are declined regularly. Pronouns in *-me* are nontruncating, but otherwise are declined regularly.[4] Examples: N. ვიღაც,

E. ვილაცამ, D. ვილაცას, G. ვილაცის, etc.; N. ვინმე, E. ვინმემ, D. ვინმეს, G. ვინმეს, etc.

14.2.3. The suffix -*ve*. The suffix -*ve* added to pronouns and adverbs generally denotes identity. With the pronoun იგი it has the meaning 'the same'. When modifying a noun it has the N. იგივე and in all other cases the form იმავე (see sec. 5.5.1). Used pronominally the cases other than the nominative have the nontruncating stem *ima-ve-*: E. იმავემ, D. იმავეს, G. იმავეს, etc. Similar to იგივე is N. ესევე, adjectival form ამავე, pronominal stem *ama-ve-* (nontruncating) 'the same' referring to antecedents closer to the speaker.[5] Other forms with the nontruncating stem -*ve* include:

ასეთივე	such an (identical, like this)
ისეთივე	such an (identical, like that)
იქვე	at (that) same place; ibid.
აქვე	at (this) same place
ახლავე	at this moment; right now

With other forms -*ve* can often be translated into English by 'very', that is, დღესვე 'this very day', მისივე სიტყვებით 'in his very own words', წყალშივე 'in the very water', 'in the water itself'. A close equivalent of Georgian -*ve* is the Russian particle же. For the use of -*(i)ve* with numerals, see sec. 10.4.4.

14.2.4. The suffix -*ǧa*. The nontruncating suffix -*ǧa* can be added to interrogative pronouns and adverbs, thereby strengthening or intensifying these interrogatives. Examples: ვი(ნ)ღა? 'who then?' 'who in the world?' რაღა? 'what in the world?' სადღა? 'where the deuce?' როგორღა? 'how in the world?' etc.

LESSON 14: Notes

1. The corresponding I. conj. form, e.g., შეაბრძანებს functions as a respectful or polite replacement for verbs in *-qvan-s*, e.g., pres. შემყავს, fut. შეიყვანს 'lead, bring in'.

2. The form გახლავთ 'he is' shows respect to the person spoken *to* (2d person) while ბრძანდება 'he is' is used to show respect to the person spoken *about* (3d person).

From the same root are the verbs ახლავს 'is, there is' (only third person) and the IV. conj. verb (with H-series markers) მახლავს (m-a-*xl*-av-s), 3sg. ახლავს 'have sthg.'. An example of the latter is: ამ ახალი გაზეთის პირველ ნომერს ბევრი ბეჭდვითი შეცდომა ახლავს. 'The first issue of this new newspaper has many typographical (= printing) errors.'

3. This is the normative rule. There is also a tendency to use the nominative case for what corresponds in other languages to the direct object when the verb is in the aorist or perfect series.

4. Older forms of declension are also found in which the case endings are added before these suffixes; e.g., D. ვისმე, რასმე; G. ვისიმე, რისამე, etc. Similar patterns are found with the suffixes *-ve* and *-ǯa* (see below, secs. 14.2.3 and 14.2.4).

5. There is a third form, ეგევე, adjectival form მაგავე; see Lesson 5, note 7.

LESSON 14: Exercises

Note: Due to the length and difficulty of the reading passages in this and the following lesson, the exercises in this lesson are restricted in number and cover chiefly the suffixed pronouns and adjectives and polite replacement for 'be'. (Lesson 15 has no exercises.) The grammatical material in this lesson and the following one are primarily for reference, although examples of some of the material will be found in the reading passages.

1. რაშია საქმე? --მკითხა ვიღაცამ.
2. მე რაღაც ვიცი იმის შესახებ.
3. როდისმე გიცხოვრიათ სოფელში?
4. ხადმე ქალაქში ვისადილებთ.
5. ჩემი ქმარი სადღაც წავიდა, მაგრამ სწორად არ ვიცი—სად.
6. შენ რაღაცით უკმაყოფილო ხარ?
7. ვინმე გაგზავნე ექიმთან!
8. დავუძახოთ ვისმე; ვინმე აუცილებლად დაგვეხმარება.
9. ასეთი რამ გაგიგონია?
10. როცა იმ მაღაზიაში იქნები, შენს ცოლს რამე უყიდე!
11. ვიღაც კაცმა გიკითხათ და რაღაც წიგნი დაგიტოვათ.
12. აქ რაღაცა აკლია.
13. ძაღლებს რამე აჭამეთ!
14. ის ეძებს რაიმე სამუშაოს.
15. თქვენ ვიღა ხართ? მე, თქვენი ჭირიმე, ლადო პაპაშვილი გახლავართ.
16. ეს დრო გახლავთ ზაფხული.
17. ეს ამბავი ვიღამ გითხრა?
18. არ ვიცი, სადღა წავიდეთ.
19. ჩვენ ერთსა და იმავე სახლში ვცხოვრობთ. აკაკიც იქვე ცხოვრობს.
20. მე იმავე პიესას ვკითხულობ, რასაც ზურაბი გუშინ კითხულობდა.
21. შოთა რუსთაველს ისეთივე მნიშვნელობა აქვს

საქართველოსათვის, როგორც შექსპირს ინგლისისათვის.

22. დღეს ისევე მხურს თბილისში ყოფნა, როგორც გუშინ.

23. ვინ ბრძანდებით? --ვერ მიცანით? თქვენი მეზობელი გახლავართ.

24. სად ბრძანდებოდით აქამდის? --სოფელში გახლდით დედის ავადმყოფობის გამო.

25. მწყემსი ჯერ კიდევ ერთსა და იმავე ადგილას დგას.

"Yard Keeper"
Artist: N. Pirosmanašvili

„მეეზოვე"
ნ. ფიროსმანაშვილი

Vocabulary

ადგილას = ადგილზე	in a/the place
ავადმყოფობა	illness; disease
ერთი და იგივე	one and the same; as adj. dat. = ერთსა და იმავე, etc.; as pronoun dat. = ერთსა და იმასვე, etc.
ვინმე	someone; anyone
ვიღა	who (in the world)?
ვიღაც(ა)	someone (pronoun); some [person] (adjective)
იგივე	(the) same (for declension, sec. 14.1.2)
ინგლისი	England
ისევე	just as; just so
ისეთი	such (a)
ისეთივე	just the same; just such a
იქვე	there (in the same place); ibid.
მნიშვნელობა	importance; significance
რაიმე (nontrunc.)	= რამე
რამე, რამ	thing; something; some (kind of)
რაღაც(ა)	something (pronoun); some [thing] (adjective)
როდისმე	at some/any time
სადმე	someplace; somewhere; anyplace; anywhere
სადღა	where (in the world)?
სადღაც(ა)	somewhere; someplace
სამუშაო	job; work
შენი (თქვენი) ჭირიმე	my good friend (affectionate form of address; literally: [may] your misfortune [come] to me).

ბრძანდები(თ)	*brjan*-d-eb-i(-t)	see sec. 14.1.1.2
გაიგონებს	ga=i-*gon*-eb-s (perfect = გაუგონია)	hear

იკითხავს, pres. კითხულობს	i-*ḳitx*-av-s	ask for s.o.; ask to see s.o.
სადილობს	*sadil*-ob-s	dine; have dinner
დატოვებს	da=*ṭov*-eb-s	leave sthg. (behind)
უძახის, fut. დაუძახებს	u-*jax*-i-s, fut. da+u-*jax*-eb-s	call s.o. (id.o.)
გახლავს	g-a-*xl*-av-s or g-*axl*-av-s	see sec. 14.1.1.2

Giorgi Saakaje
Artist: N. Pirosmanašvili

„გიორგი სააკაძე"
ნ. ფიროსმანაშვილი

Key to the Exercises

1. "What is the matter?" (lit.: in what is the matter) someone asked me.
2. I know something about that.
3. Have you ever (= at any time) lived in the country?
4. We shall have dinner (dine) someplace in the city.
5. My husband went somewhere, but I don't precisely know where.
6. Are you dissatisfied with something?
7. Send someone to the doctor's!
8. Let's call someone; someone certainly will help us.
9. Have you heard such a thing?
10. When you will be in that store, buy something for your wife.
11. Some man asked for you and left you some book.
12. Something is lacking here.
13. Feed the dogs something.
14. He is looking for some (kind of) work.
15. Who in the world are you? I, my dear friend, am (polite) Lado P̣ap̣ašvili.
16. This season (= time) is (polite) summer.
17. Who in the world told you this news?
18. I don't know where in the world we are to go.
19. We live in one and the same house. Aḳaḳi also lives there (i.e., in the same place).
20. I am reading the same play that [= what] Zurab was reading yesterday.
21. Šota Rustaveli has just the same significance for Georgia as Shakespeare for England.
22. Today I wish to be (use VN) in Tbilisi just as (much) as yesterday.
23. Who are you (polite)? Couldn't you recognize me? I am your neighbor (polite).
24. Where were you (polite) up to now (= up to here)? I was (polite) in the country because of my mother's illness.
25. The shepherd is still standing in one and the same place.

Reading Passage მზიანი ღამე

დაბადების დღე

1 ასმეშვიდე აუდიტორიაში ქრისტეს ტირილი იდგა. პოლიტეკონომიას თვითონ პატივცემული პროფესორი, კასიანე გოგიჩაიშვილი იბარებდა. ეს ამბავი მოულოდნელი არ იყო ჩვენთვის და არც ერთ ჩვენთაგანს ამის დარდი არ ჰქონია, მაგრამ როდესაც აუდიტორიიდან ლოყებდახოკილი ლუბა ნოდია გამოვიდა და გვითხრა, ყველაფერი ეყურებაო, გავშრით. ვინ იფიქრებდა, რომ ამ სათნოებით სავსე, ყრუ კაცს, რომლისთვისაც გამოცდაზე მერკანტილიზმის ნაცვლად იონჯის ფესვთა სისტემა რომ მოგეყოლა, მაინც ხუთიანს წერდა, სწორედ წელს, საგაზაფხულო სესიებზე, დაუბრუნდებოდა სმენა. ამ ამბის შემდეგ პირადად ჩემთვის გამოცდა დამთავრებული იყო, მაგრამ ცნობისმოყვარეობამ წამძლია და ლუბას მივვარდი, რომელიც გადამწიფებული ნესვივით გაყვითლებული იყო და მატრიკულში ჩაწერილ ორიანს დაშტერებოდა.

2 — რაო, გოგო? — ვკითხე ლუბას და სახელო მოვქაჩე.

— რა ვუყო ახლა ამას? — თქვა ლუბამ და უაზრო თვალები მომაშტერა.

— კი მაგრამ, არ იცოდა მაგ ოჯახდანგრეულმა, მატრიკულში ორი რომ არ იწერება? — ჰკითხა გურამმა.

— ვუთხარი და ასე მიპასუხა, აბა, რა ვიცი, გოგონი, ჩემს სიცოცხლეში პირველად ვწერ ორიანსო, რა ვქნა ახლა მე? — ისევ იკითხა ლუბამ და თვალები ცრემლით აევსო.

— მაინც რა შეგხვდა? — ჰკითხა გურამმა.

— პირველი, საქონლის წრებრუნვა. მეორე, ფულის ინფლაცია, მესამე, აღარ მახსოვს...

— ვერაფერი ვერ უპასუხე?

— დავიწყე!

— რა?

3 — როგორც შარშან, ამ ზაფხულს სოფელში ვიყავი, ბებიას ვეხმარებოდი ბოსტნის დამუშავებაში-მეთქი, ბებიაჩემი ძალიან კეთილი ქალია-მეთქი... ჰოდა, ბებიაშენი დაგიწერს ნიშანსო, ასე მითხრა. — დაამთავრა ლუბამ და მატრიკულზე დაემხო.

4 აუდიტორიის კარი გაიღო და ჩვენი ჯგუფის მამასახლისმა სია წაიკითხა:

— ბარამიძე, ჰიჰინაძე, შემოდით!

— ბ-ს მერე ჰ-ა, დეგენერატო? — ჰკითხა გურამმა.

5 — ერთი ქვევიდან, ერთი ზევიდანო! — განმარტა ეფრემმა და გადმოცვენილი თვალებით აუდიტორიისაკენ მიგვითითა, ვითომდა ჩემი რა ბრალია, პროფესორმა ასე თქვაო. მე არ ვიცი, რა ჰქვია ისეთ ავადმყოფობას, როდესაც გული ყელში ამოვარდება, ენა მუცელში ჩავარდება, შუბლზე ცივი ოფლი დაგასხამს, მუხლები მოგეკვეთება, ხელები აგიკანკალდება და თვალები დაგიბნელდება, მაგრამ როდესაც გადავხედე გურამს, რომელიც ვეებერთელა ცხვირსახოცით შუბლსა და ხელებს იმშრალებდა და გამხმარ ტუჩებს ილოკავდა, მივხვდი, რომ ეს ავადმყოფობა გადამდები იყო.

6 აუდიტორიაში ფეხაკრეფით შევედით. პროფესორი მწვანე მაუდგადაფარებულ მაგიდას უჯდა და იღიმებოდა. მას ოქროსვარაყიანი, სქელშუშიანი სათვალე ეკეთა, რომლის ორთავე ყურში შეკვეხებული ბოლოები ჩვენს დამღუპველ ორ პატარა მემბრანას უერთდებოდა.

7 — დაბრძანდით! — მიგვიპატიჟა მან. ჩვენ ადგილიდან არ დავძრულვართ.

— თქვენ ყურს ხომ არ გაკლიათ?.. მობრძანდით და დაბრძანდით! — ისევ მიგვიწვია პროფესორმა, მაგიდას მივუსხედით, რომელზეც სასიკვდილო განაჩენივით ეყარა ხელისგულის სიფართე თეთრი, ჯერ თითქმის უხმარი საგამოცდო ბილეთები.

— აიღეთ ბილეთები და მოიფიქრეთ! — გვთხოვა პროფესორმა.

8 მე ავიღე ბილეთი და ვიდრე გადმოვაბრუნებდი, უკვე ვიცოდი, რომ ეს იყო ის ბილეთი, რომელზე ფიქრიც სიკვდილამდე არ მომბეზრდებოდა. გურამმაც აიღო ბილეთი, დახედა და შავნაბადაზე შესაწირავად აყვანილი მოზვერივით მომაპყრო სევდიანი თვალები.

9 — თქვენი სახელი და გვარი? — მკითხა პროფესორმა.

— ბარამიძე თეიმურაზი. — ვუპასუხე პირველ კითხვაზე. პროფესორმა პასუხი უბის წიგნაკში ჩაიწერა.

— თქვენი? — მიუბრუნდა ახლა გურამს.

10 — ჭიჭინაძე გურამი. — ასევე ყოჩაღად უპასუხა გურამმა. პროფესორმა ისიც ჩაიწერა. მე და გურამი, როგორც ეს გამოცდაზეა მიღებული, ერთმანეთისაგან მოშორებით დავჯექით. მე საოცარი გულგრილობით დავიწყე ბილეთის კითხვა. პირველი კითხვა იყო — მიწის რენტა.

— ხომ არ დაიწყებთ? — მკითხა უცებ პროფესორმა.

— რატომაც არა! — ვუპასუხე მე, გურამმა გაკვირვებისაგან პირი დააღო.

— აბა, დაიწყეთ! — გაუხარდა პროფესორს.

11 — მიწის რენტა. მიწა კაპიტალისტურ ქვეყნებში იყიდება. საერთოდ, იქ ყველაფერი იყიდება, სინდისიც კი, სინდისი, რა თქმა უნდა, იაფად. რენტა არის მიწის გადასახადი. კაპიტალისტურ ქვეყნებში გადასახადები ძალიან მაღალია, გლეხები გმინავენ სამხედრო გადასახადების გამო, რადგან კაპიტალისტები იარაღს აჟღარუნებენ. შეიარაღებას დიდი ხარჯი უნდა... დიდ ხარჯს — ბევრი ფული, ბევრ ფულს შოვნა უნდა, საიდან? გვეკითხება მოვლენათა ლოგიკა, რა თქმა უნდა, გადასახადებისგან.

12 — რა გქვიათ თქვენ, ახალგაზრდავ? — შემაწყვეტინა პროფესორმა.

— თემო, ბატონო!

— ჩემს ლექციებს თუ ესწრებოდით?

— როგორ გეკადრებათ, პატივცემულო! — მეწყინა მე.

— რატომღაც არ მახსოვხართ, თქვენ კი, საერთოდ, არ გიცნობთ! — მიუბრუნდა იგი გურამს.

13 — ჩვენ გიცნობთ შესანიშნავად, პატივცემულო ლექტორო, თქვენ კასიანე გოგიჩაიშვილი ბრძანდებით, ყველასათვის საყვარელი პროფესორი... თქვენ ჩვენი სიამაყე ხართ, თქვენს ლექციას ვინ გააცდენს, თქვენს ლექციებს კი არ ვიწერთ, ვყლაპავთ! — ჩავარდა ექსტაზში გურამი.

14 — აბა, ერთი მომიყევით, რას ყლაპავთ? — შეაჩერა პროფესორმა. გურამი ჯერ გაქვავდა, მერე წყლიდან ამოსული ძაღლივით თავი გაიბერტყა და მე შემხედა. მე ენაზე ვიკბინე, რომ არ გამცინებოდა. ახლა პროფესორს შეხედა გურამმა.

— აბა, — შეახსენა პროფესორმა.

— ბარამიძის გამოკითხვა დაამთავრეთ, პატივცემულო? — დაინაზა ხმა გურამმა და სათნოებით სავსე ღიმილი მაჩუქა.

15 — ბარამიძე მეორე კითხვას მოიფიქრებს! — უპასუხა პროფესორმა. გურამმა კიდევ ერთხელ დახედა ბილეთს, მერე თვალები ამოატრიალა და სადღაც, შუბლზემოთ, შიგ ტვინში დაიწყო რაღაცის კითხვა. მერე, ეტყობა, ვერაფერი ამოიკითხა და ნორმალურ მდგომარეობას დაუბრუნდა.

16 — შეიძლება, ბატონო, ბილეთი გამოვცვალო? — ჰკითხა უცებ პროფესორს.

— შეიძლება! — უპასუხა პროფესორმა და ამოიოხრა. გურამის აკანკალებული ხელი ბილეთებზე დაცურდა, მერე უცებ ერთ-ერთს დააცივდა და ასე დარჩა დიდხანს.

17 — ჰიჰინაძე, თქვენს გარდა კიდევ მყავს გამოსაცდელი

ხალხი! — შეახსენა პროფესორმა. ხელი მექანიკურად ამოძრავდა, მას თან აჰყვა ბილეთი და გურამის თვალებთან გაშეშდა. გურამი ტუჩებს აცმაცუნებდა, ეტყობოდა, საკითხებს იმეორებდა.

— აბა, რას იტყვით? — თქვა პროფესორმა და თითები ნერვიულად დააკაკუნა მაგიდაზე.

— რამდენი ბილეთის გამოცვლის უფლება მაქვს, პატივცემულო? — შეეკითხა გურამი გაბზარული ხმით.

— მომეცით თქვენი მატრიკული! — გაუშვირა ხელი პროფესორმა. გურამი მოტყდა.

18 -- არ დამღუპოთ, ბატონო, სტიპენდია დამეკარგება!

-- თქვენი სტიპენდია კი არა, ოცი წლის უნახავი მეგობარი დავკარგე, მაგრამ საფლავში არ ჩავყოლივარ!

— მაგი ისედაც დაკარგული გყოლიათ. რა მოუვიდა უბედურს? — აუჩუყდა გული გურამს.

— ჭიჭინაძე, მომეცით თქვენი მატრიკული! — გაუმეორა თხოვნა პროფესორმა.

მიშველეო, გადმომხედა გურამმა.

19 — პატივცემულო პროფესორო, დიდი უსამართლობა იქნება ახლა თქვენ რომ მაგას ორი დაუწეროთ, მთელი ღამე ერთად ვსწავლობდით! — შევაწიე სიტყვა გურამს.

— ყმაწვილო, მთელი ღამე კი არა, ხუთი წელი ვსწავლობდი ჩემბერლენთან ერთად ოქსფორდის უნივერსიტეტში, მერე ის კაცი ინგლისის პრემიერ-მინისტრი გახდა, მე კი თქვენისთანა იდიოტებს ვასწავლი თბილისში, გასაგებია? — მკითხა პროფესორმა. ყველაფერი მზესავით ნათელი იყო, მაგრამ გურამს არ უნდოდა უკან დახევა.

20 — პატივცემულო პროფესორო, წარმოიდგინეთ, რომ თქვენ ხართ მილიონერი, — დაიწყო მან. — ხართ მილიონერი და გაქვთ რამდენიმე მილიონი სამიანი, მოვიდა თქვენთან მათხოვარი და გეუბნებათ — პატივცემულო მილიონერო, გაიღეთ მოწყალება, მომეცით ერთი სამიანი თუ შეიძლება, — ახლა წარმოიდგინეთ, რომ ის მათხოვარი მე ვარ და გთხოვთ...

მე ვეღარ გავუძელი მილიონერისა და ღვთის გლახის ამ დიალოგს და პირზე ხელაფარებული გამოვვარდი გარეთ. დერეფანში არავინ არ შემომგებებია და არ უკითხავს, რა მიიღეო.

Note: In the section above, from ნოდარ დუმბაძე's novel მზიანი ღამე (first appearing in the Tbilisi journal მნათობი 'Star', 'Constellation' in 1966), a group of students at Tbilisi University are taking their (oral) examination in political economy, a course which used to be considered a "snap" since the deaf professor was unable to hear the students' answers. As a consequence the students would answer his questions with any totally irrelevant thought that entered their minds. But, this year, disaster strikes: Professor Ḳasiane Gogičaišvili has a brand-new hearing aid!

Dumbaje, who is from Guria in West Georgia, often uses West Georgian features in his writing, especially in dialogues. A few of these are pointed out in the vocabularies

N.B. It is extremely important to be aware of instances of indirect speech, usually marked by *-o* (see sec. 8.5).

VOCABULARY

1 •

ქრისტეს ტირილი — loud wailing (lit., Christ's crying)
იდგა — here: was
პატივცემული — respected; honored •[see note]
ჩაიბარებს (გამოცდას) • — administer (an exam); here: political economy (examination) is the d.o.
დარდი — care, concern; **ამის დარდი** concern about this
ლოყა — cheek
დაიხოკავს — scratch
ლუბა ნოდია — (woman's name)
მოესმება — hear; be able to hear (see sec. 12.1.2.4)
გაშრება — dry (up) (intrans.); here: freeze in terror
ფიქრობს — think
სათნოება — virtue; charity; kindness
სავსე — full (+ instr.)
ყრუ — deaf
ნაცვლად — instead of (pp.)
იონჯა — clover
ფესვი — root
მოაყოლებს — tell s.o. sthg. (about)
ხუთიანი — 5 (= university grade, U.S. "A")
წელს • — = ამ წელს
სმენა — hearing
პირადად — personally
ცნობისმოყვარეობა — curiosity
წა=ს-ძლევს — sthg. overcomes s.o.
მივარდება — run to (H-series id.o. marker) (subject only singular; sec. 14.1.3); with plural subject, the form მი+ს-ცვივ(დებ)იან is used)
გადამწიფებული — overripe

ნესვი	melon
ყვითელი	yellow (E)
მატრიკული	"grade book," booklet in which course grades are written
ჩაწერს	inscribe; enter
ორიანი	2 (= university grade, U.S. "D")
დააშტერდება	stare at sthg. (H-series id.o.) (here: pluperf.)
2	
რაო	i.e., "What [did the professor] say?" See sec. 8.5.
გოგო	girl
სახელო	sleeve
მოქაჩავს	tug
რა ვუყო ამას?	[what am I to do (opt.) with/about this]
უაზრო	stunned (**აზრი** idea, opinion)
თვალი	eye
მი=/მო=აშტერებს თვალებს	stare at s.o. (H-series id.o.)
მაგ (Nom. = ეგ)	this; that (cf. ეს:ამ, ის:იმ [West Georgian])
ოჯახდანგრეული	good-for-nothing (derogatory)
ორი (= ორიანი)	(grade, = U.S. "D") •[note]
აბა	well (interjection)
გოგონი	irr. vocative of გოგონა
სიცოცხლე	life
ვქნა •	[opt. of შვრება, fut. იზამს do; make; see sec. 15.1.1]
ცრემლი	tear(s)
აავსებს	fill sthg.
რა შეგხვდა?	what happened to you? what did you encounter? here in sense of: "What question did

	you get?"
საქონელი	goods; merchandise; commodities (E)
წრებრუნვა	circulation; distribution
3	
ბოსტანი	vegetable garden (A)
დაამუშავებს	cultivate
-მეთქი	see sec. 8.5.
კეთილი	nice; kind
ჰოდა	well (interjection used to continue an interrupted conversation)
ნიშანი	here: (passing) grade (A)
ნიშანს დაუწერს	give s.o. a grade
დაემხობა	(one's head) falls down (no id.o.)
4	
ჯგუფი	group
მამასახლისი	monitor; proctor
ბ-ს = ბანს	(name of the letter ბ)
მერე	here: after (pp.)
ჭ-ა = ჭარია	(name of the letter ჭ + *-a*)
დეგენერატი	degenerate; idiot
5	
ქვევიდან ●	from the bottom
ეფრემი	(m. pr. n.)
გადმოცვენილი	downcast
მიუთითებს	show s.o. sthg.; point sthg. out to s.o.
ვითომდა	as if (to say)
ბრალი	guilt; fault
ჩემი რა ბრალია?	how is it my fault?
ისეთი	such (a)
ავადმყოფობა	disease; illness
ამოვარდება	spring up (subj. sing.)
ენა	here: tongue
მუცელი	belly; stomach (E)

ჩავარდება	fall down (subject sing.)
შუბლი	forehead
ოფლი •	sweat
მოეკვეთება მუხლი	o's knees buckle
კანკალებს	shake; quiver
გადახედავს	glance at; look over at (no d.o.; H-series id.o. marker)
ვეებერთელა	colossal; immense
ცხვირსახოცი	handkerchief
მშრალი	dry
გაახმობს	dry sthg. out (see sec. 11.1)
ტუჩი	lip
Ø=ლოკავს	lick
მი=ხვდება	recognize; notice; guess (mi=*xvd*-eb-a)
გადამდები	contagious

6

ფეხაკრეფით	on tiptoe
მაუდი	cloth
გადააფარებს	cover
გაიღიმება	smile

NB.: What follows is a description of a hearing aid built into Prof. Gogičaišvili's eyeglasses.

ვარაყიანი	gilt
სქელი	here: thick
შუშა	glass; here: lens
ეკეთება •	s.o. (dat.) is wearing (pass. of state)
ორთავე = ორივე	both
ყური	ear
შეაკვეხებს	stick sthg. in
დაღუპავს	destroy
ჩვენს დამღუპველ •	here: which would destroy us

7

დაბრძანდით	see sec. 14.1.1.1
მიიპატიჟებს	invite s.o. (d.o.) in

დაძრავს ●	move sthg.
მობრძანდით	see sec. 14.1.1.1
ისევ	again
მიიწვევს	invite s.o. (d.o.) in
განაჩენი	verdict; sentence (in court of law)
-ვით ●	like (pp. with nom. here)
ხელისგული	palm
სიფართე = სიფართოვე	(cf. ფართო 'broad', 'wide') breadth; width; here, declined as an adj. modifying ბილეთები
ჯერ	still
უხმარი	unused
ბილეთი	ticket; here: examination question
აიღებს	take
მოიფიქრებს	consider; think over (o's answer)
Ø=ს-თხოვს	ask s.o. for sthg.
8	
ვიდრე	here: before
გადმოაბრუნებს	turn sthg. over
ფიქრი	thought; thinking
მობეზრდება	s.o. (H-series id.o.) tires of sthg., loses patience with
დახედავს	look at sthg. (id.o., H-series; no d.o., see sec. 14.1.4)
შავნაბადა	mountain near Tbilisi with a church where people used to bring animals for sacrifice
შესაწირავი	sacrifice
მოზვერი	young bull
მიაპყრობს თვალს	direct a glance at/on s.o./sthg.
სევდიანი	worried
თვალი	eye (here = glance)
9	
გვარი	last name (When the family name

	precedes the given name both are declined.)
უბის წიგნაკი	notebook
ჩაწერს	write down; note
10	
ასევე	just as; equally; see sec. 14.2.3
ყოჩაღი	brave
ისიც	it, too (= ის 'he', 'she', 'it' + -ც 'also')
მიღებული	accepted; here: as was the custom
მოშორებით	at a distance (apart)
დავჯექით	according to the literary norm, the form დავსხედით should be used here; sec. 9.1.2, 14.1.6
გულგრილობა	indifference
მიწა	earth; land
რენტა	rent
რატომაც არა!	yes!, of course (lit., why not)
გაკვირვება	astonishment
დაალებს	here: = აალებს
გაუხარდება	s.o. becomes happy (here: with Teimuraz's answer) (see sec. 12.1.2.4)
11	
გაიყიდება	(II. conj. form of გაყიდის)
საერთოდ	in general
სინდისი	conscience
-ც კი	even
რა თქმა უნდა	it goes without saying; of course
გმინავს	moan
სამხედრო	military
რადგან	= რადგანაც
იარაღი	arms; weapon(s)
Ø=აჟღარუნებს	rattle (cf. English saber-rattling)
შე=ა-იარაღ-ებს	arm sthg.
უნდა	sthg. (dat.) requires sthg. (nom.)

	(with verbal nouns)
ხარჯი	expense; expenditure
დიდ ხარჯს — ბევრი ფული	i.e., great expenditure [requires] much money
ეკითხება	pres. of ჰკითხავს ask s.o. sthg.
შოვნა	finding; effort to find, to be found, acquire, get
მოვლენა	phenomenon; event
12	
შეაწყვეტინებს	interrupt
თემო	diminutive of თეიმურაზი
თუ	here: marks a question
დაესწრება	(aor. -(ვ)ესწარი, -სწრო) be present at, attend sthg. (id.o.)
ეკადრება	(only pres. series; see sec. 12.1.2.4) be proper, suitable; here: how could you think such a thing?
რატომღაც	for some reason
13	
შესანიშნავად	here: remarkably well
ლექტორი	lecturer, i.e., professor
ბრძანდებით	see sec. 14.1.1
ამაყი	proud
გააცდენს	cut (class); play hookey (E → I)
გადაყლაპავს	swallow
ჩავარდება	fall (subj. sing.; see sec. 14.1.3)
14	
ერთი ●	(with imperative:) just
მოუყვები	(aor. -(ვ)უყევი, -უყვა; perf. მოჰყოლია) tell s.o.

	sthg.
ჯერ	here: first
ქვა	stone
გააქვავებს	petrify
მერე	then
გაბერტყავს	shake
შეხედავს	look at s.o. (H-series, no d.o.)
Ø=იკბენს ენაზე	bite o's tongue
გაეცინება	be overcome with laughter (see sec. 12.1.2.4)
შეახსენებს	remind s.o. (H-series) of sthg.
გამოკითხვა	questioning; examination
დაინაზებს ხმას	lower o's voice, make o's voice soft, tender
სათნოებით სავსე	full of virtue
ღიმილი	smile
Ø=აჩუქებს	give s.o. a gift of; favor s.o. with sthg.

15

მოიფიქრებს	consider; think over
კიდევ ერთხელ	once more, once again
დახედავს	look at (H-series, no d.o.)
ამოატრიალებს	turn up
შუბლი	forehead
-ზემოთ	above (pp. with dat.; cf. *-ze*)
შიგ	inside
ტვინი	brain
ეტყობა	apparently; it seems
ამოიკითხავს	read; decipher

16

გამოცვლის	exchange (i.e., Guram wants to try a different question)
ამოიოხრებს	begin to sigh, groan (III. conj.)
აკანკალებული	shaking

დაცურდება	slip down
დააცივდება	freeze on sthg.
17 ●	
შეახსენებს	remind s.o. (*H*-series) of sthg.
ა=ა-მოძრავებს	move sthg.
აჰყვება თან	follow s.o./sthg.; here: stick to (i.e., an exam question became attached to his hand)
გააშეშებს	stiffen; freeze
ტუჩი	lip
ტუჩები ცმაცუნობს ●	(o's) lips move slightly
ნერვიულად	nervously
დააკაკუნებს	rap; tap
უფლება	right; power
შეეკითხება	ask s.o. (a question)
გაბზარული	cracked
ხმა	voice
ხელს გაიშვერს	stretch out o's hand (E → I)
მოტყდება	break; here: grow weak (II. conj. form of მოტეხს 'break sthg.')
18	
დალუპავს	ruin; destroy (note: არ + opt. expresses a negative command more as a request)
სტიპენდია	fellowship; scholarship
დაეკარგება	see sec. 12.1.2.4 ●[note]
სტიპენდია კი არა	here: don't talk to me about your fellowship
ოცი წლის უნახავი მეგობარი	a friend I hadn't seen for twenty years
საფლავი	grave
ჩაჰყვება	(aor. -ჰყევი, -ჰყვა, perf. -ჰყოლია) follow s.o. down (here in sense: it didn't kill me) (note that the ex-

	pected *h*- is absent)
მაგი	that one (i.e., the professor's dead friend)
ისედაც	in any case; anyhow
მოხდის	happen to s.o.; fut. მოუვა, aor. მოუვიდა (conjugated as a relative form of მოხვლა)
უბედური	unfortunate; ill-fated
აუჩუყებს გულს	touch s.o.'s (dat.) heart
თხოვნა	request
შველის	help s.o. (dat., H-series) (fut. უშველის)
გადმოხედავს	look over at s.o. (dat.) (no d.o.)
19	
უსამართლობა	injustice
მაგას	that one (i.e., Guram) (dat. of ეგ)
ერთად	together
შეაწევს სიტყვას	put in a good word for s.o. (H-series)
ყმაწვილი	young man; child
კი არა	not...but; i.e., not a whole night but...
ჩემბერლენი	Chamberlain (Neville)
თქვენისთანა	such as you
გასაგები	here: clear
ნათელი	clear; bright (E)
უკან დაიხევს	retreat
20	
წარმოიდგენს	imagine (E → I)
სამიანი	"C" (grade) (= "3")
მათხოვარი	beggar (A)
გაიღებს	give (usually money); grant
მოწყალება	charity; mercy
გაუძლებს	here: stand, bear sthg. (aor. -უძელი, -უძლო) (no d.o.)

ღვთის გლახა — awkward person; rogue; rascal; here: indigent person; beggar
პირზე ხელაფარებული — covering (one's) face with (one's) hands
გა(მო)ვარდება — rush out (subj. sing., sec. 14.1.3)
დერეფანი — corridor (A)
შეეგებება — meet s.o.
არ უკითხავს — (= არავის არ უკითხავს, perfect)
რა — i.e., what grade?

•ADDENDA TO VOCABULARY

TITLE
დაბადება: birth

1.
ასმეშვიდე : (No.) 107
პატივცემული: polite term of address to a professor, teacher
მოულოდნელი: unexpected
სესია: exam period (2-3 week period of examinations (administered orally)

2.
ორი, ორიანი: [Any grade below 4 results in a student losing his stipend]
ისევ: again

4.
ზევიდან: from the top

5.
და=ასხამს ოფლი: s.o. (id.o.) becomes drenched in sweat (no d.o.)

6.
რომლის: the head of this phrase is ბოლოები
მემბრანა: membrane
შე=უერთდება: sthg. becomes connected to sthg.

7.
მაკლია ყური: lit. 'I lack ear,' i.e., I am deaf:
აყრია: sup. passiv of state from აყრის.

14.
რას: here: why?

17.
თქვენს გარდა: In the 1st and 2nd person, postpositions take the possessive adjective rather than the personal pronoun. With pronouns გარდა takes the dative.
კიდევ: still
ეტყობა: it seems; apparently (verb)

18.
და=ეკარგება: s.o., sthg. is lost to s.o. (here: dies); cf. და=კარგავს lose

LESSON 15

15.1. Formal peculiarities. Unlike the peculiarities discussed in Lesson 14, these peculiarities are not so much connected with the meaning of the verbs as with their forms.

15.1.1. Suppletion. Verbs which form different series with different stems are said to have *suppletion*. In some such verbs, the present stem differs from the stem used in all remaining series, for example, present series ხედავს, fut. ნახავს, aor. ნახა, perfect უნახავს 'see'. With other verbs, the present, future, and aorist series may each have a different stem, for example, pres. ამბობს, fut. იტყვის, aor. თქვა 'say'. Most of the common verbs with suppletion have already been presented. Two highly suppletive verbs should be noted:

Verbal noun: ქ(მ)ნა[1] 'do, make'

Pres. შვრება (root II. conj.)

Fut. იზამს (I. conj.)

Aor. (ვ)ქენი(თ), ქნა (I. conj.)

Perf. უქნია (I. conj.)

The verb დადის meaning 'go' (in no particular direction, to and fro), 'wander around', 'go (regularly)'[2] is conjugated in the present series like other forms of the verb სვლა (sec. 4.5). The remaining series, however, are formed from different stems:

Verbal noun: სიარული

Pres. დადის

Fut. ივლის

Aor. (ვ)იარე(თ), იარა

Perf. უვლია

Pluperf. ევლო

In terms of the grammatical case of the subject, this verb behaves as a III. conjugation verb, with the subject in the nominative in the present and future series, in the ergative in the aorist series, and in the dative in the perfect series. Note the contrast between მიდის and დადის:

მოწაფე სკოლაში მიდის.

The pupil is going to the school.

მოწაფე სკოლაში დადის.

The pupil goes to school.

15.1.2. Changes in the preradical vowel. The following verbs have no preradical vowel in the present series and have the preradical vowel *a-* in the future and aorist series:

Pres.	Fut.	
ვნებს (H-series id.o.)	ავნებს	harm s.o.
რგებს (H-series id.o.)	არგებს	use sthg./s.o.
ს-წყენს	აწყენს (E → I)	sthg. harms s.o.
ს-ჯობნის	აჯობებს	surpass

The following verbs have no preradical vowel in the present series and have the preradical vowel *i-* in the future and aorist series:

გრძნობს	იგრძნობს[3]	feel, sense sthg.
ცნობს[4]	იცნობს	recognize

A few verbs have *H*-series id.o. markers in the present series and *u*-series markers in the future and aorist series:

მ-კბენს	უკბენს (E → I)	bite sthg.
მ-პწკენს	უპწკენს (E → I)	pinch
რქენს	ურქენს (E → I)	gore

15.1.3. Verbs conjugated with forms of არის/ყოფნა 'be'. A small number of III. conjugation and irregular verbs form the present tense (screeve) with the present tense of the verb 'be' as auxiliary: 1. *-var(t)*, 2. *-xar(t)*, 3sg. *-s*, 3pl. *-(n)an*. Some of these verbs have already been presented: სვლა 'go', 'come', etc. (sec. 4.5), დგას 'be standing', ზის, სხედან 'be sitting', წევს 'be lying' (all sec. 9.1.3); დარბის 'run' (Lesson 8, note 3), ჩანს 'appear', 'seem' (Lesson 10, vocabulary). Other verbs following this pattern are:

1.	2.	3sg.	3pl.
მოვქრივარ(თ) come fast	მოქრიხარ(თ)	მოქრის	მოქრიან
ვჰგავვარ(თ) resemble s.o.	ჰგავხარ(თ)	ჰგავს	ჰგვანან[5]

ვდუმვარ(თ)	დუმხარ(თ)	დუმს	დუმან
be silent			
ვწუხვარ(თ)	წუხხარ(თ)	წუხს	წუხან
be troubled, bothered			
ვუდრივარ(თ)	უდრიხარ(თ)	უდრის	უდრიან
be similar to, equal			

ქრის and წუხს have other series based on the future screeve forms იქროლებს and იწუხებს respectively. One verb following this pattern has the 3sg. ending *-a* and occurs only in negative sentences:

არ ვვარგი-ვარ(თ)	არ ვარგი-ხარ(თ)	არ ვარგა	არ ვარგან
not be worth			

The future is based on the form ივარგებს.

15.1.3.1. A limited number of verbs (traditionally viewed as III. conj.) have the ending *-a* in the 3sg. present screeve (instead of *-s*). These are:

თბილა	it is warm
გრილა	it is cool
ცხელა	it is hot
ცივა	it is cold
ბნელა	it is dark[6]
კმარა	it is enough

The last form is generally replaced by საკმარისია. Note also არ ვარგა above, sec. 15.1.3.

15.1.4. II. conjugation forms of root verbs in *-ev*. Root verbs in *-ev* (see sec. 3.1.4.2) form the future and present series of the II. conjugation in *i-* without adding the suffix *-eb-*. Examples:

I. conj.		II. conj.	
შეარჩევს	choose; select	შეირჩევა	
გაახვევს	wrap	გაეხვევა	
გაარკვევს	clarify	გაერკვევა	
ა=რევს	mix	აირევა	
გააქცევს	send away, make run away	გაიქცევა	run away

There is great variation in the formation of the II.

conjugation aorist series screeves of such verbs. For some II. conjugation forms of verbs in *-ev* the formation of the aorist series is as in sec. 5.1.3.c.

გაეხვევა: გა(ვ)ეხვიე(თ) გაეხვია
აირევა: ა(ვ)ირიე(თ) აირია [7a]

For others, the first and second persons are regular, but the third person loses the *-i-* (which comes from *-ev*, sec. 5.3.2.2):

შეირჩევა: შე(ვ)ირჩიე(თ) შეირჩა
გაერკვევა: გა(ვ)ერკვიე(თ) გაერკვა [7b]

A third (and much smaller) group loses the *-ev* completely in all persons; the vowel *e* is inserted before the final consonant of the root in the first and second persons; the endings are strong. The most common root following this pattern is *kcev-*:

გაიქცევა: გა(ვ)იქეცი(თ) გაიქცა

15.1.5. Irregular verbs in *-eb*, *-ob* with inserted vowel in the aorist. A very limited number of verbs in *-eb* and *-ob* which have no root vowel insert the vowel *e* or *a* in the first and second persons of the aorist. (In general, *a* is inserted before *r* and *e* elsewhere, but note იცნობს below.) Such verbs take strong endings in the first and second persons, but tend to take *-o* in the third person singular. Examples:

Future 3sg.	Aorist 2sg.	Aorist 3sg.	
გააგნებს	გააგენი	გააგნო	find the way
იკლებს (15.1.7)	იკელი	იკლო	diminish
მოასწრებს	მოასწარი	მოასწრო	precede
შეძლებს	შეძელი	შეძლო	support
Ø=ახლებს	ახელი	ახლო	touch
იგრძნობს (15.1.2)	იგრძენი	იგრძნო	feel
დაიპყრობს	დაიპყარი	დაიპყრო	conquer
დაასობს (root *sv-*)	დაასვი	დაასო	pierce
დააყრდნობს	დააყრდენი	დააყრდნო	lean on
დაუცობს	დაუცვი	დაუცო	stop sthg. up

(root *cv*-)

იცნობს (15.1.2)	იცანი	იცნო	know, recognize

Note also the following II. conjugation verb:

დათვრება	დათვერი	დათვრა	become drunk

15.1.6. "Compound" verbs with -ყოფს. The verb ყოფს[8] occurs with a limited number of adjectives and participle forms, which behave as if they were preverbs. Such "compound" verbs have no future series screeves, although the screeves of the present, aorist, and perfect series are found. Such verbs include the following (forms are 3sg. present):

უზრუნველყოფს	cf. უზრუნველი
guarantee, secure	unworried, unconcerned
უკვდავყოფს	უკვდავი
immortalize	immortal
ნათელყოფს	ნათელი
clarify	clear; bright
ცხადყოფს	ცხადი
prove	clear
უარყოფს	უარი
negate	refusal
სრულყოფს	სრული
complete, perfect	complete
უვნებელყოფს	უვნებელი
render harmless	safe; unharmed
შეურაცხყოფს	შეურაცხი
humiliate	(Old Geo.: worthless; rabble)
უგულებელყოფს	----
neglect; disregard	

Since the first element of the verb functions as a preverb, the *v*- marking the first person (as well as object markers and preradical vowels) occur after it, for example: ცხადვყოფ. Present series forms are regular. Note aorist series forms:

Aorist: ცხად(ვ)ყავი(თ), 3sg. ცხადყო, 3pl.

ცხადყვეს

Optative: ცხად(ვ)ყო(თ), 3sg. ცხადყოს

The present perfect has the form ცხადუყვია and the pluperfect ცხადეყო.

15.1.7. Present series in *-ulob-*, *-ilob-*. A small number of I. conjugation verbs have present series forms in *-ulob-* or *-ilob-*[9] but form the future series not by means of a preverb but rather with the preradical vowel *i-* and usually a future stem formant (*-eb*, *-av*, *-i*). Some of these verbs have occurred in previous lessons, for example, fut. იკითხავს, pres. კითხულობს 'read'; ისესხებს pres. სესხულობს 'borrow'; იპოვის, pres. პოულობს 'find'; იყიდის, pres. ყიდულობს 'buy'. Other verbs of this type are:

Future	Present	
ითხოვს	თხოულობს	borrow
იკისრებს	კისრულობს	take on; shoulder
იკლებს	კლებულობს	lessen; diminish
ილოცებს	ლოცულობს	pray
იმატებს	მატულობს	increase
ინატრებს	ნატრულობს	long for s.o.
ინახავს	ნახულობს	find
იტვირთებს	ტვირთულობს	take on o.s. (e.g., responsibility)
იშოვის	შოულობს	get; obtain

In addition, a few verbs may have forms in *-ulob* in the present series alongside regular formations. These verbs are:

Future	Present	
გაიგებს	იგებს or გებულობს	understand
მიიღებს	იღებს or ღებულობს	get; receive
{დაიფიცებს / დაიფიცავს}	{იფიცებს / იფიცავს} or ფიცულობს	swear
∅= იღებს თავს	იღებს თავს or ღებულობს თავს	take on o.s.

For some authorities, the two present forms are equivalent in meaning, whereas for others, the forms in *-ulob* are iterative in meaning, that is, denote regular, repeated events, while the regular formations denote one-time actions. Yet others prefer the regular forms. Compare the following:

> ეს მოწაფე კარგად სწავლობს და ხშირად ღებულობს ხუთიანებს.
>
> This pupil studies well and often receives A's.
>
> გამგე დარბაზის კარებთან იღებდა სტუმრებს.
>
> The manager *was receiving* the guests at the door of the hall.

15.1.8. "Truncated" imperatives. In the colloquial language a number of verbs have shortened imperatives alongside the regular formations. In general, in the truncated imperative the final syllable of the regularly formed imperative is dropped. Examples are:

Verb	Regular imperative	Truncated imperative	
ადგება	ადექი!	ადე!	stand up
დაჯდება	დაჯექი!	დაჯე!	sit down
შეხედავს	შეხედე!	შეხე!	look
დახედავს	დახედე!	დახე!	look
მომცემს	მომეცი!	მომე!	give me
მისცემს	მიეცი!	მიე!	give him
დაიჭერს	დაიჭირე!	დაიჭი!	catch
მოიცდის	მოიცადე!	მოიცა!	wait
წამოვა	წამოდი!	წამო!	come

15.1.9. Apparently irregular II. conjugation verbs. Most II. conjugation verbs in *i-* are derived from corresponding I. conjugation verbs. Since the roots of I. conjugation verbs and the corresponding II. conjugation verbs are generally identical in the aorist, if the I. conjugation verb is irregular in any way, the corresponding II. conjugation verb will almost always show the same irregularity. At times, however, the I. conjugation verb from which the II. conjugation form is derived is no longer in use or has acquired a different or more specific meaning so that the II. conjugation form is either the only form or the more common one. Such a II. conjugation verb may then show irregularities that are not predictable from its dictionary entry form. An example is the II. conjugation verb გარდაიცვლება 'pass away', which has *a* inserted in all persons of the aorist: გარდა(ვ)იცვალე(თ), გარდაიცვალა.

This verb has the same root as the verb შეცვლის 'change', from which the II. conjugation form შეიცვლება is derived. A form *გარდაცვლის no longer exists, however, so that the prediction of the vowel insertion is not possible for გარდაიცვლება.

15.2. Wordbuilding: Special functions of preverbs. Preverbs generally have a clear directional meaning when they occur with verbs of motion. In most other circumstances they usually serve to perfectivize and often change the meaning of the nonprefixed verb. In such instances it is difficult, if not impossible, to predict the meaning that a given preverb will give to a verb. There are some instances, however, when the preverb a given verb normally takes is replaced by another preverb, and the resultant meaning is predictable. We have seen an example of this in the use of *da-* to indicate a plural object with I. conjugation verbs and a plural subject with II. conjugation verbs (sec. 14.1.3). Other such preverbs which add a specific nuance include:

a. *gada-:* This preverb can correspond to English *re-* (in the sense of doing something again). Examples:

დაბეჭდავს	გადაბეჭდავს
print	reprint
აირჩევს	გადაირჩევს
elect	reelect
გააკეთებს	გადააკეთებს
make	remake
დაწერს	გადაწერს
write	rewrite

b. *še-:* This preverb can convey a nuance of 'a little', 'a bit', 'not quite', 'incompletely'. Examples:

გაწითლდება	შეწითლდება
blush	blush a bit
დათვრება	შეთვრება
get drunk	become tipsy
გაათბობს	შეათბობს
warm sthg.	warm sthg. a little
დაიგვიანებს	შეიგვიანებს
be late	be somewhat late

Similar meanings can be conveyed by the preverb *mo-*. Examples:

შესვამს drink მოსვამს drink a bit, some

დაბერდება grow old მობერდება age slightly

c. *c̣a-:* This preverb can have a similar meaning to that of *še-* above:

დაეხმარება help s.o. წაეხმარება help s.o. a bit

It can also denote an action that is performed superficially, hurriedly. Examples:

დაიბანს ხელს

wash o's hands

წაიბანს ხელს

wash o's hands carelessly

საუზმობს (fut.) ისაუზმებს

have breakfast

წაისაუზმებს (fut.)

have a quick breakfast

It can also denote (similarly to the Russian prefix по-) an action performed for a short time. With III. conjugation verbs the prefixed forms occur only in the future series and those series derived from it, not in the present series. Examples:

იმღერებს (fut.)

sing

წაიმღერებს

sing a little bit

ილაპარაკებს (fut.)

talk

წაილაპარაკებს

talk for a while

დაიძინებს

go to sleep

წაიძინებს

sleep for a bit

LESSON 15: Notes

1. The nouns შრომა 'labor' and ზმნა 'verb' are historically verbal nouns from შვრება and იზამს respectively.

2. This verb is somewhat similar in its usage to Russian ходить; it tends to be translated into English as 'goes' rather than as 'is going'.

3. For the aorist series of this verb, see sec. 15.1.5. The perfect is also irregular: უგრძვნია. Note also the reflexive გრძნობს თავს 'feel', i.e., როგორ გრძნობთ თავს? 'How do you feel?'

4. A present იცნობს also exists. For the aorist forms, see Lesson 7, Vocabulary.

5. In addition to მყავანან, the following verbs also have *-(a)nan* in the 3pl. of the present screeve:

მყავს:	მყავანან	have s.o. (sec. 12.1.3.b)
დგას:	დგანან	be standing (sec. 9.1.3)
წევს:	წევანან	be lying down (sec. 9.1.3)
მოსწონს:	მოსწონან	like

6. These forms, which are derived from the corresponding adjectives თბილი, გრილი, ცხელი, ცივი, ბნელი and refer to weather, cannot be replaced by sequences of these adjectives + არის; i.e., 'it is cold' can only be ცივა, never *ცივია. Compare IV. conj. forms such as მცივა 'I am cold', გცხელა 'you are hot', სთბილა 'he is warm', but წყალი ცივია 'the water is cold'.

7a. Note the formation of the 3pl. aorist of these verbs: გაეხვივნენ, აირივნენ.
7b. There is much variation in the 3rd person sing. of the aorists of these verbs: they can be conjugated regularly: გა(ვ)ერკვიე(თ), გაერკვია or the *i* can be lost in the 3rd person: გა(ვ)ერკვიე(თ), გაერკვა.

8. The verb ყოფს is the only verb in Georgian with a F/PSF *-op*. It occurs most commonly with the preverb *ga-:* გაყოფს 'divide'. With the preradical vowel *u-* it used to mean 'do', 'make', and this meaning is preserved in a few fixed expressions, such as:

რა უყო მან მას?

What did he do to him?

რა უყო მან ის?

What has he done with it?

რაც გინდა, ის უყავი მას!

Do with it whatever you want!

Note, too, that the aorist series screeves of ყოფნა 'be' are also derived from this verb.

9. Historically, these are derived from the perfect participle of the corresponding verb + the PSF *-ob*.

"Woman and children going for water"
Artist: N. Pirosmanašvili

„ბავშვიანი დედაკაცი წყალზე მიდის"
ნ. ფიროსმანაშვილი

Reading Passage „მზიანი ღამე" (Continuation)

1 მხოლოდ გულიკო გამომყვა დერეფნის ბოლომდე, ისიც უხმოდ, მერე, რომ აღარ მოვხედე, თანდათან ჩამორჩა. კიბეს ჩავყევი. ბოლო საფეხურზე რომ ჩავედი, ვიგრძენი, მიყურებდა. ზევით ავიხედე, გულიკო კიბის თავზე იდგა, ხელები ნიკაპის ქვეშ ამოედო, იდაყვებით მოაჯირს დაყრდნობოდა, თან თვალს არ მაცილებდა.

2 — რას მიყურებ? — ვკითხე. გულიკო გაიმართა, უარყოფის ნიშნად თავი გაიქნია და გაბრუნდა. მე უნივერსიტეტის ბაღში გამოვედი და სკამზე დავჯექი. ჩემს წინ ჩაცუცქული გოგონა ნიჩბით მიწას თხრიდა და ფეხებზე აყრიდა მასზე პატარა ბიჭუნას, რომელიც მორჩილად იდგა ახალდარგული ნერგივით და იღიმებოდა. გოგონა ხშირ-ხშირად ამოხედავდა ხოლმე, აბა, თუ გაიზარდაო, და მერე ისევ და ისევ თხრიდა და აყრიდა ფეხებზე მიწას, ბიჭი კი იდგა გაუნძრევლად, მორჩილად, და ალბათ ისიც გაზრდის მოლოდინში იღიმებოდა და იღიმებოდა. ბაღში მაისის მწვანე და თბილი დარი იდგა.

3 სწორედ ამ მაისის ამ თბილ დღეს ჩემი ორიანის წყალობით სახელმწიფო ბიუჯეტის გასავალი 275 მანეთითა და 40 კაპიკით შემცირდა. სტიპენდია ფულის იმ განსაცვიფრებელ კატეგორიას ეკუთვნის, რომელიც ციდან ჩამოვარდნილს გავს. მე, როგორც პატიოსან კაცს, მუდამ მიკვირდა სამი რამ — რატომ მაძლევდნენ სტიპენდიას, რატომ მიქვითავდნენ საშემოსავლოს ამ ღვთის ნაჩუქარი ფულიდან და რაში მახდევინებდნენ სწავლის ფულს. მიუხედავად ამისა, მე არ მეგულებოდა ქვეყანაზე სტუდენტი, რომელსაც ჩემზე უფრო სჭირდებოდა სტიპენდია, ან ჩემზე უფრო სცოდნოდა მისი ფასი. ჰოდა, ახლა მე, უსტიპენდიო, ვიჯექი უნივერსიტეტის ბაღში და ვუცქერდი პატარა, ბაფთიან გოგონას, რომელსაც ბიჭუნას რგვა დაემთავრებინა და მის მორწყვაზე გადასულიყო.

4 დარგულმა ბიჭმა შემომხედა და გამიცინა.

— რა გქვია, ბიჭო? — ვკითხე.

— მაგას ლაშა ჰქვია, მე ია! — მიპასუხა გოგონამ ორთავეს მაგივრად.

— მერე, წყალს რომ ასხამ ფეხებზე, არ გეშინია, რომ გაცივდეს?

— უნდა გაიზარდოს!

— ეგრე კი არ იზრდებიან. აი, მე, თქვენხელა რომ ვიყავი, ბევრს ვჭამდი, და ხომ ხედავთ, როგორ გავიზარდე. — გავიხ-

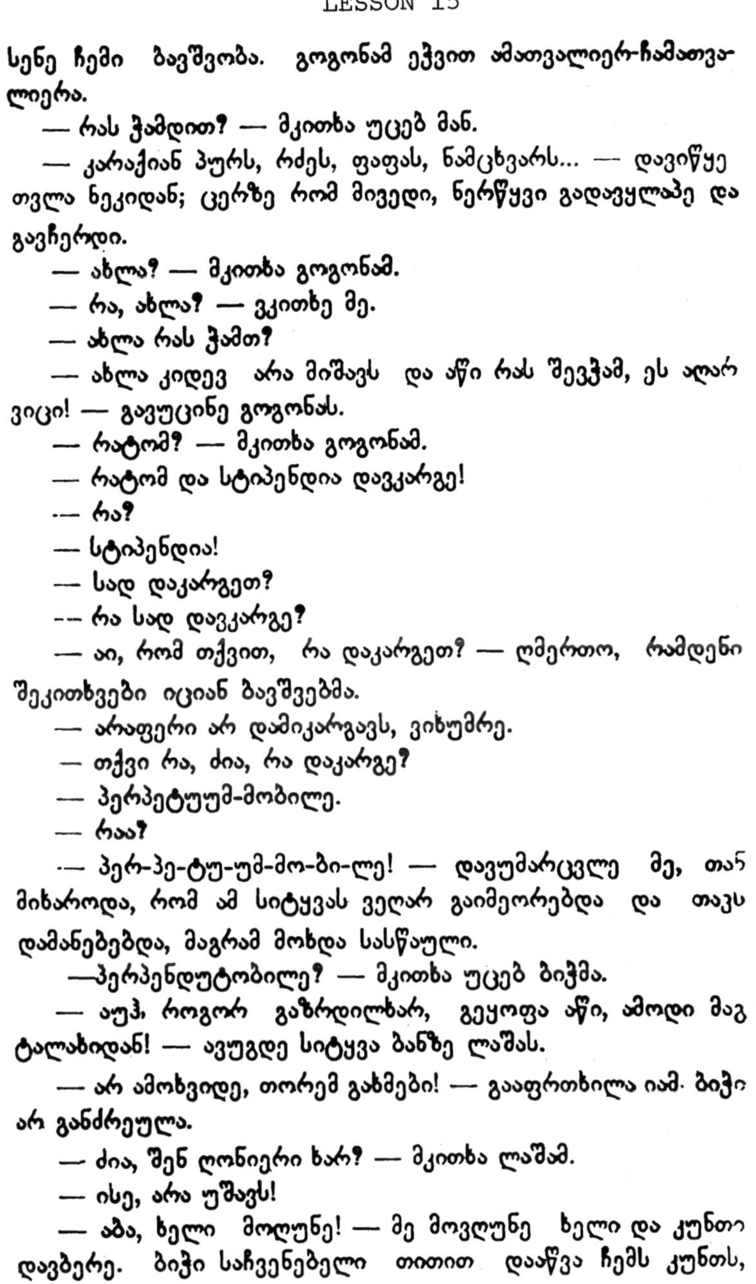

სენე ჩემი ბავშვობა. გოგონამ ეჭვით ამათვალიერ-ჩამათვალიერა.

5 — რას ჭამდით? — მკითხა უცებ მან.

— კარაქიან პურს, რძეს, ფაფას, ნამცხვარს... — დავიწყე თვლა ნეკიდან; ცერზე რომ მივედი, ნერწყვი გადავყლაპე და გავჩერდი.

— ახლა? — მკითხა გოგონამ.

— რა, ახლა? — ვკითხე მე.

— ახლა რას ჭამთ?

— ახლა კიდევ არა მიშავს და აწი რას შევჭამ, ეს აღარ ვიცი! — გავუცინე გოგონას.

6 — რატომ? — მკითხა გოგონამ.

— რატომ და სტიპენდია დავკარგე!

— რა?

— სტიპენდია!

— სად დაკარგეთ?

— რა სად დავკარგე?

— აი, რომ თქვით, რა დაკარგეთ? — ღმერთო, რამდენი შეკითხვები იციან ბავშვებმა.

7 — არაფერი არ დამიკარგავს, ვიხუმრე.

— თქვი რა, ძია, რა დაკარგე?

— პერპეტუუმ-მობილე.

— რაა?

— პერ-პე-ტუ-უმ-მო-ბი-ლე! — დავუმარცვლე მე, თან მიხაროდა, რომ ამ სიტყვას ვეღარ გაიმეორებდა და თავს დამანებებდა, მაგრამ მოხდა სასწაული.

—პერპენდუტობილე? — მკითხა უცებ ბიჭმა.

— აუჰ, როგორ გაზრდილხარ, გეყოფა აწი, ამოდი მაგ ტალახიდან! — ავუგდე სიტყვა ბანზე ლაშას.

8 — არ ამოხვიდე, თორემ გახმები! — გააფრთხილა იამ. ბიჭი არ განძრეულა.

— ძია, შენ ღონიერი ხარ? — მკითხა ლაშამ.

— ისე, არა უშავს!

— აბა, ხელი მოღუნე! — მე მოვღუნე ხელი და კუნთი დავბერე. ბიჭი საჩვენებელი თითით დააწვა ჩემს კუნთს, მოწონების ნიშნად დაასლოკინა და მკითხა:

9 — მთაზე ღონიერი ხარ?

— აბა რა!

— დათვზე?

— კი! — ავიბზუე ტუჩი.

— ძია სტალინს მოერევი? — მკითხა ბავშვმა უცებ და პასუხის მოლოდინში გაინაბა.

მე აქეთ-იქით გავიხედე. გოგონაც სმენად იყო ქცეული და ელოდა რას ვიტყოდი, მე ხმას არ ვიღებდი.

— ძია სტალინს მოერევი? — მკითხა ახლა გოგონამ.

10 — იმას რა მოერევა, ბიძია! — ვთქვი მე და ავდექი. ბავშვებმა შვებით ამოისუნთქეს.

— გეყოფა, უკვე დიდი ხარ!—ვუთხარი მე ლაშას, მხრებში ხელი მოვკიდე, ავწიე ოდნავ და მიწიდან ამოვთხარე. ბიჭმა ფეხები შეათამაშა, მერე ერთმანეთზე მიაბაკუნა და მიწა ჩამოიბერტყა.

11 — ნახვამდის, სახლში რომ მიხვალ, ძილის წინ კარაქიანი პური ჭამე და დილას სულ დიდი, დიდი ადგები. — ვაკოცე და მიწაზე დავსვი.

— მიდიხარ, ძია? — მკითხა გულდაწყვეტილმა ლაშამ.

— მივდივარ. აბა, შენი კუნთი მაჩვენე! — ლაშამ წვრილი მკლავი მოღუნა, კისრის ძარღვები დაჭიმა, სუნთქვა შეიკრა და მომაშტერდა.

12 მე თითი დავაჭირე კუნთზე.

— აუჰ, შენ ვინ ყოფილხარ, კაცო! — გამიკვირდა მე, ლაშა გაიბადრა და იას გადახედა.

— ხვალ უფრო ღონიერი ვიქნები, კარაქიან პურს შევჭამ!— დამიმედა ლაშამ.

— აბა, შენ იცი, თუ ძმა ხარ, არ დამაღალატო!. — ვთხოვე მე და ბაღიდან გამოვედი.

•

13 ჩემი ოთახი, ვარაზის ხევის მარჯვნივ რომ სახლი დგას, იმის მეოთხე სართულის შუაგულშია. აღმოსავლეთით და დასავლეთით კეთილი მეზობლები მესაზღვრებიან, ჩრდილოეთიდან ვარაზის ხევის ამოსავსებად მოთრეული ნაგავი, სამხრეთიდან კი, სამზარეულოზე გავლით, უნივერსიტეტი. ოთახის ფართობი 26 კვადრატული მეტრია, მაგრამ საბინაო სამმართველოში გატარებულია როგორც 20, ბინის ქირის შეღავათიან ფასებში გადახდის კეთილშობილური მიზნით. ოთახის ავეჯი ორი საწოლით, ერთი საწერი მაგიდით, სამი სკამითა და ერთი კარადით განისაზღვრება. კარადაში სამნახევარი თეფში და 4 ჭიქა აწყვია თავისი კოვზებითა და ჩანგლებით. რაც შეეხება ტანსაცმელს, მისი საკიდი მე თვითონ ვარ, რაც გამაჩნია, ზედვე

მაცვია, ამიტომ ოთახიდან გამოსვლის დროს გასაღებს პირველსავე შემხვედრ მეზობელს ვუტოვებ, ან კარს საერთოდ ღიად ვტოვებ.

14 კიბეზე უხალისოდ ავდიოდი. დერეფნის კარი ღია დამხვდა, ოთახის კარი შევაღე და ადგილზე გავქვავდი. ტანში ჟრუანტელმა დამიარა, მუხლები მომეკვეთა. ჩემი ოთახი სავსე იყო მეზობლებით. ისინი გარს შემოხვეოდნენ საწოლს, რომელზეც შუახნის, ჭაღარა, საოცრად დაღლილი, თეთრი სახის, გამხდარი ქალი იჯდა. იგი ოდნავ, ოდნავ იღიმებოდა და სუსტი ხმით ყვებოდა რაღაცას. ჩემთვის ყურადღება არავის მოუქცევია. ჭაღარა ქალმა მშვიდად შემხედა, ცოტა ხანს მიყურა. მერე ისევ განაგრძო ამბავი. მეზობლები სინანულით თავებს იქნევდნენ აქეთ-იქით. ჭაღარა ქალმა უცებ საუბარი შეწყვიტა და ისევ დამაცქერდა, ახლა უფრო ხანგრძლივად და დაჟინებით, მერე თვალები მეზობლებისაკენ გაექცა, მეზობლები კარებისკენ შემოტრიალდნენ. ოთახში სამარისებური სიჩუმე ჩამოვარდა. მე მესმოდა მხოლოდ ჩემი გულისცემა, ვიღაცის სკამის სულისწამღები ჭრიალი, მეტი არაფერი. ჭაღარა ქალი თვალს არ მაცილებდა, მერე მან შეშინებული თვალებით შეხედა ჩემს კარის მეზობელს, ელიკოს. ელიკომ თავი დაუქნია თანხმობის ნიშნად, მაშინ ჭაღარა ქალი ადგა, მას ხელები და ტუჩები უკანკალებდა, იგი საოცრად ჰგავდა იმ ქალს, რომელმაც ამ ოთახში 12 წლის წინ, ღამის ოთხ საათზე გამაღვიძა, პირჯვარი გადამსახა და მკერდზე მაკოცა. მერე იგი წაიყვანა ორმა მამაკაცმა, რომელთაგან ერთი შეშინებული ჩანდა, მეორე კი იღიმებოდა და პირი ვერცხლის კბილებით ჰქონდა გამოტენილი. ეს იყო ჩემი დედა. ახლა მე და მას სულ სამი ნაბიჯი გვაცილებდა. იგი მოდიოდა ჩემკენ, ნელი, ძალიან ნელი ნაბიჯით, უკვე მესმოდა მისი სუნთქვა, მინდოდა შევბრუნებულიყავი და გავქცეულიყავი, მაგრამ არ შემეძლო, მე უბრალოდ დავხუჭე თვალები და ველოდი რა მოხდებოდა. მერე მე ვიგრძენი მისი თავი ჩემს მხარზე და გავიგონე ჩუმი ჩურჩული:

15 — გამარჯობა, შვილო...

— გამარჯობა, შვილო, და ასე განუწყვეტლივ, დიდხანს, ძალიან დიდხანს, — გამარჯობა, შვილო... მე მივხვდი, რომ იგი ელოდა პასუხს, — გამარჯობა, დედა, — მაგრამ მე ვერ შევძელი.

— გამარჯობათ, ქალბატონო!.. — ვთქვი და ტირილი დავიწყე.

Vocabulary

1

გა(მო)ჰყვება	accompany s.o. (aor. irr.: -(ჰ)ყევი, -ჰყვა perf. -ჰყოლია)
დერეფანი	corridor (A); ისიც = ის + -ც
უხმოდ	silently (ხმა = voice)
რომ	here: when
მოხედავს	look at (no d.o., H-series id.o. markers)
თანდათან	gradually
ჩა(მო)რჩება	remain behind; here: fall behind
კიბე	stairs; staircase
ჩაჰყვება	go down sthg. (see გაჰყვება above for forms)
ბოლო	here: last
საფეხური	step
რომ	here: when
ვიგრძენი, მიყურებდა	I felt (that) she was looking at me (note that there is no conjunction here).
გრძნობს	feel (see sec. 15.1.5)
ზევით	up, upward(s), upstairs
Ø=უყურებს	look at s.o., sthg. (no d.o.)
აიხედავს	look up
ნიკაპი	chin
ქვეშ	under (pp.)
ამოდებს	put; place sthg. under sthg. (see Lesson 13, vocabulary)
იდაყვი	elbow
მოაჯირი	banister
დააყრდნობს	lean sthg. on sthg. (sup.) (here = relative II. conj., pluperfect)
თან	while, at the same time

მოაცილებს	tear sthg. away from s.o.
2	
რას	here: why
გაიმართება	straighten o.s. up
უარყოფა	negation
თავს გაიქნევს	shake o's head
გააბრუნებს	turn sthg. around, back
ჩაცუცქული	crouched; squatting down
ნიჩაბი	shovel (A)
მიწა	earth
Ø=თხრის	dig
მასზე პატარა	smaller than she
ბიჭუნა	little boy (nontrunc.)
მორჩილი	submissive; humble; obedient
ახალდარგული	newly planted
ნერგი	young plant; sapling
გაიღიმება	smile
ხშირ-ხშირად	very often
ა(მო)ხედავს	look up at s.o., sthg. (H-series)
აბა, თუ გაიზარდაო	well, has he grown (yet)? (presented as the thought of the little girl; note the particle *-o* at the end, = as if to say)
ისევ ●	again
გაუნძრეველი	motionless (E)
მოლოდინი	(VN) waiting; expectation
მაისი	May
დარი	(good) weather
იდგა	here: it, there was
3 ●	
ბიუჯეტი	budget
გასავალი	expense
275 მან. და 40 კაპ.	(pre-1961 currency; in post-1961 currency = 27 rubles, 54 copecks)

შეამცირებს — reduce
განსაცვიფრებელი — remarkable; astonishing (E)
ე-კუთვნის — belong to (III. conj., only pres. series)
ცა — sky
ჩამოვარდნილი — (sthg.) fallen down (participle from ჩა(მო)ვარდება)
ჰგავს — be similar to (see sec. 15.1.3) (note deletion of *h*-)
პატიოსანი — honest; honorable
მი-კვირს — be astonished (IV. conj.)
რამ (nom.) — = რამე thing
გაქვითავს — fine; tax; exact (a fine, tax, etc.)
საშემოსავლო (გადასახადი) ● — income (tax)
ნაჩუქარი — gift; given as a gift
რაში — why (lit., in what?)
გადაიხდის — pay (see sec. 11.4)
სწავლის ფული — tuition
მიუხედავად — in spite of (pp.) (here used as a preposition, so long endings)
ე-გულება — imagine; know where to find (only pres. series; sec. 12.1.2.4)
სცოდნოდა — see sec. 12.1.3
ფასი — price; value
ჰოდა ● — well
ბაფთა — ribbon
დარგავს — plant
მორწყავს — water sthg. ● [note]
4
გაუცინებს — laugh at s.o. (i.e., in s.o.'s direction, not mock; III. conj.)
ბიჭი — = ბიჭო!
მაგას — this one; that one (dat.)

ლაშა	(m.pr.n.)
ია	Violet (f.pr.n.)
ორთავე	(oblique of ორნივე = ორივე)
მაგივრად	instead of; here: for (pp.)
გა=ცივდება	catch (a) cold
ეგრე	so; in that way
რომ	here: when
თქვენხელა	as big, old as you (nontrunc.)
გაიხსენებს	remember something (deliberately)
ეჭვი	doubt; suspicion
აათვალიერებს	look at s.o. (from down up)
ჩაათვალიერებს	look at s.o. (from up down) (Note how Georgian can compound two verbs having similar meaning [here differing only in preverb]. The first verb is given up to the P/FSF and the second is conjugated fully.)

5

კარაქი	butter
რძე	milk
ფაფა	porridge; (hot breakfast) cereal
ნამცხვარი	cookie (A)
ნეკი	little finger
რომ ●	here: when. This use of რომ should be noted; it will no longer be given in the vocabulary.
ნერწყვი	spittle
გადაყლაპავს ●	swallow
არა მიშავს (რა)	I'm OK, not bad (IV. conj.)
აწ(ი)	now; from now on (West Georgian)
გაეცინებს	laugh at s.o. (id.o.)

6

რატომ და ●	why? because...
შეკითხვები	note the unusual use of the plural

after a quantifier

7

ხუმრობს	joke
ძია	uncle (nontrunc.) term of address used by children when talking to an adult
პერპეტუუმ-მობილე	perpetual motion (machine) (Latin) i.e., sthg. keeping Baramije going, a source of constant energy
მარცვალი	syllable (A)
დამარცვლავს	pronounce syllable by syllable (the Georgian equivalent of spelling a word)
თან	while; at the same time
მი-ხარია	be happy; rejoice; sthg. (nom.) makes s.o. (dat.) happy (IV. conj.)
დაანებებს თავს	leave s.o. in peace, alone
პერპენდუტობილე	(the child's attempt to say *perpetuum mobile*)
აუჰ	(interjection expressing surprise)
გეყოფა(თ)	enough! basta!
მაგ	(oblique form of demonstrative adjective ეგ) this, that
ტალახი	mud
ააგდებს სიტყვას ბანზე	change the subject (of the conversation) (lit. throw the word up on the roof)

8

თორემ	or else; lest; otherwise
გაახმობს	dry sthg. out
გააფრთხილებს	warn s.o.
გაანძრევს	move (II. conj. = გაინძრევა, aor. -ინძერი, -ინძრა)
ღონიერი	strong

ისე, არა უშავს	so-so
მოღუნავს	bend
კუნთი	muscle
დაბერავს	flex
Ø=აჩვენებს	show
საჩვენებელი თითი	index finger
დააწვება	press sthg. (superessive; sec. 9.1.2)
მოწონება	approval
ნიშანი	sign (A)
Ø=ახლოკინებს	s.o. (dat., H-series) has the hiccups; hiccups (impersonal, no d.o.)

9

აბა რა!	of course!
აიბზუებს ტუჩებს	purse o's lips
მოერევა	overcome; best; defeat; here: can you beat? (rel. II. conj. of რევს; aor. -ერიე, -ერია)
მოლოდინი	waiting (VN)
გაინაბება	stand stock still; not move
აქეთ-იქეთ	here and there; around
სმენად იქცევა	be all ears
ე-ლის	wait for (only pres. series)
ხმას ამოიღებს	say; speak

10

ბიძია	lit. uncle (also ბიძა); used by children to address an older man and, as here, by an older man to address a child affectionately
შვება	relief
ამოისუნთქავს	exhale
გეყოფა(თ)	enough! basta!
მხარი	shoulder (A)
ხელს	touch s.o. (with o's hand) (*h*- de-

მოშვილებს leted here)

ა=ს-წევს lift up (*s*- deleted here)

ოდნავ slightly; hardly

მიწა earth; ground

ამოთხრის dig out

შეათამაშებს move; cause to hop, skip, caper

მიაბაკუნებს stamp

ჩამოაბერტყავს shake off

11

ნახვამდის good-bye
(= ნახვა + -მდის)

ძილი sleep (VN of მძინავს)

კარაქი butter

დილას • in the morning.

Ø=აკოცებს kiss (H-series id.o., no d.o.)

დასვამს put down

გულდაწყვეტილი regretful

Ø=აჩვენებს show

წვრილი thin

მკლავი arm

მოღუნავს bend

კისერი neck (E)

ძარღვი vein

დაჭიმავს strain tightly

სუნთქვას შეიკრავს hold o's breath

მი/მოაშტერდება stare at s.o. (H-series id.o.)

12

დააჭერს (E → I) push; press on sthg. (superessive)

შენ ვინ ყოფილხარ! you're really something! (Note the use of the perfect here with a present tense meaning used to express surprise, astonishment.)

გაუკვირდება s.o. (dat.) becomes astonished (sec. 12.1.2.4)

გაიბადრება	here: beam
დააიმედებს	encourage (cf. იმედი hope)
თუ ძმა ხარ	please (lit. 'if you're a brother')
დააღალატებს	let s.o. down
∅=ს-თხოვს	ask s.o. for sthg. (note the omission of *ε*- after *υ*-)

13

ვარაზის ხევი	Varazi ravine (section of Tbilisi near the University)
მარჯვნივ	to, on the right of (pp.)
რომ სახლი,... იმის	= იმ სახლის(ა), რომელიც ვარაზის ხევის მარჯვნივ დგას. (Note that რომ can function as a replacement for other relatives such as რომელიც, ვინც, რაც, სადაც. იმის refers to სახლი, which has been moved from the main clause into the subordinate clause.)
სართული	story; floor (in a building)
შუაგული	center; middle
კეთილი	good; nice
ე-საზღვრება	border on (only pres. series)
ჩრდილოეთი	north
ამოავსებს	fill up
მი/მოათრევს	drag; bring; carry
ნაგავი	rubbish; garbage (A)
გავლით	by going through; passing (through)
ფართობი	area
კვადრატი	square
ბინა	apartment; housing
სამმართველო	administration; administrator's office
გაატარებს	here: enter into books; register
ქირა	rent; here = for the rent
შეღავათიანი	lowered
ფასი	price; cost; ფასებში at a cost

კეთილშობილი	noble
მიზანი	aim; goal; მიზნით with the aim, goal (A)
ავეჯი	furniture
კარადა	wardrobe; chest (for clothes), *armoire*
გან+საზღვრავს	limit to (+ instr.)
სამნახევარი	three and one half
თეფში	plate
ჭიქა	glass (for drinking)
დააწყობს	set up; arrange (root = *c̣qv-*) (d.o. plural)
აწყვია	(fut. ეწყობა) passive of state in superessive
ჩანგალი	fork (A)
შეეხება	concern
ტანსაცმელი	clothes
საკიდი	clothes hanger, clothes hook
გამაჩნია	have (IV. conj.; only pres. series)
ზედ	on (adverb) (here: on me)
პირველსავე	the very first (dat., agrees with მეზობელს)
შემხვედრი	passing (by); passer-by
დატოვებს	leave
საერთოდ	in general
ღია	open

14

კიბე	stairs; staircase
ხალისი	joy, cheer
დერეფანი	corridor (A)
დახვდება	encounter; bump into (H-series, sec. 12.1.2.4); here: find
შეაღებს	open halfway, a bit (sec. 15.2.b, cf. გააღებს)
ქვა	stone
ჟრუანტელი	shiver (E)

დამიარა	see sec. 15.1.1 (here with *u*-series id.o.)
მუხლი მოეკვეთება	o's knees buckle (sec. 12.1.2.4)
სავსე	full (+ instr.)
შემოეხვევა გარს	surround (plup.) (II. conj., see sec. 15.1.4)
შუახნის	middle-aged (gen.)
ჭაღარა	white-haired
დაღლის	tire s.o. out
გახდება	become thin (root II. conj., root -*xd*-)
ოდნავ	slightly
გაიღიმებს	smile
სუსტი	weak
მოჰყვება	tell, say sthg. (-*h*- omitted here) (aor. -ჰყევი, -ჰყვა; perf. -ჰყოლია)
ყურადღებას მი-/მოაქცევს	pay attention to (*H*-series)
მშვიდი	peaceful; quiet
შემხედა: მიყურა	შეხედავს is perfective in meaning, i.e., glance; take a look at; Ø=უყურებს is used as an imperfective or durative, note ცოტა ხანს 'a short time'.
მერე	then
ისევ	again
განაგრძობს	continue
სინანული	compassion; pity
თავს დაიქნევს	shake o's head (in agreement), nod
შეწყვეტს (E → I)	interrupt; stop for a bit
დააცქერდება	look at (*H*-series)
ხანგრძლივ(ად)	for a long time
დაჟინებით	persistently
გაიქცევა	run away; rapidly turn away (see sec. 15.1.4)
შე(მო)ტრიალდება	turn back

სამარისებური •	sepulchral
ჩამოვარდება	fall down (subject singular)
გულისცემა	heartbeat
სულისწამღები	nerve-wracking
ჭრიალი	creaking
თვალს მოაცილებს	tear o's eyes away from s.o.
შეშინებული	frightened
კარის მეზობელი	next-door neighbor
ელიკო	(f.pr.n.)
თავს დააქნევს	shake o's head, nod
თანხმობა	agreement
ნიშანი	sign (A)
ტუჩი	lip
უკანკალებს	o's (e.g., hand) shakes (only pres. series)
ჰგავს	resemble (see sec. 15.1.3)
გააღვიძებს	wake s.o. up
პირჯვარი	sign of the cross (A)
პირჯვარს გადასახავს	make the sign of the cross on s.o. (*H*-series)
მკერდი	chest; bosom
Ø=აკოცებს	kiss (only id.o.)
შეშინებული	frightened (Note: ერთი is subject here)
ვერცხლი	silver
გამოტენილი •	filled
ნაბიჯი	step
დააცილებს	separate
სუნთქვა	breathing
შებრუნდება	turn around
გაქცევა	run away (see sec. 15.1.4)
უბრალო	simple
დახუჭავს	close (eyes)
ე-ლის	wait for (only pres. series)

გრძნობს feel (see sec. 15.1.2 and note 3)
მხარი shoulder (A)
გაიგონებს hear
ჩურჩული whisper
15
გამარჯობა victory; Georgian equivalent of *hello*. Note: when used to more than one person or politely to one person takes the verb plural marker -*t*: გამარჯობათ.
განუწყვეტლივ repeatedly; over and over; here: she said over and over
მიხვდება (root = -*xvd*-) notice; see; guess
შეძლებს bring s.o. to; be able (aor. -ძელი, -ძლო)
გამარჯობათ (note the formal, polite plural)

▪ADDENDA TO VOCABULARY

2.
ბიჭი: **boy**
3.
ორიანი: **"D" (grade)**
3.
ღვთის: **Gen. of** ღმერთი; **see sec. 3.2.1.1**
Ø=უცქერს: **look at s.o./sthg. (dat.) (no d.o.)**
მორწყავს: მის მორწყვაზე **'to watering him.' The possessive adjective is used to mark the direct object in a masdar construction**
5. მიოვედი: **The verb** მიდის, **fut.** მივა, **aor.** მივიდა **means 'go and reach.' With the fut.** წავა **it means 'set out for.'**
კიდევ: **here = 'really'**

6.
დაკარგავს: **lose** *
11.
სულ: **quite**
ადგება: **get up, stand up (sec.9.1.2.1)**
14.
სიჩუმე: **silence**
სულ: **just, only (cf. German *gar*)**

---

*რომ თქვით, რა დაკარგეთ? 'what you said you lost!'

APPENDIX A

Table A.1. Noun Suffixes

<table>
<tr><th rowspan="2">Cases:</th><th rowspan="2">Consonant stem:</th><th colspan="2">Truncating vocalic stems:</th><th>Nontruncating vocalic stems:</th></tr>
<tr><th>-a</th><th>-e</th><th>-u, -o</th></tr>
<tr><td>Nominative</td><td>-i</td><td colspan="3">-∅</td></tr>
<tr><td>Ergative</td><td>-ma</td><td colspan="3">-m</td></tr>
<tr><td>Dative</td><td colspan="4">-s</td></tr>
<tr><td>before -ši, -ze:</td><td colspan="4">-∅</td></tr>
<tr><td>before -tan:</td><td>-s</td><td colspan="3">-∅</td></tr>
<tr><td>Genitive</td><td colspan="3">-is</td><td>-s</td></tr>
<tr><td>Instrumental</td><td colspan="3">-it</td><td>-ti</td></tr>
<tr><td>Adverbial</td><td colspan="2">-ad</td><td colspan="2">-d</td></tr>
</table>

<table>
<tr><td rowspan="2">Vocative form</td><td>-o</td><td>-o/-v/-∅ (sec. 6.5)</td></tr>
<tr><td colspan="2">Proper names: -∅</td></tr>
</table>

<table>
<tr><td rowspan="2">Plural:</td><td colspan="3">-eb- (+ consonantal stem endings above)</td></tr>
<tr><td>Stylistically marked plural:</td><td>nom.
erg.
gen.
dat.
voc.</td><td>-ni
} -t, -ta

-no</td></tr>
</table>

Extended case endings in -*a*: see sec. 4.3.

Derivative declension: see sec. 8.6.

Postpositions written together with the noun:

with nominative:	-vit (only with consonant stems)
with dative:	-ze, -ši, -tan; -vit
with genitive:	-tvis, -gan, -ḳen; -dan (final *s* of gen. lost)
with adverbial:	-mdis, -mde (final *d* of adverbial is lost)
with instrumental:	-urt (e.g., ცოლითურთ 'with [his] wife')

Other particles written together with the noun:

-ve	sec. 14.2.3
-c	(added to extended case ending) see Lesson 4, vocabulary)
-a	(= არის) sec. 3.1.7
-o	(indirect speech, 2d and 3d persons and 1st person plural) sec. 8.5

Table A2. Adjective Declension

Adjectives not immediately preceding their heads are declined as nouns.

Adjectives with stems ending in a consonants and immediately preceding their heads are inflected for case, not number. Adjectives with stems ending in a vowel are not inflected at all when occurring immediately before their heads.

Case	Ending	Consonant stem declension	
NOM	-i	ახალ-ი	წიგნ-(ებ)-ი
ERG	-ma	ახალ-მა	წიგნ-(ებ)-მა
DAT	-Ø	ახალ-	წიგნ-(ებ)-ს
GEN	-i	ახალ-ი	წიგნ-(ებ)-ის
INSTR	-i	ახალ-ი	წიგნ-(ებ)-ით
ADV	-Ø	ახალ-	წიგნ-(ებ)-ად
VOC	-o	ძვირფას-ო	ბატონ-(ებ)-ო

SUMMARY OF CONJUGATIONS

CONJUGATION	MOST COMMON MEANINGS
I.	transitive verbs
II.	intransitive: passives in *i-*, change of state in *-d-* (become sthg.)
III.	intransitive *activities*
IV.	verbs of feeling, emotion, states of being

(It is important to note that there are many exceptions to the above meanings in each conjugation.)

SUMMARY OF CASE MARKING

I., III. CONJ. ⇒ SERIES ⇓	Subject	Direct Object (normally only I. conj.)	Indirect Object
Present/Future*	NOM	DAT	DAT
Aorist	ERG	NOM	DAT
Perfect	DAT	NOM	(postposition -tvis)

*The irregular verb იცის 'know' takes the ergative in the present series and the dative in the future series; see secs. 9.1.4, 12.1.3.e.

II. CONJ.	Subject	Indirect Object
	NOM	DAT

IV. CONJ.	Subject	Object
	DAT	NOM

SUMMARY OF SCREEVES

SERIES ⇒	PRESENT	FUTURE	AORIST	PERFECT
NON-PAST	present	future	—	—
PAST	imperfect	conditional	aorist*	present perfect
MODAL	conjunctive present	conjunctive future	optative	pluperfect

*The positive imperative is generally identical to the 2nd person aorist; see sec. 6.3.

Hints for Looking Up Verbs in Dictionaries

1. Remember that most bilingual Georgian dictionaries list verbs only under the verbal noun (masdar).

2. Consider the possibility of a change from *e* to *i* in the aorist and pluperfect of root I. conjugation verbs and in II. conjugation verbs in *i*- derived from them. (See sec. 5.3.1.c.)

3. a. Remember that *v* regularly is dropped before *o* (sec. 1.11.1). Example: გამოაცხობს 'bake,' but aorist გამოვაცხვე, გამოაცხვე, გამოაცხო, perfect გამოუცხვია.

b. Consider the possibility of the metathesis of *v* (sec. 1.11.2); e.g., მოიკვლება 'be killed' from მოკლავს 'kill.'

4. Remember that a number of irregular verbs insert the vowels *e* or *a* in all persons of the aorist or in the first and second persons of the aorist. For details, see sec. 9.1.

5. Remember that a sequence such as *ga*- can be the preverb *ga*-, the 2nd person object marker *g*- plus the preradical vowel *a*-, or the beginning of the root. Compare the following:

გააღებს	he will open it	გა- = preverb
გახსოვს	you remember it	გ-ა- = person marker plus preradical vowel
გალობს	he is singing	გალ- = root

6. Remember that some verbal roots (usually denominal) can begin with the vowels *a, e, i, u,* and that, similarly, roots can end in *av, eb, am,* etc. Examples:

ამაყობს	he is proud	root = ამაყ-
ერთდება	be united	root = ერთ-
განიარაღდება	he will arm himself	root = იარაღ-
უმჯობესდება	it will improve	root = უმჯობეს-
შეღება	he painted it (aor.)	root = ღებ- (< შეღებავს)

APPENDIX B: Verbal Affixes

The following charts list the affixes that can occur in individual verb forms. It is important to remember that not all the affixes listed can co-occur and that, except for the root, all of the other "slots" can be empty; for instance in a present tense root verb such as ჭერ 'you are writing' only the root is found. This absence of a marker is very often significant, for example, in determining when the subject of a given verb form is second person (object in IV. conj. and perfect series verbs).

References in the charts indicate where more detailed information can be found.

The marker of indirect speech -*o* (sec 8.5) is often found added to the end of a verb form.

Table B.1. Verbal Affixes: I., II., and III. Conjugations, Future, Present, and Aorist Series

1A. PREVERBS	1B. *-mo*	2. SUB-JECT	3. OBJECT PERSON PREFIX	4. PV	5.	6. II. CONJ.	7. P/FST	8. CAUS-ATIVE	9. IMPERF, COND., CONJ.	10. SCREEVE MARKERS	11. 3D PERSON	12. PLURAL MARKER
a(ğ)- da-* ga(n)- ga(r)da- mi- mo-* še- ča- šta- ça(r)- **2.2.1** *da-* 14.1.3 ***ča-, gada-,*** ***še-* 15.2**	-mo- **7.2.4** **7.2.5**	1. v- **2.1** 2. x- **3.1.7** **4.6.3**	1.sg. -m- 2. -g- 1 pl. -gv- id.o.: 3. -s-/-h- **7.1-2**	-a- -i- -u- -e- **13.5**	**R** **O** **O** **T**	-d- **3.1.2**	-am -av -eb -ob -i **2.0** (-op) **L.15,** **n.8**	(-ev) -in (-eb-) **11.4**	-d- I conj. III conj. -od- II. conj. III conj. with PSF *-i-*. **2.2.3;** **3.1.5;** **4.1.1;** **8.1.2**	-i II. conj. present, future; imperf., cond. -e conj.; aorist (weak); opt. (II. conj. in *-d-* -o opt. (weak) -a opt. (strong)	*Singular:* -s pres., fut. (I, III conj.); conjunctive; optative -a pres., fut. (II. conj.); imperf/cond; aorist -o aorist (5.4.1) *Plural:* -en pres, fut. -nen imperf/ cond/conj; aorist, opt. (II. conj.) -es aorist -n optative	-t **2.1;** **7.1.2:** **rules** **3-5**

Note: Many of the above affixes are mutually exclusive and cannot co-occur in one and the same form. No forms will contain all eleven types of affixes. Only the root is obligatory; i.e., slots 1-4 and 6-12 can be blank. (For irregularities in conjugation not treated above, see sec. 15.1.)

* Doesn't combine with *mo-*.

Table B.2. I. and III. Conjugations, Perfect Series

1.	2.	3-4.		5.	7.	8.	9.	10.	11.		12.
PRE-VERBS, *-mo*	OBJ. PERS. PREF.	SUBJECT PERSON PREFIX Perf	Plup.		P/FST	CAUS-ATIVE MARKER	NASAL INFIXES	SCREEVE MARKERS	OBJECT MARKER Perf.	Plup.	PLURAL MARKER
as above	1. v-	1.sg. mi- 1 pl. gvi- 2. gi- 3. u-	me- gve- ge- u-	**ROOT**	-am/-m -av/-v -eb **10.1.1.1**	as above	-n- in some III. conj. verbs in both perf. and plupf. **10.1.1.1-2** -in- in plupf. of regular I. conj. verbs in *-eb*. **10.1.1.2.**	-i- perfect -i- pluperfect (strong) -e- pluperfect (weak)	1. -var 2. -xar 3. -a; -s	 3. -a -o	-t **7.1.2, rules 3-5; 10.1.2.1**

Table B.3. II. Conjugation Perfect Series: Absolute (see Lesson 11)

1. Preverb	2. Subject prefix	3-4. Participle prefix	5. Root	7. P/FSF	8-9. Participle suffix	10-11. Subject person/ screeve markers: perfect	pluperf.	12. Plural marker
as above	v- 1st	m- (11.1)		-m (< -am) -eb -ob-	-il- -ul- -ar- -al- (11.1)	1st -var 2d -xar 3sg. -a 3pl. -an	-iqavi -iqo -iqvnen	-t

Table B.4. II. Conjugation Perfect Series: Relative (see Lesson 11)

1. Preverb	2. Subject prefix	3. Id.o. prefix	5. Root	7. P/FSF	9. Pluperfect marker	10. Screeve markers	11. Subject markers	12. Plural marker
as above	v- 1st	-m- 1sg. -g- 2d -s- 3d -h- 3d -gv- 1pl.		-eb- -v- (< -av) -m- (< -am) -ob-	-od-	-i (perf. and plu- perf.)	perfect 1st -var 2d -xar 3sg. -a 3pl. -an pluperf. 3sg. -a 3pl. -nen	-t

Table B.5. IV. Conjugation: Present, Future, and Aorist Series (See sec. 12.1.2)

1.	2.	3.	4.	5.	7.	9.	10.	11.	12.
PRE-VERBS	OBJ. PERS. PREF.	SUBJECT PREFIX	PV		P/FST	IMPERFECT, COND., CONJ. MARKER	SCREEVE MARKERS	OBJECT MARKER	PLURAL MARKER
(rare)	1. v-	1sg. m- 1pl. gv- 2. g- 3. h- s-	Present series: i-/u- a- ——— Remaining series: e-	ROOT	Present series: -av -i ——— Future series: -eb	Present series: -d- -od- ——— Future series: -od-	-i- imperf., cond., future -e- conjunc. aorist -o- optative	Present: 1. -var 2. -xar 3. -s, -a ——— -a imperf. aor. -s conj. opt.	-t **12.1.2.1**

The perfect series is formed according to the pattern of relative II. conj. verbs, except that inversion occurs; i.e., what marks the indirect object in the relative II. conj. verb marks the subject in the IV. conj. verb, and what marks the subject in the relative II. conj. verb marks the object in the IV. conj. verb.

Table B.6. Passives of State: Present Tense; Future and Aorist Series (see sec. 13.4)

2. Subject prefix	3. Object prefix	4. Preradical vowel	5. Root	7. P/FSF	9. Cond., conj. marker	10. Screeve markers	11. Subject suffixes	12. Plural marker
v- 1st	forms as above	as above		present: none	Future series:	-i- pres., future	as above	-t
				Future series: -eb-	-od-	-e- conj., aorist		
						-o- opt.		

Perfect series forms are conjugated like II. conj. perfect series, absolute or relative.

APPENDIX C: Summary of Screeve Endings

Present, Future:

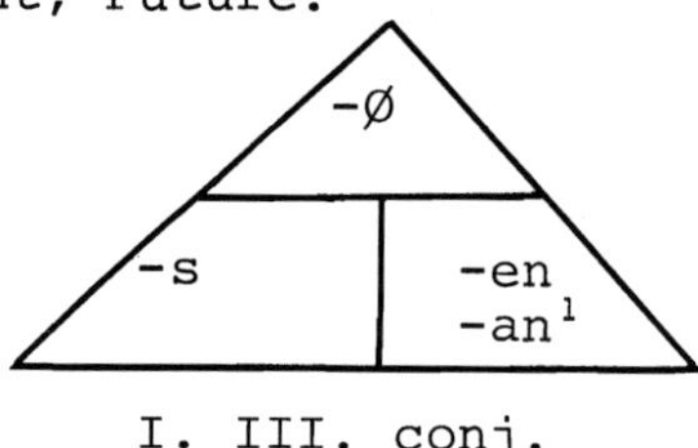

I. III. conj.

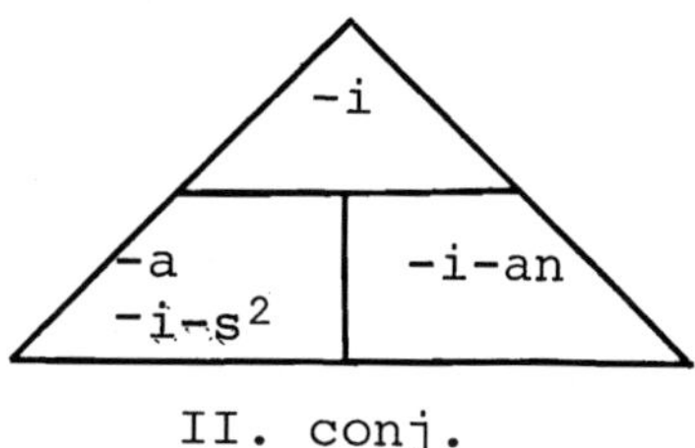

II. conj.

Imperfect, Conditional, Conjunctive:

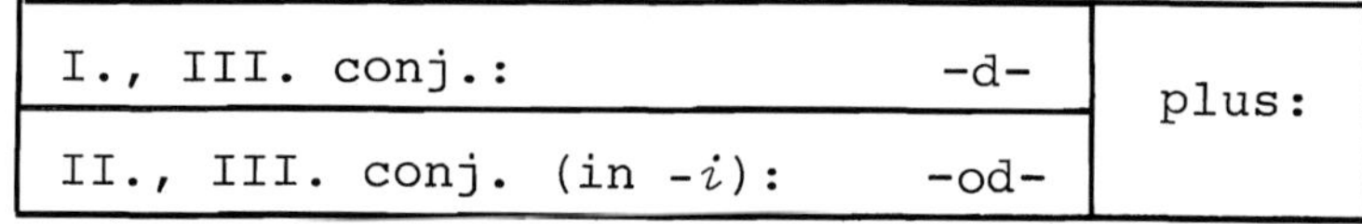

I., III. conj.:	-d-	plus:
II., III. conj. (in -*i*):	-od-	

a. Imperfect, Conditional b. Conjunctive

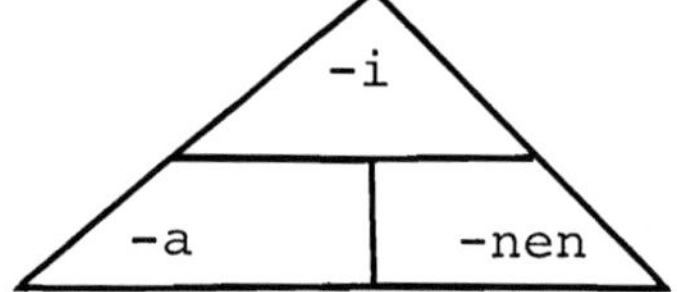

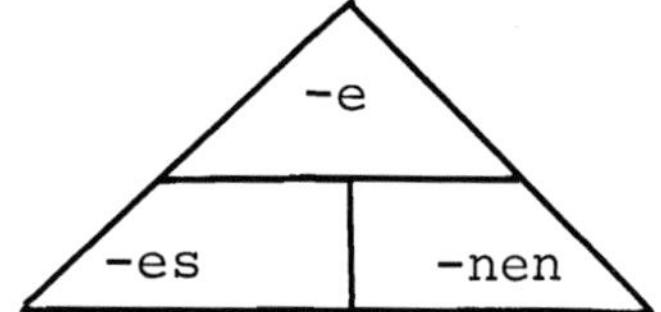

Aorist:

a. I., III. Conj.

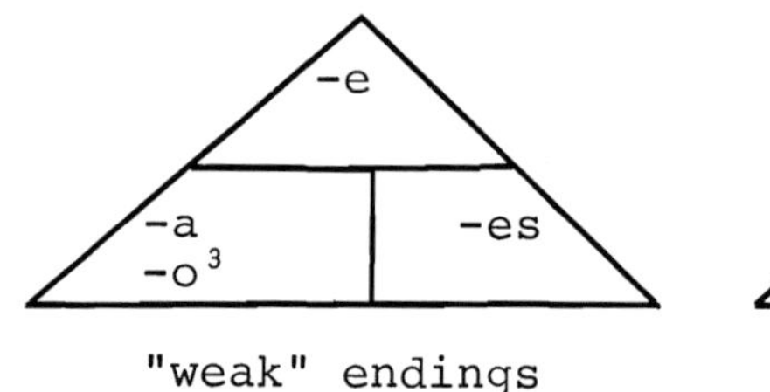

"weak" endings

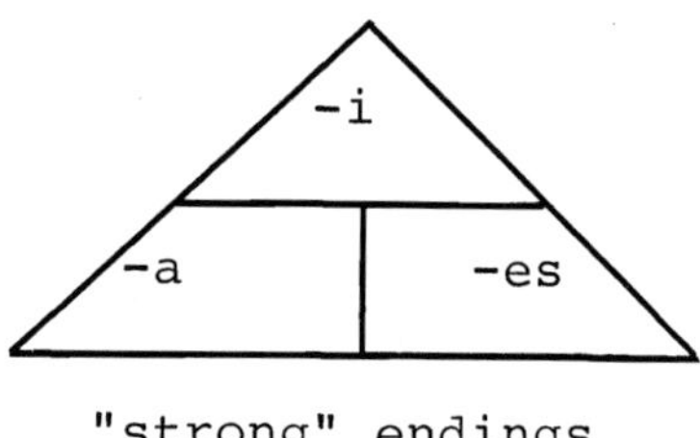

"strong" endings

b. II. Conj.

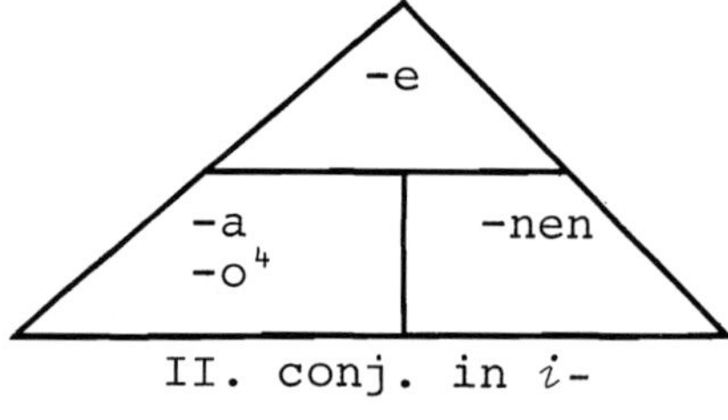

II. conj. in *i*-

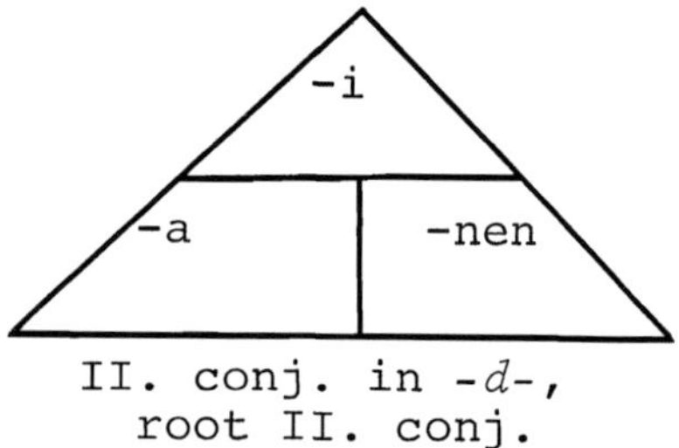

II. conj. in -*d*-, root II. conj.

Optative:

a. I. Conj., III., Conj., II. Conj. in *i*-:

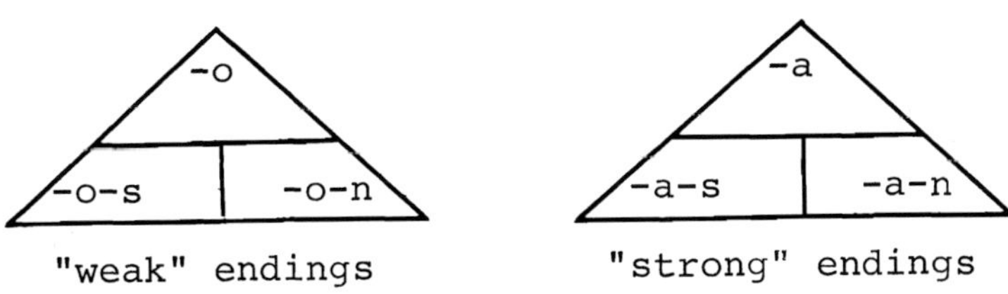

"weak" endings "strong" endings

b. II. Conj. in -*d*- and Root II. Conj.:

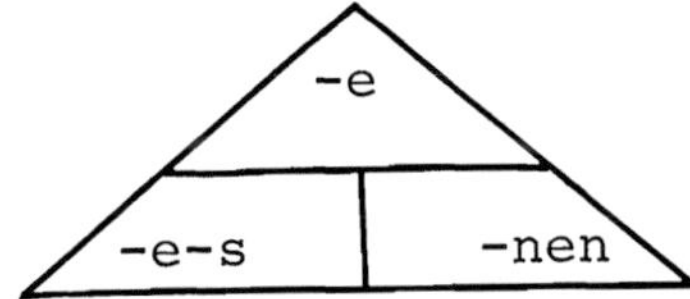

(The verb მიცემა (მოცემა) 'give' also takes these endings, except 3pl. მიეცენ.)

1. With P/FSF -*i*.
2. See secs. 3.1.4.3, 3.1.4.4.
3. With I. conj. verbs with no root vowel and P/FSF -*eb*, -*ob*.
4. In II. conj. verbs derived from verbs described in note 3, above.

APPENDIX D

Summary of the forms of ყოფნა 'be'

Present subseries: (only present tense)

Present:	1.	ვარ(თ)	3sg.	არის
	2.	ხარ(თ)	3pl.	არიან

Future subseries:

Future:	1-2.	(ვ)იქნები(თ)	3sg.	იქნება
			3pl.	იქნებიან

(Remaining screeves of the future subseries are regular II. conj. verbs in *i*-.)

Aorist series:

Aorist:	1-2.	(ვ)იყავი(თ)	3sg.	იყო
			3pl.	იყვნენ
Optative:	1-2.	(ვ)იყო(თ)	3sg.	იყოს
			3pl.	იყვნენ, იყონ

Perfect series:

Perfect:	1.	ვყოფილვარ(თ)	3sg.	ყოფილა
	2.	ყოფილხარ(თ)	3pl.	ყოფილან
Pluperfect:	1-2.	(ვ)ყოფილიყავი(თ)	3sg.	ყოფილიყო
			3pl.	ყოფილიყვნენ

Summary of the forms of სვლა 'go', 'come', etc. (სვლა will be exemplified with the preverb *mo*- = 'come'.)

Present subseries:

Present:	1.	მოვდივარ(თ)	3sg.	მოდის
	2.	მოდიხარ(თ)	3pl.	მოდიან
Imperfect:	1-2.	მო(ვ)დიოდი(თ)	3sg.	მოდიოდა
			3pl.	მოდიოდნენ
Conjunctive:	1-2.	მო(ვ)დიოდე(თ)	3sg.	მოდიოდეს
			3pl.	მოდიოდნენ

Future subseries:

Future:	1.	მოვალ(თ)	3sg.	მოვა
	2.	მოხვალ(თ)	3pl.	მოვლენ

Conditional:	1.	მოვიდოდი(თ)	3sg.	მოვიდოდა
	2.	მოხვიდოდი(თ)	3pl.	მოვიდოდნენ
Conjunctive:	1.	მოვიდოდე(თ)	3sg.	მოვიდოდეს
	2.	მოხვიდოდე(თ)	3pl.	მოვიდოდნენ
Aorist series:				
Aorist:	1.	მოვედი(თ)	3sg.	მოვიდა
	2.	მოხვედი(თ)	3pl.	მოვიდნენ
Optative:	1.	მოვიდე(თ)	3sg.	მოვიდეს
	2.	მოხვიდე(თ)	3pl.	მოვიდნენ
Imperative:	მოდი(თ)!			
Perfect series:				
Perfect:	1.	მოვსულვარ(თ)	3sg.	მოსულა
	2.	მოსულხარ(თ)	3pl.	მოსულან
Pluperfect:	1-2.	მო(ვ)სულიყავი(თ)	3sg.	მოსულიყო
			3pl.	მოსულიყვნენ

APPENDIX E: Common Phrases and Expressions

Hello!	გამარჯობა! გამარჯობათ!
Hello: (response)	გაგიმარჯოს! გაგიმარჯოთ!
Good morning!	დილა მშვიდობისა!
Good evening!	საღამო მშვიდობისა!
Good night!	ღამე ნებისა!
Goodby!	ნახვამდის!; კარგად იყავი(თ)!
Farewell!	მშვიდობით!
How are you?	როგორ(ა) ხარ(თ)?
I'm well, thank you.	გმადლობთ, კარგად.
How do you feel?	როგორ გრძნობ(თ) თავს?
Pleased to meet you.	სასიამოვნოა შენი (თქვენი) გაცნობა!
Please	გთხოვ(თ); გეთაყვა
Thank you	გმადლობ(თ)
Excuse me	უკაცრავად!; ბოდიში!
Forgive me	მაპატიე(თ)!
Happy birthday	გილოცავ(თ) დაბადების დღეს!
Happy New Year	გილოცავ(თ) ახალ წელს!
Bon voyage	გისურვებ(თ) ბედნიერ მგზავრობას!
To your health (toast)	იცოცხლე(თ); იდღეგრძელე(თ)!
Do you speak English?	თქვენ ლაპარაკობთ ინგლისურად?
What time is it?	რომელი საათია?
It is 10:00.	ათი საათია.
It is 10:20.	ათი საათი და ოცი წუთია.
It is 10:15.	თერთმეტის თხუთმეტი წუთია.*
It is 10:30.	თერთმეტის ნახევარია.*
It is a quarter to 11.	თერთმეტს აკლია თხუთმეტი წუთი.
At 6:00 p.m.	საღამოს ექვს საათზე.

*Note that the *following* hour in the genitive is used in these expressions.

Days of the week:

Sunday	კვირა	On Sunday	კვირას
Monday	ორშაბათი		
Tuesday	სამშაბათი		
Wednesday	ოთხშაბათი		
Thursday	ხუთშაბათი		
Friday	პარასკევი		
Saturday	შაბათი		

Months of the year:

January	იანვარი (A)	In January	იანვარში
February	თებერვალი (A)		
March	მარტი		
April	აპრილი		
May	მაისი		
June	ივნისი		
July	ივლისი		
August	აგვისტო		
September	სექტემბერი (E)		
October	ოქტომბერი (E)		
November	ნოემბერი (E)		
December	დეკემბერი (E)		

Seasons:

Summer	ზაფხული
In summer	ზაფხულში
Autumn	შემოდგომა
In the autumn	შემოდგომაზე
Winter	ზამთარი (A)
In winter	ზამთარში
Spring	გაზაფხული
In spring	გაზაფხულზე

Money

Copeck	კაპიკი	Ruble	მანეთი
5 copecks	შაური	10 rubles	თუმანი (A)
20 copecks	აბაზი		

APPENDIX F: Bibliography

Grammars.

Руденко, Б. Т. *Грамматика грузинского языка*. Moscow, Leningrad, 1940. Reprint, 's-Gravenhage, 1972. [A brief survey of Georgian grammar concentrating mainly on inflection rather than on meaning and uses of forms.]

Tschenkéli, Kita. *Einführung in die georgische Sprache*. 2 vols. Zurich, 1958. [A superlative work, rich in detail, covering almost all aspects of the language. A combination grammar-textbook. Volume 2 consists of graded exercises and a chrestomathy of Georgian literary selections. Indispensible for the serious student.]

Vogt, Hans. *Grammaire de la langue géorgienne*. Oslo, 1971. [A thorough, solid, linguistically sophisticated analysis of Georgian by an outstanding linguist. Has excellent examples taken from Georgian literature.]

Dictionaries.

Cherkesi, E. *Georgian-English Dictionary*. Oxford, 1950. [Good selection of vocabulary, though no grammatical information is given. Verbs are listed under verbal noun.]

Gvarjaladze, Isidore, and Gvarjaladze, Tamar. *English-Georgian and Georgian-English Dictionary*. Tbilisi, 1974. [A pocket-sized two-way dictionary. No grammatical information given; verbs are listed under verbal noun.]

Gvardjaladzé, Isidore, and Lébanidzé, E. *Dictionnaire géorgien-français*. Tbilisi, 1971. [Large selection of vocabulary but no grammatical information. Verbs are listed under verbal noun.]

Gvarjaladze, Isidor, and Gvarjaladze, Thamar. *Georgian-English Dictionary*. Tbilisi, 1979. [Large selection of vocabulary but no grammatical information. Verbs are listed under verbal noun.]

Канкава, М. В. *Краткий грузинско-русский словарь*. Tbilisi, 1965. [No grammatical information. Verbs are listed under verbal noun.]

Meckelein, Richard. *Georgisch-deutsches Wörterbuch*. Berlin, Leipzig, 1928. [Good, large selection of vocabulary. No grammatical information; verbs listed under verbal noun.]

Tschenkéli, Kita. *Georgisch-deutsches Wörterbuch*. 3 vols. Zurich, 1965-74. [*The* indispensible dictionary. It is in essence a translation of the 8-volume

Academy dictionary, but far superior in its treatment of verbs. Grammatical information is outstanding, often far more complete than in the Academy dictionary. Verbs are listed by root.]

Major Georgian sources.

აკაკი შანიძე, ქართული გრამატიკის საფუძვლები. [Fundamentals of Georgian grammar.] Tbilisi, 1973. [The standard and most complete Georgian grammar.]

არნოლდ ჩიქობავა, ქართული ენის განმარტებითი ლექსიკონი. [Explanatory dictionary of the Georgian language.] 8 vols. Tbilisi, 1950-64. [The official "unabridged" Academy dictionary.]

APPENDIX G: SOURCES OF ILLUSTRATIONS

PAGES

73. Tsitsishvili, Irakli. *Tbilisi: Architectural Landmarks and Art Museums, an Illustrated Guide*. Leningrad (Aurora): 1985, p. 133.
79. Kvirkvelija, T. R. *Arxitektura Tbilisi*. Moskva (Strojizdat):1985, p. 53.
98. Xucišvili, G. *Tbilisi čerez veka i gody*. Tbilisi (Sabçota Sakartvelo): 1983, p. 68.
100. Beridze, V. V. *Iskusstvo Gruzinksoj SSR*. Leningrad (Avrora): 1972, plate 15.
107. Amiranašvili, Š. *Vklad Gruzii v sokrovišču xudožestvennoj kul'tury*. Tbilisi (AN GSSR): 1963, plate 8.
141. Loladze, M. V. *On the Highways of Georgia*. Tbilisi (Sabçota Sakartvelo): 1975, p.2.
159. Javakhishvili, A. and G. Gvelesiani, eds. *Soviet Georgia, its Geography, History and Economy*. Moscow (Progress): n.d., facing p. 41.
168. *Georgian Soviet Socialist Republic*. Moscow (Novosti): n.d.
188. Davitaja, F. F. otv. red. *Sovetskij Sojuz: Gruzija*. Moscow (Mysl'): 1967, facing p. 80.
231. -----. *Georgian Soviet Socialist Republic*. Moscow (Novosti): n.d.
249. -----. *Iraklij Moiseevič Toidze*. Moscow-Leningrad (Sovetskij xudožnik): 1950.
253. -----. *Georgian Soviet Socialist Republic*. Moscow (Novosti): n.d.
266. Davitaja, F. F. otv. red. *Sovetskij Sojuz: Gruzija*. Moscow (Mysl'): 1967, 131.

282, 298, 331, 369. Xucišvili, G. *Tbilisi čerez veka i gody*. Tbilisi (Sabçota Sakartvelo): 1983, p. 47, 123, 149, 89.

320. -----. *Science, éducation, culture*. Tbilisi (Edition de la Chambre de commerce et d'industrie de la R.S.S. de Géorgie): 1975.
351. -----. *Kartuli xelnaçerebi*. Tbilisi (Xelovneba): 1970, plate 3.

396, 413, 415, 443. (From a collection of postcards of Pirosmanašvili's works.)

APPENDIX G: Sources of Readings

Lesson 5. „თბილისი." შ. თაბუკაშვილი, ვ. რამიშვილი, თ. ჩერქეზიშვილი, ქართული ენა, III კლასის სახელმძღვანელო, თბილისი, 1957, გვ. 90.

Lesson 6. „კავკასიური ენები." ა. ჩიქობავა, ზოგადი ენათმეცნიერება, I., თბილისი, 1939, გვ. 116-117.

Lesson 7. „ქუთაისი." საქართველოს სსრ, მოკლე ისტორიულ-ეკონომიკური ნარკვევი, თბილისი, 1970, გვ. 264-265.

Lesson 8. „მოხევეების საოჯახო ყოფა." ვალერიან ითონიშვილი, მოხევეების საოჯახო ყოფა, თბილისი, 1970, გვ. 3-4.

Lesson 9. „საქართველოს სსრ მოსახლეობა." ლ. კარბელაშვილი, გ. გეხტმანი, საქართველოს სსრ ეკონომიური გეოგრაფია, IX კლასის სახელმძღვანელო, თბილისი, 1961, გვ. 3-4.

Lesson 10. „ზაქარია ფალიაშვილი." 50 ოპერა, თბილისი, 1966, გვ. 329-331.

Lesson 11. „რეპორტაჟი საქართველოდან." მიხეილ დავითაშვილი, რეპორტაჟი საქართველოდან, თბილისი, 1971, გვ. 11-13.

Lesson 12. ალ. ლონტი, „ძველი ქართული თარიღები," დროშა, 1977, № 12, გვ. 10.

Lesson 13. „ნიკო ფიროსმანიშვილი." შალვა ამირანაშვილი, ქართული ხელოვნების ისტორია, თბილისი, 1971, გვ. 494-495.

Lessons 14-15. „დაბადების დღე." ნოდარ დუმბაძე, მზიანი ღამე, თბილისი, 1967, გვ. 5-14.

GEORGIAN-ENGLISH VOCABULARY

This vocabulary contains all the words in the exercises to the lessons except for proper names. Names of countries and of historical provinces of Georgia are included in the main vocabulary; other geographic names are listed separately after the main vocabulary. Words occurring only in the reading selections and personal names are not given here.

Verbs are listed and alphabetized by root. Preverbs, preradical vowels and object markers follow the root, present or future stem formant and person markers except for IV. conjugation verbs, whose entries (although alphabetized according to root) begin with the 1st person subject marker. Examples:

I. conjugation

-სწორებს, გა=ა　　root = *sc̣or-*　　გაასწორებს

-სწავლის, Ø=ა　　root = *sc̣avl-*; present and future are identical　　ასწავლის

II. conjugation

-რჩება, და=　　root = *rč-*　　დარჩება

-ცვლება, გარდა+ი　　root = *cvl-*　　გარდაიცვლება

II. conjugation

მღერის　　root = *mğer-*　　მღერის

-ცინის, ი-　　root = *cin-*, *i-* = preradical vowel　　იცინის

IV. conjugation

მი-ყვარს　　root = *qvar-*, listed under ყ　　მიყვარს

მე-სმის　　root = *sm-*, listed under ს　　მესმის

Grammatical information about irregular forms is not given in this vocabulary but can be found in the vocabularies to the exercises of the individual lessons. Words in this vocabulary marked with an asterisk (*) show such irregularities and should be checked in the lesson. For verbs of motion, see sec. 4.5.

The symbol ‖ represents the entry word, so that under the entry for -მარტავს, გან = the listing ‖სი-ტყვას represents განმარტავს სიტყვას.

Other symbols, etc. are as used in the vocabularies to the individual lessons. •Addenda, p. 526.

ა

აგვისტო 6 August

ადამიანი 8 human being, person

ადგილი 6 place

ადგილას 14 in a, the place

ადვილი 3 easy

ადმირალი 12 admiral

ადრე 4 early

აეროპორტი 7 airport

ავად 5 sick

ავადმყოფი 10 patient, sick person

ავადმყოფობა 14 disease, illness

ავტონომიური 6 autonomous

ავტორი 3 author

აზერბაიჯანი 5 Azerbaijan

აი 8 here is, are; there is, are

აივანი(A) 9 balcony

აკადემია 3 academy

აკადემიკოსი 8 academician

აკრძალული 8 forbidden

ალბათ 3 probably

ალბანეთი 11 Albania (both in Caucasus and Balkans)

ამას წინათ 5 recently, a short time ago

ამბავი* (A) 9 story, information, news; thing

ამდენი 13 so much, this much

ამერიკა 4 America

ამიერკავკასია 5 Transcaucasia (lit., Cis-Caucasia)

ამინდი 4 weather

ამირბარი 12 (archaic term for 'admiral')

ამიტომ 10 therefore

ამხანაგი 6 comrade

ან 7 or [non-interrogative]

ანალიზი 4 analysis

ანბანი 2 alphabet

ანგარიში	9	bill, account; calculation
ანდაზა	8	proverb
ანი	8	name of the letter 'ა'
ანუ	6	or, in other words
აპრილი	9	April
არ, არა	2	not
არა	2	no
არაბი	12	an Arab
არამედ	4	but rather
არავითარი	11	no (kind of) (adj.)
არავინ*	13	no one
არასოდეს	10	never
არაფერი (E)	13	nothing
არაყი (A)	5	vodka, brandy
არდადეგები (pl.)	4	vacation
არია	8	aria
-არსებს, და=ა	8	establish
არსად	13	nowhere, not ... anywhere
არსებობს	9	exist, be
არქიტექტურა	6	architecture
არც.... არც	10	neither ... nor
ასე	6	so
ასეთი ●	6	such (a)
ასული	6	daughter
აუცილებლად	12	certainly, without fail
აფხაზი	6	an Abkhaz
აქ	3	here
აქამდის	11	up to now
აქცენტი	4	accent
აღარაფერი (E)	7	nothing any more (see sec. 6.4.2)
აღმაშენებელი (E)	6	builder, restorer
აღმოსავლეთი	4	east(ern)
აჭარა	6	Adjaria
აჭარელი (E)	6	an Adjarian

ახალგაზრდა	7	young; youth (person)
ახალი (A)	2	new
-ახლ		see -ხლ
ახლა	2	now
ახლანდელი (E)	11	present(-day)
ახლოს	6, 9	adverb, pp. near
ახსნა-განმარტება	10	explanation

ბ

-ბადებს, და=	5	bear, bring into the world
დაიბადება	5	be born
ბავშვი	3	child, baby
ბაზარი (A)	9	market
ბალეტი	8	ballet
-ბანს, და=	7	wash
ბანი	8	name of the letter 'ბ'
ბაჟი	7	(customs) duty
ბასკი	6	a Basque
ბატონი	6	Mr. (see lesson 6, note 9)
ბაღი	6	garden
ბაყაყი	9	frog
ბგერა	4	sound
ბებია	7	grandmother
ბევრი	6	much, many
ბერი	5	monk
ბერძენი (E)	4	a Greek
-ბეჭდავს, და=	3	print
ბეჯითი	3	diligent
ბიბლია	4	Bible
ბიბლიოთეკა	6	library
ბიოგრაფია	3	biography
ბიძა	7	uncle
-ბნევს, და=ა	10	confuse
ბნელი	4	dark
ბოდიში	9	excuse, apology

ბოდიშს ვიხდი	9	excuse me!
ბოთლი	7	bottle
ბოლო	4	end, conclusion
ბოლშევიკი	8	Bolshevik
ბომბა	13	bomb
ბრალდებული	9	accused
ბრინჯი	10	rice
-ბრუნებს, და=ა	6	return
-ბრუნდება, მი=	8	return
ბრუნვა	10	(grammatical) case
-ბრძანებს, ∅=	6	order, command
ბრძანდები(თ)	14	(see sec. 14.1.1.2)
ბრძოლა	8	struggle, battle
ბუნება	12	nature
ბუნებრივი	12	natural
გ		
-გებს, გა=ი	4	understand; learn, find out; hear
-გებს, მო=ი	13	win
-გებს, წა=ა	13	lose
გადასახადი	13	tax
გაერთიანება	6	unification
გაზაფხული	9	spring
გაზეთი	2	newspaper
გათენება	8	dawn, dawning
გაკვეთილი	2	lesson
გამო	4	(pp.) because of, on account of
გამოგონება	11	invention
გამომგონებელი (E)	11	inventor
გამომქვეყნებელი (E)	5	publisher
გამომცემლობა	3	publishing house
გამოფენა	6	exhibit
გამოცდა	3	examination
გამყიდველი	7	salesperson

განათლება 11 education, instruction
განვითარება 10 development, education
განმავლობაში 10 (pp.) in the course of, during
განსაკუთრებით 12 particularly, especially
გარდა 12 (pp.) in addition to, except for, besides
გარეთ 3 outside
გარკვეული 4 clear, explicit; (a) certain
გასაღები 7 key
გასული 5 last, previous
გემო 12 taste
გენერალი (A) 7 general (military rank)
გენეტიკა 6 genetics
გეოგრაფი 12 geographer
გერმანია ● 5 Germany
-გვიანებს, და=ი 5 be late (intrans.)
გვიან 3 late
გვირგვინი 13 crown, wreath, garland
გზა 4 road, way
-გზავნის, გა= ● 7 send
გიჟი 8 crazy
გლეხი 11 peasant
გმირი 6 hero
გოგონა* 13 little girl
მ-გონია 12 think, seem
-გონებს, გა=ი 14 hear
გრამატიკა 2 grammar
გრილი 12 cool
-გრძელებს, გა=ა 2 continue
-გრძელებს, და=ა 7 lengthen
გრძელი* 9 long
გრძნობა 12 feeling, sense
გული 13 heart
გუნდი 8 choir, chorus; team

გუშინ	2	yesterday
გუშინდელი (E)	3	yesterday's
გუშინწინ	10	day before yesterday
დ		
-დებს, და=*	13	put down
და	2	and
და	4	sister
დაახლოებით	6	approximately
დათვი	8	bear
დამოწმებული	5	attested
დამწერლობა	11	writing system, writing
დანა	3	knife
-დარებს, შე=ა	6	compare
დასავლეთი	4	west(ern)
დაფა	13	blackboard
და-ძმა	12	brother(s) and sister(s), siblings
დახურული	10	closed
-დგება, ი-*	9	be standing
-დგება, და=*	9	stand up
-დგება, წარ+*	9	appear (before)
-დგამს, და=	9	put down
დგა-		see -დგება
-დგენს, და=ა	11	fix, determine
-დგენს, წარმო=ა	6	present; perform
-დგენს, წარმო+ა	10	represent, be [only present series]
დედა	2	mother
დედალი(A)	13	hen; female (of animals)
დედაქალაქი	4	capital city
დევს*	13	be lying
დეკემბერი (E)	9	December
დემოკრატიული	9	democratic
-დექ-		see -დგება
-დვ-		see დევს
დიახ	2	yes

დიდი	2	big, large; great
დიდხანს	8	for a long time
დილა	6	morning
დინამო	13	dynamo; name of a sports team
დისერტაცია	9	dissertation
დოქტორი	9	doctor (Ph.D.)
დრო	4	time
დროზე	4	on time
დროს	4	(pp.) during
დუმს*	8	be silent
დუღს	8	boil
დღე	2	day
დღეს	2	today
დღესასწაული	8	holiday
ე		
ეგრისი	6	Colchis (West Georgia)
ევროპა	4	Europe
ე.ი.		see ესე იგი
ეკლესია	4	church
ეკონომიკა	3	economics
ელავს*	8	(be) lightning
ელჩი	7	ambassador
ენა	2	language; tongue
ეპისკოპოსი	7	bishop
ერა	6	era
ჩვენს ერამდე	6	B.C.
-ერთებს, შე=ა	7	unite
ერთად	4	together [see Lesson 4, note 5]
ერთადერთი	11	only one, the only, a single, unique
ერთ-ერთი	9	one (of several)
ერთი	4	one
ერთი და იგივე*	14	one and the same
-ერთიანებს, გა=ა	6	unite
ერთმანეთი	7	each other

ერთხელ	9	once, one time
ერი	5	people, nation
ესე იგი	9	that is, i.e.
ექიმი	4	doctor (of medicine)
ექსპორტი	12	export
ვ		
ვაჟიშვილი	6	son
ვარდი	6	rose
ვახშამი (A)	10	supper
-ვე	11	(particle indicating identity; same)
ვეფხისტყაოსანი (A)	4	*The Knight in the Tiger Skin* (poem by Šota Rustaveli)
ვიდრე	9	than
ვინ*	4	who?
ვინმე*	14	someone, anyone
ვინაიდან	5	because
ვიღა?*	14	who (in the world)?
ვიღაც(ა)*	14	someone; some (person)
-ვიწყებს, და=ი	6	forget
-ვიწყდება, და=ა	12	forget (see sec. 12.1.2.4)
ვრცელი	7	extensive, long
ზ		
ზი-		see -ჯდ-
ზამთარი (A)	8	winter
ზანური	6	Zan (= Mingrelian and Laz)
ზარი	8	bell
ზაფხული	12	summer
ზეგ	3	day after tomorrow
ზმნა	2	verb
ზოგი	6	some
ზოგიერთი	7	several
-ზრდის, აღ=	9	raise, bring up
-ზრდის, გა=	9	raise, grow
ზუსტი	8	exact

თ

თაგვი	8	mouse
-თავებს, გა=ა	3	finish
თავაზიანი	9	polite
თავგადასავალი (A)	8	adventure
თავდაპირველი	11	original, initial, first
თავი	3	head; chapter
თავიანთი	8	their own
თავისუფალი (A)	10	free
თამადა	9	toastmaster (at Georgian banquet)
თამაშობს	8	play (games, roles)
თამაში	6	game
თანამედროვე	11	contemporary
თარგმანი	2	translation (i.e., book, article)
-თარგმნის, გადა=	2	translate
თარიღი	6	date
თბილი	9	warm
თეატრი	4	theater
თეთრი	2	white
თეორიული	11	theoretical
-თესავს, და=	10	sow
თვე	9	month
თვითმფრინავი	8	airplane
თვითონ	12	(one)self
-თვლის, ჩა=	3	consider (as + Adv.)
თითი	8	finger
ფეხის თითი	8	toe
თითქმის	6	almost
თოვს	8	to snow
თუ	3, 4, 10	a. if (sec. 4.1.2), b. or (in questions), c. intensifies a question
თუ შეიძლება	9	if possible

თუმცა	3	although
თურმე	10	apparently
თურქი	6	a Turk
-თქვამს, წარმო+	2	pronounce
-თქვ-		see -ტყვ-
თქვენი ●	2	your, yours (pl.)
თხზულება	3	composition, (literary) work
-თხრ-		see -ტყვ-

ი

იატაკი	13	floor (as opposed to ceiling)
იაფი	7	cheap, inexpensive
იბერია	6	Iberia (East Georgia)
იგივე	14	the same (see sec. 14.1.3)
ივლისი	4	July
ივნისი	10	June
იმდენი ●	7	that much
იმ დროს, როდესაც; იმ დროს, როცა	5	while
იმიტომ	4	for that reason
იმიტომ, რომ	4	because
ინგლისი	14	England
ინგლისური	2	English (adj.)
ინდოეთი	12	India
ინსტიტუტი	4	institute
ირემი(E)	9	deer
ისე	9	so, thus
ისე..., რომ	9	so ... that
ისევე	14	just so, just as
ისეთი	14	such (a)
ისეთივე	14	just the same, just such (a)
ისრაელი	9	Israel
ისტორია	3	history
ისტორიკოსი	5	historian
იტალია	5	Italy

იუმორისტული 8 humorous
იქ 3 there
იქვე 14 there (in the same place), ibid.
იქნებ(ა) 6 perhaps (+ opt.)

კ

კაბა 7 dress
კავკასია 6 Caucasus (region)
კავშირი 5 union
კათალიკოსი 5 catholicos (patriarch of the church)
კალათბურთი 8 basketball
კალამი (A) 3 pen
კანტორა 9 office
კაპიკი 7 copeck
კარგი 3 good
 კარგად 2 well
კარი 5 door; gate
კატა 7 cat
კაცი 5 man
კახეთი 11 Kakhetia (province in East Georgia)
კბილი 10 tooth
კედელი (E) 13 wall
-კეთებს, გა=ა 2 do, make
-კეთებს, გადა+ა 11 remake, alter
კვარტეტი 2 quartet
-კვდება, მო= 8 die
კვერცხი 13 egg
კვირა 6 week; Sunday
კვლავ 6 again
-კვლევს, გამო=ი 3 investigate
კი 2, 8 however, and (see sec. 2.6); yes
-კიდებს, ჩამო= 13 hang
-კითხავს, Ø=ჰ 8 ask s.o. sthg.
-კითხავს, ი-* 14 ask for s.o., ask to see s.o.

-კითხავს, (წა+)ი* 2 read

-კითხებს, (წა=)ა 11 cause s.o. to read, have s.o. read

კითხვა 3 reading; question

კილო 6 dialect

კინოფილმი 2 movie, film

-კლავს, მო= 9 kill

მ-ა-კლია* 12 lack

კლასი 3 class

კლასიკური 2 classical

კმაყოფილი 3 satisfied (+ Instr.)

კნავის* 8 meow

კოვზი 3 spoon

კოლექტივიზაცია 9 collectivization

კოლმეურნე 10 collective farmer (kolkhoznik)

 კოლმეურნეობა 9 collective farm (kolkhoz)

კოლხეთი 6 Colchis (West Georgia)

კომბოსტო 9 cabbage

კომისია 9 commission

კომპოზიტორი 6 composer

კონიაკი 12 (grape) brandy, cognac

კონცერტი 2 concert

-კრავს, და=უ 12 play (musical instrument; no id.o.)

კრება 3 meeting, gathering

კრემლი 4 Kremlin

კუთხე 11 corner; angle; region

კულტურა 5 culture

ლ

-ლაგებს, გა(ნ)=ა 11 locate

-ლაგებს, და=ა 11 arrange, order

 ალაგია 13 be arranged (passive of state)

ლაზი 6 a Laz

ლამაზი 3 pretty, beautiful, good-looking

ლაპარაკობს 8 speak

ლეგენდა 8 legend

ლეგენდარული	8	legendary
-ლევს, და+*	5	drink
ლექსი	2	poem
ლექსიკონი	4	dictionary
ლექცია	3	lecture
ლიმონი	12	lemon
ლინგვისტი	6	linguist
ლინგვისტიკა	2	linguistics
ლიტერატურა	3	literature
ლობიო	9	beans (collective)
-ლოდება, Ø=ე	7	wait for, expect
ლოზუნგი	13	slogan
ლოკომოტივი	13	locomotive; name of a sports team
ლურჯი	3	blue
მ		
მაგალითი	6	example
მაგიდა ●	4	table
გ-მადლობ(თ)	8	thank you
მავზოლეუმი	4	mausoleum
მათემატიკა	3	mathematics
მაინც	9	however, at least, still
-მალავს, და=	3	hide
-მალავს, და=უ	7	hide from s.o.
მალე	3	soon
მამა	2	father
მამაკაცი	8	man (male human being)
მამალი (A)	8	rooster
მანეთი	7	ruble
მარგანეცი	12	manganese
მართალი (A)	13	true
მართლა	13	truly
მართლმადიდებელი (E)	9	an Orthodox (Christian)
მარილი	13	salt
-მარტავს, გან=	7	explain

|| სიტყვას 7 define
მარტო 8 only, alone
მარხავს, და= 9 bury
მარჯვენა 11 right (not left); right hand
მასალა 3 material
მასპინძელი (E) 9 host
მასპინძლობს 8 act as host
მასწავლებელი (E) 2 teacher
მასხარა 8 clown
-მატებს, და=უ 11 add sthg. to sthg.
 -მატება, და=ე 11 (II. conj. form)
მატჩი 13 (sporting) match, game
მაღაზია 7 store
მაღალი (A) 8 high, tall
მაშინ 3 at that time, then
მაწონი* 12 yogurt
-მბ- see -ტყვ-
მდგომარეობა 5 situation
მდიდარი (A) 4 rich
მდინარე 8 river
მეგობარი (A) 4 friend
მეგრული 6 Mingrelian
მედუქნე 5 shopkeeper
მეექვსე 5 sixth
მეზობელი (E) 7 neighbor; neighboring
მეთაური 5 head (of an organization)
-მეთქი 8 (see sec. 8.5)
მელანი (A) 3 ink
-მეორებს, გა=ი 2 repeat
მეორე 3 second
მეპურე 5 baker
მესაზღვრე 7 border guard
მესამე 3 third
მეტი 7 more

მეტისმეტად 7 too, overly
მეფობს 8 reign
მეფე 5 king
  მეფის 6 (gen.) tsarist
მეფობა 6 reign
მეცნიერება 8 science
მეცნიერული 3 scientific
მეცხვარე 5 shepherd
მეხუთე 5 fifth
მეხსიერება 12 memory
-მზადებს, და=ა 3 prepare
-მზადებს, მო=ა 6 prepare
მზად 3 ready
მზე 4 sun
  მზიანი 3 sunny
მთა 4 mountain
მთავარი (A) 3 main
-მთავრებს, და=ა 3 finish, end
მთავრობა 7 government
მთარგმნელი 5 translator
მთაწმინდა 13 lit., 'holy mountain,' mountain overlooking Tbilisi
მთელი 4 whole, entire
მიერ 4 (pp.) by
მილიონი 6 million
მილიცია 8 police
მინერალი 12 mineral
მიხედვით 6 (pp.) according to
მკვლელი 10 murderer, killer
მმართველი 6 ruler
მნიშვნელობა 14 importance, significance
მნიშვნელოვანი 2 important, significant
მოედანი (A) 4 (public) square
მოკლე 7 short

მოლაპარაკე 6 speaker
მომდევნო 11 following
მონათესავე 11 related
მონასტერი (E) 5 monastery
მონაწილეობს 9 participate (only present series)
მორფოლოგია 3 morphology
მოსავალი 9 harvest, yield
მოსამართლე 9 judge
მოსაწვევი ბარათი 11 invitation
მოსახლეობა 10 population
მოულოდნელი 7 unexpected
მოქცევა 11 conversion
მოღვაწე 13 (public) figure, leader
მოწაფე 2 pupil
მოწმე 10 witness
მოხსენება 6 report
მოხუცი 8 old man
მრავალი (A) 8 many
მსახიობი 10 actor
მსგავსი 9 similar
  მსგავსად 9 (pp.) like, similar to
  მსგავსება 9 similarity, resemblance
მსოფლიო 12 world
მსხვერპლი 10 victim
მსხვილი 8 thick
მტერი (E) 7 enemy
-მტკიცებს, და=ა 6 maintain, prove
მუდამ 3 always
მუზეუმი 12 museum
მუსიკა 2 music
მუსლიმანი 6 Moslem
მუშაობს 8 work
მუხლი 13 knee, lap
მღერის 8 sing

მღვდელი (E) 7 priest
-მყარებს, და=ა 8 establish, found
მშვენიერი* 11 beautiful
მშობლები 7 (pl.) parents
მძიმე 13 heavy
მწერალი (A) 3 writer
მწვადი 12 shish-kebab, shashlik
მწვანე 3 green
მწვანილი 9 vegetable
მწყემსი 10 shepherd
მხატვარი (A) 11 artist, painter
მხოლოდ 2 only
-მჯობინებს, Ø=ა 11 prefer sthg., s.o. to sthg., s.o.

ნ

ნადირობს 9 hunt
-ნათესავება, და=ე 11 be related to
ნათესაობა 11 relationship
ნავთობი 12 oil, petroleum
ნაკლებობა 8 lack, shortage
ნამდვილი 9 real, actual
ნარკვევი 12 essay, study
ნაწარმი 12 product
ნაწარმოები 9 derivative, work
ნაწილი 3 part, section
ნახავს* 2 see
-ნახავს, და+ი 8 catch sight of, see
-ნახავს, შემო=ი 11 keep, preserve; save (e.g., money)
ნახევარი (A) 10 half
ნახშირი 12 coal
მი-ნდა* 12 want
მ-ნებავს* 12 (would) like (polite)
ნელი 3 slow
ნელა 3 slowly
-ნთებს, და=ა 13 light (a fire)

ნიმუში 6 model, specimen
-ნიშნავს, ალ+ or ალ= 2 mean
ნოემბერი (E) 7 November
ნოხი 7 carpet, rug

ო

ოთახი 4 room
ოთხშაბათი 8 Wednesday
  ოთხშაბათს 8 on Wednesday
ოლქი 6 region
ომი 4 war
ოპერა 2 opera
ორთოგრაფია 13 spelling, orthography
ორივე 8 both
ორშაბათი 8 Monday
  ორშაბათს 8 on Monday
ოსტატი 7 master; craftsman
ოქრო 10 gold
ოქტომბერი (E) 9 October
-ოხრებს, ა=ა 6 overrun, ravage, devastate
ოჯახი 11 family

პ

პაკეტი 5 package
პანთეონი 13 pantheon; cemetary in Tbilisi where famous people are buried
პაპა 6 grandfather
პაპიროსი 7 cigarette
-პარავს, მო=პ 10 steal from s.o.
პარკი 10 park
პარლამენტი 9 parliament
პასუხობს* 8 answer s.o.
პასუხი 4 answer
-პატიჟებს, და= 13 invite
პატარა* 7 small, little
პატიმარი (A) 13 prisoner

პერანგი 7 shirt

პერიოდი 5 period

პიანინო 12 piano

პიესა 2 (theater) play

-პირებს, და=ა 6 intend

პირველი 3 first

პირველ ყოვლისა 13 first of all

პირი 7 face; mouth

პირობა 9 condition

პოემა 5 (longer) poem

პოეტი 4 poet

-პოვის, ი-* 9 find

-პოვება, მო+ი 9 be found (only present series)

პოლიტეკონომია 10 political economy

პოლიტიკა 9 politics

პორტრეტი 6 portrait

პრინციპი 13 principle

პროგრამა 5 program

პროტოტიპი 8 prototype

პროფესიული 11 professional

პროფესორი 3 professor

პური 3 bread

ჟ

ჟურნალი 2 magazine

რ

რა? 2 what?

რადგანაც 8 for, because

რადიო 5 radio

რადიოგადაცემა 2 radio program

რაიმე 14 (= რამე)

რამ, რამე 14 thing; something, some kind of

რამდენი? 6 how much?, how many?

რამდენიმე 6 several

რამდენიც 7 as much

რასაკვირველია	6	of course
რატომ	3	why?
რაღაც(ა)	14	something; some (thing)
რაც	5	what, which, that (rel.)
რაც + comparative ... მით + comparative	12	the more ... the more
-რბის, გა+*	13	run away
-რბის, შე+*	9	run in(to)
-რბენ-		see -რბ-
რედაქტორი	3	editor
რედაქცია	11	redaction, edition
რევოლუცია	9	revolution
-რეკავს, და=უ *	7	telephone s.o.
რესპუბლიკა	5	republic
რესტორანი (A)	4	restaurant (also without syncope)
რექტორი	12	rector (head of a university)
რეცენზია	7	review, critique
-რეცხავს, გა=	13	wash something (inanimate)
რვეული	3	notebook
რიგი ●	9	row, order, series
როგორ?	8	how?
როგორი?	8	of what kind?, how?
როგორც	10	as
როდესაც	2	when
როდის?	2	when?
როდისმე	14	at some time, at any time
რომ	4, 6	a. in (in conditionals, sec. 4.1.2), b. that
რომანი	2	novel
რომელი (E)	4	which?
როცა	2	when
რუსი	4	a Russian
რუსული	2	Russian (adj.)
-რქვ-		see -ქვ-

-რქმევ- see -ქვ-

-რჩება, და= 9 remain

-რჩება, მო= 9 be healed

მი-რჩევნია* 12 prefer

-რჩენს, მო=ა 9 heal

მ-რცხვენია* 12 be ashamed

ს

საათი 6, 8 hour; watch, clock

საბეჭდი მანქანა 13 typewriter

საბუთი 6 document, proof

დამამტკიცებელი || 6 evidence

საბჭო 3 council

საბჭოთა 5 Soviet (adj.)

საგანი (A) 9 subject, object

სად? 3 where

სადაც 6 where

სადგური 7 station

სადილობს 14 dine, have dinner

სადილი 10 dinner

სადილობა 10 dinnertime

სადილობისას 10 during, at dinnertime

სადმე 14 someplace, somewhere, anywhere

სადღა? 14 where (in the world)?

სადღაც 14 someplace, somewhere

სადღეგრძელო 9 toast

საელჩო 7 embassy

საენათმეცნიერო 3 linguistic

საესტრადო 7 pertaining to the stage; popular

სავარჯიშო 2 exercise

საზოგადო 10 general

საზოგადოება 3 society

საზოგადოებრივი 9 social

საზღვარი (A) 7 border, frontier, limit

სათვალე 7 (eye)glasses

საიდან 9 whence

საინტერესო 2 interesting

საკითხი 7 question

საკმარისი 10 sufficient, satisfactory

სალარო 9 cashier's (booth)

სამზარეულო 7 kitchen

სამიკიტნო 13 inn, tavern

სამუშაო 14 job, work

სამშობლო 8 homeland

სამწუხარო 4 unfortunate

სამხრეთი 8 south(ern)

სამხრეთ ოსეთი 6 South Ossetia

სანამ* 13 (conjunction) until, before

საოცარი (A) 7 surprising

საპატიმრო 13 prison

სარკე 7 mirror

სასადილო 7 dining room

სასამართლო 9 court (judicial)

სასახლე 7 palace

სასწაული 9 miracle

საუბარი (A) 9 conversation

საუკეთესო 13 best

საუკუნე 5 century

საფუძველი (E) 13 base, basis, foundation

საქართველო 2 Georgia

საქმე 5 affair, matter, job

საღამო 2 evening

  საღამოს 2 in the evening

საყიდელი (E) or საყიდი 7 (in order) to buy

საშინაო დავალება 3 homework

საშიში 8 dangerous

საშუალო 4 middle, average

  საშუალო სკოლა 4 middle school (roughly, high school)

საჩუქარი (A)	7	gift
საწერი	13	for writing, writing-
საწოლი	7	bed, bedroom
საწყალი (A)	7	pitiable, poor
საჭიროა	6	it is necessary (+ opt.)
საჭმელი (E)	4	food
სახე	13	face; image; form
სახელი	3	name; noun
სახელმძღვანელო	10	textbook
სახელმწიფო	6	(national) state
სახელოვანი (A)	11	famous
სახლი	4	house
სეიმი	9	"seim", i.e., parliament
-სესხებს, ი-*	6	borrow
სექტემბერი (E)	10	September
სვამს		see -ლევ-
სვანი	6	a Svan
სვეტიცხოველი (E)	6	"Church of the Living Pillar" in Mcxeta
სია	3	list
სიამოვნება	7	pleasure
სიდიდე	10	bigness; size
სიკვდილი	9	death
სიმართლე	8	truth
სიმინდი	10	corn (maize)
სიმფონია	2	symphony
სიმღერა	8	song
სინათლე	13	light
სინამდვილე	8	reality
სინტაქსი	3	syntax
სირაქლემა	8	ostrich
სიტყვა	2	word
სიყვარული	12	love
სკამი	7	chair

სკოლა	5	school
მე-სმის*	12	hear
-სმენს, მო=ი	2, 5	listen to
სომეხი (E)	4	an Armenian
სოფელი (E)	10	village
სოფელში	10	to, in the country
სოციალისტური	6	socialist
სპარსი, სპარსელი	6	a Persian
სპორტსმენი	10	sportsman
სტამბა	3	printing house
სტატია	2	article
სტრუქტურა	4	structure
სტუდენტი	3	(university) student
სტუმარი (A) ●	4	guest
სულელური	5	silly (of things)
სული	8	soul
მ-სურს*	12	wish
სურათი	5	picture
სურვილი	9	wish
სუფრა	7	banquet; (dining) table; table-cloth
სქელი	9	fat
სცენა	9	stage
-სწავლის, Ø=ა	4	teach
-სწავლის, ი-*	2	study, learn
-სწავლის, შე+ი	6	learn
სწავლა	4	learning
-სწორებს, გა=ა	3	correct
სწორი, სწორე	4	precise, exact
-სხამს, და=ა	9	pour
-სხდებიან, ი-*	9	be sitting
-სხდებიან, და=*	9	sit down
სხდომა	3	session, meeting
-სხედ-		see -სხდ-

სხვა 4 (an)other
სხვადასხვა 11 different
სხვისი 11 someone else's
-სჯის, და= 9 punish

ტ

-ტან- see -ქვ-
ტანი 13 body
ტაძარი (A) 9 cathedral
ტახტი 10 throne
-ტევს, შე=ე 7 attack (no d.o.)
ტერიტორია 6 territory
ტექნიკა 11 technique
ტექსტი 4 text
-ტეხს, გა= 13 break into pieces
-ტეხს, მო= 13 break off
ტიკინა 8 doll, puppet
ტირის 8 cry
-ტკენ- see -ტკივ-
მ-ტკივა* 12 sthg. hurts s.o.
-ტკინ- see -ტკივ-
-ტოვებს, და= 14 leave sthg. behind
ტრადიცია 11 tradition
-ტყდება, გა= 13 break (intrans.)
ტყე 9 forest
-ტყვის, ი- * 8 say
-ტყვის, ე- * 8 tell s.o., say to s.o.
ტყუის 8 lie (tell a lie)

უ

-უბნ- see -ტყვ-
უდიდესი 6 greatest
უდური 11 Udi (NW Caucasian language)
უთუო 8 doubtless, sure
უკან 4 (pp.) behind
უკანასკნელი 8 last; (the) latter

უკვე	3	already
უკრაინა	4	the Ukraine
უმეტესი	6	most (greatest number)
უმრავლესობა	8	majority
უმცროსი	12	younger, junior
-უმჯობესებს, გა=ა	4	improve
უნდა*	6	must (+ opt.)
უნივერსიტეტი	3	university
ურთიერთობა	6	relationship
უფრო	4	more
უფროსი	12	elder
უცებ	7	suddenly
უცნაური	8	strange, unknown
უცნობი	9	unknown
უცხო, უცხოური	4	foreign
უჯრა	4	drawer
ფ		
ფანქარი (A)	3	pencil
ფანჯარა (A)	4	window
-ფარებს, გადა=ა	13	spread (e.g., tablecloth)
ფაქტი	6	fact
ფედერაციული	9	federative
ფერწერა	11	painting
ფეხი	7	foot, leg
ფეხბურთი	8	soccer (football)
ფიზიკა	2	physics
ფილმი	2	film
ფირფიტა	4	(phonograph) record
ფოლკლორი	6	folklore
ფონეტიკა	4	phonetics
ფონოგრაფი	13	phonograph
ფორთოხალი (A)	12	orange
ფოსტა	12	post-office; mail
ფრანგი	4	a Frenchman, Frenchwoman

-ფრენ-		see -ფრინ-
ფრთა	8	wing
ფრთხილი	3	careful
ფრინავს*	8	fly
-ფრინდება, გა=	8	fly off
-ფრინდება, ჩა=	8	fly down
ფრინველი	8	bird
ფრონტი	4	front
ფული	7	money
-ფუძნება, და=ე	11	be based on
ქ		
-ქებს, Ø=ა or -ქებს, შე=ა	7	praise
ქალაქი	3	city
ქალბატონი	6	Ms., Miss, Mrs.
ქალი	8	woman
ქალიშვილი	6	daughter
ქარავანი (A)	8	caravan
ქართველი	4	a Georgian
ქართველური	4	Kartvelian
ქართლი	6	Kartli
ქართული	2	Georgian
მ-ქვია*	12	be named, be called, s.o.'s name is
მა-ქვს*	12	have sthg.
მა-ქვს, გა(მო)+*	12	bring, carry out; export
მა-ქვს, მი+ *	12	bring, take sthg.
მა-ქვს, მო+ *	12	bring sthg.
მა-ქვს, შე(მო)+*	12	bring, carry in; import; introduce
ქვეყანა (A)	5	country, world
-ქვეყნებს, გამო=ა	3	publish
ქიმია	2	chemistry
ქმარი (A)	11	husband
-ქმნის, შე=	9	create
-ქნ-		see -მა-ქვ-ს

-ქონ- see მა-ქვ-ს
ქრისტიანი 6 a Christian
ქურდი 7 thief
ქუჩა 4 street
ქუხს 8 thunder

ღ

-ღებს, გა=ა 5 open
-ღებს, მი=ი 4 receive, get
ღალატობს* 10 betray
ღამე 3 night
ღარიბი 11 poor (not rich)
ღებულობს ● 10 gets, receives (iterative, only present series)
ღვინო* 4 wine
მ-ღვიძავს 12 be awake
-ღვიძებს, გამო=ა 8 wake s.o. up
ღმერთი* (E) 8 God

ყ

მ-ყავს* 12 have someone
-მ-ყავს, მი+* 12 lead someone
ყავა 13 coffee
-ყალიბებს, ჩამო=ა 6 form
ყელი 12 throat
ყეფს 8 bark
-ყვ- see -ყავ-
მი-ყვარს 12 love
-ყვან- see -ყავ-
ყველა* 6 all; everyone, everybody
 ყველაზე 8 most
ყველაფერი (E) 4 everything
ყველი 4 cheese
ყვირის 8 shout
-ყვირებს, შე+ 13 shout out
-ყიდის, ი-* 7 buy

-ყიდის, გა=	7	sell
-ყიდის, მი=ჰ	7	sell to s.o.
ყივის*	8	crow
ყიყინებს	9	croak
ყოველთვის	4	always
ყოველი (E)	2	every
ყოველდღე	8	every day
-ყოლ-		see -ყავ-
-ყრის, და=	13	scatter, throw down (plural d.o.)
ყურძენი (E)	9	grapes
შ		
შავი	3	black
შარვალი (A)	7	trousers
შარშან	8	last year
შედგენა	3	composition; composing
-შენებს, ა=ა	7	build
შეერთება	6	union
შეერთებული	8	united
შეიძლება	6	be able, can (+ opt.; see sec. 6.2)
შეკითხვა	5	question
შემდეგ	2, 4	then, after that; (pp.) after
შემოდგომა	9	autumn, fall
შემქმნელი	11	creator
შენი	4	your, yours (sg.)
შესავალი (A)	13	entrance
შესაძლებელია	6	it is probable, possible (+ opt.)
შესახებ	4	(pp.) about
შეუძლებელი	6	impossible
შეყვარებული	11	beloved (person)
შეცდომა	8	mistake
შვილი	13	child (son, daughter)
შვილიშვილი	7	grandchild
მ-შია*	12	be hungry
-შივდება, მო+	12	become hungry

შე-შინია*	12	be afraid of, fear
-შინებს, შე=ა	7	frighten
შინ	3	(adverb) home, at home
-შლის, და=	9	dissolve, take apart, dissect
შორის	4	(pp. with dat.) among, between
შტატი	8	state (in U.S.A.)
შუა	4	(pp. with dat.) between, among
შუა საუკუნეები	11	Middle ages
ჩ		
ჩაი*	8	tea
ჩანს*	10	appear, seem (only present series)
ჩემი	4	my, mine
-ჩენს, აღმო+ა*	5	discover
-ჩერებს, გა=ა	7	stop
-ჩერებს, შე=ა	8	stop for a bit, briefly
ჩვენი	4	our, ours
ჩვენთვის	7	for us
ჩვეულებრივი	6	usual, ordinary
ჩვეულებრივ	6	usually, ordinarily
ჩივის*	8	complain
ჩრდილო	6	north(ern)
ჩქარი	12	fast, rapid, quick
ჩქარა	12	quickly, rapidly
ც		
-ცის, ი-*	9, 12	know (sthg.) (see secs. 9.1.4, 12.1.3.e)
-ც-		see -ცემ-
-ც (-აც after consonants)	4	also (written together with the preceding word)
-ც და ...-ც	4	both...and (written together with the preceding words)
-ცავს, და=ი*	9	defend
-ცან-		see -ცნ-
-ცდის, გამო=	9	test, examine
-ცდება, შე=	9	err, make a mistake

წელიწადი (A)	8	year
-წერს, აღ+	2	describe
-წერს, ა+უ	7	describe to s.o.
-წერს, გადა+	2	copy
-წერს, და=	2	write
-წერს, მი=ს, მო=(ს)	7	write to s.o.
წერილი	2	letter; article
წერილობითი	4	written (of a language)
-წვება, ი-*	9	be lying down
-წვება, და=*	9	lie down; go to bed
წვიმს	8	rain
წიგნი	2	book
წითელი (E)	2	red
-წითლებს, გა=ა	2	make blush, make red
წინ	4	(pp.) in front of, before; (adverb) before
წინადადება	9	sentence, clause
წინათ	6, 10	(pp.) ago; (adverb) before, previously
წინაპარი (A)	11	ancestor
წინაშე	9	(pp.) in front of, opposite
წკრიალებს	8	tinkle, ring
მ-წონს, მო+	12	like
წრე	3	circle; club
წუთი	8	minute, moment
წუხელ	3	yesterday evening
-წყებს, და=ი	2	begin
წყალი (A)	8	water
წყალობით	4	(pp.) thanks to
წყარო	6	source, spring
-წყვეტს, გადა=*	9	decide
მ-წყინს *	12	be annoyed, find unpleasant
მ-წყურია	12	be thirsty (only present series)
-წყურდება, მო+ს	12	become thirsty

ჭ

ჭადრაკი	8	chess
-ჭამს, Ø=	10	eat
-ჭამს, შე=	11	eat up, consume
ჭანი	6	a Č̣an (Laz)
-ჭირდება, და=ს	12	need (see sec. 12.1.2.4)
ჭირიმე, შენი	14	my good friend (affectionate form of address)
-ჭმევს, Ø=ა*	11	feed (animals)
-ჭრის, გა=ი	13	cut one's (e.g., finger)
-ჭრის, და=	9	wound, cut
-ჭრის, მო=	3	cut, cut off
-ჭრევინებს, მო=ა	11	cause to cut off

ხ

ხალხი	7	people, folk
ხალხური	2	(adj.) folk
ხანჯალი (A)	13	dagger
ხარჩო	12	(Geo. soup made with mutton, rice, plums)
-ხასიათებს, და=ა	10	characterize
-ხატავს, და=	11	draw, paint
ხატი	6	icon
-ხდება, გა=	9	become (+ nom.); be transformed into (+ adverbial)
-ხდება, მო=	10	happen, occur
-ხდის, გადა=ი	9	pay
-ხედ-		see -ნახ-
ხელი	3	hand
ხელისუფლება	8	(political) power
ხელმძღვანელი	9	leader
ხელნაწერი	3	manuscript
ხელოვნება	6	art
ხეობა	5	(mountain) valley
ხვალ	2	tomorrow
ხვალინდელი(E)	3	tomorrow's

-ხვდება, და=	10	meet s.o. (e.g., at railroad station)
-ხვდება, შე=	9	encounter, meet
-ხილავს, გან=ი	2	discuss, examine, investigate
ხილი	9	fruit
გ-ა-ხლავს	14	(see sec. 14.1.1.2)
ხმადაბალი (A)	13	low, soft (of voice)
ხმადაბლა	13	softly (of voice)
ხმამაღალი (A)	8	loud
ხმამაღლა	8	loudly
-ხმარება, და=ე	7	help
ხოლმე	2	(indicates iterativity; see sec. 2.2.3)
ხოლო	9	and, but, however
ხომ	5, 10	but, however; interrogative particle, in affirmative sentences expects the answer 'yes', in negative sentences, 'no'
ხორბალი (A)	10	wheat
ხორცი	13	meat
-ხსნის, ა=	11	solve, explain
მ-ა-ხსოვს*	12	remember
ხსოვნა	9	memory
-ხსომ-		see -ხსოვ-
ხშირად	2	often
ჯ		
ჯალათი	11	executioner
ჯარი	7	army
ჯარისკაცი	4	soldier
-ჯდება, ი-*	9	be sitting (see sec. 9.1.3)
-ჯდება, და=*	9	sit down (see sec. 9.1.2)
-ჯდება, მო=უ*	13	sit down near, next to
-ჯდომ-		see -ჯდ-
ჯერ კიდევ	5	still, yet
-ჯექ-		see -ჯდ-
ჯვარი (A)	9	cross

ჯილდო 4 prize

ჰ

ჰაერი 12 air

ჰავა 9 climate

ჰალსტუკი 7 necktie

ჰოლანდიური 4 Dutch

GEOGRAPHIC NAMES

In the following the names of cities, states, provinces, etc. are given. Names of countries are to be found in the general vocabulary. Glosses are not given for locations within Georgia.

ბათუმი

ბეთლემი Bethlehem

ბოლნისი

ბორჯომი

ბაქო Baku (Azerbaijan)

გორი

ერევანი (A) Yerevan (Armenia)

ვირჯინია Virginia

თბილისი

იალბუზი Mt. Elbrus

იერუსალიმი Jerusalem

ლენინგრადი Leningrad

ლონდონი London

მოსკოვი Moscow

მცხეთა

ნიუ-იორკი New York

პარიზი Paris

რომი Rome

სოჭი Sochi (Russia)

ქუთაისი

ყაზბეგი Mt. Kazbek

ჩიკაგო Chicago

INDEX

The index is divided into three parts: 1. an index of grammatical terms, 2. an index of affixes (listed in English alphabetical order, and an index of Georgian words (in Georgian alphabetical order). References are to lesson and section. *L.* = Lesson, *n.* = note, App. = appendix.

1. Index of grammatical terms.

2. Index of affixes. Note: for most verbal affixes and for case markers, see Appendixes A, B and C.

3. Index of Georgian words. Note: Verbs of motion which take a great variety of preverbs are listed under the preverb *mi*-.

●ADDENDA TO VOCABULARY

ასო	11 letter (of the alphabet)
გვარი	12 last name, family name
გთხოვ(თ)	7 please
-თქმის, ი-*	12 be said
იმ დროს	5 at that time
მაგრამ	3 but
რიცხვი	11 number
-სულ-	11 (perfect participle root of სვლა ; see sec. 11.1.)
ღვთ-	8 (see ღმერთი)
ძალა	12 force, strength

ADDENDA & CORRIGENDA

[P. = 'page,' No. = 'exercise number ...,' l. = 'line'; ↑ = 'from the bottom'; → = 'replace with ...']

P. 51. No. 10., l. 2. Change word order to: ხვალ ინგლისურ გაკვეთილს გადავწერ.

P. 112, add to end of §5.3:
In general, a negated aorist conveys the nuance that the action was not performed because one didn't want to perform it; e.g., ოთახში არ შევედით 'we didn't go into the room [because we didn't want to].' To express negation without this nuance of volition, see §10.1.3.1.b.

P. 185, No. 26: Change text in square brackets to read: [Whan a word occurs before a monosyllabic verb, it often adds *-a*, as here, ვინცა.]

P. 186, No. 40, l. 1: ქუჩაზე → ქუჩაში.

P. 186, No. 45, l. 2: გადავიდეთ, რომ → გადავუდეთ და

P. 194, No. 40, l. 1: on the street → on (lit., 'in') the street.

P. 195., No. 45, l. 2: in order to → and to.

P. 217, Note 5, l. 6: fut. ებრძოლებს → fut. შეებრძოლებს

P. 237, l. 8 ↑: Add to მთავარი entry: უმთავრესი mainly

P. 250, No. 2: ძველი ლეგენდა არსებობს, რომლის მიხედვითაც → არსებობს ძველი ლეგენდა, რომლის მიხედვითაც

P. 250, No. 3: ვერ მოკლა, არამედ → არ მიკლა, არამედ.

P. 259, No. 3.: He couldn't kill → He didn't kill.

P. 291, to entry ჩადის, ჩამოდის: arrive → arrive (from a distance, by travelling)

P. 297, l. 17, to entry ფუძემდებელი: add to translation: (see §8.6.1)

P. 304, l. 10 ↑: it is written → it is/has been written

P. 304, l. 8 ↑: it was written → it was/had been been written

P. 314, bottom line: მხატავი → დამხატავი

P. 315, No. 6, l. 3: ეს იგო → ის იყო.

P. 315, No. 12, l.. 2: მის მიერ დახატულა → მის მიერაა დახატული.

P. 316, No. 24, l. 3: გადაწერილა → გადაწერილია

P. 317, No. 38, l. 2: სვეთიცხოველი → სვეტიცხოველი.

P. 318, col. 1, l. 6, to entry ასო: letter → letter (of the alphabet)

P. 319, col. 2, l. 10, to შანიძე entry: (1887-) → (1887-1987)

P. 321, No. 6, l. 3: This was → He was.

P. 323, NOTE, l. 4: მოუჭრეს → მოაჭრეს.

P. 355, to entry მ-წყინს add: be offended

P. 375, l. 15: ახალი სუფრა ფენია → ახალი სუფრა აფენია

P. 390, l. 10 ↑, to entry ჩააცმევს: The first and second columns should read: ჩააცმევს or ჩააცვამს (ტანს, ტანზე) ča=H-a-*cmev*-s or ča=H-a-*cv*-am-s (aorist ჩა(ვ)აცვი(თ), ჩააცვა; perfect: ჩაუცმევია) Passive of state as from ჩაიცვამს above.

P. 401, l. 17, to entry საქებარი: of praise; praiseworthy; laudable (A) → of praise; praising, to praise (A)

P. 451, 5, l. 11 ↑, add entry: თვლა counting, (to) count

P. 452, 7, l. 17 add entry: ვეღარ here = never

P. 455, l. 3, add entry: შენ იცი mind you!

ADDITIONS TO VOCABULARY

P. 510: add -ცვამს, ჩა=ა- see ცმევს, ჩა=ა-

P. 512, to: მ-წყინს add: be offended